DIRECTING THE DOCUMENTARY

Third Edition

Michael Rabiger

Focal Press

Boston   Oxford   Johannesburg   Melbourne   New Delhi   Singapore

Focal Press is an imprint of Butterworth–Heinemann.

Copyright © 1998 by Butterworth–Heinemann

ℛ A member of the Reed Elsevier group

All rights reserved.

Butterworth–Heinemann supports the efforts of American Forests and the Global ReLeaf program in its campaign for the betterment of trees, forests, and our environment.

Library of Congress Cataloging-in-Publication Data
Rabiger, Michael.
    Directing the documentary / by Michael Rabiger.—3rd ed.
       p.   cm.
    Includes bibliographical references and index.
    ISBN 0-240-80270-5 (pbk. : acid-free paper)
       1. Documentary films—Production and direction. I. Title.
    PN1995.9.D6R33 1997
070.1′8—dc21   97-6582
                                                         CIP

British Library Cataloguing-in-Publication Data
A catalogue record for this book is available from the British Library.

The publisher offers special discounts on bulk orders of this book.
For information, please contact:
Manager of Special Sales
Butterworth–Heinemann
225 Wildwood Avenue
Woburn, MA 01801–2041
Tel: 617 928-2500
Fax: 617 928-2620

For information on all Focal Press publications available, contact our World Wide Web home page at: http://www.bh.com/focalpress

10 9 8 7 6 5 4

Printed in the United States of America

For
Paul, Joanna, and Penelope

CONTENTS

Preface to the Third Edition   vii

PART 1: INTRODUCTION, HISTORY, AND FUTURE

1   Introduction   3
2   A Brief and Functional History of the Documentary   13

PART 2: IDENTITY AND AUTHORSHIP

3   Finding Your Creative Identity   37
4   Developing Your Story Ideas   44

PART 3: SCREENCRAFT

5   Screen Grammar   55
6   Screencraft Analysis Projects   70
7   Basic Shooting Projects   97

PART 4: PREPRODUCTION

8   Initial Research and the Proposal   113
9   Research Leading Up to the Shoot   127
10   Developing a Crew   143
     Preproduction Checklist   149

PART 5: PRODUCTION

11   Equipment Selection   155
12   About Lighting   164
13   Avoiding Problems   169
14   Interviewing   173
15   Directing Participants   188
16   Directing the Crew   202
17   Authorship   207
18   Production Projects   212
     Production Checklist   235

PART 6: POSTPRODUCTION

19   A Postproduction Overview   241
20   The Paper Edit: Designing a Structure   249
21   Editing: The First Assembly   255
22   Editing: The Process of Refinement   268
23   Narration   276
24   Editing: The End Game   288
25   Postproduction Projects   303
     Postproduction Checklist   307

PART 7: AESTHETICS AND AUTHORSHIP

26   Documentary Theory and the Issue of Representation   315
27   Elements of the Documentary   321
28   Form, Control, and Identity   344
29   Re-enactment, Reconstruction, and Docudrama   351
30   Ethics, Authorship, and Documentary Mission   356

PART 8: CAREER TRACK

31   Education   367
32   Getting Work   381

PART 9: OTHER INFORMATION

Filmography of Director Michael Rabiger   391
Glossary   393
Bibliography and Film Sources   407
Index   413

PREFACE TO THE THIRD EDITION

Anyone interested in learning how to make a documentary film or video should find here everything they need, both technically and conceptually. Using a hands-on, project-oriented approach, this book leads you through the necessary steps toward using the screen as a tool of inquiry and self-expression. It can take you from absolute beginner, if that's what you are, to advanced levels of competency. If you are already a professional, you may find new ways of seeing and a greater wholeness and logic in the world of your work.

This edition has been thoroughly revised and compressed to allow for new material while holding down size and cost. The explanations and practices have developed from my long background in both filmmaking and in teaching. Workshops and seminars that I have taught in recent years in a number of countries have been especially valuable. They have confirmed how similar the needs and practices of documentary makers are in different parts of the world. Although this book cites mainly English language films, many of them made by American independents, its practices and methods work in a wide range of cultural settings.

This new edition includes:

- the same popular checklists at the end of each production-oriented phase
- discussion of significant new films
- educational and career chapters extensively revised
- a fuller list of international film schools
- more about project development, the proposal process, and the prospectus
- more about documentary language and method
- more on new technology and the market possibilities that it brings
- more hands-on production projects,
    to also develop proficiency in reflexive, compilation, and essay filmmaking
    divided into direct cinema and cinéma vérité projects covering all the common shooting situations

in handheld and tripod modes for each

that develop proficiency and awareness in sound

- a new sound troubleshooting guide
- new chapters on

    current issues in documentary theory

    screen grammar and editing theory

- a new part devoted to authorial identity, with exercises to help you find and articulate your artistic identity as a director—a focus generally absent in film schools and the film industry alike. This will enable you to

    define the themes arising from the marks your life has left on you.

    develop an artistic self-profile.

    develop documentary "story" variations that truly grow out of your experience, interests, and tastes.

Recognizing how many people, like myself, are experiential learners and temperamentally unsuited to absorbing masses of untried information, the book is laid out to be accessible to all kinds of users:

- You want conceptual preparation before production work. Each production-related phase includes a thorough introduction followed by graduated projects to help you develop skills, judgment, and confidence.
- You learn best from doing, not from masses of preparation. If so, jump straight into the projects and use the text to problem solve as solid issues take shape.
- You are a teacher who wants to give students the best in documentary training, and you need methods of assessment. These are provided, and the book has evolved specifically to take the burden of instruction off your shoulders so you and your students can get on with the truly fascinating relationship that develops over their work.
- You want to direct fiction but realize that documentary will prepare you wonderfully for eventual features work and offer more of a living meantime.
- You are already in the film industry, trapped in craft work that has become routine, and are longing to learn how to move up to directing. This book is for you too!

Developments in documentary narrative techniques have blazed the trail for screen fiction, and fiction directors-in-training learn how to search out the authentic and the behavioral—both in life and in actors—from making documentaries. They also gain the confidence to improvise and to make use of open-ended spontaneity.

Teachers facing the educational climate that requires more defined learning outcomes and that expects performance assessments will note that the projects and exercises in this book come with judgment criteria and an assessment system. By offering multiple ways to judge film work, the book will help both teachers and learners to see more deeply into the work and to make judgments through shared and evident criteria.

The documentary these days is in better shape worldwide. With fresh approaches and new causes to champion, the independent documentary is stirring public interest and appearing again in cinema runs. To quicken the momentum, digital video equipment and desktop computer postproduction seem set to revolutionize screen production in general and the documentary in particular. The future has never looked more exciting for independent filmmakers.

I would like to express my sincere thanks for ideas and help to Peter Attipetty, Camilla Calamandrei, Dr. Judd Chesler, Michael Ciesla, Dan Dinello, Dennis Keeling, Cezar Pawlowski, Barb Roos, and her students at Grand Valley State University. Thanks to Bill Yancey for help with the text, and to Dirk Matthews and Milos Stehlik for pictures and pictorial sources. My grateful thanks to Dean Mary Schmidt Campbell, Ken Dancyger, and the film faculty and students at the Tisch School of NYU for giving me the rare privilege of working with them. I owe a large debt of gratitude to Columbia College students: Dear friends, both past and present, you are too many to name, but you showed me the way to writing and rewriting this book.

Lastly, heartfelt thanks to my wife, Nancy Mattei, for sharp proofreading and her usual constructively tough criticism.

Michael Rabiger, Chicago, 1997

P A R T 1

INTRODUCTION, HISTORY, AND FUTURE

CHAPTER 1
Introduction 3

What Is a Documentary? 3
Objectivity and Fairness 6
The Director's Craft 7
A "Contract" with the Audience 8
The Filmmaker and the Media 10
Film or Video? 10
Bearing Witness 12

CHAPTER 2
A Brief and Functional History of the Documentary 13

On Film Language 13
Authorship and Factual Footage 14
The Invention of the Documentary Film 16
New Technology Leads to Advances in Form 23
Direct Cinema and *Cinéma Vérité* 25
The Documentary and Television 29
Technology: More Walls Come Tumbling
   Down 30
The Documentary's Future 33

C H A P T E R   1

INTRODUCTION

WHAT IS A DOCUMENTARY?

Put two documentarians together and they will probably argue about what is, or isn't, a documentary. And as decades pass, the parameters keep enlarging and the disputes are taken up by new generations. But uncontested is what is central to documentary's spirit—the notion that documentaries explore actual people and actual situations.

Documentary and time: Usually documentaries cover the present or the past, but documentaries can also project into the future. Peter Watkins' *The War Game* (1965) uses the knowledge from World War II bombings of Dresden, Hiroshima, and Nagasaki to hypothesize a major nuclear attack on London. Documentary sometimes uses actors when authentic means are not legitimately available to render the spirit of actuality.

Documentary as the creative treatment of actuality: Documentary's founding father John Grierson—to whom we shall return later—defined the documentary as the "creative treatment of actuality." This is conveniently imprecise, for it embraces all nonfiction forms, such as nature, science, travelogue, industrial, educational, and even certain promotional films. But films under these categories may not be documentary at all.

Documentary as socially critical: The documentary seems concerned with uncovering further dimensions to actuality and implying some kind of social criticism. The better ones do not go in for hand wringing or promoting a product or service, and may not even be concerned with objectively measurable facts. A factual film about the way workers manufacture razor blades would be an industrial film, but a film showing the effect on workers of repetitive precision manufacturing, and *that invites the spectator to draw socially critical conclusions*, can only be called a documentary—however well it might also relay the physical process of manufacturing. Concern for the quality and justice of human life normally takes the documentary beyond the merely factual into moral and ethical dimensions, where it scrutinizes the organization of human life and furthers humane consciousness. The best are models of disciplined passion, showing the familiar in an unfamiliar way and inviting us to function at a heightened level of awareness.

Documentary, individuality, and point of view: Emile Zola said, "A work of art is a corner of Nature seen through a temperament." If we amend this to "a documentary is a corner of reality seen through a human temperament," it fits beautifully, since each documentary examines the actual through the lens of a human temperament. Memorable films of all kinds present their characters and events through the lens of an identifiable, authorial persona. In fiction, Hitchcock, Godard, Bergman, Wertmuller, and Altman have their recognizable concerns and style, just as in the documentary do Rouch, Wiseman, Kopple, the Maysles brothers, and many others. Each brings a fresh, special, and engrossing involvement with the human condition.

Artists are usually the first in society to see what is at the edge of society's consciousness, and any art museum or gallery shows a great historical range of visions. Documentarians, like painters, make their critical distinctions guided by conviction, conscience, ideology, or interest in form, and they too seek to persuade. But an artist is not necessarily an individual working alone. A fifteenth century Italian painting might be attributed to Fra Angelico or Uccello, but it is really the work of a team of apprentices and specialists. Each expert handled special details, such as landscape background, hands, or drapery. Likewise, in film aspects of a film's vision are handled by a team and not just an individual. *Hoop Dreams* (1994), codirected by Steve James, Fred Marx, and Peter Gilbert, shows how superb screen authorship arises out of shared rather than individual values (Figure 1-1). Given how collaborative the medium is, and that it is shown to a collective audience, this is hardly surprising.

Documentary as an organized story: Successful documentaries, like their fiction counterparts, also need a good story with interesting characters, narrative tension, and an integrated point of view. These elements are fundamental to all stories and are present in myth, legend, and folktales—humankind's earliest narratives.

Where does this organization come from, and who has the right to impose it? T.S. Eliot claimed this work for the artist when he said, "It is the function of all art to give us some perception of an order in life, by imposing an order on it." The documentary gives us a perception of life's underlying organization by demonstrating cause and effect.

Documentary's range of forms: Imposing an order, or demonstrating cause and effect, can be accomplished any number of ways. A documentary can be controlled and premeditated, spontaneous and unpredictable, lyrical and impressionistic, starkly observational, have commentary or no speech at all, interrogate its subjects, catalyze change, or even ambush its subjects. It can "impose an order" using words, images, music, or human behavior. It can use literary, theatrical, or oral traditions and partake of music, painting, song, essay, or choreography.

Fidelity to the actual versus realism: There are no limits to the documentary's possibilities, but it always reflects a profound fascination with, and respect for, actuality. But what *is* actuality? To the materially minded it is something objective that we can all see, measure, and agree on. The wealthy TV network or funding agency, wary of lawsuits, wants a documentary to contain only what can be seen, proved, and defended in court. Not surprisingly, these organizations are much

FIGURE 1-1 ———————————————————————————————

Superb screen authorship arising from shared values in *Hoop Dreams* (1994), codirected by Steve James, Fred Marx, and Peter Gilbert. (*Hoop Dreams* Copyright 1994, Fine Line Features. All rights reserved. Photo appears courtesy of New Line Productions, Inc.)

readier to produce informational films or controlled corporate journalism than they are true documentary, which includes individual social criticism and conscience at work.

But documentary reflects the richness and ambiguity of the whole of life, and this takes it beyond objective observation. Under pressure human reality becomes surrealism and hallucination, as one sees so brilliantly in Erroll Morris' *The Thin Blue Line* (1988). So along with outward, visible reality we include ways to represent the inner lives of those we film, because even their thoughts, memories, dreams, and nightmares are part of actuality. Writers have always been able to shift levels between their characters' inner and outer dimensions, and have sometimes included the storyteller's perceptions as part of the rich resulting narrative. Film is still in the process of developing these freedoms.

Documentary as a presence and consciousness: The modern documentary differs from its earlier and more scripted form because technology allows us to record events and authorial consciousness *as they unfold.* This produces the sensation of spontaneous life and adaptation familiar from the heightened moments in our own lives. Take, for example, Nicholas Broomfield and Joan Churchill's fine *Soldier Girls* (1981). Ostensibly it shows how the U.S. Army trains its women soldiers, but it reveals a great range of both formal and informal moments, including sadistic training and humiliations that are all the more disquieting when applied by white men to minority women. The film avoids confronting its central paradox until late: Because warfare is brutal and unfair, a caring instructor cannot kindly train soldiers to survive, no matter what gender. But this argument stretches thin after what we have seen, and leaves us disturbed by larger questions about military traditions and mentality—just as the film's makers surely intended. The film shares what moved or disturbed Broomfield and Churchill but never tells us what to feel or think. Instead, *by exposing us to evidence that is contradictory and provocative* it jolts us into realization and inner debate.

Documentary as a social art: The documentary is a construct of evidences. It aims to induce in its audience the progression of its makers' experience as they grapple to understand the meaning of particular events. Films are usually made collaboratively, so this sensibility can arise collectively in several individuals. The resulting film is then consumed by another collective—the audience. Film, and particularly the documentary, is a truly social art form.

OBJECTIVITY AND FAIRNESS

Objectivity: People frequently assume documentaries are "objective" because factual television likes to balance out opposing points of view. Adversarial balance, runs the argument, ensures a fair, unbiased view of the events and personalities in question. This is a tactic inherited from journalism because it serves to minimize dangers and responsibilities to the news institution. One is being proved wrong because this would bring discredit or even lawsuits. Another is the accusation of political bias. So part of a journalist's professionalism has been, and still is, to seem objective. A newspaper will do this by prescribing a uniform and faceless "house" writing style, and will take steps to camouflage staff attitudes by presenting them indirectly as the opinion or the conflicts of others. In the 1930s this fixation with equipoise led reputable British newspapers to report the trouble brewing in Hitler's Germany as a petty squabble between communists and blackshirts, something whipped up by "Red troublemakers." With hindsight we see that no commentator could possibly sit on the fence and write in this hands-off way. This was not being "fair" or responsible when the Nazis had already begun enacting their philosophy of genocide. It was necessary, then and now, to *interpret* events and to decide where the cause of justice and humanity lay in specific issues.

Fairness: Equally important in a world full of ambiguity is the responsibility of documentarians to be fair. If, for example, you were telling the story of a malpractice accusation against a surgeon, it would be prudent not only to cover allegations from both sides but to cross-check everything that can be independently verified. This is what good journalists and successful detectives do everywhere.

Clarification not simplification: What interests documentarians is seldom clear cut, but an ever-present temptation exists to render it so. Nettie Wild's *A Rustling of Leaves* (1990) is a courageous and sympathetic account of the populist guerrilla movement in the Philippines, but the partisan nature of her beliefs makes one feel guiltily skeptical throughout. She makes heroes of the left-wing peasants in their struggle against right-wing thugs, and though her sympathy is clearly justified, we know that resistance cannot long remain honorable. Soon both sides commit atrocities and the waters become too muddy for the story to be one of moral rectitude. Here fairness means not only relaying the protagonists' declared principles but exposing the ugly and paradoxical aspects of liberation through violence. Wild tries to do this, showing, for instance, the trial and execution by guerrillas of a youthful informant. But one doubts if much justice survives once the camera is no longer around. A film should be accurate and truthful, but it will still fail unless it is also perceived as such. This may mean establishing whether something is generally or only narrowly true. Handling your audience well means anticipating the film's impact on a first-time viewer every step of the way and knowing when justifiable skepticism requires something special from the film's discourse. The more intricate the issues, the more difficult it will be to strike a balance between necessary simplification, on the one hand, and fidelity to the complexity of human life, on the other.

Documentary is often wrongly labeled: Anything nonfiction is routinely called a documentary when it may be factually based advertising sponsored by a branch of the travel industry, or a pet care film that shows how necessary Doggo Coat Conditioner is to the well-being of man's best friend. True documentaries are concerned with the values that determine the quality of human life, not with selling a product or service. Then, again, the language used about documentary is often confusing. Penetrating but fair-minded exposure of a subject's issues will be called "objectivity," yet the same word will be used for the fence-sitting favored by news organizations, who make up a balance in order to sidestep any charges of political commitment. Worse yet, the artful ways that news and documentary practitioners use to disguise their own biases beguile the public into thinking that documentary itself is objective. Nothing could be less true.

A documentary is a subjective construct: The alluring notion that a camera can ever record anything objectively disintegrates once one confronts one or two practical considerations. What, for instance, is an "objective" camera position, because someone must place the camera somewhere? How does one "objectively" decide when to turn the camera on and off? And as one views the resulting material, how does one spot the "objective truth" that should be used? These are all editorial decisions. They are inextricably bound up with film art's need to compress what in life is lengthy and diffuse into a brief and meaningful essence.

Quite simply, filmmaking is a series of highly significant choices of what to shoot, how to shoot it, what to use, and how most effectively to use it. If your film is to be perceived as fair, balanced, and objective, you will need a broad factual grasp of your subject, material that is persuasive and self-evidently reliable, and the courage and insight to make interpretive judgments about its use. Almost every decision involves ethical choices, many of them disquieting and involving sleepless nights. Whatever your intentions, the medium itself plays a very big part in the message. You will be showing to your audience not the events themselves but rather an artful representation, a construct having its own inherent logic, dynamics, and emphases.

THE DIRECTOR'S CRAFT

Like many craftspeople, most screen directors operate from a gut recognition that is really a process of internalized logic. Working more by reflex than by conscious deduction, they recognize what "works" and what will be effective. Of course, this is maddeningly inaccessible to the novice and seems calculated to shut him out. Even professional crew members routinely nurture quite distorted ideas of the directorial process, especially the stages before and after shooting. They think that directors are a special breed who make decisions in some remote and arty compartment of their being. Because this echoes how we tend to separate art from technology anyway, this cultural apartheid is especially damaging among documentary makers, whose responsibility is to create and maintain wholeness and integration.

Let's be clear. Directing is not a mystical process. If a director at work appears inscrutable, it's probably because a strenuous inner process monopolizes most of his or her energies. No film—indeed, no artwork of any kind—emerges except by more or less conscious and responsible decisions. The conventions of cinema art thrust the director into selecting and interpreting cause and effect every step of the way. Although cinematography seems to place the viewer in direct contact with the subject, the record is not unmediated reality because it has been constructed knowing that *the audience has been led by its viewing experience to expect every aspect of every shot to carry meaning.* This is active interpretation, not the generalized recording of C-Span.

Directing well takes a highly evolved consciousness, both of the world you are filming and of the process by which it will be presented. How do you get to that stage? By practice. So be prepared for your first work to be clumsy and naive. Be prepared for an incredibly long and demanding process. Be prepared to grow from being wrong over and over again, and know that it sometimes takes great persistence to keep going, especially when you feel defeated.

The rewards of making documentary are that you can involve yourself in life's mysteries and travel deeper and deeper into the unknown. You will find wonderful travel companions and, by trying to raise your own and others' consciousness, you will never doubt that you are attempting something honorable and useful.

A "CONTRACT" WITH THE AUDIENCE

How a filmmaker engages with the audience often proceeds from deep and unexamined assumptions about who "other people" really are and how one relates to them. These assumptions arise from a lifetime of omnivorous film viewing, but what you decide will affect your choice of cinematic language and how well your film conveys its scope and perspective. There are different levels of respect for the audience's intelligence, and whichever is used becomes part of an implied contract between communicator and audience.

The advertiser or propagandist, wanting to condition the audience, produces only the evidence that supports predetermined conclusions. He will often use jokiness or sensation to coerce his audience into buying the premise. Moving up the scale of respect, there is the "binary" communicator mentioned earlier, who gives "equal coverage to both sides" in any controversy, as if issues only ever have two sides. By showing a world full of matched opponents, this type of film implies we need do nothing except stay tuned to those in the know. Here too the audience is considered a passive mass to be informed and entertained, but not challenged to make judgments.

At a higher level is a discourse—and this is equally true of narrative fiction—that aims not at conditioning or diverting but at sharing something in all its complexity. Ira Wohl's *Best Boy* (1979) is about an elderly couple uneasily yielding up their mentally handicapped son to an institution in preparation for the time they can no longer care for him (Figure 1-2). Delicately but perceptibly, the film touches on all the regret, pain, and failure connected with the son's position as a handicapped member of a family.

A film such as this does not set out to sell or convert, but rather to expand one's mind and emotions by drawing us through a series of events fraught with meaning and ambiguity. It invites us to make difficult judgments about motive and responsibility, and it makes us accomplices during an honest, painful quest for goodness and truth.

A good film, like a good friend, engages us actively, and never patronizes or manipulates either its subjects or its audience.

Consciously or otherwise, every film signals how it means to treat its audience and under what general premise. This I think of as a "contract" struck with the audience. Like good storytellers, the better films set their terms in the opening moments so that the audience faces the enjoyable prospect of suspense and promise.

FIGURE 1-2

Best Boy by Ira Wohl. Pearl must let her "best boy" Philly leave home to enter a supportive institution. (Ira Wohl)

THE FILMMAKER AND THE MEDIA

Nowadays documentary makers rely almost wholly on television or cable to show their work. For the company executives who control these corporations, the notion that truth may reside more powerfully in the vision of an individual than in the consensus of the boardroom is a prickly issue, suspended as they are in the web of myth and litigiousness generated by our mercantile democracy. Corporations by definition are committed to audience figures, survival, and profits; they decide programming by subtracting what may hurt profitability by offending a sector of the audience, the sponsor, or the self-appointed guardians of public morals. Dissenting individuals or groups are only safe to honor later as historical heroes, so dissident views take unending struggle to get on television.

But, paradoxically, it has been either enlightened corporations, philanthropic endowments, or embattled individuals within them whose commitment to free speech has kept the documentary alive, and (by extension) its contribution alive to democratic pluralism.

Today, the diversification of television consumption, through cable, satellite, the Internet, and video facilities—with production equipment becoming smaller, better, and cheaper—makes video presentations possible that were once prohibitively difficult and expensive. Distribution is evolving toward the diversity of book publication, so a growing need for diverse screen authorship already exists. Lowered production costs and an increased outlet should mean increased freedom for the individual voice—the kind of freedom presently available in the print media. If logic prevails (a very big "if"!), this broadening expression means a more democratic and healthy society.

FILM OR VIDEO?

At the risk of aggravating purists, I have termed a work in either medium a *film.* But this book covers the concepts and methodology behind directing any documentary, and although I implore you to learn your ABCs using video, nothing of importance is exclusive to one delivery medium. Most of this book holds true for other nonfiction forms, such as the *industrial, nature, travelogue,* and *educational* film, and even for *fiction* filmmaking because all screen forms operate out of a common fund of techniques, use the common screen language understood by audiences, and rely on common dramatic principles for their effectiveness. I will assume that you are embarking on the wonderful adventure of experimenting with documentary using video for economic reasons.

Acquisition in video: Using even the simplest video equipment, extensive and fascinating study is immediately possible. With film, expensive and time-delaying laboratory work is necessary before you see your material, so there is a delay in assessing results.

I personally care very little whether I work in film or tape. I get a superior image on film but must worry constantly about the amount of stock I am consuming. Film equipment is now larger, less portable, and little more reliable than video, and video editing of film is now universal. *Hoop Dreams* was actually made on Betacam video and in finished form was transferred to 35mm film for theatrical release. I doubt if many in the audience knew or cared.

So for your economy and morale, don't shoot documentary on film until you have performed extensively and successfully in video. At the time of writing, you can put a 30-minute video film in Hi8 or digital format on the screen for $400 or less in tape costs, while its 16mm film equivalent (negative purchase, developing, work-printing, release printing, sound processing charges) would cost upward of $15,000. While other factors enter any calculation professionals make over which medium to use, the novice can expect the same successes, problems, and faults to show up regardless of the medium used. One avenue of learning is twenty times as expensive as the other, and much more labor intensive to edit.

Linear video editing: However, videotape editing on linear (noncomputer) equipment has one huge drawback. Because it involves selectively transferring scenes onto one uncut piece of tape, the edit is accumulated in a linear fashion. This means you can't go back and shorten or lengthen one scene without retransferring everything that follows. In practice, there are sometimes ways to wriggle out of this straitjacket, but the overall hindrance remains.

Nonlinear editing: Editing by random access in a computer restores the flexibility of film editing while dispensing with all the splicing and filing that made for so much drudgery. In nonlinear postproduction the film or video rushes (also known as "dailies") are transferred to a massive hard disk as a video version in

FIGURE 1-3

Sony DCR VX1000. Consumer models of digital camcorder now approach broadcasting standards. (Courtesy of Sony Electronics, Inc.)

compressed digital form. This permits the assembly and manipulation of any number of cut versions with the same speed and efficiency one takes for granted in word-processing. Since the first edition of this book, film editing in the world's high-tech production centers has virtually vanished.

Digital desktop production: With the proliferation of digital camcorders (Figure 1-3) and desktop nonlinear editing, now more than ever one can learn film making at low cost and rapidly. Shooting and editing to online (broadcasting) quality can now be done with a $15,000 package (a digital camcorder; fast audio-visual computer with a high-speed, high-capacity hard drive; video and sound editing software; and digital output). Until recently the cost was at least ten times as much (a Betacam camcorder, off-line suite, and online suite for making a digital master.)

BEARING WITNESS

If you have investigated local records in search of your forebears, you have probably found only names, occupations, births, marriages, and deaths, and little else about the genetic heritage you carry. I would love to know more about a particular branch of my family who in the nineteenth century were village chimney sweeps just north of London. Only two pieces of information, evocative in their contradiction, have been handed down: that the boys had saltpeter rubbed into their torn knees and elbows to toughen the skin ready for the brutal job of climbing inside chimneys, and that the family believed itself descended from nobility.

How much is authentic I cannot say, but one universal fact stands out: ordinary people know virtually nothing about the lives and minds of their progenitors, especially if poor and illiterate. The great mass of humanity has left nothing save what can be glimpsed in the records of their time, in their folk music and cautionary sayings, and in the marks they made on the landscape. Of humble individuals one can learn nothing unless they tangled with the law or did something remarkable. Their collective history was written for them, if recorded at all, by their masters, who were neither expert nor unprejudiced.

You and I need not pass so silently from life. Future historians will have as their resource documentaries that are grassroots visions, not just what was preserved by an elite and its servants. You and I can use cinematic language—the twentieth century's great contribution to universal understanding—to create a record of family, friends, and surroundings; to pose ideas and questions; and to convey what we see and feel. We can propose the causes, effects, and meanings of the life that we are leading. We can bear witness to these times, reinterpret history, and prophesy the future. The consequences for democracy, and for a richer and more harmonious tapestry of cultures, are incalculable. This is the art and purview of the documentary film.

CHAPTER 2

A BRIEF AND FUNCTIONAL HISTORY OF THE DOCUMENTARY

In a book like this it is impractical to take more than a brief look at the documentary's development so I make no claim to historical or geographical balance. Instead here is an unapologetically selective account to serve as a backdrop to the rest of the book. Although the films listed are classics, they are not readily available. Many video stores carry a few documentaries, but specialized films are hard to find. If you live near a university, you may be able to view films in their library. In North America, you can try the video rental and sales specialists listed in the Bibliography and Film Sources section near the back of the book. If you live outside the United States, try your library service for an interlibrary tape loan, or call your national film institute (every country seems to have one) for advice.

ON FILM LANGUAGE

Art enables us to vicariously experience other realities than our own and to connect emotionally with lives, situations, and issues that would otherwise remain alien. Finding ourselves reacting within a new context, we open up to other ways of seeing. For example, although the facts of something fairly distant such as World War II are unchanged, our emotional perspective can be stirred up anew. Even the monolithically evil image of Nazi Germany is undergoing change. Works such as Wolfgang Petersen's *Das Boot,* Werner Herzog's *Signs of Life,* and Steven Spielberg's *Schindler's List* have affirmed strands of normality and even goodness within the Third Reich. Such films make it not less evil, just more dangerously human.

Because film is so recent on the scene compared with other arts, its language and effect are only coming to be understood, especially as screen language is itself still in vivid evolution. To complicate matters, filmed action, such as the "facts" of history, draws its meaning both from the perspective of the viewer's times and from the interpretative structure imposed by the film's makers. Even at a cellular level, two film shots placed together form a suggestive juxtaposition that would be quite different if their order were reversed. Relativity and comparison are therefore the heart and soul of film language.

Film is also more a medium of experiencing than of contemplation, and one cannot become a good filmmaker without grasping the differences. Literature can easily place the reader in the past or in the future, while film holds the spectator in a constantly advancing present tense. Even a flashback quickly becomes its own ongoing present. Literature is experienced as a contemplative and intellectual activity in which the reader, moving at his own pace, shares the mental and emotional processes of the author and her characters. Film is a dynamic experience in which cause and effect are inferred by the spectator, even as the events appear to happen. Like music, its nearest relative, film grasps the spectator's heart and mind with existential insistency. Because we seldom want to stop, slow, or repeat any part of the show, we are less likely to fully appreciate the means of persuasion or the extent of our emotional subjugation. Film's verisimilitude lulls us into passively watching "events" as though they were real, so that authorship and an authorial voice appear to be absent. Nothing could be further from the truth. Documentaries are authored constructs no less than fiction films, with which they have much in common.

Documentary's history is a David and Goliath saga where subject matter has weight and substance, while authorship—a preeminently attractive aspect in all other artworks—is almost invisible. Exceptions have been the high points in the history of the genre, but now there is a movement toward films with an authorial "voice." Video and nonlinear postproduction will accelerate this evolution because they liberate filmmakers to filter, freeze, slow motion, superimpose, or interleave texts at will. This unshackles us from the tyranny of real time and realism, and permits a subjective and impressionistic treatment of original footage. The PBS series *The Great War* (1996) demonstrated how positively such a treatment can affect a historical narrative.

AUTHORSHIP AND FACTUAL FOOTAGE

Before the documentary form was invented and named in the 1920s, nonfiction cinema had existed for more than two decades. The first moving pictures transfixed for the world's wonderment pieces of reality, such as workers leaving a factory, a baby's meal, a train arriving to disgorge its passengers, and a rowing boat going out to sea. These earliest recorded moments of daily life are deeply touching because they are the human family's first home movies.

From its beginnings as a fast-buck optical trick, the fiction cinema quickly expanded its subject matter, following contemporary audience tastes in the direction of vaudeville, the music hall, and popular theater. Early fiction cinema includes staged comedy, historic reenactment, magic illusions, farce, and melodrama. The camera never stopped gathering factual footage of all kinds for newsreels, always very popular. During World War I, vast amounts of footage covered all phases of the hostilities and film became an important medium of communication and propaganda for wartime governments and their populations. Of all the early factual footage, that of World War I must be the most familiar to us today. It is also the most obviously biased in its attitudes and omissions. At our remove in time, the footage and its intertitles seem like jingoistic and naive posturing, with "our side" as heroes and "the enemy" as a malevolent and inhuman machine.

Are newsreels also documentary films? Plainly each is documentary material, but because newsreels are episodic and disjointed, they lack the comprehensive vision of a true documentary. Instead, footage is event centered while the event's meaning and relationship to any larger dimension remains out of sight. More than sound track is missing from those early film documents of the Great War. Absent is the interpretive vision already visible in a contemporary fictional work, such as *Birth of a Nation* (1915), even though Griffith's vision was flawed with southern racist attitudes. The fiction cinema was lucky in having superb role models in literary fiction. A filmmaker looking for a treatment of war could, for instance, pick up Tolstoy's *War and Peace*. It uses the historical novel form to subvert historical attitudes that assumed the overriding influence of kings, generals, and ambassadors during the Napoleonic wars. Tolstoy's experience as a soldier at Sebastopol told him that wild rumors, inadequate equipment, or even mistaken ideas about the enemy could put an army to flight just as easily as poor leadership. He did not need to alter any of the facts of the French invasion of Russia; he simply viewed them as an ordinary Russian, instead of from an elitist historical vantage. Tolstoy's largeness of view, his compassion for the humble soldier and for the precious coherence of family life, as well as for the more abstract idea of Russia herself, help us see not just those wars, but all war, as a tragic human phenomenon to be avoided at almost any cost.

Early actuality films entirely lack any of this coherence and largeness of vision. So where in literature might nonfiction filmmakers have looked for clues? There is no obvious form or body of work. Persuasive factual reporting was previously delivered through government reports, specialized journals, or newspapers. Mayhew's *London Labour and the London Poor* (published 1851 to 1862) is much nearer the documentary form and uses interview methods that allow his subjects to speak with their own words and ideas (Figure 2-1). But in its presentation of a whole interconnecting web of injustices, the book is quite passive.

Possibly painting or caricature are the documentary's true antecedents, and its values and concerns can be found in the work of artists such as Bruegel, Hogarth, Goya, Daumier, and Toulouse-Lautrec. Goya's vision of war or Daumier's of the urban poor helped show the way for the documentary film, from an individual and emotionally committed perspective to cast an unblinking eye on the terrible beauty of the twentieth century.

Newsreels made a large contribution to the public knowledge of World War I, but the context was also set by newspaper and government reports, letters, eyewitness accounts, fiction, poetry, and photography. Historians, repossessing that silent footage, have since reworked it to reveal rather different perspectives of the Great War, a revised outlook formed with hindsight's overview, of course, but that could only come from a radically different political and social consciousness than that of the period's ruling class. How ironic that the same footage can support such different representations.

Film's mere existence may have shifted the world's notions of truth, because its self-evident plasticity dramatizes how *truth is relative rather than absolute*. As

FIGURE 2-1

Henry Mayhew interviewed London's poor. (Illustration from Mayhew's *London Labour and the London Poor.*)

more World War I information becomes available, as new researchers uncommitted to earlier viewpoints look at the complex pattern of actions and events, they propose new relationships and more broadly embracing explanations. That war, of course, is only a single example among numberless documentary subjects.

THE INVENTION OF THE DOCUMENTARY FILM

The spirit of documentary is perhaps to be found first in Russia with the Kino-Eye of Dziga Vertov and his group. A young poet and film editor, Vertov produced educational newsreels that made a vital bid for followers during the Russian Revolution. He came to believe passionately in the value of real life captured by the camera and, in keeping with the spirit of the time, to abhor the stylized fictional life presented by bourgeois cinema. Vertov served as a leading theorist during the Soviet Union's period of great cinema inventiveness in the 1920s.

The term *documentary* is said to have been coined by John Grierson while reviewing Flaherty's *Moana* in 1926. Flaherty, an American whose earlier *Nanook of the North* (1922) is acknowledged as documentary's seminal work, began shooting his ethnographic record of an Eskimo family in 1915 (Figure 2-2). While editing his footage in Toronto, he inadvertently set fire to his 30,000 feet of negative and had to gather funds to reshoot it.

Owing to the constraints of a hand-cranked camera, insensitive film stock requiring artificial light, and appalling weather conditions, Flaherty had to ask his subjects to do their normal activities in special ways and at special times. Because of Nanook's liking for Flaherty and because he knew they were placing on record a vanishing way of life, Nanook and his family both provided and influenced the content, enabling the filmmaker to shoot his "acted" film about a battle with the elements as if it were a fictional story (Figures 2-2 and 2-3).

Having gotten to know his "actors" for such a long time, Flaherty's relationship with them was so natural that they could quite un-self-consciously continue their lives before his camera. The film's participants and their lives were so inarguably authentic that the film transcended mere acted representation. Just as important was the fact that Flaherty's unsentimental vision of Eskimo daily life elicits the larger theme of man in a struggle for survival.

Distributors at first refused to accept that *Nanook* would interest the public, but they were proved wrong when it drew large crowds. Yet while audiences lined up to see the film, its subject died on a hunting trip in the Arctic. One cannot imagine a more ironic endorsement of the truth in Flaherty's vision.

However, with *Man of Aran* (1934) and other films made later in his career, Flaherty came under fire from Grierson, Rotha, and others for being more interested in creating lyrical archetypes than in observing the true, politically deter-

FIGURE 2-2

Nanook warming his son's hands from *Nanook of the North*. (The Museum of Modern Art/Film Stills Archive.)

FIGURE 2-3 —————————————————————————————————————

From *Nanook of the North*. A family to feed. (The Museum of Modern Art/Film Stills Archive.)

mined conditions of his subjects' lives. Not only did he assemble an ideal family from assorted islanders, but he carefully avoided showing the big house of the absentee landlord—the individual largely responsible for the islanders' deprivations. George Stoney and Jim Brown's *How the Myth Was Made* (1978) goes to Aran and explores Flaherty's process with some of the film's surviving cast.

From *Nanook* onwards, factual cinema began showing real life in ways that went beyond the fragmented presentation of news footage. By turning events into a story, the documentary cinema could not avoid interpreting its subject and implying, sometimes with considerable and unconscious self-revelation, its makers' ideas about social cause and effect. Grierson, who was to pilot the British documentary movement, described the documentary form as the "creative treatment of actuality." In the development of national cinemas that was to come, American documentaries often followed Flaherty's example by showing the struggle between man and nature. Paradoxically it was Pare Lorentz's films made for the U.S. government, *The Plow That Broke the Plains* (1936) and *The River* (1937), that showed rather too explicitly the connection between government policy and ecological disaster (Figures 2-4 and 2-5). Their success as indictments ensured that American documentary makers were soon turned loose to work without government funding.

FIGURE 2-4

The Plow That Broke the Plains. (The Museum of Modern Art/Film Stills Archive.)

In Britain, after the ravages of World War I, Grierson's self-proclaimed mandate, as he worked for the British Government in the late 1920s, was "somehow we had to make peace exciting, if we were to prevent wars. Simple notion that it is—that has been my propaganda ever since—to make peace exciting." Grierson endorsed Brecht's statement, "art is not a mirror held up to reality, but a hammer with which to shape it." The people who collected around him were socialists committed to the idea of community and communal strength. The British documentary school's achievement was revealing the dignity in ordinary people and their work. *Night Mail* (1936) and *Coal Face* (1936) recruited some of the brightest artistic talents, such as the composer Benjamin Britten and the poet W.H.

FIGURE 2-5 ————————————————————————————

The River. (The Museum of Modern Art/Film Stills Archive.)

Auden, to assist in producing works that have since become famous for their celebration of the rhythms and associations of humble work.

A few years later, with the onset of World War II, Humphrey Jennings emerged as the poet of the British screen. His *Listen to Britain* (1942) and *Fires Were Started* (1943) neither preach nor idealize; instead, through innumerable vignettes of ordinary people adapting to the duress of war, Jennings produced a moving and unsentimental character portrait of Britain itself.

In Russia of the 1920s, with the revolution scarcely completed, the new government found itself needing to control a huge nation of peoples who neither read nor understood each other's languages. Silent film offered a universal language with which the citizens of the new Soviet republic could confront the diversity, history, and pressing problems of their nation with optimism. Because the government wanted the cinema to be both realistic and inspirational, and to get away from what it considered the falseness and escapism of western commercial cinema, much thought in those idealistic days went into codifying the cinema's function. One outcome was a heightened awareness of the power of editing, and another was Dziga Vertov's articulation of Kino-Eye, a cinema intended to record life without imposing on it. It was the precursor of the Direct Cinema movement that is discussed later.

Vertov's *Man with the Movie Camera* (1929) is an exuberant record of the camera's capability to move, to capture life in the streets, and even to be reflexively aware of itself. He believed that by compiling a rapid and ever-changing montage of shots, life itself would emerge free of any point of view other than that of the all-seeing camera. Despite his intention to produce an egoless film, the chaotic profusion of imagery, the humor, and the catalogue of events and characters could only be Vertov's.

Sergei Eisenstein, the grey eminence of the Soviet cinema, never made a documentary, but his historical reenactments, most notably *Strike* (1924) and *The Battleship Potemkin* (1925), have a quality of documentary realism in their presentation of recent Russian history and are the precursors of docudrama.

European documentaries of the 1920s and 1930s, coming from societies neither recently settled, like America, nor torn by revolution, like Russia, tended more toward reflecting the onset of urban problems. In centuries-old cities bursting at their seams with dense, poverty-stricken populations, filmmakers such as Joris Ivens, Alberto Cavalcanti, and Walter Ruttmann produced experimental films that have since been labeled "city symphonies" (Figure 2-6). Films of the period made in France, Holland, Belgium, and Germany are characterized by inventive, impressionistic shooting and editing. One is struck by the romantic attitude of these films to the busy rhythms of daily life and for the stress of living in poor, cramped quarters. The paradox is that, in spite of hardship, the ordinary people in their worn and dirty surroundings show the vitality and humor of their medieval ancestors whose hands originally built the environment. It is as though Bruegel has returned with a camera.

In Spain, Luis Buñuel's *Land Without Bread* (1932) portrayed the appalling poverty and suffering in a remote village on the border with Portugal. Eloquent

FIGURE 2-6

Berlin: Symphony of a City. (The Museum of Modern Art/Film Stills Archive.)

and impassioned, the film leaves the spectator seething with anger at a social system too lethargic and wrapped in tradition to bother with such obscure citizens.

More than any other power group, the Nazis realized the potency of film in a generation addicted to the cinema. In addition to propaganda films using carefully selected actors to show Aryan supremacy and the preeminence of Hitler's policies, the regime produced two epics so accomplished in the compositional and musical elements of film that they undeniably belong with the great documentaries of all time. Leni Riefenstahl's *Olympia* (1938) presented the 1936 Olympic Games as a paean to the physical being of athletes and, by association, to the supremacy of the Weimar Republic. Along with Riefenstahl's *Triumph of the Will* (1937), this film is regarded as a pinnacle in the exploitation of nonfiction cinema's potential (Figure 2-7).

What is so sinister in this valuation is that *Triumph of the Will* has also been acknowledged as the greatest advertising film ever made. Its apparent subject was the 1934 Nazi Congress in Nuremberg, but its true purpose was to mythicize Hitler and show him as the god of the German people. It is an abiding discomfort that great cinema art should eulogize such a monstrous figure, but Riefenstahl's

FIGURE 2-7

A Hitler massed rally in *Triumph of the Will*. (The Museum of Modern Art/Film Stills Archive.)

FIGURE 2-8

Resnais' impassioned plea for humane watchfulness in *Night and Fog*. (Films Inc.)

career stands as a reminder of how reality needs wise and responsible interpretation if art is to be on the side of the angels.

World War II, which immolated half of Europe, was a time of prodigious factual filming. Most documentaries were government sponsored and focused on the consequences of massive warfare: the destruction of cities, homelessness, the plight of the millions of refugees, as well as the lives of the soldiers, sailors, and airmen who fought for their countries. Ironically, it was the Nazis' own film records that contributed such damning evidence to Alain Resnais' *Night and Fog* (1955), possibly the single most powerful documentary ever made about the human capacity for destroying our own kin (Figure 2-8).

NEW TECHNOLOGY LEADS TO ADVANCES IN FORM

The documentary film remained tethered to the limitations of its clumsy technology well into the 1950s, when bulky cameras and huge, power-hungry sound recorders were all that was available. Although location sync sound was possible, equipment limitations turned documentary participants into stilted actors. One has only to see a late Flaherty film, such as *Louisiana Story* (1948), to sense the subjugation of content and form to an inflexible technology. Even Jennings' excellent *Fires Were Started* (1943) is so self-consciously arranged and shot that one has to remind oneself after dialogue sequences that the people and the scenes of wartime London ablaze are actual war footage.

Life was too often staged and too seldom caught as it happened. But technological advances changed all this. One was magnetic tape sound recording, which permitted a relatively small, portable audio recorder, and another was the Eclair self-blimped (mechanically quiet) camera, which made handheld sync filming possible. Its magazine design also allowed quick reloading with only seconds of down time during magazine changes. Yet another advance came from Ricky Leacock and the Robert Drew group at Time Inc. in New York. They solved the problem of recording sync without having to link the tape recorder and camera with constricting wires.

By the beginning of the 1960s these advances transformed every phase of location filming, from news gathering and documentary to improvised dramatic production. The outcome was a revolution in the relationship between camera and subject. Now truly mobile and flexible, the camera and recorder became observers adapting to life as it unfolded. A handheld unit could be operated by two people and follow wherever the action might lead. The camera became an active observer, and this showed on the screen in the immediacy and unpredictability of the new cinema form.

FIGURE 2-9

Flaherty shooting silent footage for *Louisiana Story.* Sound was impractical on location. (The Museum of Modern Art/Film Stills Archive.)

DIRECT CINEMA AND *CINÉMA VÉRITÉ*

The new spontaneous mobility evoked two very different philosophies concerning what was most truthful in the relationships between the camera and its subjects. In America, the Maysles brothers, Fred Wiseman, and others favored *direct cinema*. Their observational approach intruded as little as possible in order to capture the spontaneity and uninhibited flow of live events. The emphasis was on shooting informally without special lighting or evident preparations, and waiting for events of significance to take shape.

Direct cinema proponents claim a certain purity for the method, but unless the camera is actually hidden—an ethically dubious practice at best—participants are usually aware of its presence and cannot help but modify their behavior. Certainly audience members feel like privileged observers, but the authenticity of what they think they are seeing is often questionable. The integrity of observation claimed by direct cinema proponents is more illusory than actual, because its appearance is sustained by editing out material where the illusion is broken, such as when participants glance at the camera. Direct cinema works best when events consume participants' attention; it works progressively less well as the camera gains visibility and priority.

The second approach was called *cinéma vérité* and originated with Jean Rouch in France. He had learned from his ethnographic experience in Africa that making a documentary record of a way of life was itself an important relationship. Like Flaherty with Nanook, Rouch found that authorship could usefully and legitimately be shared between participants and the filmmaker. Permitting and even encouraging interaction between the subject and director, *cinéma vérité* legitimized the camera's presence and let the director be a catalyst for what took place on the screen. Most importantly, it authorized the director to initiate characteristic events and to prospect for privileged moments rather than passively await them.

Eric Barnouw, in his excellent *Documentary: A History of the Non-Fiction Film* (London: Oxford University Press, 1974), sums up the differences as follows:

> The direct cinema documentarist took his camera to a situation of tension and waited hopefully for a crisis; the Rouch version of *cinéma vérité* tried to precipitate one. The direct cinema artist aspired to invisibility; the Rouch *cinéma vérité* artist was often an avowed participant. The direct cinema artist played the role of uninvolved bystander; the *cinéma vérité* artist espoused that of provocateur.

Direct cinema found its truth in events available to the camera. *Cinéma vérité* was committed to a paradox: that artificial circumstances could bring hidden truth to the surface.

Since both approaches capitalized on the spontaneous, neither could be scripted. Freed from the tyranny of the blueprint, film editors began inventing a film language that involved building in a freer, more intuitive form, using counterpointed voice tracks and flexuous, impressionistic cutting to abridge time and space. These poetic advances were adopted by the fiction feature film.

The *cinéma vérité* practitioner affects filmed reality willingly, and the direct cinema proponent does so unwillingly, but in practice the two approaches really have much in common. The claim of fidelity to the actual is all the more questionable if one acknowledges that editing routinely brings together on the screen what in life is separated by time and space. Like the fiction film, the documentary is plainly channeled through a well-defined human point of view despite its appearance of objectivity and verisimilitude. In the end, it summons, as best it can, the spirit of things rather than the letter, and it is all the more exciting because of this.

How then can we judge a film's claim to fairness and truth? Only the audience and the audience's knowledge of life can determine if a film is "truthful." This is subjective and requires emotional and experiential judgments.

In the United States, actor John Cassavetes used the new portable 16mm equipment to shoot his first film, a fiction piece that capitalized on the power of Method dramatic improvisation. *Shadows* (1959) was grittily shot and difficult to hear, but undeniably powerful in its spontaneity. The intrepid Albert and David Maysles (Figure 2-10), who had cobbled their own equipment together, produced their documentary, *Salesman* (1969). It uses observational or direct cinema to follow a band of hard-nosed bible salesmen on a sales drive in Florida. With humor and sympathy, it shows how American salesmen are tormented on the rack of success, and to what limits they go in order to meet company-dictated quotas. It also proves how accurately Willy Loman in *Death of a Salesman* epitomizes the dilemma of the American corporate male. Few works expose the operating costs of the American dream with more deadly wit.

The Maysles brothers' *Gimme Shelter* (1970) followed the Rolling Stones to their gigantic outdoor concert at Altamont, California. Many camera crews were

FIGURE 2-10

Albert and David Maysles—a complete film unit ready to go. (Wolfgang Volz.)

deployed, and the film continually cuts from position to position in the swollen, restless crowd. Showing the mean, dangerous side of the 1960s counterculture, the film culminates with the murder of a troublemaker in the crowd by the Hell's Angels. The film is mainly remarkable for its omniscient view of a mass movement.

A fine French film benefitting from the new mobility was Pierre Schoendoerffer's *The Anderson Platoon* (1967) (Figure 2-11). With his crew, Schoendoerffer, who was originally a French army cameraman, risked his life following a platoon of GIs in Vietnam who were led by a black lieutenant. We accompany the Anderson platoon for many days, experiencing what it is like to grapple with an invisible enemy, to fight without real purpose or direction, and to be wounded or dying far from home. The film honors the ordinary soldier without ever romanticizing war; compassionately it watches and listens, moving on the ground and in the air with the depleted patrol. Making frequent use of music, the film achieves the eloquence of a folk ballad.

Another filmmaker whose art developed out of mobility is the American Fred Wiseman. Originally a law professor, he was moved to make a film about an institution to which he normally brought his class. *The Titicut Follies* (1967) shows life among the inmates of Bridgewater State Hospital in Massachusetts, an institution for the criminally insane. The staff, unaware of how they looked to the out-

FIGURE 2-11

The Anderson Platoon, a ballad of an unwinnable war. (Films Inc.)

side world, allowed Wiseman to shoot a huge amount of footage, which he accomplished using minimal equipment and no special lighting. The result is a violently disturbing, haunting film that shows scene after scene of institutionalized cruelty, thought by those outside the profession to have ended in the eighteenth century. The film caused a furor and was immediately banned by state legislators from being shown in Massachusetts.

A more retrospective study, Marcel Ophuls' magnificently subtle analysis of the spread of fascist collaboration in France during World War II, *The Sorrow and the Pity* (1970), helped to open the discussion of an era of shame for the French. In the United States, Peter Davis' *Hearts and Minds* (1974) was a similarly excellent, hard-hitting work that examined the roots of American involvement in Vietnam.

Cinematographer Haskell Wexler has been involved with documentaries since the 1960s. He covered the 1965 March on Washington with *The Bus* (1965), filmed a personal journey through North Vietnam in *Introduction to the Enemy* (1974), and shot footage for Joseph Strick's *Interviews with My Lai Veterans* (1971). He used his experience as a camera operator to develop a fiction film, *Medium Cool* (1969), which is set among actual events that took place during the 1968 Democratic Convention riots in Chicago. The latter film portrays a news

FIGURE 2-12

Harlan County, USA, a film showing real-life violence in the making. (Krypton International Corp.)

cinematographer jerked out of the cocoon of his craft to a growing political awareness. It crystallizes the unease Americans were feeling at the violence, both inside and outside the country, being perpetrated by their government in the name of democracy.

Another fine American documentary is Barbara Kopple's *Harlan County, USA* (1976), which follows the development of a Kentucky miners' strike and shows that the bad old days of company intimidation and violence are still with us (Figure 2-12). In the finest tradition of the genre, Kopple shows us the close-knit ties and stoic humor of this exploited community. Surely no film has more graphically spelled out the ugly side of capitalism or the moral right of working people to protect themselves from it. Her *American Dream* (1990) documents the divisions within another lengthy strike, this time at the Hormel meat factory. In an America that is downsizing, hostile to organized labor, and on the cusp of massive changes in the patterns of employment and consumption, the workers were destined to lose this battle.

THE DOCUMENTARY AND TELEVISION

In the 1960s, increased camera mobility was matched by improvements in color-stock sensitivity. Shooting in color increased the price of filmmaking, and the stock budget became an increasing obstacle to documentary production. By this time, television had bitten deeply into cinema box-office figures, and the documentary had migrated from the cinemas to the home screen. Always potentially embarrassing to its patron, the documentary now had to exist by permission of giant television networks whose executives have always been susceptible to commercial, political, and moral pressure groups. Even the BBC, with its relatively liberal and independent reputation, drew the line at broadcasting *Warrendale* (1967), a Canadian film about a controversial treatment center for disturbed adolescents (Figure 2-13).

Likewise, Peter Watkins' chilling *The War Game* (1965), a BBC docudrama founded on facts known from the firebombing of Dresden and made to show the effect of a nuclear attack on London, waited 20 years to be broadcast (Figure 2-14). It is hard to see this kind of censorship as anything but blatant paternalism.

For better or for worse, the ever-insecure documentary maker now depended on the approval and good will of television companies for survival. But documentaries, even when mandated in a communications charter, are a minority interest; they tend to concentrate on problems and areas of concern. They are awkward to absorb into an entertainment system because their length and content are best determined by an individual's judgment. They are quite often slow, make demands on the audience's concentration, and are thought to be "unentertaining." They garner low ratings and from the position of an anxious television executive are dispensable.

The documentary is, however, a vitally dramatic form for surveying actuality. In a pluralistic society committed to principles of free speech, it plays a critically important role in informing public opinion. Because they make no profits from advertisers, documentary filmmakers depend on enlightened sponsorship to fund their work, or on finding ways to make documentaries more widely relevant and

FIGURE 2-13

Disturbed children on the razor's edge from *Warrendale*. (The Museum of Modern Art/Film Stills Archive.)

appealing. This is, in fact, happening and documentaries are becoming more popular.

TECHNOLOGY: MORE WALLS COME TUMBLING DOWN

The spread of cable television, the ubiquitous video rental store, and video on demand delivered via phone lines together promise some fascinating changes. The familiar network control that gives the viewer so little real choice is giving way to diversity. Cable companies such as Home Box Office are actually financing nonfiction films, while the Discovery Channel shows nothing else, and shows it worldwide.

Digital and interactive video, in which computerized operation allows the user to choose a path through the available material, offers a variety of instructional and entertainment possibilities. In addition, the video industry is getting ready to upgrade standards for picture sharpness and sound fidelity in what was to be called high definition television, but will probably turn into a merging of technologies. A relationship between music, television, the computer, the Internet, and home entertainment is evolving rapidly as all of these systems incorporate digital electronics. Because of all of these changes, the film/video industry seems

FIGURE 2-14

The War Game, a frightening view of nuclear disaster that was kept from the public. (Films Inc.)

set to follow the more flexible, venturesome publishing operation that has long been the norm in the music recording industry. All that can be said with confidence is that the electronics industry is evolving products of enormous potential for the home and workplace, and is doing it faster than the average person can even follow in newspapers and journals.

Not only are distribution cartels changing, but the tremendous cost of making videos seems likely to become a thing of the past. A new generation of digital video camcorders is appearing, with picture and sound quality in a $4,000 machine that rival those of Betacam, the previous industry state-of-the-art system. An hour of color sync recording can now be made on a 6mm tape cassette costing no more than a decent meal. Just as 16mm film superseded 35mm as the medium for television filming, so tape formats are shrinking in size and cost. The truckloads of equipment and engineers previously needed for location recording were replaced by a large camcorder, and this is being replaced by small, one-person-operated digital instruments capable of high-quality color and sound recording. Digital 6mm videorecording is producing impressive audio and video quality at modest prices from pint-sized instruments. The professional models do even better. Either can feed almost directly into a computer hard disk, and with the development of lower priced nonlinear postproduction, the day is soon arriving when desktop production will be able to produce broadcast quality output with compact disk

(CD) quality sound (Figure 2-15). What is truly revolutionary is that generations of copies can be made digitally that are every bit (no pun intended) identical to the original. The days of generational loss are at last passing, and a longer lasting archiving medium is now in sight.

Higher resolution, large screens, and high-fidelity sound will transform society's forum for ideas and entertainment, although the cinema, as a place to see a show with a large audience, will probably always endure.

Developments in technology always herald innovations in form. One-person, broadcast-quality video filmmaking is now a reality. What Ross McElwee did with difficulty and at great expense in his delightful *Sherman's March* (1989), that is, filming a series of serendipitous encounters unaided, can now be done as easily and quickly as making a tape recording. Not only can the filmmaker record with little fuss, he or she can go home and edit on a home computer as if writing on a word processor. The consequences for new forms of film authorship are exciting. Admirers of the brilliant Chris Marker, for example, can build on the diary form used in his intensely personal essay films. The BBC series *Video Diaries* does this by equipping non-filmmakers who have interesting jobs or an inherently dramatic

FIGURE 2-15

D-Vision OnLINE desktop postproduction screen. Using a PC with WindowsNT and a Targa 2000DTX, this system can post-produce to broadcast quality picture and CD quality sound. (Photo courtesy of D-Vision Systems, Inc.)

life situation with a miniature camera, and then providing expert help in editing. The results are often fascinating and significant, because a non-filmmaker with only a little basic training can now document a journey or reunion and reflect publicly on its impact and meaning. Thus an adoptee in search of her biological parents can record every major step in this most fundamental and moving of all journeys, and with the help of a highly skilled editing and producing team, can share the frustrations and revelations of self-discovery.

Soon high school students may begin to use the screen with the same freedom offered a writer using a computer and paper. As everyone knows, there is more to writing than paper, but undeniably the low cost of paper allows writers to experiment and evolve. Evolution for filmmakers has never been easy. The medium is hard to use competently, and previously only the lucky, the aggressive, or the privileged could even make an attempt. Just as inexpensive magnetic recording facilities unlocked the door to impoverished musicians in the 1960s, access to video facilities is democratizing the hands at the controls in the film and video world. There is no reason why original films should not reach a selective and fair-sized audience as the delivery mechanisms expand and their hunger for product grows. That, after all, is what capitalism is good at.

THE DOCUMENTARY'S FUTURE

This brief survey of the documentary's history—little more than a personal sketch of its highlights—is meant to show that the documentary is increasingly a medium for the individual, committed voice. The required crew is small and getting smaller, and the approach is intimate, while accommodating a balance of structured preparation and existential spontaneity. A documentary is the sum of relationships during a period of shared action and living, a composition made from the sparks generated during a meeting of hearts and minds.

Documentary makers have an ardent respect for the integrity of the actual, for the primacy of the truth in the lives of real people both great and small. The documentary maker's mission is not to change or evade destiny but rather to embrace its substance, to speak passionately of the lessons of history and the choices still available for making a more humane and generous society. Experimentation with and learning about this mission is opening up because technological advances are putting new tools in ordinary people's hands.

We are also seeing an awakened public interest in actuality films, from "info-tainment," cop shows, and popular shows that exploit home movie clips, all the way to the work of serious independent filmmakers. The Public Broadcasting Service (PBS), in its *POV* series, has begun showing the work of independents on a variety of controversial subjects. American documentaries are penetrating the cinemas. A number of documentaries, such as *Sherman's March* (1989), *The Thin Blue Line* (1989), *Roger and Me* (1989), *Brother's Keeper* (1992), *Hoop Dreams* (1994), and *Crumb* (1994), have all made it to the big screen. The audience choice of best movie for the 1989 Chicago International Film Festival was *Roger and Me*, and critics have noted two years running that in the Sundance Festival of independent filmmakers, documentaries have greater vitality than fiction.

The popularity of any film lies in finding fresh language and innovative form, which are discussed in more detail later, but there is also a movement toward what may be called the ordinary person's "voice." It is particularly strong and pertinent in re-examining history, as *Yesterday's Witness* showed in England. Said to be the world's first television oral history series, *Yesterday's Witness* started production in the late 1960s and ran to over 100 episodes. Overview histories have yet to be made by those outside the establishment, and although the man in the street has been the subject of documentary since the form's inception, only now is he (and she, of course) becoming the author.

As electronic publishing on cable, by satellite, and through the Internet becomes more extensive, and more responsive to minority interests, there will be an increased demand for personal films about actuality and for films with imaginative and committed authorship. The medium needs new products, new approaches, and new voices.

Your time has come.

P A R T   2

IDENTITY AND AUTHORSHIP

CHAPTER 3
Finding Your Creative Identity   37

Find Your Life Issues   39
Projects   39
    3-1 The Self-Inventory   39
    3-2 Alter Egos   41
    3-3 Using Dreams to Find Your
       Preoccupations   42
    4-4 Goals Summary   42
Finding Your Work's Path   42

CHAPTER 4
Developing Your Story Ideas   44

Collecting Raw Materials   44
    Journal   44
    Newspapers and Magazines   45
    History   45
    Myths and Legends   45
    Family Stories   46
    Childhood Stories   46
    Social Science and Social History   46
    Fiction   47
Testing a Subject   47
Using the Medium   49
Local Can Be Large   50
Subject-Driven versus Character-Driven
    Films   50
Subjects to Avoid   51
Displace and Transform   51

C H A P T E R 3

FINDING YOUR CREATIVE IDENTITY

Reflecting contemporary life by making documentaries is a wonderful and life-enhancing profession. You are reading this book because this work calls to you. It is a quest for meaning—a fundamental and noble human drive if ever there was one. Like all true learning, it makes one feel completely alive.

Even before you have acquired technical control of the screen, you will want to shoot films that have meaning for you. You are attracted to working in the arts for a purpose. By nature human beings are seekers and one's chosen art form is the vehicle for the quest. You want your filmmaking to be *about* something and you face a central question: How am I to use my developing skills in the world? What kind of subject should I tackle? What can I be good at? Do I have a creative identity, and if so, what is it?

You will probably first make documentaries by looking at something that fascinates you in life and concentrating on how to capture it with the camera. This is quite reasonable, but something will be missing. You. You are missing. If documentary really is "a corner of nature seen through a temperament," then you must also study the heart and mind that are making the choices.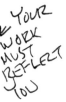

Marketa Kimbrell, the much-respected directing teacher at New York University, says "If you want to put up a tall building you first have to dig a very deep hole." She means that it takes a strong foundation in self-knowledge to build an acting performance or to direct a complex dramatic work. Likewise, to practice documentary effectively and well, one needs insight into the foundation of one's own subjectivities in order to be able to assess and value those of others. A documentary maker tries to get inside other people's realities, to see the world as they see it.

The work we do well is that for which we are specially suited. I believe that we must start by recognizing how life has marked us, and what passions and compulsions each of us harbors as a result. This means seeing nonjudgmentally what long-term tensions we carry, and to what personality traits we resonate. Each of us treads a path largely of our own making. Novalis put it memorably as, "Character is destiny."

However, we are used to seeing ourselves as *acted upon,* and we seldom comprehend how we act on others. We are particularly blind to the consistency of purpose in our less conscious and less commendable actions. This is good enough perhaps as an instinctual way to live one's life, but for anyone working in the creative arts it is no better than sleepwalking. Film exists to create a sophisticated stream of consciousness in an audience, so we can do no less in ourselves. Undertaking this won't be a quick fix, indeed it implies a lifetime of inward work to match the outward professional career.

Having watched the evolution of a good many directors, I believe that we may be best served by making a good provisional profile of our formation and fascinations. Then, through filmmaking, we test, amend, and extend it. I recommend that you only profile who you are and what you are doing *for the purposes of making the film in hand.* By seeing through the eyes of a characterized self, your vantage will be stabilized and you will be able to get the film made. Developing knowledge of oneself is a work in progress, and each film is a stage, in both senses of the word. However, using filmmaking to search for a final or ultimate self is not recommended; it leads into a hall of mirrors and to making egocentric films that are either unwatchable, or unfinishable.

Those with dramatic life experience (say, of warfare, survival in labor camps, or of being orphaned) seldom doubt which subjects to tackle. But for the rest of us who live more ordinary lives, placing an identity on our own undoubted sense of mission can be baffling. We face a conundrum; we can't make art without a sense of identity, yet identity is also what we are seeking through making art.

Many are attracted to the arts because they feel the need for self-expression, but this phrase has a variety of applications. The most prevalent is that of self-affirmation, but this suggests that art and therapy are synonymous. I think art is about doing work in the world, while therapy is about acquiring a sense of normality and well-being. There's nothing wrong with that. Self-affirmation in the arts, however, can become the slippery slope to self-display, and any inventory of beliefs and achievements leads rather too easily to homily.

Another approach to self-expression rests with form. Some people feel that by mastering particular styles and genres, they can carve out an identity, but I fear that this is another misguided quest for individuality in a society uncomfortably locked together by mass media. We live in an age that has elevated individuality to godhood. It tells us that Self is that which is different from everyone else. But historically this is a recent western idea that gathered force during the Renaissance when man began making himself, rather than God, the center of the universe. The Hindus see things differently. To them, Self is that which you *share* with all creation. Significantly, this is inclusive while the western ideology is isolating. Most who are trying to create something actually subscribe to both ends of the spectrum. They want to be individual and recognized, but they also want to create something universal—another conundrum.

You may be asking, does all this really matter so early in one's career? Maybe not, but most of us are anxious to find what we are best equipped to handle, and I think these instincts are right. Indeed, without some persuasions about cause and effect in life, without a perception of its order, we lack the vision to create vision. How, then, do we go about defining ourselves in order to direct documentaries?

Actually the choices are mercifully few. Our lives have marked us irrevocably, and these marks—whether we know it or not—largely determine what we pursue. We can struggle against this, and deny the marks we carry, but this is a waste of effort and merely evidences their power over us. People achieve only what matters to them. In looking back, we see patterns to our lives, and we see what has been driving us all along. And we see the patterns compelling those we know well even more clearly.

FIND YOUR LIFE ISSUES

You carry the marks of a few central issues. Reminders unfailingly arouse you to strongly partisan feelings. Though the issues may be few and personal, exploring them sincerely and intelligently will deeply touch your audience and keep you busy for life. We are not talking about autobiography, but about the themes arising from the core of your experience, which offer endless variations.

To find your own life issues means paring away whatever is outside your abiding concerns. Because of the shimmering, ambiguous nature of reality, this is not easy. What is real? What is cause and what is effect? Most filmmakers, unlike writers or painters, seem to stop much too readily at a superficial understanding of their own drives. Documentary is a branch of drama, and if your drama is to be original you *must* develop a dialogue—with yourself, and between yourself and your audience—through the conduit of the stories you tell. Here are a few projects to help begin the process.

PROJECTS

PROJECT 3-1: THE SELF-INVENTORY

To discover your real issues and themes, and what you can truly give to others, make a nonjudgmental inventory of your most moving experiences. This is not difficult since the human memory retains only what it finds significant. If you already think you have a good handle on your underlying issues, try making the inventory anyway—you may be surprised. Honestly undertaken, this project will reveal which life events have formed you, and knowing of their existence will urge you to work to explore the underlying issues. You will probably find that you have resonated with these issues all along when you consider your affinities in music, literature, and films, not to mention the choices you have made in your friendships, love affairs, and family relationships.

Here's what to do:

1. Go somewhere private and write rapid, short notations of each major experience just as it comes to mind. Keep going until you have at least ten or a dozen experiences in which you were deeply moved (to joy, to rage, to panic, to fear, to disgust, to anguish, to love, etc.).

2. Now stand back and organize them into at least two or three groups. Name each grouping and define the relationships between them. Some moving ex-

periences will be positive (with feelings of joy, relief, discovery, laughter), but most will be painful. Make no distinction, for there is no such thing as a negative or positive truth. To discriminate is to censor, which is just another way to prolong the endless and wasteful search for acceptability. Truth is *truth*—period!

3. Now examine what you've written as though looking objectively at someone else's record. By placing yourself in a different light, you should find trends, even a certain vision of the world, clustering around these experiences. In profiling yourself, don't be afraid to be provisional and imaginative, as though developing a fictional character. Your object is not to psychoanalyze yourself or to find ultimate truth. That would be impossible. Just fashion a storytelling identity, a role that you can play with all your heart. Because it's a role, you can change it, evolve it, improve it as you go.

4. Now write notes that, without disclosing anything too private, will enable you to describe objectively, aloud, and to friends or documentary colleagues:

a. The **main marks your life has left on you** during formative experiences. Keep your description of the experiences to a minimum and concentrate on their effects.
    Example: "Growing up in an area at war, I was someone who had an early fear and loathing of uniforms and uniformity. When my father came home after the war, my mother became less accessible, and my father was closer to my older brother, so I thought of myself as having to do things alone."

b. Two or three **themes** that emerge from the marks you carry.
    Examples:
    "Too much separation breeds self-sufficiency but inability to fit in."
    "Someone who takes what you value can also give you the courage to
        fight back."
    "Fighting enemies is a cover for lack."
    "Good work often gets done for the wrong reasons."

c. Five or six very **different characters toward** whom you feel unusual empathy. These can be people you know, or people who exist and whom you could contact.
    Examples:
    A friend who grew up in an orphanage who has trouble with women
        and intimacy
    A friend who avoids his real issues by putting all his energies into the en-
        vironmental protest movement
    An older woman who is fighting back because her boss claimed she was
        incompetent when he wanted to replace her with someone younger
    People whose emotional control has put them in a situation of crisis
    Loners who construct their own self-contained worlds
    People who swim against the tide or who distrust authority
    Anyone searching for something he or she has lost

d. Three or four **provisional film topics.** Make them as different from each other as possible, but all should be alternative ways to explore your central concerns. Displacing one's concerns into other areas of life avoids autobiography and lets you enter new worlds that you will nevertheless see with knowledge-able eyes. Choose ones that reflect the concerns to which you are already committed.

Examples:

Anyone whose existence is made difficult by having to keep their real
identity secret, such as a gay person in the military

Someone entering a situation where she feels unacceptably different

Anyone who has begun to seriously doubt the validity of his work

Anyone embattled who thinks he has truth and right on his side, and
who doesn't

Anyone forced into a lesser role and who must find ways to still feel she
still has value

PROJECT 3-2: ALTER EGOS

Some people believe there is a single "true" self, while others believe that we are made of multiple personalities, each evoked by particular circumstances. The latter view, whether true or not, is convenient for storytelling, which is what documentary really is. So, another approach to one's deeper aspirations and identifications is by uncovering those characters or situations to which you particularly resonate. The aim here is supplement what you did in the previous exercise with an additional and, if possible, rather different self-characterization.

1. List six or eight characters from literature or fiction with whom you have a special affinity. Arrange them by their importance to you. An affinity can be hero worship, but it becomes more interesting when one is responding to darker or more complex qualities.

2. Do the same thing for public figures, such as actors, politicians, sports figures, etc.

3. Make a third list of people you know or have known and who have had an influence on you, but leave out immediate family if they complicate the exercise.

4. Take the top two or three in each list and write a brief description of what, in human or even mythical qualities, each person represents, and what dilemma seems to typify them. One person top on my list would be a young nurse in the Spanish Civil War who, faced with a corridor of seriously wounded young soldiers, had to choose the few who would come under the care of the only surgeon. To me she represents the unlucky person suddenly facing tragic responsibilities and who loses her carefree youth forever because she will never be free of doubt whether she chose well.

5. Using only what the resonances suggest, write a self-profile as truthfully as you can manage. If a different character emerges, don't worry. The aim is not to define who you are (you'll never succeed) but to build a provocative and active picture of *what you are looking for and how you intend to act in the world.* Don't hesitate to imaginatively round out the portrait as though it were a fictional character.

6. Discuss what kind of work this person should be doing.

PROJECT 3-3: USING DREAMS TO FIND YOUR PREOCCUPATIONS

Keep a log of your dreams, for here the mind expresses itself unguardedly and in surreal and symbolic imagery. Unless you have a period of intense dream activity, you will have to keep a record over many months before common denominators and motifs begin showing up. Keep a notebook next to your bed, and awake gently so that you hold onto the dream long enough to write it down. When you get really interested in this work, you will automatically awake after a good dream so that you can write it down. Needless to say, this will not be popular with a bedroom partner.

Dreams often project a series of forceful and disturbing images. By keeping track of the dream rather than an interpretation, you can return and reinterpret as you amass more material. These images are often key to your deepest thematic concerns.

PROJECT 3-4: GOALS SUMMARY

To summarize your goals try answering the questions below. Deal honestly with what you know and are, and try to avoid taking refuge in optimism or escapist fantasy.

1. The theme or themes that arise from my self-study are _____

    _____

2. The changes for which I want to work are _____

    _____

3. The kinds of subject for which I feel most passionately are _____

    _____

4. Other important goals I have in mind are _____

    _____

FINDING YOUR WORK'S PATH

The self-profile that has emerged should bring you closer to an inner self who has all along been searching for his or her own path. Your life has given you special understanding of certain forces and the way they work in the world. As you commit yourself to showing them at work, expressing something of what you feel about them, the process of your work will release further understanding. This is the creative process, something that is cyclical, endlessly fascinating, and that brings us closer to others.

In documentary the learning process is lengthy and demanding. At the beginning you get clues, clues lead to discoveries, discoveries lead to movement in your work, and movement leads to new clues and a new piece of work in which to evolve them. Work—whether a piece of writing, a painting, a short story, a film script, or a documentary—is therefore both the evidence of movement and a prime mover in discovering more meaning. Our work becomes the trail and the vehicle for our own evolution.

Filmmaking has risks. It is an intensely socializing process, and you can easily lose yourself amid all the orthodoxies and criticisms of the people around you. Film is made and viewed collectively, so you will need a strong sense of purpose and self if you are to hold on to the meanings in your work.

Finding and acting on the self-discovery material in this chapter means taking chances and trusting that it will lead somewhere. If you work closely with other people (as I hope you do), you will need to take chances, because having people listen and react to your story is important to discovering and accepting it yourself. The person who chooses to take the bull by the horns and become an artist cannot remain private. In any group you'll see the courageous who go out on a limb, and others too afraid to show themselves. Telling your own story to creative partners is the prerequisite, for we cannot urge liberation in others until we have first liberated ourselves.

Not every environment supports this kind of work. Depending on traditions and leadership, some are intensely competitive because perquisites, patronage, or other advantages are at stake. This is an unfortunate fact of life, to be deplored but also to be circumvented. You cannot wait around for ideal circumstances before doing what's important to your forward movement in life. The best work situations are nurturing yet demanding, and here you see people flower and evolve over a period of time.

If you feel you are not making good progress, don't despair. Production work puts you constantly in situations of change and growth. Facing and overcoming dilemmas is an important part of developing your creative identity, which isn't completed before entering production, but goes on all the time—from film to film, from cradle to grave.

C H A P T E R 4

DEVELOPING YOUR STORY IDEAS

Making documentary has something in common with writing fiction. The first step is to find and develop an idea. Writers habitually change hats and the two worn most often are "story discovery" and "story development and editing." These modes use quite different parts of your mind: One is looking for the subject or topic that brings a "shock of recognition," and this takes imagination and instincts. The other is a deliberate analysis, testing, and structuring of what one finds to see if it can be made into a good cinematic tale.

Let's first examine where documentary ideas are waiting to be found.

COLLECTING RAW MATERIALS

The seeker is the person committed to searching for meaning among the many baffling clues, hints, and details in life. If you are one, you are probably using some of what I'm about to describe—ways of collecting and sifting material for a story, *the* story you need to tell. When you examine your collection diligently, you will actually see the outlines of the collector, the shadowy Self that is implacably assembling what it needs to represent its own preoccupations, and nowhere more so than in a journal.

JOURNAL

Keep a journal and note down anything that strikes you, no matter what its nature. This means always carrying a notebook and being willing to use it publicly and often. If you have a computer, try copying incidents into a simple database under a variety of thematic or other keys, so you can call up material by particular priorities or groupings. A computer isn't better than, say, index cards, except that it lets you juggle and print your collection, and experiment with different structures.

Rereading your journal becomes a journey through your most intense ideas and associations. The more you note what catches your eye, the nearer you move to your current themes and underlying preoccupations. You may think you know them all, but you don't.

NEWSPAPERS AND MAGAZINES

Real life is where you find the really outlandish true tales. Keep clippings or transcribe anything that catches your interest and classify them in a system of your own. Again, categorizing is creative busywork because it helps you discover underlying structures, both in life and in your fascinations.

Newspapers are a cornucopia of the human condition at every level, from the trivial to the global. Local papers are particularly useful because the landscape and characters are accessible and reflect local economy, local conditions, and local idiosyncrasies. The agony columns, the personals, even the ads for lost animals can all suggest subjects and characters. With every source, you have possible characters, situations, plots, and a meaning to be found.

HISTORY

History doesn't happen, it gets written. Look at *why* someone makes a record or *why* someone writes a historical overview, and you see not objective truth but someone's interpretation and wish to mark or persuade. History is all about point of view—that's why they say that historians find what they look for.

The past is full of great and small figures who have participated in the dramas that interest you. In *Luther* the playwright John Osborne explored the predicament of the antiestablishment rebel through Martin Luther; Alan Bennett in *The Madness of King George* investigated paternal authority as it veers over the brink of insanity; and Steven Spielberg brought alive Oskar Schindler in *Schindler's List* so he could explore the awful predicament of being Jewish in Nazi-dominated Europe. History is the full canvas of human drama, full of repetitions, and thus full of analogues to contemporary situations. Even within living memory there are millions of wonderful stories waiting to be told.

If history excites you, maybe your job is to tell the stories that have force and meaning for you. Do it well and you will move and persuade others to act a little differently ("those who forget history are condemned to relive it").

MYTHS AND LEGENDS

Legend is inauthentic history; by taking a real figure and examining the actuality of that person in relation to the legend, one can discover what humankind fashions out of figures who catch public imagination. This is the subject of Mark Rappoport's *From the Journals of Jean Seberg* (1995), which uses a look-alike actress to play the part of a hypothetical Jean Seberg, who, instead of dying at 40, looks back questioningly at her earlier life.

Every culture, locality, community, or family has its icons who reflect the national or local sense of saints, fools, demons, and geniuses. When you can find them or resurrect them, they make powerfully emblematic film subjects. All these cultural units also have their own myths, many translatable into a modern setting. Myth is useful because it expresses particular conflicts that humans have found enduringly insoluble, and which must therefore be accommodated. The human truths in Greek mythology (for instance) do not lead to easy or happy resolution, but instead leave the bittersweet aftertaste of fate and prove to be unexpectedly uplifting. Yes, that's how it *is!*

Each generation regenerates myths for its own purposes, using them to frame contemporary characters and action that are otherwise unresolvable. This quality of paradox and the unanswerable is peculiarly modern. Virtually every character of magnitude in a documentary is reenacting one or more myths, so finding out what mythical roles your characters represent is a powerful part of discovering what thematic thrust lies dormant and waiting to be released in your documentary.

FAMILY STORIES

All families have favorite stories that define special members. My grandmothers both seem like figures out of fiction. My mother's mother was said to find things before people lost them. In all respects conventional, she had mild kleptomania, especially where flowers and fruit were concerned. At an advanced age, during breaks in long car journeys, she would hop over garden walls to borrow a few strawberries or liberate a fistful of chrysanthemums. How a family explains and accommodates its most eccentric member is a tale in itself.

My other grandmother began life as a rebel in an English village, became an Edwardian hippie, married an alcoholic German printer, who beat her and abandoned her in France, where she stayed the rest of her life. The lives of Winifred and her children are too fantastic to be credible in fiction, but there are many aspects that could make a documentary. Family tales can be heroic or they can be very dark, but being oral history they are often vivid.

CHILDHOOD STORIES

Everyone emerges from childhood as if from a war zone. If you did the creative identity exercise in the previous chapter, you surely wrote down several traumatic things that happened when you were a child and that are thematic keys to your subsequent life.

One that springs to mind as I write this is when, at the age of seventeen, I overheard on the studio set a misogynistic comment about my editor. On returning to the cutting room, I naively repeated this to her as something absurd, but she flushed scarlet and sped out of the room to find him. I died several deaths waiting for what I felt sure would be murder and mayhem. What a lesson in the price of indiscretion.

The incident has rich thematic possibilities: we are sometimes spies, sometimes guardians, sometimes defenders, sometimes denunciators. When life hands us power, how should we use it? So many invisible influences direct our destiny. How far have you explored yours? What are the documentary correlates to what seared you into consciousness?

SOCIAL SCIENCE AND SOCIAL HISTORY

Social science and social history are excellent resources for documentarians. If one of your themes happens to be the way the poor are exploited, you would find excellent studies of farm, factory, domestic, and other workers. With each will be a bibliography to tell you what other studies have been done. The more modern your source, the bigger the bibliography. Some books now contain filmographies too.

Case histories are a source of trenchant detail when you need to know what is typical or atypical. Case histories usually include both observation and interpretation, so you can see how your interpretation compares with that of the writer. Social scientists are chroniclers and interpreters; their work can inform you from a huge and carefully considered knowledge base. You can use their work also to tell whether your feelings and instincts in a particular area have support elsewhere.

FICTION

Don't separate and discard fiction because you are working with actuality. Works of fiction are sometimes intensely well observed and can give one, in a very concentrated form, an inspiriting sense of guidance. Jane Smiley's *A Thousand Acres* is not only an excellent novel that reinterprets *King Lear* in a midwestern rural setting, it is a superbly knowledgeable evocation of farmers and farming. To read it in association with intended work on, say, the depopulation of the land as big agribusiness takes over family farms, is to be reminded at every level of what a documentary maker should seek.

TESTING A SUBJECT

Testing the power of a subject takes research (to find out what is there) and some self-questioning (to find out if it's for you). Most important is to ask, "Do I *really* want to make a film about this?" An absurd question? Look around and see how often beginners attach themselves to subjects for which they lack knowledge or any emotional investment.

Why do people take on subjects for which they later lose interest? Television has so conditioned us that we tend do what's familiar by unthinking reflex. For Americans, "documentary" means those worthy, laudatory reports made to satisfy station licensing requirements for socially responsible programming. They often lack any critical edge and present a closed, approving view that prevents the audience from making any judgments of its own. No matter how commendable the topic and the judgments, this is propaganda, not real documentary. Good documentaries go beyond factual exposition or let's-all-share-our-goodness boosterism, and tackle areas of life that are complex, ambiguous, and morally taxing.

Making a documentary—I want to say this loud and clear—is a long, slow process. Be prepared for initial enthusiasms to dim over the long haul. You must wed yourself to more than a passing attraction. Try asking questions that dig into your own and the topic's makeup, rather as if you were choosing a new country of residence:

- Is there an area in which I am already knowledgeable and even opinionated?
- Do I feel a strong and emotional connection to it—more so than to any other practicable subject?

- Can I do justice to the subject?
- Do I have a drive to learn more about this subject?

Honestly answered, these questions flush out one's level of commitment. The wish to *learn* is a very good indicator of one's ability to sustain interest and energy. Be careful not to bite off more than you can chew—a common impulse. Simple economics will keep you out of many topics that are only open to large companies. For example, a biographical study of a movie actor would be impossible without corporate backing because the actor's work is only visible in heavily copyrighted works.

Another inaccessibility may arise when one chooses an institution as one's subject. To film the police or the army, for instance, would be insurmountably difficult without very high-level approval. Even a local animal shelter may be hedged around with politics and suspicions. Most institutions have nothing to gain from letting in unverifiable filmmakers who might dig up, or manufacture, damaging evidence. Some institutions make fascinating topics for films but many don't because they are unremarkable and a film merely confirms commonsense expectations.

Narrow your sights and pick a manageable subject area. One gets no awards for failed good intentions, so treat yourself kindly and take on what matches your capabilities and budget. Not for a moment need this confine you to small or insignificant issues. If, for instance, you are fascinated by the roots of the Vietnam War, and you have no access to combat or archival footage, there are always other approaches open to the inventive. You might find that the man who sells newspapers on your street corner is a Vietnam veteran with a fascinating and representative experience. You may then find that he has a network of friends who have snapshots, home movies, and mementos. Now you can make your tale about how Everyman goes to war wanting to believe he's defending freedom.

Ingenuity and a willingness to reject the obvious is the way to refine good subjects. Be aware that one's first and immediate ideas for a subject are generally those everyone else has already had, so to avoid clichés ask yourself:

- What is this subject's underlying significance to me?
- What do most people—like myself—already know?
- What would I—and most people—like to really discover?
- What is unusual and interesting about it?
- Where is its specialness really visible?
- How narrowly (and therefore how deeply) can I focus my film's attention?
- What can I *show?*

Confronting the personal impact of a subject, instead of trying to see everything from an omniscient or audience point of view, usually takes one into new and exciting directions. Trying to discover the unexpected or reveal the unusual is vital if you are to produce a fresh view, and this always seems to involve narrowly defining what you really want to show and what you really want to avoid.

You might, for the sake of argument, want to make a film about inner-city life. But to encompass the whole subject is both impossible and ill advised. Trying to cover too many aspects will lead to thinly supported generalizations, which any mature viewer will reject. On the other hand, profiling a particular café from dawn to midnight might reveal much, and in very specific terms.

Think small. Think local. There are many good films to be made within a mile or two of where you live. Most people do not think of exploiting their own "turf." Think small and local, and, to begin with, think short too. Try your skills on fragments at first, or you risk being overwhelmed and discouraged.

USING THE MEDIUM

Documentary should act on our hearts, not just our minds; it exists *to change how we feel about something*. For example, one can know that women's compositions are seldom played, that virtually no women conduct orchestras, and yet one can have no special feelings about this—after all, the world abounds with worse injustices. It takes *Antonia* (1974) by Jill Godmillow and Judy Collins to change all that. The makers draw us into liking and identifying with Antonia Brico; she had all the qualifications to conduct an orchestra except one: she was not a man. Although this was just one woman's heartbreak, I think of her every time I see an orchestra and I look to see if the leadership roles are any more balanced.

The veteran BBC producer Stephen Peet believes that the best documentaries deliver an emotional shock. This could be in one memorable scene or it could be the sum of a whole biographical film, as in *Antonia*. Really using documentary's potential means going beyond facts and opinions, vital though they may be, to show evidence that will make a strong impact.

"What can I show?" is the key issue, for the screen really is different from other forms of persuasion. Film portrays people and situations by externals, by what can be seen in action. People describing a feeling or an event do not involve us and move us like people seen living through the event and the feelings it evokes. Doing is more interesting, more inherently credible, than talk about doing. Can you collect enough material to tell a story without speech? True, some subjects cannot be anything other than talking heads. And under the right circumstances, a talking head film can be incredibly dramatic. But for many topics, the talking head option ought to be rejected. *Behavior, action, and interaction are always more effective and involving to watch, because they invoke our own thoughts, feelings, and judgments.*

A tough test of any idea is to *imagine that you must make it as a silent film*. This lets you discover quickly whether you are thinking like a journalist or a filmmaker. Choosing the latter forces you to create with the camera instead of the microphone.

Why do we so easily conceive ideas in terms of speech instead of action and image? Perhaps we are all deeply indoctrinated with the habit of show-and-tell. One reaches for an abstraction and then reaches for images to illustrate it. Imagine a journalistic *Nanook of the North*; the film would be based on narration, interview, or a reporter and would use small parts of the action as cutaway illustration. This would be a travesty because it demotes an observed experience, with all its mystery and suspense, to the status of a dreary TV lecture.

The challenge is to scrutinize living reality for ideas that are already incipient and symbolized. When your search is successful, the action of each shootable scene will impart a clear, strong feeling and an implied idea (such as "sons have to kill their fathers in order to become themselves"). No description or corroboration in words will be necessary. You have found drama instead of a sociology illustration.

Good cinematography and good action tend to create a strong *mood*. This predisposes viewers to enter the movie wholeheartedly and opens them to the film's more abstract values. Once a film is freed from the tyranny of the interview with illustrations, it can become more sensual, more lyrical, and more sensitive to atmospheres, lighting, and small but significant details. These build the strong aura of subjectivity a viewer will recognize from her own personally felt experience (don't I wish I'd remembered this during my directing career).

By the way, when you come to edit, assemble all your visual, behavioral material first and develop what it suggests, rather than start with speech organized as a paper edit. This can help prevent speech coming to dominate at the editing stage.

Another way to plan a series of moods through your film is to predesign a sound composition. Audition sound materials indigenous to your intended locations. Using these or other added authentic sound means you can build up a layered and effective sound track. Much of film's power to enter the imagination lies not in the visuals but in sound. As Robert Bresson has said, "The eye sees but the ear imagines." Music, properly used, can make a subtle authorial comment or give focus and dimension to the inner lives of the characters. You should be considering these possibilities when you are auditioning subjects.

A good place to develop a sense of sound design is at an outdoor event, such as a street market, which usually has a profusion of voices, sounds, and music played over radios or speaker systems. Spend some time concentrating on what you hear as if you were a blind person trying to "see" through sound, and make an inventory of what to record.

LOCAL CAN BE LARGE

Try to make films that are thematically large enough for the outside world, and not just aimed parochially at capturing the attention of your peer group. You can, however, take the most localized material and, if your eye is wise, reveal universal truths. This is difficult and comes from evolving your grasp of what it portends. Figuratively this is like starting out blind and willing oneself to see better and better. At any moment one wants to give up and say, "This is all that exists." But it seldom is. This, in fact, is all we have yet seen. There is more, and more.

SUBJECT-DRIVEN VERSUS CHARACTER-DRIVEN FILMS

One way to avoid the didactic film, which lectures or illustrates concepts, is to spurn messages altogether and look instead for characters of magnitude. By this I mean someone of large spirit who is trying to get or do something appreciable in the world. The essence of drama is effort and opposition, so filming people with these qualities means that there will always be ideas and thematic meaning for you to discover and reveal. You have to find these things, and make sure that your film clarifies their nature.

SUBJECTS TO AVOID

Many subjects come to mind easily because they are in our immediate surroundings or are being pumped up by the media. Stay away from

- worlds you haven't experienced and cannot closely observe
- any ongoing, inhibiting problem in your own life (you won't find a new perspective on it while directing a film unit; see a good therapist)
- anything or anyone that is "typical" (nothing real is typical, so nothing typical will ever be interesting or credible)
- preaching or moral instruction of any kind
- films about problems for which you already have the answer (so does your audience)

DISPLACE AND TRANSFORM

After a period of careful inquiry and reflection, take your two or three best subjects and, even though temporary and subject to change, assume they are your own real ones. If you are working directly from events and personalities in your own life, use documentary to find others who have similar situations, so that you can *transform what's on the screen and move to a useful distance from the originals.* This has numerous benefits. It frees you from self-consciousness and allows you to tell all the underlying truths instead of only those palatable to friends and family. Most importantly, it allows you to concentrate on dramatic and thematic truths, instead of getting tangled up in biographical accuracy.

Every film I have ever made has been about imprisonment and trying to escape. It took me many years to discover this. A colleague said that underlying all his films has been the search for a father (his own died when he was young). We are all marked in particular ways, and are deeply moved and motivated by this. Direct autobiography is usually inhibiting, but any of the limitless analogues can be freeing and fascinating.

Research, development, and writing a proposal for a chosen subject are handled in Part 4: Preproduction. First, however, let's look at screen language to clarify how film, and particularly documentary, language works. Keeping your chosen subject in mind will be useful because it will keep you thinking practically rather than in the abstract.

P A R T 3

SCREENCRAFT

CHAPTER 5
Screen Grammar   55

The Shot   56
Shot Denotation and Connotation   57
Shots in Juxtaposition   57
The Axis   59
The Actor and the Acted Upon   60
Subtext   62
Horizontal Movement through Space   62
Vertical Movement through Space   62
Screen Direction   62
Changing Screen Direction   63
Different Angles on the Same Action   63
Abstraction   65
Subjectivity versus Objectivity   66
Duration, Rhythm, and Concentration   66
Sequence   67
Transitions and Transitional Devices   67
Screen Language in Summary   67

CHAPTER 6
Screencraft Analysis Projects   70

Project 6-1: Picture Composition Analysis   70
   Strategy for Study   71
   Static Composition   71
   Visual Rhythm   73
   Dynamic Composition   73
   Internal and External Composition   74
   Composition, Form, and Function   75
Project 6-2: Editing Analysis   76
   First Viewing   77
   Analysis Format   77
   Making and Using a Floor plan   77

   Strategy for Study   78
   First Impressions   78
   Definition and Statistics   79
   Use of Camera   80
   Use of Sound   80
   Editing   81
   Point of View   82
   Defining Point of View and Blocking   82
Project 6-3: Lighting Analysis   84
   Lighting Terminology   84
   Lighting Setups   88
   Strategy for Study   91

CHAPTER 7
Basic Shooting Projects   97

Sound Theory   97
Finding the Problems   98
Finding the Solutions   99
Project 7-1: Voice Recording Experiments
   for Interiors   100
Project 7-2: Voice Recording Experiments
   for Exteriors   101
      Sound Troubleshooting Chart   102
Camera Handling Theory   104
Camera Handling Projects   105
Project 7-3: Tripod: Interview, One Subject   105
Project 7-4: Handheld: Tracking on Static
   Subject   107
Project 7-5: Handheld: Tracking Forward
   on Moving Subject   108
Project 7-6: Handheld: Tracking Backward
   with Moving Subject   108

C H A P T E R   5

SCREEN GRAMMAR

Don't bypass this chapter, thinking it's conventional screen grammar. It isn't. Rather, you'll find here an approach to film language that will keep you from losing your bearings once, as a director, you get caught up in the demands and delights of technique. Making films is really about communicating with audience members, who imbibe film as they do music, not for a demonstration of theories or technical virtuosity, but instead to enter unfamiliar realms of feeling and idea.

This chapter explains how much film language is really an analogue for human perception, action, and reaction. If you never let go of this, your filmmaking will come from the heart as well as the head.

All languages including film have their grammar and conventions. Film's developed from the 1890s, when the early cameramen and actors (and eventually directors) competed to put simple stories before audiences. At first their films were naïvely simple, but within a couple of decades, and in spite of the absence of sound, they invented most of the screen language that we now take for granted. In the various filmmaking centers of the world, they found out what worked by trial and error, with the Russians alone making a concerted effort in the 1920s to formulate what the screen could do. In fact, theory among working filmmakers is still notable for its absence. We should not be surprised; spoken languages of great subtlety flowered long before anyone thought of philology.

Film language is a set of collectively generated conventions that enable us to tell each other stories through the orchestration of images, actions, sounds, and words in time. It exists because human beings of every culture share complex processes of perception and logic. Those in the time arts who routinely make creative decisions—at no matter what level of sophistication—focus most of their discussion on how some aspect of drama "works." Over and over again, the criterion applied to an action, a shot, a line, or a character's motivation is whether it "works." The implication is important; artistic decisions are made in the light of shared instincts of recognition. If it were otherwise, cinema and stage drama could not exist.

Most people learn film technique by copying other filmmakers. This is as natural and risky as actors studying other actors, so we too should heed Stanislavsky's warning that actors should search for the roots of their craft in life itself, not among other actors. Put another way, a copy of a copy is always degraded. Your ideas and feelings about life should be preeminent, and you should use screen techniques as the vehicle for their realization. We certainly learn to speak that way, acquiring language because it gets us what we need. My elder daughter's first sentence was "Meat, I like it." Language is a tool to do or get something (more meat!).

From this rather fundamental perspective, let's look at the different units of film language.

THE SHOT

A shot is a framed image placed on record by someone who thinks it holds meaning. If you view someone else's *rushes* or *dailies* (i.e., footage straight out of the camera), you find yourself constantly trying to figure out what the makers (camera operator and director) were thinking, feeling, and seeking. You assess this not only from what is in the shot, but also *from what it excludes*. A shot of a man staring offscreen may exclude what he sees, and in the process, focuses us on how, rather than what, he is studying.

The more remote the material is in time and place, the easier it is to see the filmmaker searching for meanings, and to see how susceptible he or she was to the received wisdom of the day. The corollary is true: we are more likely to accept present-day footage of familiar scenes as "objective" and value free. But records, whether of actuality or of life enacted or re-enacted, are always *constructs*, they are always subjective, and they always invoke a triangular relationship between content, storyteller, and viewer.

Let me elaborate. Imagine you are hunting through archival shots in a film library, as I once did at the Imperial War Museum in London. After you recover from the atmosphere of a place so packed with sad ghosts, you notice from the library stockshots that by today's standards their cameras and film stock were less developed. Even so, each shot testifies, in addition to its subject, to different kinds of involvement from its makers, that is, different emotions, emphases, and agendas.

Imagine you run a shot that some librarian has labeled, "Russian soldiers, vicinity of Warsaw, running into sniper fire." From the first frame you notice how emotionally loaded everything seems: It's shot in high contrast black-and-white film stock that accentuates the mood, and the air is smoky because lighting comes from behind the subjects. Though here, as elsewhere, filming is undeniably a mechanical process of reproduction, everything is polarized by the interrelationship of human choice, technology, subject, and environment, and all of these things are contributing to what you feel. The camera enters the soldiers' world because it runs jerkily with them instead of shooting from a sheltered tripod. You catch your breath when a soldier falls because the cameraman almost trips over his fallen comrade. The camera recovers, and continues onward, leaving the wounded soldier to his fate. Then suddenly it plunges to the ground. The camera motor runs out framing some out-of-focus mud. With slow horror you realize you have just accompanied a cameraman in his last seconds of work. Feeling desolation, you replay his shot several times. You notice that when you hold on particular frames, it seems as though time and destiny can be replayed, re-entered, and relived. Even when you replay something and "know" what's going to happen, *film is always in the present tense.*

Now someone brings you a photo of a dead cameraman lying face down on the battlefield, his camera fallen from his hands. It's him. Your poor cameraman. You recognize the knob of mud from his last seconds of film. Left alone with him, you ponder the combination of forces that made him willing to gamble his life to do this work. You wonder whom he left behind, and whether they learned how he died. You are his witness, but you have also *become* him, taken on his destiny. He will always be with you, somewhere. You have grown and will always *be* him, somewhere in the recesses of your own being.

Really, a shot's meaning can go very far beyond its subject.

SHOT DENOTATION AND CONNOTATION

If you can identify a shot's content you know what a shot denotes, but to grasp its connotations means looking beyond surfaces and interpreting how and why it might be used to imply more than it depicts. This speculation, in turn, prompts us to wonder about the heart and mind behind its making. This is very obvious when a shot communicates the death of its maker, but much less so when we see calm shots of a flower or a hand lighting a candle. The shots *denote* a flower and a candle being lit but, depending on context, might *connote* "natural beauty," "devotion," or a host of other ideas. Connotation is a cultural activity that depends on how far the filmmaker can draw the audience along a path of metaphysical association.

SHOTS IN JUXTAPOSITION

When two images are juxtaposed, or cut together, we infer a meaning from their relationship. Figure 5-1 give some examples with explanations.

The examples in Figure 5-1 illustrate an engaging disagreement between two early Russian editing theorists. Examples 1 to 5 illustrate Pudovkin's categories of juxtaposition, in which exposition and building a story line are paramount. Examples 6 to 12 show some of the preferred categorizations of Eisenstein, to whom the essence of narrative art lay in conflict and dialectics. His juxtapositions, therefore, highlight contrast and contradiction, and argue as much as they inform.

Meaning and signification, like all communication, are culturally based and are in slow but inexorable evolution. Signification depends on a collusion between audience and communicator, a set of conventions that must be learned before their purpose becomes evident. For instance, ethnographers have remarked, after projecting edited footage to isolated tribesmen, that their subjects understood the "story" until the film cut to a close-up. The tribesmen lost concentration because they could not understand why the camera eye suddenly "jumped close." They were about to learn that a close-up does not collapse space so much as temporarily diminish the field of attention and clear away what surrounds and obscures the center of interest.

	Shot A	Shot B	Shot B in relation to A	Type of cut
1	Woman descends interior stairway	Same woman walking in street	Narrates her progress	Structural (builds scene)
2	Man runs across busy street	Close shot of his shoelace coming undone	Makes us anticipate his falling in front of a vehicle	Structural (directs our attention to significant detail)
3	Hungry street person begging from doorway	Wealthy man eating oysters in expensive restaurant	Places one person's fate next to another's	Relational (creates contrast)
4	Bath filling up	Teenager in bathrobe on phone in bedroom	Shows two events happening at the same time	Relational (parallelism)
5	Exhausted boxer takes knockout punch	Bullock killed with stun-gun in an abattoir	Suggests boxer is a sacrificial victim	Relational (symbolism)
6	Police waiting at road block	Shabby van driving erratically at high speed	Driver doesn't know what he's going to soon meet	Conflictual (still vs. the dynamic)
7	Giant earth-moving machine at work	Ant moving between blades of grass	Microcosm and macrocosm coexist	Conflictual (conflict of scale)
8	Geese flying across frame	Water plummeting at Niagara Falls	Forces flowing in different directions	Conflictual (conflict of graphic direction)
9	Screen-filling close-up of face, teeth clenched	Huge Olympic stadium, line of runners poised for pistol start	The one among the many	Conflictual (conflict of scale)
10	Dark moth resting on white curtains	Flashlight emerging out of dark forest	Opposite elements	Conflictual (dark vs. light)
11	Girl walks into funfair	Distorted face appears in funfair mirror	The original and its reflection	Conflictual
12	Driver sees cyclist in his path	In slow motion driver screams and swings steering wheel	Event and its perception	Conflictual (real time vs. perceived time)
13	Driver gets out of disabled car	Same image, car in foreground, driver walking as a tiny figure in distance	Transition—some time has gone by	Jump cut

FIGURE 5-1 ——————————————————————————

Examples of juxtaposed shots or cuts.

But *whose* center of interest? The film technician or film reviewer will answer, "the audience's." Our answer is more complex, and infinitely more useful to directing films because it places the persona of a storyteller ahead of the audience's reception of the story.

Perception by a camera is a mechanical process in which a focal plane is affected by incoming light. Perception by you and me is different because we evolve an intellectual and emotional framework within which to organize what our senses tell us. The convention of the internal monologue, or *voice-over* illustrates this because it verbalizes this process. For our purpose, let's say that *perception is our inner life of ideas and feelings proceeding in counterpoint with our environment of outer, visible, and audible events.* I want to stress that this interior activity is not just passive reaction; it also directs our attention as we move to confirm impressions, hopes, fears, interests, and hypothetical explanations. The object of the oral or literary storyteller is to recapture, sustain, and modulate this vital activity. However, because film is always in the present tense, the film storyteller is a presence guiding our attention rather than a reteller. You can't retell the present; but you can observe, navigate, and even narrate it, and interpret it as it unfolds.

We are going to examine the way this perceptual process works in a notional figure I'll call the Concerned Observer. This person is an involved onlooker who forms ideas and anticipations while seeing and hearing. At a later point we are going to make the Observer into the more active and participatory Storyteller, whose function is absolutely central to conscious, integrated film directing.

Here I want to emphasize how constant and important perception really is, because it is so routine during everyday life that we are unaware of *how* or why we observe what we do. Even the word *observe* has misleadingly passive, scientific associations, whereas, in reality, it is a highly active process and freighted with an intricate interplay of feelings, associations, and ideas, all of which lead constantly to actions.

THE AXIS

Next time you are near two people having an animated discussion, notice how your attention shifts from one to the other. Figure 5-2 represents A and B being watched by the observer O. It's useful to think of O as a child, because children are highly observant, have strong emotions, and are often invisible to their seniors. As the Observer, your eyeline moves back and forth, led from A to B and back again as they talk. Your awareness follows the line of tension between them, the active pathway of words, looks, awareness, and volition. This is called the *scene axis* and is really the subject-to-subject axis.

Every scene has, in addition to one or more subject-to-subject axes, an Observer-to-subject axis, which in my example is at right angles to the scene axis between A and B. This is called the *camera axis* or camera-to-subject axis. But the term is misleading because it makes it technical-sounding when really it is intensely human. The Observer (yourself watching the two people in conversation, for instance) has a strong sense of his own relationship to each person (his axis), to the invisible connection between them (their axis), and to what passes between them.

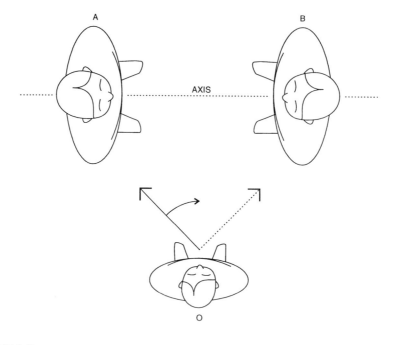

FIGURE 5-2 ————————————————————————————————

The Observer watching a conversation.

In turning to look from person to person, the Observer can be replaced by a camera *panning* (i.e., moving horizontally) between the two speakers. Now let's see in Figure 5-3 what happens when O moves closer to A and B's axis. To avoid missing any of the action, the Observer must switch quickly between A and B.

Human beings in this circumstance avoid seeing the unpleasant blur between widely separated subjects by blinking their eyes. To the brain this produces two static images with virtually no period of black in between. Cutting between two camera angles taken from the same camera position reproduces this familiar experience. Historically this cinematic equivalent probably emerged when someone tried cutting out a nauseatingly fast pan between two characters. It "worked" because its counterpart was already part of human experience.

THE ACTOR AND THE ACTED UPON

During a conversation you sometimes merely turn to look at whoever speaks. Other times, when the talk becomes heated, you find yourself looking at the listener, not the speaker. What's going on here? Any human interaction is like a tennis game. At any given moment, one player *acts* (serves the ball), the other is *acted upon* (receives the ball). When a player prepares an aggressive serve, our eye runs ahead of the ball to see how the recipient will deal with the onslaught. We see her run, jump, swing her racquet, and intercept the ball. As soon as we know she's go-

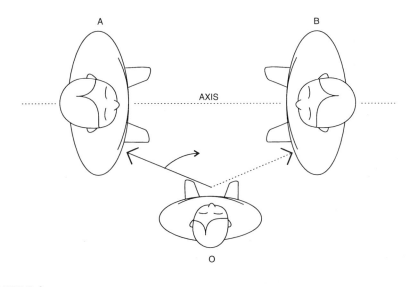

A   B

AXIS

O

FIGURE 5-3 ————————————————————————————

The Observer moves close to the characters' axis.

ing to succeed, our eye flicks back to see how the first player is placed, how she will handle the return. The whole cycle has been reversed because our eye jumps back to the original player before the ball returns.

We monitor every human interaction like this because we know that, consciously or otherwise, everybody is *constantly trying to get or do something,* no matter where, what, or who the people are. A tennis game ritualizes this exchange as a competition for points, but a conversation is likely to be just as complex and structured.

Of course, nice middle-class people like myself hate to think of ourselves making *demands.* We imagine ourselves as patient, tolerant victims acted upon by a greedy and selfish world. Seldom do we see ourselves as acting upon others, except during our occasional triumphs. But the fact is—and you must take this to heart if you intend to work in documentary, which is a branch of drama—that *everyone acts upon those around them, even when they use the strategy of passivity.*

To the Observer, at any given moment one person is the actor and the other is the acted upon. Often the situation alternates rapidly, but it is via their action and reaction that we routinely assess a person's character, mood, and motives.

Now look at how you watch two people conversing. Your eyeline switches according to your notion of who is acting upon whom. As in watching tennis, you'll find that as soon as you've decided how A has begun acting on B, your eye switches in midsentence to see how B is taking it in. Depending on how B adapts and acts back, you soon find yourself returning to A.

Once one understands this principle, most shooting and editing decisions become obvious.

SUBTEXT

While you watch a conversation you search for behavioral clues to unlock the hidden motives and inner lives of the characters. Beneath the visible and audible surface, which we might call the text of the situation, lies the situation's *subtext,* or hidden meaning—something we are always seeking. But why do they say what they say, and do what they do? Their underlying reasons are the subtext, something developed in drama by the director and the actors, and something continuously developing during rehearsal, shooting, and even in editing, where it is the editor's job, in addition to putting the piece together, to liberate those subtextual possibilities that eluded everyone else.

HORIZONTAL MOVEMENT THROUGH SPACE

Dollying, tracking, or *trucking* are names given to any movement where the camera itself moves horizontally through space. In life we are sometimes motivated by our thoughts and feelings to move closer or further away from what commands our attention. We move sideways to see better or to avoid an obstacle in our sightline. Sometimes, in accompanying someone important, we look sideways at them. The point to remember is that camera movements all need *motivation,* either in response to the action or, more interestingly, as part of the strategy of story revelation adopted by the Storyteller.

VERTICAL MOVEMENT THROUGH SPACE

Craning up or craning down is a movement vertically up or down, and is similarly motivated. The movement corresponds with the feeling of sitting down, or standing up—sometimes as an act of conclusion, sometimes to "rise above," sometimes to see better.

SCREEN DIRECTION

Screen direction is a term describing a subject's direction or movement in a frame, or in a sequence when a subject's movement links several shots, as in a chase (Figure 5-4). An important screen convention is that *characters and their movements are generally observed from only one side of the scene axis.* Let's imagine you ignored this and intercut one part of a parade moving screen left to right (L-R) with another going R-L. The audience would expect the two factions to collide, such as when police move up to a position where they can block a demonstration.

Now suppose you run ahead of the parade in order to watch it file past a landmark. In the new position, you would see marchers entering an empty street from the same screen direction. But in life you might cross the parade's path to watch it from the other side. This would be unremarkable because you initiated

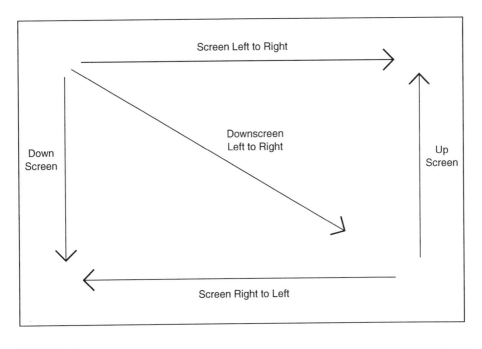

FIGURE 5-4

A range of screen directions and their descriptions.

the relocation. But in film to simply cut to a camera position across the axis must be specially set up on the screen or the audiences becomes confused.

CHANGING SCREEN DIRECTION

Screen direction of an ongoing event can be altered, but we must see the change on-screen. You can make a parade change screen direction by filming at an angle to a corner (Figure 5-5). The marchers enter in the background going R-L, turn the corner in the foreground, and exit L-R. In essence they have changed screen direction. If subsequent shots are to match, their action will also have to be L-R. Another solution to changing screen direction, during a gap in the parade, for instance, is to dolly so the camera *visibly* crosses the subject's axis of movement (Figure 5-6). Remember that any change of observing camera orientation to the action must be shown on-screen.

DIFFERENT ANGLES ON THE SAME ACTION

So far we have found everyday human correlations for every aspect of film language. But can there be one to justify using very different angles to cover the same action? We said earlier that cutting together long and closer shots taken from a

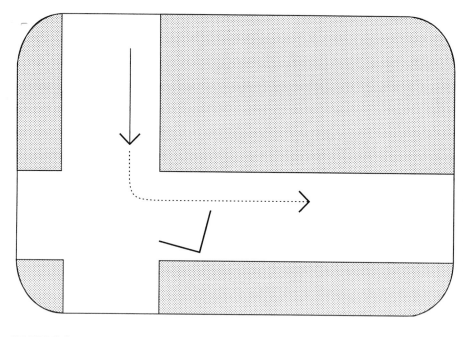

FIGURE 5-5 ──────────────────────────

By shooting at a corner, a parade or moving object can be made to change screen direction.

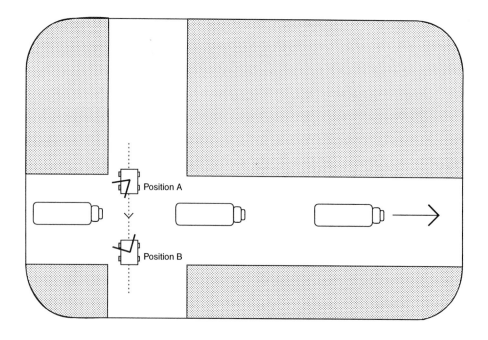

FIGURE 5-6 ──────────────────────────

Dollying sideways between floats in a parade changes the parade's effective screen direction, but the dollying movement must be shown.

single axis or direction suggests, by excluding the irrelevant, an observer's changed degree of concentration. But now imagine a scene of a tense family meal that is covered from several very different angles. Although it's a familiar film convention, surely it has no corollary in life. Ah, but wait. This narrative device—switching viewpoints during a single scene—was a prose convention long before film was invented; so it probably has rather deep roots.

In literature multiple points of view imply not physical changes of location but shifts in psychological and emotional point of view. The same is true when this strategy is used on-screen. But film is misleading because, unlike literature, it seems to give us "real" events. So we must constantly remind ourselves that film gives us a *perception* of events, a "seeming" that is not, despite appearances, the events themselves.

Here's an example from your own life. When you're a bystander during a major disagreement between friends, you get so absorbed that you forget all about yourself. Instead, you go through a series of internal agreements and disagreements, seeing first one person's point, then another's. You get so involved that you virtually experience each of the protagonists' realities.

Screen language evokes this heightened subjectivity by using a series of privileged views. These correspond with the way an observer may identify with different people as a situation unfolds. His sympathy and fascination migrates from person to person as events unfold. What's important in screencraft is that the *empathic shifts must still be rooted in a single "storyteller's" sensibility* if they are to have a naturally integrated feel. The state of heightened and embracing concentration is not one we normally maintain for long.

ABSTRACTION

The opposite of probing emotional inquiry is withdrawing into mental stocktaking, or a state of abstraction. In this way we can alter our examination from the whole to a part, or from a part to the whole. Watch your own shifts of attention; you will find that you often do this to escape into a private realm where you can speculate, contemplate, remember, or imagine. Often detail that catches your eye turns out to have symbolic meaning, or is a part that stands for the whole. Thus a car door handle near a swirling water surface can stand for a whole flood. This much used principle in film is called *synecdoche* (pronounced sin-eck-dockee). Often our eye is directed toward something symbolic, that is, something conventionally representative, much as a scale represents justice, or a flower growing on an empty lot might represent renewal.

This act of abstraction can, of course, have different causes. It may not be withdrawal or refuge by the Observer, but rather looking inward in an intense search for the significance of a recent event. Selective focus is a device used to suggest this state. When an object is isolated on the screen, and its foreground and background are thrown out of focus, it strongly suggests abstracted vision, as does abnormal motion (either slow or fast). These are just a few of the ways we can represent how we routinely dismantle reality and objectively distance ourselves from the moment. We may be searching for meaning, or simply refreshing ourselves through imaginative play.

SUBJECTIVITY VERSUS OBJECTIVITY

We experience a world full of dualities, oppositions, and ironic contrasts. You drive your car very fast at night, and then, stopping to look at the stars, you become aware of your own insignificance under their light that has taken millions of years to reach your eyes. Human attention shifts from subjectivity to objectivity, from past to present and back again, from looking at a crowd as a phenomenon, to looking at the lovely profile of a woman as she turns away. Screen language exists to replicate every aspect of an Observer's attention. In your films, if you make the shifts in the stream of images consistently human, you will create the sensation in your audience of an integrated being's presence—that of our invisible, thinking, feeling, all-seeing Observer.

DURATION, RHYTHM, AND CONCENTRATION

Human beings are directed by rhythms that originate in the brain and control our heartbeat and breathing. We tap our feet to music, or jump up to dance when the music takes us. Everything we do is measured by the beat, duration, and capacity of our minds and bodies. The maximum duration of films is said to be governed by the capacity of the human bladder! Screen language is governed by other human capacities. The duration of a shot is determined by how much attention it demands, just as the decision when to cross the road is governed by how long we take to assess the traffic. The speed of a movement on the screen is judged by its context, where it is going, and why.

Speech has inherently powerful rhythms. The Czech composer Leos Janacek was so fascinated by language rhythms that his late compositions drew on the pacing and tonal patterns of people talking. Films, particularly those with long dialogue scenes, are similarly composed around the speech and movement rhythms of the characters. Here screen language mimics the way an Observer's senses shift direction, and reproduces the way we maintain concentration by refreshing our minds thorough search. These are the most difficult scenes to get right in editing because subtextual consistency depends on delicate nuances.

Rhythm plays yet another important role in film viewing. Early and enduring stories, such as the Arthurian legends and the Norse sagas, were composed in strict rhythmic patterns because it made memorization easier for the troubadours reciting them from court to court. Equally significant is the fact that when spoken language has strong rhythmic structure, audiences can concentrate for longer periods.

Film language makes use of every possible rhythm. Many sounds from everyday life—bird song, traffic, the sounds from a building site, or the wheels of a train—contain strong rhythms to help in composing a sequence. Even static pictorial compositions contain visual rhythms, such as symmetry, balance, repetition, opposition, and patterns, to intrigue the eye.

SEQUENCE

In life there is a flow of events and only some are memorable. A story about a life takes only the significant parts of a life and bridges them together, as happens when one dreams. The building blocks are segments of time (the hero's visit to the hospital emergency room after a road accident), the events at a location (the high points of his residency in Rome), or of a developing idea (as he builds his own home his wife loses patience with the slowness of the process). Because time and space are now being indicated rather than exhaustively played out, the junctures between the building blocks must be either indicated or hidden, as the story demands.

TRANSITIONS AND TRANSITIONAL DEVICES

Most of the transitions we make in life—from place to place, or time to time—are slow or imperceptible because we have other preoccupations. Stories either replicate this by hiding the seams between sequences, or instead by indicating or emphasizing them draw attention to time passing. An action match cut between a woman drinking her morning fruit juice and a beer drinker raising his glass in a smoky dive minimizes the scene shift by drawing attention to the act of drinking. A dissolve from one scene to the other would indicate, in somewhat dated screen language, "and time passed." A simple cut from one place to the next invites the audience to fill in the blank. However, a scene of a teenager singing along to the car radio in a long, boring drive, followed by flash images of a truck, screeching tires, and the teenager yanking desperately at the steering wheel, is intentionally a shock transition. It replicates the violent change we go through when taken nastily by surprise.

Sound can be a transitional device. Hearing a conversation over an empty landscape can draw us forward into the next scene (of two campers in their tent). Cutting to a shot of a cityscape while the bird song from the campsite is still fading out gives the feeling of being confronted with a change of location while the mind and heart lag behind in the woodland. Both these transitional devices imply an emotional point of view.

All transitions are in fact narrative devices, ways of handling the necessity of moving, montage fashion, between discontinuous time or space. Each implies an attitude or point of view, either on the part of characters or the Storyteller.

SCREEN LANGUAGE IN SUMMARY

Screen language is routinely misunderstood as some kind of professional packaging. Used as a technique for documenting events for an audience, it can easily lack soul. But whenever, as viewers, we sense the integrity of a questing human intelligence at work, life on-screen becomes human and potent instead of mechanical and banal.

Imagine you go to your high school reunion and afterwards see what another participant filmed with his little video camera. It is his eyes and ears, recording whatever he cared to notice. When you see what he shot, you are struck because his version of the events gives such a characteristic idea of his personality. You see not only who he looked at and who he talked to, but how he spent time and how his mind worked. From his actions and reactions, you can see into his mind and heart, even when he says nothing from behind the camera.

Likewise, a good fiction film's handling of its events and personalities creates an overarching heart and mind doing the perceiving. Under the *auteur* theory of filmmaking, this is the director's vision. But controlling how a whole film crew and actors create the perceptual stream is simply beyond any one person's control, so I prefer to personify the intelligence behind the film's point of view as that of the Storyteller. This is not the simple "I" of the director, not the reactive passivity of the Observer, but a fictional entity that is as proactive, complex, and dependent on artistic serendipity as any created by an actor or novelist.

This is also evident in documentary and, to a lesser extent, in other nonfiction forms. All are constructs, even when they take their materials directly from life. At its most compelling, *screen language implies the course of a particular intelligence at work as it grapples with the events in which it participates.* People who work successfully in the medium seem to understand this instinctively, but if you happen to lack this instinct, simply pattern your work around the natural, observable processes of human perception, human action, and human reaction. You can't go far wrong if you are true to life. As you do this, your film will somehow take on a narrative persona all its own, and this you should encourage.

To prepare yourself for this responsibility, you can either read all of Proust and Henry James, or if you don't have the time, simply get into the habit of monitoring your own processes of physical and emotional observation, especially under duress. One constantly forgets to do this homework because we are imprisoned to the point of forgetfulness within our own subjectivity. In ordinary living we see, think, and react automatically, and notice so very little. Now compare this with what you are used to seeing on the screen. The camera's verisimilitude makes events unfold with seeming objectivity. Well used, it gives events the force of *inevitability,* like perfectly judged music. Students often assume that the cinema process itself is an alchemy that will aggrandize and ennoble whatever they put before the camera. But the cinema process is primarily a framer and magnifier: It makes truth look more true, and artifice more artificial. Small is big, and big is enormous. Every step by the cinema's makers relentlessly exposes their fallibilities along with their true insights.

The process, far from automatically delivering objective and inevitable cinema, delivers a metamorphosis of scale. Anyone present when something was filmed who later sees the film version has experienced how different it is from on-the-spot impressions. Not only has content been inescapably chosen and mediated by a string of human judgments, but it has been transformed by the lenses, lighting, film stock, or video medium used, and even the context in which one saw the movie (crowded cinema, motel TV, with your family, etc.).

To use the medium successfully you need knowledge of the human psyche. You need to know what your audience will make of what you give it. This is rooted not in audience studies or theory, but in shared instincts about human truth and human judgments.

Let's say it again: A film delivers not just a filtered version of events but also, by mimicking the flow of a human consciousness at work, implies a human heart and mind doing the observing. Screen the world's first filming and the Lumieres brothers are palpably present behind their wooden box camera, winding away at the handle until their handmade film stock runs out. It is through their minds as well as their cameras that we see workers leaving the Lumieres' factory, or the train disgorging those passengers who are so unaware of the history they are making.

Film conventions are modeled on the dialectical flow of our consciousness whenever we are following something of importance to us. Our emotional responses play a huge part in this by literally directing our sight and hearing. You can test this out. Try noting down what you remember from a striking event you experienced. What most people recall of an accident, say, is highly visual, abbreviated, selective, and emotionally loaded. Just like a film!

CHAPTER 6

SCREENCRAFT ANALYSIS PROJECTS

PROJECT 6-1: PICTURE COMPOSITION ANALYSIS

The object is to study

- how the eye reacts to a static composition
- how the eye reacts to dynamic composition
- visual elements for composing more consciously

A highly productive way to investigate composition is in a group. But what follows can also be undertaken solo if need be. I haven't found a need to formally log one's reactions, though if you are working alone, notes or sketches will reinforce what you discover. Help from books is not easily gained since composition texts tend to make the whole business intimidating and formulaic. Trust your eye to find what is there, and your own nonspecialist vocabulary to describe it.

Equipment Required: Video player, with freeze-frame and variable-speed scan functions. For the best sound, connect the VCR sound output to a stereo. A slide projector and/or an overhead projector is useful but not indispensable.

Study Materials: Any visually arresting sequence from a favorite fiction movie (any Eisenstein movie is a good standby); a book of figurative painting reproductions (best used under an overhead projector so that you look at a big image); a dozen or more 35mm art slides, also projected as large images (I find impressionist paintings ideal because they usually make an interpretation of a recognizably "real" scene, but the more eclectic your collection the better).

STRATEGY FOR STUDY

If you're leading the group, explain what is wanted more or less as follows:

> *I'll put a picture up on the screen. First notice how your eye is drawn into the composition, then what course it takes as you examine the rest of the picture. After the image has been on the screen for about 30 seconds, I'll ask one person to describe how her eye behaved. Please avoid guessing what the picture is "about," even if it suggests a story. We're interested in how each person's perception worked.*

Rotate through the class. Not everyone's eye responds in the same way, so there will be interesting discussions about variations. Out of the general agreement come ideas about visual reflexes and about those components of compositions that the eye finds attractive and engrossing. After the group has seen enough pictures, ask members to formulate guidelines for leading the spectator's eye.

After the group has worked with paintings, I like to show both good and bad photos. Photography tends to be accepted less critically because it seems to offer fewer artistic choices. It's interesting to uncover just how much control goes into a photograph that at first seemed like a straight record. Now move the group on to more abstract images, even to completely abstract ones, and let them find the same principles at work.

STATIC COMPOSITION

Here are questions to help one see more critically. Apply them after seeing a number of images, or direct the group's attention to each question's area as it becomes relevant.

1. *Why did your eye go to its particular starting point in the image?* Was it the brightest point? The darkest place in an otherwise light composition? An area of arresting color, or a significant junction of lines creating a focal point?

2. *When your eye moved away from its point of first attraction, what did it follow?* Commonly lines—perhaps actual ones, such as a fence or outstretched arm, or implied ones, such as sightlines between characters. Sometimes the eye simply moves to another significant area in the composition, jumping from one organized area to another, avoiding the intervening "disorganization."

3. *How much movement did your eye make before returning to its starting point?*

4. *What specifically drew your eye to each new place?*

5. *Are places in your eye's route specially charged with energy?* Often these are sightlines, such as between a Virgin's eyes and her baby's, between a guitarist's eyes and his hand on the strings, or between two field workers, one of whom is facing away.

6. *If you trace out the route your eye took, what shape do you have?* Sometimes a circular pattern, sometimes a triangle or ellipse, but perhaps many shapes.

Any shape at all can point out an alternative organization that helps to see beyond the wretched and dominating idea that "every picture tells a story."

7. *How do you classify the compositional movement?* It might be geometrical, repetitive textures, swirling, falling inwards, symmetrically divided down the middle, flowing diagonally, and so forth. Making a translation from one medium to another—in this case from the visual to the verbal—helps one discover what is truly there.

8. *What parts do the following play in a particular picture?*
a. Repetition
b. Parallels
c. Convergence
d. Divergence
e. Curves
f. Straight lines
g. Strong verticals
h. Strong horizontals
i. Strong diagonals
j. Textures
k. Non-naturalistic coloring
l. Light and shade
m. Depth
n. Dimension
o. Human figures

9. *How is depth suggested?* This is an ever-present problem for the camera operator, who is liable, unless trained otherwise, to place human subjects against a flat background and shoot. Unless there is something angling away from the foreground to suggest a receding space, the screen is like a painter's canvas and looks very much what it is—two dimensional.

10. *How are the individuality and mood of the human subjects expressed?* Commonly through facial expression and body language, of course. But more interesting are the juxtapositions the painter has made between person and person, person and surroundings, all of the people to a total design. The message here for documentary makers is that framing is arranged—as far as is legitimate—according to an interpretation of the subject's meaning; composition helps define the subtext. The good camera operator is therefore the person who *sees in terms of relatedness* and uses that vision responsibly to further the ends of the film.

11. *How is space arranged around a human subject, particularly in portraits?* Usually in profiles there is more space in front of the person than there is behind him, as if in response to our need to see what the person sees.

12. *How much headroom is given above a person, particularly in a close-up?* Sometimes the frame cuts off the top of a head or does not show a head at all in a group shot.

13. *How often and how deliberately are people and objects placed at the margins of the picture so that parts are cut off?* By using a restricted frame in such a way, the viewer's imagination has to supply what is beyond the edges of the picture.

VISUAL RHYTHM

I have stressed an immediate, instinctual response to the organization of an image because this is how an audience must read a film. Unlike responding to a photograph or painting, which can be leisurely and thoughtful, the filmgoer must interpret within a relentless onward movement in time. It is like reading a poster from a moving bus; if the words and images cannot be assimilated in the given time, the message goes past without being understood. If the bus is crawling in a traffic jam, however, you have time to see it in excess and become critical, even rejecting, of it.

This analogy shows how there is *an optimum duration for each shot* depending on its content (or "message") and the complexity of its form (how much work the viewer must do to interpret the message from the presentation). That duration is also conditioned by a third factor, audience expectation. We either work fast at interpreting each new image or slowly, depending on how much time we were given for preceding shots.

This principle by which a shot's duration is determined by content, form, and inherited expectation is called *visual rhythm.* As you would expect, a filmmaker can either relax or intensify a visual rhythm, just as a musician can. There are consequences for both the rate of cutting and the tempo of camera movements.

Ideal films for the study of composition and visual rhythm are those by the Russian Sergei Eisenstein, whose origins as a theater designer made him very aware of the impact of musical and visual design on an audience.

Designers' sketches and the comic strip are perhaps the progenitors of the *storyboard,* which is much used by ad agencies and the more conservative elements in the film industry to lock down what each new frame will convey. The wish to exert such total control over the vagaries of the creative process are both admirable and somewhat totalitarian. As in its political counterpart, there may be a price to pay for what it takes to get the trains running on time. Needless to say, there is little call for storyboarding in documentary, which derives so much of its power and authenticity from accommodating the spontaneous. There is, however, all the more need for internalized compositional and relational skills while shooting.

DYNAMIC COMPOSITION

Once you work with moving images rather than still ones, more principles come into play. When image components move, it is called a *dynamic composition* and a new problem emerges. A balanced composition can become disturbingly unbalanced if someone moves or leaves the frame. Even the movement of a figure's head in the foreground may posit a new sightline and a new scene axis (about which, more later), that demands a compositional rebalancing. Even a zoom into close shot almost always demands reframing because compositionally there is a drastic change, even though the subject is the same.

To study this, use a visually interesting film sequence. A chase scene makes a good subject and the slow-scan facility on your VCR (if it has one) becomes very useful. Determine how many of the following aspects you can see:

1. *Reframing because the subject moved.* Look for a variety of camera adjustments.

2. *Reframing because something/someone left the frame.*

3. *Reframing in anticipation of something/someone entering the frame.*

4. *A change in the point of focus to move the attention from the background to foreground or vice versa.* This changes the texture of significant areas of the composition.

5. *Different kinds of movement (how many?) within an otherwise static composition.* Across the frame, diagonally, from the background to foreground, from the foreground to background, up frame, down frame, and so on.

6. *What makes one feel close to the subjects and their dilemmas?* This concerns point of view and is tricky, but, in general, the nearer one is to the axis of a movement, the more subjective is one's sense of involvement.

7. *How quickly does the camera adjust to a figure who gets up and moves to another place in frame?* Usually subject movement and the camera's compositional change are synchronous. The camera move becomes clumsy if it either anticipates or lags behind the movement.

8. *How often are the camera or the characters blocked (i.e., choreographed) in such a way as to isolate one character?*

9. *What is the dramatic justification for zeroing in on one character in this way?*

10. *How often is composition more or less angled along sightlines, and how often do sightlines extend across the screen?* Here there is often a shift in point of view from subjective to objective.

11. *What does a change of angle or a change of composition make you feel toward the characters?* Maybe more or less involved, and more or less objective.

12. *Find a dynamic composition that forcefully suggests depth.* An obvious one is where the camera is next to a railroad line as a train rushes up and past.

13. *Can you locate shots where camera position is altered to include more or different background detail in order to comment upon or counterpoint foreground subject?*

INTERNAL AND EXTERNAL COMPOSITION

So far we have dealt with composition within, and therefore internal to, each shot. But another form of compositional relationship is that between an outgoing image and the next or incoming shot. Called *external composition,* this is a hidden part of film language because we are unaware of how it influences our judgments and expectations.

An example might be as follows: The point where a character exits the frame in shot A leads the spectator's eye at the cutting point to the very place in shot B where an assassin will emerge from a large and restless crowd. Here the eye is conducted to the right place in a busy composition.

Another example of external composition might be the framing of two complementary close shots in which two characters have an intense conversation. The compositions are similar but symmetrically opposed (Figure 6-1).

FIGURE 6-1

Complementary compositions in which external composition principles call for balance and symmetry.

Use your VCR's slow-scan facility to help you see compositional relationships at the cutting point. Find aspects of internal and external composition by asking yourself:

1. *Where was your point of concentration at the end of the shot?* Trace with your finger on the monitor's face where your eye travels. Its last point in the outgoing shot is where your eye enters the incoming shot composition. Interestingly, the length of the shot determines how far the eye gets in exploring the shot—so shot length influences external composition.

2. *Is there symmetry and are shots complementary?* These are shots designed to be intercut.

3. *What is the relationship between two same-subject but different-sized shots that are designed to cut together?* This is revealing; the inexperienced camera operator often produces same-scene medium and close shots that cut together poorly because proportions and compositional placing of the subject are incompatible.

4. *Does a match cut when run very slowly show several frames of overlap in its action?* Especially in fast action, a match cut, to look smooth, needs *two or three frames of the action repeated* on the incoming shot because the eye does not register the first two or three frames of any new image. Think of this as accommodating a built-in perceptual lag. The only way to cut on the beat of music is thus to place all cuts two or three frames before the actual beat point.

5. *Do external compositions make a juxtapositional comment?* Cut from a pair of eyes to car headlights approaching at night, from a dockside crane to a man feeding birds with his arm outstretched, and the like.

COMPOSITION, FORM, AND FUNCTION

If form is the manner in which content is presented, visual composition goes beyond mere embellishment to become a vital element in communication. While interesting and even delighting the eye, composition in the right hands can be *an organizing force that dramatizes relationships and projects ideas*. It makes the subject (or "content") accessible, heightens the viewer's perceptions, and stimulates critical involvement—like language used by a good poet.

How should one plan a compositional approach? One can first involve oneself with a subject then find an appropriate form to best communicate that subject. Or, if you are more interested in language than subject, choose your form and then look for an appropriate subject. The difference is one of purpose and temperament.

PROJECT 6-2: EDITING ANALYSIS

The object is to

- learn the conventions of film language so that they can be used with confidence
- analyze a sequence using standard abbreviations and terminology
- analyze how a whole film is constructed
- consider a film's sound track as a composition

Equipment Required: Video player as in Project 6-1. Your monitor set can be a domestic television set, but route the sound into the line input of a stereo for better reproduction.

Study Materials: Any good live-action documentary—many are now available on tape at accessible prices. Compilation films (i.e., compiled from archive footage) make heavy use of narration to bind together otherwise unrelated material and are mainly useful for studying how narration can be written and placed to make sense out of otherwise unrelated shots.

Making a documentary requires that you find a structure for the whole during the editing stage because there is no hard and fast blueprint in the beginning. Individual scenes are constructed—even contrived—out of available material, which may not cut together all that elegantly. Though the spontaneity and realism of *cinéma vérité* shooting is still tempered with the storytelling devices that accompany a concern for style and cinematic elegance, the documentary maker's hands are often tied by concern for the integrity of actuality, so there are many compromises. To study the full range of editing expression, one should study the fictional form.

A well-made feature film with a wealth of editing techniques is Nicolas Roeg's *Don't Look Now* (1973). An adaptation of a Daphne du Maurier short story, the film is set in Venice and makes full use of its exotic location. The narrative style is admirably compact and allusive, relying heavily on editing to telescope events into a brief montage of essential moments. Roeg was a cameraman prior to becoming a director, so he values the visual above the spoken, and his composition and camera use are masterly. The film also has a dense and highly evocative sound track. The narrative, which develops out of the trauma a couple suffer at the loss of their child, moves freely backward and forward in time, and this is particularly evident in the love-making scene.

Another feature recommended for documentarians to study is Carroll Ballard's *The Black Stallion* (1979). Ballard, originally a documentary maker, sometimes uses documentary shooting methods. The island scene, where the boy first tames the horse, is superbly lyrical and spontaneous.

FIRST VIEWING

Whatever film you choose, *first see the whole film without stopping,* and then see it a second time before you attempt any analysis. Write down any strong feelings the film evoked in you, paying no attention to order. Note from memory the sequences that sparked those feelings. You may have an additional sequence or two that intrigued you as a piece of virtuoso storytelling. Note these down too, but whatever you study in detail should be something that stirred you at an emotional rather than a merely intellectual level.

ANALYSIS FORMAT

Before you go ahead and analyze one of your chosen sequences, you may need to review standard film terminology (see Glossary) so that your findings can be laid out on paper in a form that any filmmaker could understand. What you write down is going to be displayed in split-page format, where all visuals are placed in the left half of the page and all sound occupies the right half (Figure 6-2).

It is better to do a short sequence (say, 2 minutes) very thoroughly than to do a long one superficially because your objective is to extract the maximum information about an interesting passage of film language. Make a number of shot-by-shot passes through your chosen sequence, dealing with one or two aspects of the content and form at a time. Your "script" should be written with wide line spacing on numerous sheets of paper so that you can insert additional information on subsequent passes.

Some of your notes, say, on the mood a shot evokes, will not fit into the script format, which must primarily be concerned with *what can be seen and heard.* Keep notes on what the viewer *feels* as a separate entity. First, you should deal with the picture and dialogue, shot-by-shot and word-by-word, as they relate to each other. The initial split-page script might look like Figure 6-2.

Once this basic information is on paper, you can turn to such things as shot transitions, internal and external composition of shots, screen direction, camera movements, opticals, sound effects, and the use of music.

MAKING AND USING A FLOOR PLAN

In the case of a sequence containing a dialogue exchange, make a floor plan sketch (Figure 6-3) to help determine what the room or location looked like in its entirety, how the characters moved around, and how the camera was placed to show this. Knowledge of this kind can help you decide where to place your camera later when you start shooting.

Action	Sound
Fade in L.S. FARMHOUSE. EXT. DAY	Fade up birdsong, (music fades in.)
MS Farmhouse, burned out barn in B/G	Karen's V/O: "But I thought you said that whole business was being put off! When we last talked about it, you said..."
Cut to KITCHEN, INT, DAY	
CU Ted	Ted: "Everything's changed."
	K: "Everything's changed?"
2S Ted & Karen	T: "We're not to blame. You know that."
CU Karen, worried, shocked	
MS Karen moves L-R to stove	
MS Ted moves slightly after her	T: "There's a buyer . . . (Music fades out) someone's interested."
Karen turns sharply to face him	
BCU Ted, eyes waver & drop	K: "Ted, Ted! What are you telling me?"
Cut to O/S on to Karen	
Cut to O/S on to Ted	K: "You told me . . . (dog begins barking) . . . you promised me . . .
Cut to OTHER SIDE KITCHEN DOOR	(V/O) you said you'd never let the lawyer
Anna, 4, clutching Raggedy Ann doll,	swindle us out of this place...You said...."
looking frightened.	Ted's V/O: "The agent said it's now or never. We've got to make up our minds."

FIGURE 6-2 ───────────────────────────────────

Example of split-page format script.

STRATEGY FOR STUDY

The action side of your split-page log should contain descriptions of each shot and its action, and on the sound-side note the content and positioning of dialogue, music start/stopping points, and featured sound effects (i.e., more than mere accompaniment).

The scrutiny of a film sequence proceeds by categories. I have listed them below in a logical order for inquiry, but reorder my list if something else works better for you. To avoid overloading yourself, concentrate on a few of the given aspects at a time. Find at least one example of everything so that you understand the concepts at work. If you feel overwhelmed, do what is rewarding and interesting.

FIRST IMPRESSIONS

What progression of feelings did you have while watching the sequence? It is important to learn to read *from* film rather than read *into* it. Film is a complex and deceptive medium; like a glib and clever acquaintance, it can make you uneasy about your perceptions and can make you accept too easily what "should" be

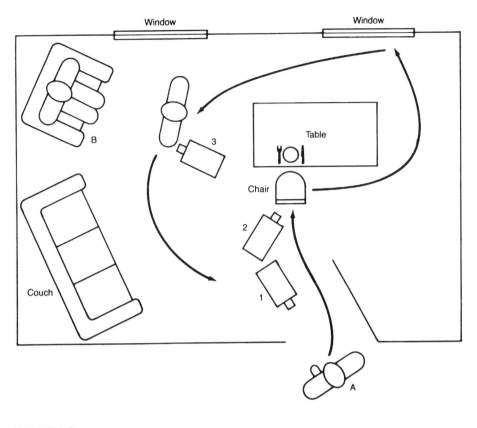

FIGURE 6-3

This floor plan shows the entry and movement of Character A within a room in relation to the seated Character B. The three numbered camera positions cover all of the action.

seen or "should" be felt. Instead, recognize what you did feel and connect your impressions with what can actually be seen and heard in the film.

Following are questions to help you round up important information:

DEFINITION AND STATISTICS

- *What determines the beginning and end points of the sequence?*

  Is its span determined, for instance, by being at one location or by representing a continuous segment of time?

  Is the sequence determined by a particular mood or by the stages of a process?

- *How long is the sequence in minutes and seconds?*

- *How many picture cuts does the sequence contain?* The duration of each shot and how often the camera angle is changed are aspects of a director's style but are also just as likely to be derived from the sequence's content. Try to decide whether the content or its treatment is driving the cutting.

USE OF CAMERA

- *What motivates each camera movement?*

    Does the camera follow the movement of a character?

    Does it lay out a landscape or a scene geography?

    Does the camera move closer and intensify our relationship with someone or something?

    Does the camera move away from someone or something so we see more objectively?

    Does the camera reveal significant information by moving?

    Is the move really a reframing to accommodate a rearrangement of characters?

    Is the move a reaction, panning to a new speaker, for instance?

    Is the move a Storyteller revelation, motivated by an expectant point of view rather than content?

- *When is the camera used subjectively?*

    When do we directly experience a character's point of view?

    Are there special signs that the camera is seeing subjectively (e.g., an unsteady handheld camera for a running man's point of view)?

    What is the dramatic justification?

- *Are there changes in camera height?*

    To accommodate subject matter (e.g., to look down into a barrel)?

    To make you see in a certain way (e.g., to look up from child's point of view at a stern teacher's face)?

USE OF SOUND

- *What sound perspectives are used?* Does a particular passage of sound:

    Complement camera position (near mike for close shots, far from mike for longer shots—replicating camera perspective)?

    Counterpoint camera perspective? (Altman films are fond of giving us the intimate conversation of two characters distantly traversing a large landscape.)

    Remain uniformly intimate in quality (as with a narration or with voice-over and "thought voices" that function as a character's interior monologue)?

- *How are particular sound effects used?*

    To build atmosphere and mood?

    For punctuation?

    To motivate a cut? (Next sequence's sound rises until we cut to it.)

As a narrative device? (Horn honks, so woman gets up and goes to window, where she discovers her sister is making a surprise visit.)

To build, sustain, or defuse tension?

To provide rhythm? (Meal prepared in a montage of brief shots to the rhythmic sound of a man splitting logs.)

EDITING

- *What motivates each cut?*

  Is there an action match to carry the cut?

  Is there a compositional relationship between the two shots that makes the cut interesting and worthwhile?

  Is there a movement relationship (e.g., cut from car moving L-R to boat moving L-R) that carries the cut, or does someone or something leave the frame (making us want to see a new frame)?

  Does someone or something fill the frame, blanking it out, and permitting a cut to another frame, which starts blanked and then clears?

  Does someone or something enter the frame and demand closer attention?

  Are we cutting to follow someone's eyeline, to see what she sees?

  Is there a sound, or a line, that demands that we see the source?

  Are we cutting to show the effect on a listener?

  What defines the "right" moment to cut?

  Are we cutting to a speaker at a particular moment that is visually revealing, and, if so, what defines that moment?

  If the cut intensifies our attention, what justifies that?

  If the cut relaxes and objectifies our attention, what justifies that?

  Is the cut to a parallel activity (something going on simultaneously)?

  Is there some sort of comparison or irony being set up by the juxtaposition?

  Are we cutting to a rhythm, say, of music?

  Are we cutting to the rhythmic cadences of speech?

- *What is the relationship of words to images?*

  Does what is shown illustrate what is said?

  Is there a difference, and therefore a counterpoint, between what is shown and what is heard?

  Is there a meaningful contradiction between what is said and what is shown?

  Does what is said come from another time frame (e.g., a memory of one of the characters or a comment on something in the past)?

  Is there a point at which words are used to move us forward or backward in time?

Can you pinpoint a "change of tense" in the film's grammar? (This might be done visually, as in the old cliché of autumn leaves falling after we have seen summer scenes.)

- *What is the impact of the first strong word on each new image?*

  Does it clarify the new image?

  Does it give it a particular emphasis or interpretation?

  Is the effect expected (satisfying perhaps) or unexpected (maybe a shock)?

  Is there a deliberate contradiction?

- *Where and how is each music segment used?*

  How is it initiated (often when the characters or story begin some kind of motion)?

  What does the music suggest by its texture, instrumentation, and so forth?

  How is it finished (often when the characters or story arrive at a new location)?

  What comment is it making (ironic, sympathetic, lyrical, or revealing the inner state of a character or situation)?

  From what sound does it emerge at its start?

  Into what other sound does it merge at its close? (Sound dissolves like these are each called a *segue* [pronounced "seg- way"].)

POINT OF VIEW

Here *point of view* (POV) means more than just whose eyeline we occasionally share, it refers to *whose reality the viewer most identifies with at any given time.* This is a complex and interesting issue since a film, like a novel, can present:

- a main POV (probably through a "POV character")
- the multiple, conflicting POVs of several characters
- an omniscient, all seeing POV
- an authorial POV

The authorial POV is seldom used, except in documentaries narrated by their directors. Normally POV arises from the situations and how the characters emerge. Yet a film's appearances can be deceptive unless you look very carefully. Point of view can migrate during a scene, and a multiplicity of viewpoints can contribute richness and variety to figures who, though secondary or even unsympathetic, nevertheless make up the central character's world.

DEFINING POINT OF VIEW AND BLOCKING

Here are some practical ways of digging into a sequence to establish how it is structuring the way we see and react to the participants. A word of caution, though. Point of view can only be confidently specified by considering the aims and tone of the whole work. Taking a magnifying glass to one sequence may or may not verify your overall hypothesis. How the camera is used, the vibrancy of the action, the frequency with which one person's feelings are revealed, and the amount of development the protagonist undergoes all play a part in enlisting our sympathy and interest.

Blocking is a term borrowed from the theater to describe how the participants and camera move in relation to the set. Who and how we see affect where our sympathies go, so blocking cannot be separated from POV.

1. *To whom is the **dialogue** or narration addressed?*

a. From one character to another?
b. To himself (thinking aloud, reading a diary or letter)?
c. To the audience (narration, interview, prepared statement)?

2. *How many **camera positions** were used?* Using your floor plan, show:

a. Basic camera positions and label them A, B, C, etc.
b. Camera dollying movements with dotted lines leading from one to another.
c. Shots in your log, marked with the appropriate A, B, C camera angles.
d. How the camera stays to one side of the scene axis, or the main subject-to-subject axis, to keep characters facing in the same screen direction from shot-to-shot. When this principle is broken, it is called *crossing the line*. The effect is disorienting for the audience.

3. *How often is the camera close to the crucial axis between characters?*

4. *How often does the camera **subjectively** share a character's eyeline?*

5. *When and why does it take an **objective** stance to the situation* (either a distanced viewpoint or one independent of eyelines)?

6. *Character blocking: How did the characters/camera move in the scene?*

a. To the location and camera movement sketch you have already made, add dotted lines to show the participants' movements (called *blocking*). You can use different colors for clarity.

7. *What **point(s) of view** did the "author" engage us in?*

a. Whose story is this sequence if you go by gut reaction?
b. Taking into account the angles on each character, whose POV were you led to sympathize with?
c. How many viewpoints did you share? (Some may have been momentary or fragmentary.)
d. How much are audience sympathies structured here by camera angles and editing?
e. How much are sympathies molded independently by the action or the situation itself?

For a more extended discussion see Point of View in Chapter 27, Elements of the Documentary.

PROJECT 6-3: LIGHTING ANALYSIS

The object of this project is to

- analyze common lighting situations found in both fiction and nonfiction films
- understand what goes into creating a lighting mood

Equipment Required: VCR as previously. At first, turn down the monitor's color control so you can see light distribution in a black-and-white picture. Adjust the monitor's brightness and contrast controls so the greatest range of gray tones is visible between video white and video black.

Study Materials: Any fiction or documentary film having a range of lighting situations; that is, interiors, exteriors, night shots, day-for-night, dawn, and so on. Erroll Morris' *A Brief History of Time* (1991) has a number of elaborately lit interiors.

LIGHTING TERMINOLOGY

Here the task is to recognize different types and combinations of lighting situations in order to become familiar with the look and effect of each and to be able

FIGURE 6-4 ──

A *high-key* image lighting style.

to name them with the appropriate standard terminology. Unless you are specifically interested in color, turn down the color control on your monitor so you see just *light* and not chrominance. Following is some basic terminology.

A *high-key picture* is a shot that looks bright overall with small areas of shadow. In Figure 6-4, the shot is exterior day, but the interior of a supermarket might also be high key.

A *low-key picture* is a shot that looks overall dark with few highlight areas. These are often interiors or night shots, but in Figure 6-5 there is a backlit day interior that ends up being low key.

Graduated tonality shots have neither very bright highlights nor deep shadow, but mainly consist of an even range of midtones if they were viewed without color. This might be a rainy landscape or a woodland scene, as in Figure 6-6. Here an overcast sky is diffusing the lighting source, and the disorganized light rays scatter into every possible shadow area so there are neither highlights nor deep shadows.

FIGURE 6-5 ——————

A *low-key* image lighting style.

FIGURE 6-6

A *graduated-tonality* image, illustrating lighting from a diffused source.

High-contrast picture shots may be lit either high key or low key, but there is a big difference in illumination level between highlight and shadow areas. This would be as true for a candlelit scene as it is for Figure 6-4. Figure 6-7 is a clearer example of a high-contrast scene because it contains a much more obvious area of shadow.

Low-contrast picture shots can either be high or low key but have shadow area illumination not far from the highlight levels. The country post office scene in Figure 6-8 and the woodland scene in Figure 6-6 are both low contrast.

Hard lighting describes light quality and can be any light source that creates hard-edged shadows (e.g., sun, studio spotlight, candle flame). The barn scene in Figure 6-7, with its sharply defined shadow, is lit by hard sunlight.

Soft lighting describes light quality from any light source that creates soft-edged shadows (e.g., fluorescent tubes, sunlight reflecting off a matte-finish wall, light from an overcast sky, studio soft light). Figures 6-6 and 6-8 are both illuminated by soft light and lack any defined shadows.

Key light is not necessarily an artificial source because it can be the sun. It is a light source that contributes the shot's intended shadows, and these in turn reveal the angle and position of the supposed source light. In Figure 6-7 the key light is coming from above and to the right of the camera, as revealed by the line of shadow. Like all lighting, this indicates time of day and helps to set a mood.

FIGURE 6-7

A *high-contrast* image, showing a big difference in illumination levels.

Fill light is the light source used to raise illumination in shadow areas. For interiors, it will probably be soft light thrown from the direction of the camera. This avoids creating additional visible shadows. Fill light, especially in exteriors, is often provided from matte white reflectors. In Figure 6-5, the girl would not be visible unless some fill light was being thrown from the direction of the camera.

Back light is a light source shining on the subject from behind, and often from above as well. A favorite technique is to put a rim of light around a subject's head and shoulders to create a separation between the subject and background. You can see this in Figure 6-5, where the girl's arm and shoulder are separated from the background by a rim of backlight. Although Figure 6-9 is high key, the key light comes from above and behind, so the boy is backlit. This gives texture to his hair and makes him stand out from his background.

FIGURE 6-8

A *low-contrast* image contains little range between levels of illumination.

A *practical* is any light source that appears in frame as part of the scene (e.g., a table lamp, overhead fluorescent). The elderly couple in Figure 6-10 not only has practicals in frame (the candles) but is lit by them. Each candle tends to fill the shadows cast by the others, so the overall effect is not as hard as the light normally associated with a candle flame's point light source.

LIGHTING SETUPS

In Figures 6-11 to 6-15, the same model is lit in various ways. The effect and mood in each portrait vary greatly as a result. In the diagrams, I have only shown key and fill lights, but most of the portraits contain other sources, including backlight, which is shown separately. In floor-plan diagrams such as these, one cannot show the *height* of the shadow-producing light sources, only the *angle of throw* relative to the *camera-to-subject axis*. Heights can be inferred from the areas of highlight and their converse shadow patterns.

Frontal lighting setups have the key light close to the camera/subject axis so that shadows are thrown backward out of the camera's view. You can see a small shadow from the blouse collar on the subject's neck. Notice how flat and lacking in dimensionality this shot is compared with the others (Figure 6-11).

FIGURE 6-9

A back-lit image can also be a high key picture, but with the light source behind the subject.

FIGURE 6-10

A *practical* is any lighting source that appears in frame, no matter whether or not it is a functional source.

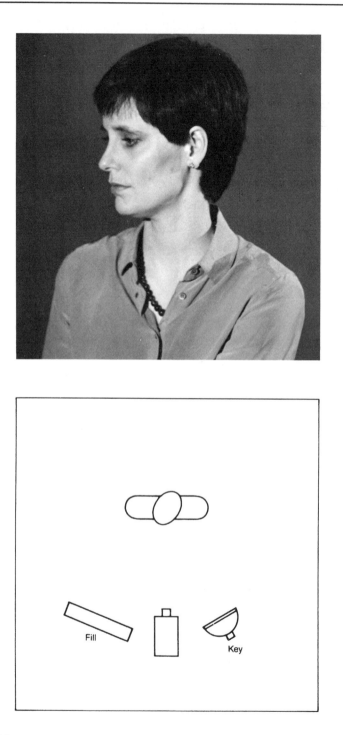

FIGURE 6-11

Example of *frontal lighting* and the setup diagram. (Dirk Matthews)

Broad lighting setups have the key light to the side so that a broad area of the subject's face and body is highlighted. If you compare this shot to the previous one, you will see how skimming the key across the subject reveals her features, neck contours, and the folds in the blouse. We have pockets of deep shadow, especially in the eye socket, but these could be reduced by increasing the amount of soft fill light (Figure 6-12).

Narrow lighting setups have the key light to the side of the subject, and perhaps even beyond, so that only a narrow portion of the woman's face is receiving highlighting. Most of her face is in shadow. This portion of the model is lit by fill. Measuring light reflected in the highlight area and comparing it with that being reflected from the fill area gives the *lighting ratio*. It is important to remember when you are taking measurements that fill light reaches the highlight area but not vice versa, so you can only take accurate readings with all the lights on (Figure 6-13).

Back lighting setups have the key light coming from above and behind the subject, picking out the body outline and putting highlights in the hair and profile. Some additional fill would make this an acceptable lighting setup for an interview. Backlight is a component in each of Figures 6-12 and 6-13, and helps to suggest depth and roundness. Figure 6-11 looks so flat because it lacks both shadow and highlights. Some backlight would put highlights around the edges and give it the sparkle and depth of the other portraits (Figure 6-14).

Silhouette lighting has the subject reflecting no light at all, so the subject shows up only as an outline against raw light. This lighting is sometimes used in documentaries when the subject's identity is being withheld (Figure 6-15).

STRATEGY FOR STUDY

Locate two or three sequences with quite different lighting moods and, using the definitions given earlier, classify them as follows:

a. Style   High key/low key/graduated tonality?

b. Contrast   High or low contrast?

c. Scene   Intended to look like natural light or artificial lighting?

d. Setup   Frontal/broad/narrow/backlighting setup?

e. Angles   High/low angle of key light?

f. Quality   Hard/soft edges to shadows?

g. Source   Source in scene is intended to be _____

h. Practicals Practicals in the scene are _____

i. Time   Day-for-day, night-for-night, dusk-for-night, day-for-night?

j. Mood   Mood conveyed by lighting is _____

Among feature films, two classic, superbly lit black-and-white films are Welles' *Citizen Kane* (1941), with cinematography by the revolutionary Gregg Toland,

and Jean Cocteau's *Beauty and the Beast* (1946), whose lighting Henri Alekan modeled after Dutch painting, especially its interiors. Also fascinatingly lit is Louis Malle's *Pretty Baby* (1978), a film set in 1917 New Orleans; it was lit by the great Sven Nykvist, Bergman's cinematographer, who once said that one of his achievements was to work with increasingly simpler lighting setups over the years.

Information on lighting instruments can be found in Chapter 10, Equipment Selection, and on lighting practice in Chapter 11, About Lighting, which deals with the rudiments of lighting for the low-budget documentary maker.

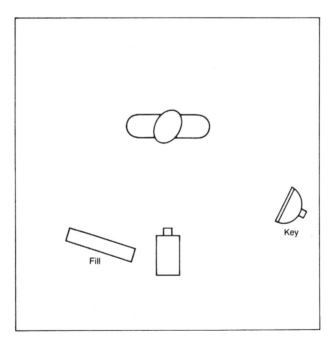

FIGURE 6-12

Example of *broad lighting* and the setup diagram. (Dirk Matthews)

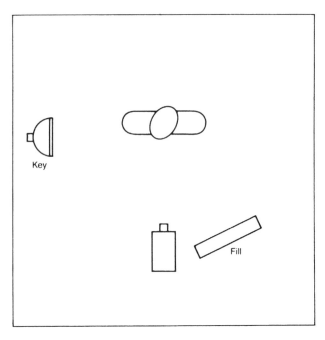

FIGURE 6-13 ——————————————————————————————————————

Example of *narrow lighting* and setup diagram. (Dirk Matthews)

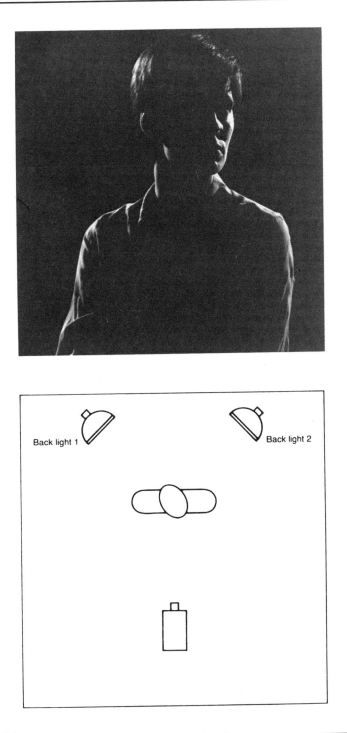

FIGURE 6-14

Example of *back lighting* and setup diagram. (Dirk Matthews)

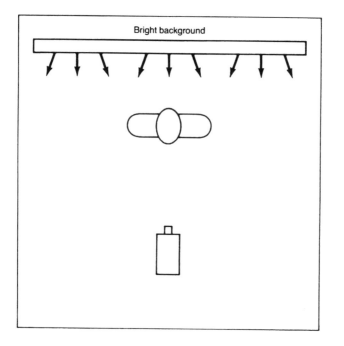

FIGURE 6-15

Example of *silhouette lighting* and setup diagram. (Dirk Matthews)

CHAPTER 7

BASIC SHOOTING PROJECTS

Carrying out these projects will equip you with a range of invaluable skills and awarenesses. Ahead in Chapter 17, Production Projects, are assignments demanding conceptual and authorial skills, but here your work will focus on gaining the prerequisite control over the tools and basic techniques. The sound experiments can often be combined with camera handling assignments. In a class, it may be better if each group does different work, from which all can learn, than if everybody does the same few exercises.

SOUND THEORY

The object is to

- give basic understanding of how sound behaves
- familiarize your ear
- learn necessities for successful voice recording

Film students tend to disregard sound, and pay for it dearly. Inconsistent or badly recorded sound is seldom the fault of equipment, but rather the way it is used. Some analytic experience will train you to recognize and correct a range of common failures. Let's look first at categories to be found in any location voice recording. Figure 7-1 is a diagram of a voice recording taking place in a noisy office that has busy street traffic outside. All sound recordings have four basic components:

1. **S = Signal:** desired recording subject, in this case a speaker.
2. **A = Ambience:** background sound inherent in the location; here it includes the typewriter and phone nearby, and traffic from the street outside.

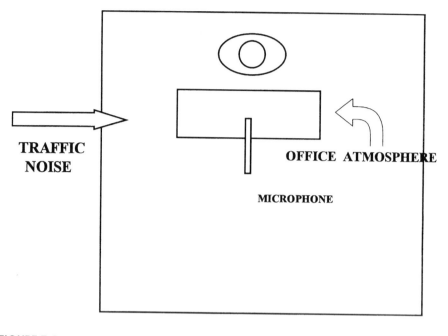

FIGURE 7-1

Diagram of typical sound situation involving a speaker covered by one microphone in a noisy office with traffic outside.

3. **R = Reverberation:** sound derived from the signal bouncing from sound-reflectant surfaces. Reverb muddies the signal's clarity because reflections arrive at the mike in varying degrees of delay.

4. **N = Noise:** sound system hiss, hum, or interference. Unless sound is entirely digital, system noise is amplified with each generation of sound transfer.

FINDING THE PROBLEMS

One can evaluate a voice recording by posing these questions:

1. *S:A. How well is the signal separated in level from ambience?*
Think of our ambience (office atmosphere) competing with signal (the speaker) as a comparison, or *ratio* of signal to ambience, abbreviated as S:A. A high S:A ratio is desirable because it means high signal to low ambient sound, which yields good, intelligible speech. A low S:A might would deliver a signal hardly louder than the ambience, putting undue strain on the audience and sabotaging intelligibility.

2. *S:R. How much reverberation is muddying the signal?*
Location reverberation is S:R, that is, the ratio of the signal to its reverberant "reflections" returning from sound-reflective surrounding surfaces, such as the floor, walls, and ceiling. These prolong the signal by shuttling it in complex patterns and

superadding delayed versions to the original. Reverb helps the audience to identify with the mood of a particular enclosure—a large or small room, bare or furnished, high or low ceiling, and so on.

There are, in fact, two kinds of reflected sound:

Echo is delayed sound you hear when the signal is reflected after a uniform delay (such as when you clap your hands some distance from a single tall building).

Reverberation is reflected signal being returned by multiple surfaces and containing multiple delays. In a large space, such as an indoor swimming pool, the reverb delays are long and every signal is confused by a massive "tail" of reverb. In an average room, delays are very short but their effect colors any recording.

The recordist makes a location *sound test* by loudly clapping hands just once. After the sudden *transient* of the hand clap (signal), its aftereffect (reverb) can be heard as either long or short, loud or soft. In the final mix, ambience or reverb can be added to a recording, but never subtracted, so *dry* (nonreverberant) original recordings are always preferable.

3. *S:N. How much system noise is there?*
Old sound amplification and recording systems had a low signal-to-noise (S:N) ratio, as fans of old movies know well. Modern amplification systems are very clean, but analogue recording (on videotape or worse, 16mm optical sound) is often anything but. Make the best possible original recording because each generation of copy augments and worsens noise levels. Digital recordings—both audio and video—can be copied for many generations without degradation.

4. *How cuttable is the sound?*
This is treacherous because inconsistencies only become obvious once sections are cut together.

Inconsistency in S:A. Imagine a 2-hour interview shot in the back room of a restaurant. You want to cut together two sections that fit well together, but that have utterly different S:A levels. The segment shot early has little restaurant atmosphere, the late one has a lot—a big but not insoluble problem. In the final mix you may be able to add a room tone to material with less ambience, and make it match the noisy segment.

Inconsistency in S:R. This is virtually insoluble. These occurs with complementary angles when they are cut together with inconsistent miking. The result is that when cutting from a medium shot to a close shot, a voice changes wildly in quality because the longer shot is full of reverb. It cannot be "fixed in the mix." Needless to say, documentary shot on the run often suffers from these problems.

FINDING THE SOLUTIONS

When you take the role of recordist or mike operator, *always* wear headphones and concentrate not on what people say, but on sound quality as they say it. The golden rule is always to place a mike as close to the signal source (the speaker) as possible to give a high signal amplitude and the best S:A and S:R ratios. In film, this ideal may be confounded by the need to hide the mike and allow one's subjects the freedom to move.

The recordist uses two main types of *microphone reception pattern.* Each appears in various kinds of mikes and each has its uses and drawbacks.

Omnidirectional.   Usually giving better fidelity, the omni picks up sound equally from all directions and is useful for covering spontaneous group conversations. Lavalier (chest) mikes are "omnis" and are useful because they are small, easily hidden, and remain close to the speaker or signal. Lavaliers are often used with radio transmitters to give excellent sound and freedom of movement to wearers, but speech from someone in movement lacks all perspective changes because the mike, unlike the camera, remains a fixed distance from the speaker. The omni's big drawback is that it cannot be angled to help separate signal from ambient sound.

Directional.   Often called a *cardioid* because of its heart-shaped pickup pattern, this type discriminates usefully against sound coming from off-axis. During a shoot in a noisy street, angling the mike toward the speaker and away from the traffic direction can enhance dialogue intelligibility and suppress off-axis traffic. Superdirectional mikes do not bring sound "nearer" or make it inherently louder; they simply discriminate more effectively against off-axis sound—but at some cost to fidelity.

Producing good sound means training yourself to hear sound coverage differences and recognizing the effect of an environment. Editing your work together is really important because sound inequities begin to intrude as juxtaposition makes them glaringly apparent. Listen to edited versions repeatedly and with your eyes closed. You should hear sound components as clearly as a conductor hears the instruments in a quartet.

PROJECT 7-1:
VOICE RECORDING EXPERIMENTS FOR INTERIORS

Use a fairly large, minimally furnished room. Shoot a seated person reading in an even voice and holding the text so that it never gets between the mouth and microphone. A basic camcorder setup with headphones, equipped with both directional and omnidirectional mikes, if possible, is all you need.

1.   *Hearing ambience.* In the barest room you can find, set up a wide shot about 12 feet from a seated person. Station a radio playing music, as a source of constant ambient sound, near the camera. Using either an omni or directional mike near the camera, listen through monitor headphones, and set the radio sound level so that it makes the reader difficult but not impossible to understand. Neither moving nor changing the voice and radio, now shoot 15 seconds each of wide shot, medium shot, and big close-up (BCU), using an appropriately changed mike position for each. Now edit the three shots together for a dramatic illustration of how signal-to-ambience ratio changes as the mike approaches the speaker.

2.   *Hearing sound perspective changes and reverberation.* Repeat the experiment without the radio playing. Shoot wide-angle and close-up shots with appro-

priate mike positions, then reverse the logic by shooting a close-up picture with a wide-shot mike position, and a wide shot using close-shot sound. Edit the resulting footage together in different permutations. You will see that changing the mike positioning itself produces a sound perspective change and that close-shot sound is acceptable over a wide shot but not vice versa. Notice the hollow and "boxy" sound quality of the wide shot. Its recording contains a considerable admixture of reverberant sound compared with that of the close-up.

3. *Hearing microphone axis changes.* Take a continuous medium shot of your reader with the mike in shot and directly before the speaker at about 4 feet distance. During a continuous reading, point a directional mike on axis (directly at the speaker's mouth) for 10 seconds, then rotate it smoothly and silently to a position 90 degrees from axis, hold this position for 10 seconds, then rotate it a further 90 degrees so it now points at the camera and away from the speaker. Hold this for a further 10 seconds. View/listen to rushes, then make an edited version that shows only the three static mike positions. Always *when sound is cut together one really hears the changes.* Notice, as the mike leaves the axis, how the voice quality becomes thinner and the reverberant component increases. You might try a blindfold assessment, and while listening, describe how the mike is situated at different times.

4. *Hearing optimum speaker axis.* Speech, in particular the all-important consonants, comes out of a person's mouth directionally. Shoot a medium-close shot of the reader, taking 10 seconds of speech with a mike (preferably omnidirectional) handheld 2 feet in front of the person's face. Be careful not to introduce any handling noise. Keeping the mike at the same distance and always pointing towards the speaker, circle around to the speaker's side, holding steady there for 10 seconds. Finish by circling to the rear of the speaker, again holding for 10 seconds. View/listen to rushes, then edit the three positions together for an illustration of what happens to a voice's quality when the mike moves progressively away from the speaker's axis. Compare consonant clarity and the fidelity of other shots with the best (on-axis) recording, and note any changes in the ratio of signal to reverberant sound.

PROJECT 7-2:
VOICE RECORDING EXPERIMENTS FOR EXTERIORS

1. *Hearing perspective changes.* In a quiet, open grassy space, use a directional or omnidirectional hand mike to shoot a speaker first in close, then wide, shot (camera about 20 feet distance). Edit back and forth between the two shots for an illustration of sound perspective changes that this time lack reverberant sound.

2. *Hearing signal to ambience ratio and camera distance.* Shoot in the open near some constant source of outdoor ambient, sound such as a highway, fountain, or playground. Using a directional hand mike, shoot a minute of interview with the camera and mike pointing toward the ambient sound's source and the speaker's back to it. Then turn the action around and shoot a minute with the mike at the same distance but its axis, this time, away from the sound's source. Intercut the two tracks several times. Because there is virtually no reverberant sound, the mike's degree of discrimination will be readily apparent at the cuts.

3. *Hearing signal to ambience and how it affects choice of microphone.* In the same noisy exterior setup, shoot an additional section for the interview in point 2 above using a lavalier mike. Intercut close shot (CS) sound from point 2 with lavalier sound to discover the differences between the two forms of mike coverage. Discuss the ratios of signal-to-ambience in your coverage.

Sound Trouble Shooting Chart

Problem effect	*Cause*	*Solution*
Speaker obscured by high background noise.	Lack of insulation or separation.	1. Close windows to reduce exterior atmosphere. 2. Move shoot away from source. 3. Reduce ambient source.
	Low S:A.	1. Get mike closer. 2. Use lavalier for high S:A. 3. Move directional mike so ambience is off-axis, signal is on-axis.
Speaker's voice not clear.	Lack of sibilants.	1. Get mike on-axis to speaker. 2. Mike from above, not below.
Speaker's voice "edgy."	Overmodulating.	1. Reduce recording level so peaks are contained below 0 dB.
	Too much sibilance or sibs "popping."	1. Try moving mike progressively off-axis. 2. Experiment with mike in relation to reverb—it may be reinforcing certain frequencies.
	Two mikes picking up the same signal but out of phase.	1. Cover situation with one mike. 2. Move mikes closer to respective speakers so S:A ratio is higher. 3. Rewire one mike or use phase-reverse switch if there is one.
Feedback howl.	Mike picking up headphone or speaker to create feedback loop.	1. Greater separation between mike and secondary sound source. 2. Move mike off-axis to secondary sound source. 3. Reduce secondary source level.
Speaker obscured by room acoustics.	High location reverberation.	1. Dampen reflective surfaces by carpeting floor, hanging sound blankets on off-camera walls. 2. Move mike closer to source or use lavaliers for higher S:R ratio. 3. Change location. 4. Place cloth on table if there is one, and don't place mike on or near highly sound-reflective surfaces.

Problem effect	Cause	Solution
Sound inconsistent on cuts.	Inconsistent ambience.	1. Shoot presence track so you can boost quieter track to match louder. 2. Angle mike to control S:A ratio.
	Inconsistent voice quality.	1. Try to use consistent mikes and miking. 2. Keep mike at more consistent distance. 3. Minimize mike changes when camera position changes. Close-shot sound can always be thinned to sound like long shot, but not vice versa.
	Inconsistent reverb.	1. Minimize mike axis and position changes. 2. Muffle reverberant surfaces as above. 3. Improve S:R by using closer or lavalier miking.
	Inconsistent voice levels.	1. This can be fixed in the mix. 2. Watch recording level meter more carefully. 3. Check rerecording procedures for workprint. A standard 0 dB tone on original is there to help standardize copy levels.
Unwanted noises in mike.	Air currents.	1. In windy location use blimp or windshield on mike. 2. Alter miking if speaker's breath rattles mike diaphragm.
	Mike handling.	1. Hold hand mike more carefully and monitor via headphones. 2. Use mike shock-mount. 3. Check that taut or dragging cables aren't transmitting handling noise. 4. Consider different type of mike.
High system noise	Undermodulating or replay system at fault.	1. Record at higher level. Sound should generally peak at 0 dB. 2. If original tape is OK make new workprint copies. 3. A sound head may need demagnetizing. A magnetized head partially erases the track, the top frequencies disappearing first.
Mike creating shadows.	Positioning in relation to lighting.	1. Mike from below frame instead of from above it. 2. Keep mike still so shadow doesn't draw attention to itself by moving. 3. Use wireless mikes so no boom is required. 4. Try to get DP to alter lighting (!)

CAMERA HANDLING THEORY

Documentary camerawork can be divided into two different categories, tripod and handheld, each serving a different purpose.

Tripod
When camerawork is done from a tripod, it

- usually is used only in stable and relatively predictable shooting situations
- makes very controlled transitions from subject-to-subject possible
- makes very controlled image transitions possible
- makes stable close-ups possible at the telephoto end of the zoom lens
- conveys the cool, assured view familiar from studio television and feature films
- is associated with an invulnerable, omniscient point of view
- is associated with careful, elegant lighting

Though invaluable for anything requiring a rock-steady camera, the tripod-mounted camera is virtually immobile and handicapped when it comes to covering spontaneous events. Either a moving subject must be covered with multiple cameras, or the action must be interrupted to allow moving the single camera to a new position. This limits coverage to subjects that can be made subservient to the needs of the camera.

Handheld
The handheld camera

- can be placed on the shoulder
- can be held low, even at ground level
- allows the operator to walk, stand, or sit while shooting
- is most justified when motivated by events
- can move under, over, or through obstacles with the ease of a human being
- can react to events much as we do in life
- implies a spontaneous, event-driven quest
- must often judge how best to cover action and reaction as they happen
- sometimes makes humanly imperfect movements and reactions
- conveys a subjective, even vulnerable, point of view
- is associated with shooting by available light
- becomes increasingly shaky as the operator zooms in

The handheld camera is usually on the operator's shoulder so that it can pan or track with the subject at will. During a protest march this could allow one to follow a single demonstrator throughout a day or to cover the main elements—

speaker, marshals, police, contingents of demonstrators—that make up the event's totality. When events move with any speed, the operator, after being directed to "Roll camera," must make on-the-spot decisions about subject framing, camera moves, and whether to favor either action or reaction at any given moment. The challenge is to minimize the jerkiness and indecision of the human being supporting the camera.

To reduce unsteadiness, use a Steadicam or keep your lens on wide angle, and when you need close or wide shots physically move your camera close to, or distant from, the subject.

CAMERA HANDLING PROJECTS

Over a number of assignments, your strengths and weaknesses will emerge. It is good for individuals in a class to rate each other's work ahead of the instructor, because assessing someone else's work helps you develop the quick and experienced eye you will need in the field.

From here onward, each project is accompanied by italicized criteria that can be rated by degrees of agreement, thus:

Outstandingly true = 5

Considerably true = 4

Acceptably true = 3

Somewhat true = 2

Only slightly true = 1

Not at all true = 0

PROJECT 7-3:
TRIPOD: INTERVIEW, ONE SUBJECT

Read the section on interviewing. Look at the judgment criteria below: they are goals and contain a lot of information and reminders. Place the interviewer's head right under the lens, so the interviewee appears to address the viewer.

Action: For approximately 4 minutes of screen time, shoot an interview lasting 5 minutes with a seated subject. Use three image sizes:

Wide shot (top of head down to knees)

Medium shot (head and top of shoulders)

Big close-up (forehead to chin)

Sound: A lavalier mike is ideal for this setup. The interviewer shouldn't be miked because the questions are to be eliminated during the edit.

Directing: Arrange a touch signal between the director/interviewer and camera operator to request zoom changes. Image size changes must be considerable and compositions must intercut, because this exercise is intended to result in a seamless, questionless, and "transparent" flow of on-screen statements.

Interviewing: Good short interviews require compact expository information, a center or focus that develops, some significant change, and an outcome or resolution. The speaker and interviewer must not overlap because eliminating the interviewer's voice (a prime object here) becomes impossible. If an overlap happens, get the interviewee to repeat the reply without an overlap. Ensure that no answer depends on your question, that is, make sure each answer comes out as a freestanding statement. To succeed in this, you must really listen, not think ahead.

Suggested Subjects

1. How a special person helped the interviewee resolve a major conflict in his/her life.

2. The worst period in the interviewee's life, how it came about, and how it ended.

3. A pivotal event in the interviewee's life, how it happened, and what it helped decide.

Edit using Project 25-1 guidelines in Chapter 25.

Criteria

Good sound and no mike visible

Interviewer's voice successfully eliminated

Interviewee is at ease

Composition proportions match on cuts between different-sized images

Interviewee's body position and expression matches between cuts

Zooming and recomposing happen simultaneously and smoothly

Editing maintains natural rhythm of speaker's speech

Interview successfully restructured to develop meaningfully

Tends to use wide shot for new subject matter

Tends to cover moments of intensity in BCU

Interviewee's story has enough expository information

Story builds to a climactic or pivotal moment

Story arrives at a resolution

Story told with intensity throughout

Story has an impact

Film leaves a sense of meaning and purpose

PROJECT 7-4:
HANDHELD: TRACKING ON STATIC SUBJECT

Action: Using the wide-angle end of your zoom, make a slow, walking track at 45 degrees to a brick wall at 3 feet distance (Figure 7-2). The bricks should slide past, neither bobbing up and down nor swaying nearer to and further from camera. To track smoothly, make the camera into a solid part of your head and shoulders, walk with legs a little bent so you can glide, and make your footsteps fall in a straight line to eliminate swaying. As you walk, draw your feet over the ground surface. This helps transfer your weight smoothly from foot to foot without a pounding motion. It also permits your sliding foot to encounter obstacles or irregularities in time to accommodate them.

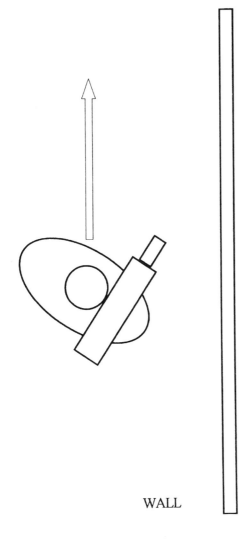

FIGURE 7-2 —————————————

Ground-plan sketch for handheld walking track exercise.

WALL

Criteria

Camera stays upright

Maintains 45 degree angle to the wall

Maintains 3 feet distance

Camera does not bob or sway

PROJECT 7-5:
HANDHELD: TRACKING FORWARD ON MOVING SUBJECT

Walk behind a stranger in the street, staying about 8 feet distance and at 45 degrees to the person's axis. Keep your subject steady and appropriately composed in the frame. Feature the background meaningfully. Have something pleasant to say in explanation if your subject becomes aware of you!

Criteria

Camera "in sync" with subject

Stays at appropriate closeness

Subject steady in frame

Composition adapts to subject changes

Background meaningful and interesting

PROJECT 7-6:
HANDHELD: TRACKING BACKWARD
WITH MOVING SUBJECT

Action (two versions)

a.   Arrange for a subject to walk facing you as in Figure 7-3. The camera operator walks backward, guided through a light touch by an assistant for safety's sake. Frame the subject in a wide shot, and hold that shot for about 15 seconds, then let the subject gain on you until you have a medium shot. Hold this size shot for a while, then allow the subject to gain on you again, this time holding for about 15 seconds of big close-up. Remember to include lead space (more space ahead of a moving subject than there is behind him) in the composition. You may need to give your subject mental work to do so that he can forget the camera.

b.   Now do the same thing again but this time, as in Figure 7-4, with the camera shooting at about a 30 degree angle to the subject's axis. Experiment with the framing and background to find the most acceptable shot.

Editing: When cutting between different image sizes, be careful to preserve the footstep rhythm.

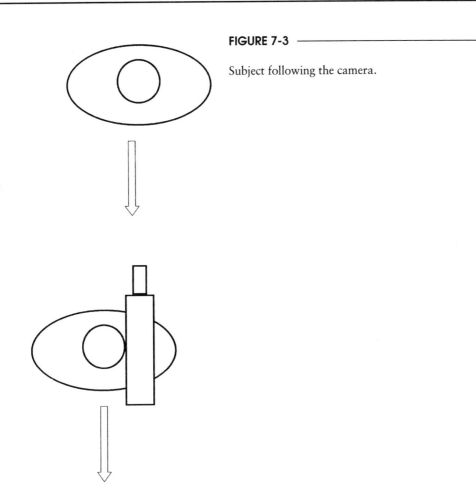

FIGURE 7-3 ————————————

Subject following the camera.

Discussion: What combination of subject size, angle, and background seems to produce the smoothest shot? How much of a problem is it for the subject to have the camera in her eyeline? Can you intercut the on-axis and off-axis material at all elegantly?

Criteria

Person relaxed and un-self-conscious
Camera glides as if on wheels
Wide shot (WS) well framed
Medium shot (MS) well framed
BCU well composed
Backgrounds (B/Gs) used effectively
The two cuts look natural

FIGURE 7-4 —————————————————

Subject following camera with the
camera at 30 degrees to axis.

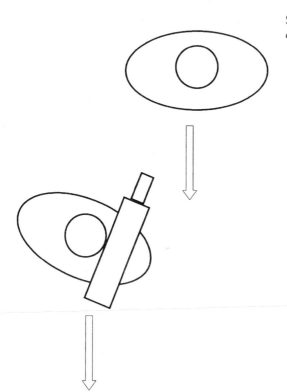

Now you've covered some basics. The next shooting work will come in Chapter 18, Production Projects. Each project represents a typical documentary situation and a particular genre of documentary work. Out of this you gain the broad experience of a working documentarian. The work will require sophisticated handling of the camera and microphone, and poses a series of exciting authorial challenges.

PART 4

PREPRODUCTION

CHAPTER 8
Initial Research and the Proposal   113

On Preproduction   113
Research Overview   114
The Documentary Proposal   116
    Documentary Project Proposal Helper   117
The Treatment   119
Budget Planning Form   119
The Prospectus   124

CHAPTER 9
Research Leading Up to the Shoot   127

A Sample Subject for Discussion   127
Research Relationships   128
Two Research Strategies   128
Deciding the Action and Casting the Players   130
The Value of Assigning Metaphorical Roles   130
The Preinterview and How People Alter in
    Front of the Camera   131
Developing the Film's Thematic Structure   132
Double-Checking One's Findings   132
Developing the Working Hypothesis and
    Finding the Dielectics   133
The Working Hypothesis as a Necessity   135
The Need for Development, Conflict, and
    Confrontation   135

The Dramatic Curve   136
Facts and Narration   139
Research Partnership   139
Setting Up the Shoot: Logistics and the
    Schedule   139
The Personal Release Form   140
Permission to Film at Location Facilities   141

CHAPTER 10
Developing a Crew   143

Using People with Experience   143
Developing Your Own Crew   143
Crew Members' Temperaments Are
    Important!   144
Clearly Define the Areas of Responsibility   145
Crew Roles and Responsibilities   145
    Director   145
    Camera Operator   146
    Gaffer   147
    Sound Recordist   147
    Grip   148
    Production Manager (PM)   148
Equipment Selection: Drawing Up a Want
    List   149
Preproduction Checklist   149

CHAPTER 8

INITIAL RESEARCH AND THE PROPOSAL

ON PREPRODUCTION

The preproduction period is that which covers all the decisions and arrangements prior to shooting. For a documentary, this includes choosing a subject; doing the research; assembling a crew; choosing what equipment will be necessary; and deciding the method, details, and timetable of shooting.

There is a good reason why even seasoned filmmakers seldom rely on spontaneous inspiration, expressed succinctly by Werner Herzog when questioned after a show of his work. Asked about "the intellectual challenge during shooting," he replied caustically that "filmmaking is athletic, not aesthetic." In no uncertain terms, he proceeded to tell his startled questioner that most filming is so grueling that rarefied thought is impossible.

François Truffaut makes a similar point in *Day for Night,* the central character of which is a director whose movie runs into a thicket of problems and compromises. Played by Truffaut himself, the director says at one point that he always starts shooting convinced the film will be superb, but halfway into the schedule hopes only to finish. My own fantasy, which returns at least once every shoot, is to escape further filming by miraculously turning into the owner of a rural grocery.

The depth of thought you invest at this time and the extent to which you foresee problems and obstacles go very far indeed to ensure a successful shoot; more important, this preparation largely determines whether the movie will be a coherent entity. Directing a documentary, contrary to the impression of instant "auteurism," is less a process of spontaneous inquiry than one guided by preliminary conclusions reached during research. In other words, the shoot may largely be collecting "evidence" for underlying patterns and relationships identified earlier.

RESEARCH OVERVIEW

Let's assume you have chosen a subject and now face the initial research phase leading up to a written proposal. No two people research alike, but some steps are fairly universal. Research methods tend to develop from the exigencies of the subject, so you must heed practicalities, that is, recognize as early as possible whether you have the makings of a film. This process is also about the realism behind deciding *what* film is possible, because a documentary cannot be made from good intentions, only from what can be captured with a camera.

Following are some recommended steps. You will often be forced by circumstances to take them out of the ideal order, or to take several concurrently. When you hit an impediment, turn and work elsewhere so you don't waste time. Filmmaking demands lateral thinking; progress in one area changes what has been decided in another, so one must constantly readjust the whole, which is frustrating until you get used to it.

This list of steps really covers the whole of research, but because documentary makers often have several irons in the fire, most proposals are written from partial rather than conclusive research. Even when research is rather thorough and complete, there is usually a fallow period while funds and sponsoring organizations are being sought, so there will always be preproduction research leading up to the first day of shooting.

- *Define an off-the-top-of-your-head working hypothesis for the subject* (see Hypothesis section of Documentary Project Proposal Helper later). Don't sit on the fence until you know more. Start now. You should often return to this step.

- *List the action sequences,* and decide how far they alone would go toward making an interesting and coherent silent film. This shows how inherently cinematic your film is, or how much it relies on speech. (Radio with pictures!)

- *Check reality.* During preproduction check often whether

    What you want is accessible.

    The people are amenable and interested.

    Releases and permissions really will be available.

    You can afford it.

    You should narrow the film's topic, either for its own good or because of an obstacle in any of the previously mentioned points.

- *Check existing resources,* that is,

    Study publications covering your subject, such as magazines, newspapers, journals, and even fiction. All are useful repositories of ideas and observations. Read up, and don't reinvent the wheel. You'll find much overlap between them. Can you show something new?

    See films on the your subject, but *not* if you feel vulnerable to their influence.

    Develop a list of fundamental points your film must make.

    Develop your own angle, defining what will be different in your film.

Define goals and what you want to avoid in content or style.

- *Develop trust.* Make yourself and your purpose very generally known to those you may want to film. Keep this broad because you do not want to tie yourself down. But you must create overall trust in your motives and interests.

- *Do the legwork.* Spending time with your subjects over a period is the most valuable thing you can do. Make sure that you:

  Know what's typical of the world that you want to film.

  Know the people and places, their rhythms and routines.

  Make a private list of what is normal, and what you notice is atypical.

  Decide who are the possible protagonists.

  Know what life role each acts in the drama you are beginning to perceive.

  Try to get multiple perspectives on each person or facet, especially when there are ambiguities. But avoid being intrusive or divisive.

- *Develop a reliable working hypothesis.* You should be revisiting your definition of your subject often because it changes. Making a hypothesis (described later) is the best way to lock down your thematic purpose. If you put this off, you won't know what to shoot or how to shoot it. The result? You shoot everything that moves.

- *Preinterview.* Under the guise of preliminary research, do audio or video preinterviews of whoever you're considering for the film. But ask no searching questions—you want to ask these only when you are shooting. Listen to the tape to see who comes across well. Good quality audio can be used later as voice-over.

- *Make the final draft proposal revision.* Even when you have nobody to satisfy but yourself, work over all the considerations prior to shooting. This will be invaluable mental preparation.

- *Make a rough budget* (see the budget form later in this chapter.)

- *Write a treatment.* This is optional and consists of writing the film you see in your head after developing the research. A treatment is probably a necessity if you are applying for money. See The Treatment (later).

- *Obtain permissions.* Approach those you wish to film and secure a promise of their time and involvement. If you intend to shoot in special locations, secure written permissions beforehand.

Once shooting becomes definite,

- *Secure your crew.*
- *Make a shooting schedule* and make plans to deal with foreseeable difficulties.
- *Plan shooting style* and special strategies to secure the film you envision.
- *Do any necessary trial shooting* to

    "audition" doubtful participants

    work out communications with a new crew

    test new or unfamiliar technology

THE DOCUMENTARY PROPOSAL

Everyone dreads writing proposals. They are an unavoidable part of communicating one's intentions, particularly when it comes to fundraising. But they do have another important function: They force one to greatly clarify the organizational and thematic analysis developed during research. Then as the time comes to pitch your film (i.e., to seek support through making a verbal presentation), you will make a much clearer and more forceful argument when you need to solicit support from the crew or financiers.

An even more useful aspect of making a proposal is that it also helps prepare you to *direct* the film, that is, to shoot materials designed to say something instead of blindly collecting stuff that you hope can be beaten into shape during editing.

The proposal should show you can fulfill the conditions of documentary itself. It should:

- Tell a good story.
- Not relay value-neutral information like a textbook.
- Aim to relay a personal, critical perspective on some aspect of the human condition.

To dramatize human truths, both large and small, the successful documentary usually incorporates:

- interesting characters who are trying to do or get something
- well-placed exposition of necessary information or context, not too much and placed not too early
- tension and conflict between opposing forces
- dramatic suspense—not usually the kind in which people hang off cliffs, but situations that intrigue the spectator and have her judging, anticipating, wondering, comparing
- considerable development of at least one character or major situation
- confrontation between main factions or elements
- a climax of opposing elements or forces
- a resolution

These criteria may look as though they only apply to traditional narrative, but they actually apply to almost any kind of film, even (in its own terms) the most experimental.

Your proposal should demonstrate how these implicit expectations of the form will be met. The proposal helper that follows will help you figure out what is needed for each category, which is like the pigeonholes in a mail sorting office. A well-researched film will have something substantial and different in each pigeonhole. If you find you've put similar material into more than one classification, go to further drafts until material is presented *only once and in its rightful place.*

Keep on writing and rewriting until your proposal is succinct, free of redundancy, and effortless for the reader to assimilate. Experienced readers know that a mind that thinks well and writes well can probably work effectively in a more difficult medium such as filmmaking.

DOCUMENTARY PROJECT PROPOSAL HELPER

The worksheet below with its set of prompts will help you develop the kind of information and knowledge you need to write a proposal or develop a prospectus package as the prelude to searching for financial support.

Working title _____   Format _____

Director _____   Camera _____

Sound _____   Editor _____

Others: _____ (role) _____   _____ (role) _____

1. WORKING HYPOTHESIS and INTERPRETATION. What are *your* persuasions about the world you are going to show in your film, the main "statement" that you want to emerge out of the film's dialectics? Write a hypothesis statement incorporating the following wording:

In life I believe that _____

My film will show this in action by exploring (situation) _____

The main conflict is between _____ and _____

Ultimately I want the audience to feel _____

and to understand that _____

2. TOPIC and EXPOSITION. Write a concise paragraph about

   a. Your film's *subject* (person, group, environment, social issue, and so on).

   b. *Background information* the audience needs to understand the enclosed world you intend to present and how this information will be established.

3. ACTION SEQUENCES. Write a brief paragraph for each intended sequence that shows an activity. (A sequence is usually delineated by being in one location, one chunk of time, or an assembly of materials to show one topic.) For each, try to cover the following:

   a. The sequence's action will be _____

   b. The factual information it contributes to the film will be _____

   c. The conflicts it evidences will be _____

   d. The metaphor I'd use to convey its subtextual meaning is _____

   e. The events in the sequence are structured around/by _____

   f. I expect the sequence to contribute to the film as a whole by _____

   g. Specifically it contributes to the film's hypothesis that _____

   h. I expect to get from it the following special, perhaps emblematic imagery _____

4. MAIN CHARACTERS. Write a brief paragraph about your main characters, including for each:

   a. The person's identity—name, relationship to others in film, and so on.

   b. What this person contributes to your film's story.

   c. The metaphoric role you see this person occupying in relation to who and what else is in the film.

   d. What this character wants to get or do in relation to the others.

   e. Any direct speech quotations that say freshly and directly what this person is about.

5. CONFLICT. What is at issue in this film? Define,

   a. What conflict the characters know they are playing out.

   b. What other principles (of opinion, view, vision, and so on) you can see in opposition.

   c. How we will see one force finally meet with the other (the "confrontation," very important).

   d. What possible developments you see emerging from this confrontation.

6. AUDIENCE, ITS KNOWLEDGE AND BIASES. Your documentary must presume some knowledge, right or wrong, and some expectations in your audience that the film must extend, subvert, or endorse. Complete the following:

   a. My intended audience is _____ (don't write "Everyone")

   b. I can expect the audience to know _____ but not to know _____

   c. Audience biases are _____ (both positive and negative ones may coexist)

   d. Alternative facts, ideas, or feelings my audience needs to understand are _____

   e. My audience will see these new truths because of _____

7. TO-CAMERA INTERVIEWS. "Talking heads" are less and less in favor but do make good safety coverage. When well recorded, the track can be used as voice-over narration or interior monologue. For each interviewee list:

   a. Name, age
   b. Job or profession
   c. Metaphoric role in your film's dramatic structure
   d. Main elements your interview will seek to establish

8. STRUCTURE. Write a brief paragraph on how you hope to structure your film. Try to include:

   a. How you will handle the progression of time in the film.

   b. How specially important information will be made to appear and, if possible, when (try to make exposition emerge unobviously and as it's needed).

   c. What you imagine will be the climactic sequence or "crisis" and where in the structure this might go.

   d. How other sequences will build toward this "crisis" and how others will become the falling action after it.

   e. Sequences or interviews you intend to have on hand for parallel storytelling. (This is important safety coverage because being able to cut between parallel stories allows you to use only the essence of each.)

9. FORM AND STYLE. Special considerations in shooting or editing style that might augment or counterpoint your film's content. You might comment on:

   a. Narration (if there is to be any, and by whom)
   b. Lighting

    c.   Camera handling
    d.   Rhythms, type, and amount of intercutting or parallel storytelling
    e.   Juxtaposition of like or unlike materials to create comparison, ironic tension, etc.

   10. RESOLUTION. You film's ending is your last word and has a disproportionate influence on the film's final impact. Write a brief paragraph about how you imagine your film ending, and what meaning you foresee it establishing for the audience. If events could go in more than one direction, hypothesize different endings, because this is an entirely realistic consideration.

THE TREATMENT

Treatments and proposals are both written to convince a sponsor, fund, or broadcasting organization that you can make a film of impact and significance, but they go about it in different ways. While the proposal presents the intended film as a list of categorized information, the treatment describes what an audience would experience from the screen. It will be a matter of judgment how to present the best case, according to whom you are going to approach.

A treatment is a present-tense short story narrative that excludes any philosophy or directorial intentions. To begin, take the information you worked up in the proposal draft and:

- Restructure it into a sequence by sequence presentation, one paragraph per sequence.
- Write as a present tense narrative only *what will be seen and heard from the screen.*
- Write colorfully so the reader can visualize the film you have in your head.
- Where possible, convey information and the nature of your characters by using their own words as brief, spirited quotations.
- Don't write anything that the reader thinks you cannot produce.

Many sources of financial support are institutions attracting large numbers of applications who publish their own strict guidelines. When you apply, you must follow their specifications closely, or you will waste your time and theirs. Often you will be expected to fulfill something like the prospectus format that follows.

BUDGET PLANNING FORM

Your final budget, or a budget summary sheet, should wherever possible be done using a budget software program. Here is an all-purpose form to remind you what you will need and to help you plan out costs. Note that two figures, a high and a low, are compiled. These are optimistic and pessimistic approaches and keep you from a painful underestimation. A contingency percentage is always added at the end of a film budget to cover the unforeseen, such as bad-weather delays, reshoots, additions, or substitutions.

Budget Worksheet

Working Title:			Film length: ___m ___secs
Name	Address	Home phone	Work phone
(Director)			
(Camera)			
(Sound)			
(Editor)			
Format (circle all that apply):	VHS / Hi8 / DV/ Betacam / Other _____	Film: B&W/color 8mm / 16mm / 35mm	
Project is at stage of (circle one):	Research / Preproduction / Production / Postproduction		
Schedule	Preproduction	Production	Postproduction
From			
To			
Brief description of subject:			
Working hypothesis of film is:			

Preproduction Costs

Item	Low Estimate	High Estimate
Director/researcher @ _____ per day for ____ / ____days		
Travel		
Phone		
Photocopying		
Food		
Accommodation		
Tests		
Research (library, etc.)		
1: Preproduction SUBTOTAL		

Production Costs

Role	Daily rate	Min days	Max days	Low estimate	High estimate
Director					
Camera Operator					
Sound Operator					
Gaffer					
Other					
2a: Production personnel SUBTOTAL					
Equipment					
Camera (film)					
Camcorder					
Magazines (film)					
Changing bag (film)					
Clapper board (film)					
Lenses					
Filter kit					
Exposure meter					
Color temp. meter					
Tripod					
Baby legs					
Hi-hat					
Tilt head					
Spreader					
Video monitor					
Nagra package (film)					
Headphones					
Mike boom					
Extra mikes					

Equipment	Daily rate	Min days	Max days	Low estimate	High estimate
Mixer					
Batteries					
Sun gun					
Lighting package					
Tie in cables					
Extension cords					
Other _____					
Other _____					
2b: Production equipment SUBTOTAL					

Materials	Type	Cost per unit	Min days	Max days	Low estimate	High estimate
Camera raw stock						
Nagra tape						
Develop negative						
Make workprint						
Sound transfer						
Sound stock						
Videocassettes						
Other _____						
Other _____						
Miscellaneous	Type	Per day	Min	Max		
Insurance						
Transport						
Food						
Accommodation						
Location or other fees						
Other _____						
2c: Production materials/miscellaneous SUBTOTAL						

Postproduction Costs

Role	Cost per day		Min days	Max days	Low estimate	High estimate
Editor						
Assistant editor						
Narrator						
3a: Postproduction personnel SUBTOTAL						
Materials	Type	Amount	Min	Max		
Archive footage						
Time coding						
Window dub						
Off-line editing equipment						
Music						
Titling						
Online (video)						
Sound mix						
Transfer mag master to optical (film)						
Conforming (film)						
First answer print (film)						
First release print (film)						
3b: Postproduction materials/processes SUBTOTAL						
Production office						
Legal						
Insurance						
Phone/fax, assistance, and other production office expenses						
Production manager						
Other _____						
Other _____						
4: Production office SUBTOTAL						

Budget Summary

Phase	Category	Subtotal		Minimum Estimate	Maximum estimate
Preproduction	1: Personnel & materials TOTAL				
Production	2a: Personnel				
	2b: Equipment				
	2c: Materials/miscellaneous				
	TOTAL				
Postproduction	3a: Personnel				
	3b: Materials/processes				
	TOTAL				
	4: Production office				
	FINAL SUBTOTAL				
	Contingency (add 12% of final subtotal)				
PRODUCTION GRAND TOTAL					

THE PROSPECTUS

This is a presentation package or portfolio you put together to communicate your project and its purposes to prospective funders. It should be thoroughly professional and contain:

Cover letter: This succinctly communicates the nature of the film, its budget, the capital you want to raise, and what you want from the addressee. If you are targeting many small investors, this may have to be a general letter, but wherever possible fashion a specific letter to a specific individual.

Title page: Finding a good title usually takes inordinate effort but does more than anything to arouse respect and interest. An evocative photo or other professional-looking artwork here and elsewhere in the prospectus can do much to make your presentation exciting.

One liner: A simple, compact declaration of the project. For example,

1. A Midwest theater director goes to live as one of the Los Angeles homeless so she can knowledgeably direct a play about homelessness.
2. Marriage as seen in the ideas and play of 7 year olds from across the social spectrum.

3. Three people, of different ages and from different countries, relive their near-death experiences and explain how profoundly their lives changed afterwards.

Synopsis: Brief recounting of the documentary's intended story that captures its flavor and style.

History and background: How and why the project evolved and why you feel compelled to make this particular film. This is the place to establish your commitment.

Research: Outline what research you've done and what it contributes. This is the opportunity to establish the factual foundation to the film, its characters, its context. If special cooperation, rights, or permissions are involved, here is where you assure the reader that you've secured them.

Reel: A 3–5 minute specially edited trailer that shows the characters, landscape, style, and other attractions to which you lay claim. It may be a single sequence of great power, or a montage of material. This is your chance to let the screen make your argument. Be aware that when there are four hundred applications, reels must be of distinguished material that makes its point extremely rapidly. Include an overview list to make viewing an alluring prospect.

Budget: Summary of main expected expenditures. Don't understate or underestimate—it makes you look amateurish and leaves you asking for too little.

Schedule: Approximate shooting period (or periods, if shooting is broken up) and preferred starting dates.

Resumés of creative personnel: In brief paragraphs, name the director, producer, camera operator, sound operator, and editor, and briefly summarize their qualifications. Append a one-page resumé from each. Your aim is to present the team as professional, exciting, and specially suited.

Audience and market: Say who the film is intended for, and outline a distribution plan to show convincingly that the film has a waiting audience. Copies of letters of interest from television stations, channels, film distributors, or other interested parties are very helpful here.

Financial statement: Outline your financial identity as a company or group, make an estimate of income based on the distribution plan, and say if you are a bona fide not-for-profit company, or working through one, because this may permit investors to claim tax breaks.

Means of transferring funds: A model letter from the investor back to your company committing funds to your production account.

Each funding agency may have its own preferred form of presentation, so research the fund's identity and track record to know how best to present your work. Every grant application is potentially the foundation for a lengthy relationship, so your prospectus and whatever proposals follow it should be clear, individual, and professional work that personably convey your project and its purpose. Each prospectus should be tailored to the particular addressee, but this doesn't mean you should promise different things to different people.

At this stage you are what you write, so try to secure desktop publishing facilities to give your work really professional-looking graphics and typesetting. This is a tricky time because you probably have been unable to do more than basic research and must minimize your uncertainties. Once the project is feasible and funds have been secured, then research and development can begin in earnest.

CHAPTER 9

RESEARCH LEADING UP TO THE SHOOT

Your proposal has received the green light, or, as an independent, you have decided, after suitable reflection, that you are going ahead with this subject. Now you are entering the preproduction phase of research, a period of concentrated discovery and decision making prior to shooting.

A SAMPLE SUBJECT FOR DISCUSSION

Let us assume that you want to make a film about a local school band that you've been following for a while and that you find fascinating for particular reasons. You want to go further than merely showing how the band rehearses or how it absorbs new members since that would merely illustrate what common sense alone would expect. Your purpose is to try and lay bare the fanaticism and quasi-military discipline underlying the band's success.

Before shooting anything, find out whether such an idea is feasible. This is one of the prime purposes of research. By the way, if you have to produce a film in a given time, it is a good idea to pursue the fundamentals of *several* possible ideas from the outset. Projects have a nasty habit of folding up. Permission to shoot might be a stumbling block, but sometimes one loses all conviction during research that any really meaningful film is possible. Recognizing this in time is somehow always easier if you have standby alternatives.

We are going to pursue the possibilities of this school band through the various stages of preproduction. Researching means initially surveying the general area to see if it is promising and beginning by making a "shopping list" of possible sequences. To do this you must start visiting for informal chats.

RESEARCH RELATIONSHIPS

Be purposely tentative when you tell people during research about the project you have in mind. Keeping to generalities lets you feel your way, indicates that you are open to suggestions, and allows participants a stake in determining the film.

To get to the bandmaster in our hypothetical school, you would start with the school principal. You might say that you live nearby and have been thinking about making a film on the school's marching band. If he asks for a full description of the project, or a script to show to his board, this is a bad sign. It signifies fear, a bad precedent, excessive caution, a lack of authority, or all of the above. In all probability, he will be delighted and will tell the bandmaster to expect you. When you arrive, approval of your project is already implied because the signal has come from the top. In dealing with any kind of institutional structure, it is usually best to work from the top downward.

When you first make a research visit, take a notebook and nothing else. Explain who you are and what you have done previously. Present yourself in a friendly, respectful way and try to reassure those you meet about your motives. You are there to learn from experts; that is your role, and that is what you should project. It is a truthful presentation of your purpose (though not the whole truth perhaps), and it is a role to which most people respond appreciatively.

At this point you really do not know what your future film might contain, nor do you have more than the vaguest notion of what it will really be about. It is therefore not only prudent but also truthful to keep your options open and to parry questions with a request for *their* ideas. Often people ask to see a script. Explain that in modern documentary filmmaking, one films events that are real and spontaneous, so documentarians cannot make scripts.

Your role as a researcher should be one of extremely wakeful passivity, watching and listening and correlating what you receive. Even the innately suspicious are usually intrigued by a moviemaker's interest, lowering their barriers as they come to know you. This takes an investment of time on your part, but keep in mind that *documentaries are only as good as the relationships that permit them to be made.* Few relationships of trust are achieved quickly so expect to proceed at your subject's own speed. This may mean you spend days, weeks, or even months getting to know your subjects and letting them come to trust you.

TWO RESEARCH STRATEGIES

Two ways to elicit opinions but still not commit you to any particular point of view are to play the "student of life" role and sometimes that of devil's advocate. Instead of saying to the bandmaster, "I think you are tough and inflexible toward those kids," you probe in a more general and depersonalized way, no matter what your convictions may be, by saying, "Some of the people I've spoken to say you are pretty definite about what you want. Do you find there's opposition to this?" And perhaps later, you might hazard something like, "Your experience seems to have shown you that kids need a strong sense of direction." Without committing yourself to agreement, you have shown that you appreciate the band-master's convictions. Most people assume that because you can accurately describe their convictions, you also share them. While this is sometimes true, it is more likely to be a convenient misunderstanding. It would be unproductive to correct it.

Why does the student-of-life approach find such ready acceptance? Initially you will probably feel yourself trying to fake a confident, relaxed interest that you are too anxious to really feel. Do not worry; this is researcher's stage fright, and it always seems to accompany the initial stages of a new project, even for old hands. Yet you will be amazed at how readily your presence, and your right to ask all sorts of questions, is usually accepted. And then you will be passed eagerly on from person to person.

Have you stumbled upon exceptionally cooperative people? Probably not. Rather, you have uncovered a useful facet of human nature. Most of us seem privately to consider we are living in undeserved obscurity and that nobody properly recognizes our achievements or true worth. When someone comes along wielding the tools of publicity—the pen, microphone, or camera—it offers the fulfillment of a deep-seated yearning. In addition, there are more people than you would imagine with a philanthropic desire to tell the world a few truths it should know. All this, I think, helps explain why people may receive you with surprising enthusiasm and respond so gratefully to the recognition your attention confers.

With this comes an obligation on your part to act responsibly and to treat respectfully the lives you enter. More often than not, you will leave the scene of a documentary feeling that your participants have not only given you dinner but have shared something profoundly personal with you and your camera. You carry a strong sense of obligation not just to "the truth," which is an abstract thing, but to those who gave you something of themselves. It gets tricky when you feel similarly obligated to those whom you neither like nor approve. Making documentaries poses many awkward questions of moral obligation.

One cardinal rule during the research period: *Never even hint you will film any particular scene or any particular person unless you are absolutely certain that you are going to.* Most people are longing to be interviewed or filmed working, no matter how cool they are on the outside. If you don't commit yourself, you will avoid disappointing people and making them feel you have rejected them. Stress the tentative and uncertain aspects of your research as long as you possibly can. You may yet have to shoot certain scenes or interviews, just to keep someone happy. Diplomacy of this kind costs time and money, and is to be avoided.

Another cardinal rule: *Never say you will show footage to participants, either cut or uncut, if you think there is the remotest possibility that pressure will be brought on you to make undesirable changes.* Participants in a film, whether documentary or fiction, are generally appalled by their own appearance and mannerisms. They are the worst people to help you make judgments about balance and content. A reporter does not have to show his notebook to anyone before the article comes out in the newspaper, and you should likewise avoid actions that lead to loss of editorial control. This is ultimately in your participants' interest as well as your own, because their initial shock and embarrassment usually changes later to pleasure and self-acceptance when an assembly of people is approving.

DECIDING THE ACTION AND CASTING THE PLAYERS

I mentioned earlier that you should start making shopping lists of possible sequences. In the hypothetical band project you have begun researching, you would
spend time at the school getting to know the band's personalities and routine. You
would start listing the possible action sequences, such as:

Band auditioning

Band practicing

Band marching

Playing in practice

Special performances

Social activities between members either before or after sessions

Social activities between members in between times

Like a fiction movie, you have been finding locations and pieces of action. Now
you need to set about "casting players." You should begin making private, confidential notes on outstanding individuals. What kind of people are they? What
does each represent in the whole? One may be the clown, another might be the
diplomat, another the uncertain kid who is uncomfortable with the band's milita-
rism but values being a member too much to leave. There may be senior kids who
act as "policemen" and enforcers of the band's discipline. There may be a few eccentrics whose presence is tolerated because their playing outweighs their oddities.

THE VALUE OF ASSIGNING METAPHORICAL ROLES

It is extremely helpful to develop not only functional descriptions for your characters but a *metaphorical* characterization for each as well. All this, of course, is for
your private use and not to be divulged to your subjects, as they might think you
were mocking them. By producing a metaphorical vision of the group and their
situation, you are compelling yourself to define each person's underlying and unacknowledged role. Fred Wiseman's *Hospital* (1969) makes us think of purgatory,
where souls are rescued or sent onward. The image is so prevalent and so sustained that one realizes how, through the force of his own vision, he has made us
see a New York emergency room as an embodiment of classical mythology. Before
our eyes the doctors, nurses, policemen, and patients become players in a renewed
version of mythology. Similar human archetypes probably underpin every successful documentary.

So your obligation as documentarian and artist is more than just reflecting reality. A mirror does the same, and sends back what is value-neutral and banal.
Your film should reveal more of your subject than anyone would expect. You
want to demonstrate that it contains the characters, passions, atmospheres, and
struggle proper to any human tale. The key lies in not only categorizing your characters as a sociologist would, but in using the eyes of a poet or dramatist so that

you see the constants of myth and legend that are constantly regenerated in everyday life.

Giving a name to each of the metaphorical roles you see being enacted by the participants (e.g., king, queen, jester, prophet of doom, diplomatic troubleshooter, sentry, earth mother) is important. It means you are taking the first steps toward recognizing how, like most established groups, they have unconsciously set up a microcosmic society with its own roles, rules, values, and sanctions. With this golden key in hand, your film can go about compactly portraying this complete world in miniature.

Let us imagine that the band begins to look like a militaristic, patriotic, and authoritarian microcosm. It seems to say a lot about the ideology and background common to the teachers and students. You now want to supplement the band activities, which suggest the contradictory values of both collaboration and dictatorship, with interviews. These you hope will give your audience access to the way the students and their teachers think. From chatting with people and absorbing many different points of view, you realize which individuals best represent the conflicting ideals you want to make visible. Certainly the bandmaster is a charismatic figure, and his power is accepted by most as a beneficial imposition. Talk to key instrumentalists and to other teachers, and casually cross-check your own impressions by asking each for a view of the others.

THE PREINTERVIEW AND HOW PEOPLE ALTER IN FRONT OF THE CAMERA

During research you investigate the subject, but also test the behavior of potential interviewees as they go on record. Someone with an unsuppressed yearning to "be famous" (which is what people associate with film and television cameras) may come across as a show-off or clam up from sheer nervousness. This could derail your shooting and you can't risk that.

At a subsequent research visit, take along an audio cassette recorder. I always ask permission before turning my machine on. When recording begins, most people are self-conscious and rather constrained. Soon they begin to speak more freely and with feeling, though some do not. Some people become monosyllabic or show an accentuated tendency to digress or to qualify everything they begin to say.

Take your audio recording and just *listen*, making note of your thoughts and realizations. Informal audio interviews show who will give you the most, who remains undistorted by character hang-ups, and who, on the other hand, cannot or will not deliver when he goes on record. Sometimes an interesting and likable person simply does not record well. His voice may be flat or uncongenial, or he does not construct verbal pictures in a logical, communicative way. Still others prove to be monotonous or expressionless and their affect negates whatever they say or do on screen. Even the voice quality itself matters greatly. Henry Kissinger's harsh voice, for example, may have been a major factor in his unpopularity.

For some reason, none of this is easy to see until you are out of the person's presence and can listen with relative objectivity. Recognizing what does or does not work at this early stage will save time, money, and heartache later. Often, of course, a recording simply augments what you already knew: This person is a delight to hear, and you are sure you want to use her. By now you know your priorities, and the key participants—each representing different and probably opposed aspects in your underlying framework—have become the natural choice.

These preinterviews can be used later as voice-over if you take care to record well, in a quiet place, and without letting voices overlap.

DEVELOPING THE FILM'S THEMATIC STRUCTURE

Let us suppose that you become convinced that the band is really a viable analogue for an aspect of your country's political structure with its charismatic father figure at the helm. This analogy is by no means farfetched. Peter Davis' *Hearts and Minds* (1974) repeatedly uses scenes of American sports and the team spirit atmosphere as an analogy for the values expressed by supporters of war in Vietnam. The makers imply through the comparison that a sports mentality conditioned young Americans to enter an ideological conflict under the tragically simplistic notion of "our team" and "their team." Only in the field did the young GIs begin to question what "playing for the team" really meant. By such conditioning and metaphors in peacetime, the film implies, we prepare our sons to go out to suffer and die. Finding such paradigms, the documentarian can draw attention to the invisible substructures in a society.

Leadership in society is often exerted by those who name truths convincingly. Richard Nixon, Ronald Reagan, and Margaret Thatcher seduced electorates with their ad men and their populist messages; it is our job to use our minds and our more powerful art to penetrate the superficial and to reveal countervailing and more pervasive truths.

DOUBLE-CHECKING ONE'S FINDINGS

During research, talk to many people and collect as many relevant viewpoints as you can. Initial judgments are often based on brief and sometimes unrepresentative exposure, so testing one's assumptions against the impressions of people whose lives make them expert helps you sift out as much reliable information as possible.

It is fascinating to realize how people, especially the highly visible or powerful, are perceived quite differently according to who you question. Partisan viewpoints and biases are inevitable, but you need to know what they are based on. Cross-checking people's impressions of your major "characters" enables you to avoid superficial judgments and allows you to build into your film the richness and diversity of affinities and tensions that bind any group of people together.

By now you are almost oppressively knowledgeable about the people and practices that surround the school's marching band. You need to withdraw and decide your priorities, because if you were to shoot now you would lack clear direction.

DEVELOPING THE WORKING HYPOTHESIS
AND FINDING THE DIELECTICS

Whatever your initial motives were for looking into the marching band, they must now be reviewed in the light of your much more extended exposure. Earlier I said that a film qualifies as a documentary when it implies a critical attitude toward some aspect of society. Here we face some problems inherent in film, because as Richardson says in *Literature and Film,* "literature has the problem of making the significant somehow visible, while film often finds itself trying to make the visible significant." In film generally, and especially in documentary, there is an oversupply of verisimilitude. A torrent of surface trivia obscures underlying meanings. It is not enough to merely *show* something: we must also indicate where its significance lies. How is this achieved?

[handwritten margin note: SOMETHING THAT APPEARS REAL]

Most of what is significant—in issues as well as in individuals—exists because some kind of conflict is at work. It may be conflict between people of different opinions, different convictions, or different ambitions. It may, like Nanook's, be between the individual and his environment or between the parts of an individual torn between allegiances to class, generation, race, nation, or a system of belief. Conflict often exists internally when an individual is torn between conflicting desires.

Jean-Luc Godard once said, while rejecting formulas as a means of creating screen characters, that in real life we never gain possession of some magic psychological key to another's thoughts and feelings. He might also have added that we never stop looking. Everything we learn about another person is suggestive, fragmentary, and pieced together from that person's external behavior alone. Godard's method of revealing personality was to concentrate on a character's contradictions, because these showed most clearly what was unresolved and therefore most active in a person's inner life.

To show the pressing truths of human life, documentary must uncover the ambiguities and contradictions in its characters' "unfinished business" and focus on those aspects of its topic that are truly in flux. In your research into the band, you suspect that the band exemplifies how the country talks eternally about democracy, yet hungers for "strong leadership" to sort out the misfits for their own good. But now you hit a snag. Although the bandmaster is an authoritarian of the worst kind, bands need leaders and a lot of the kids like him. Even more confounding is that, in spite of disagreeing with all his ideas, you find yourself liking him too.

What to do? Give up? Surely you have stumbled on a truly interesting subject, all the more so because you yourself have contradictory, ambivalent feelings toward him and toward the situation that he has projected around himself.

For your own clarity, you must now define the focus, the underlying and implicit concept of your film. This should not be shared with anyone outside your crew, but it is absolutely vital in determining any shooting to come. A helpful example comes to mind from a feature film. You may have seen *The Orchestra Rehearsal* (1979), a ribald Fellini movie shot for television about a fictitious orchestra that rebels against its conductor and descends into anarchy. On the surface the movie is a comedy, but it uses the orchestra as a metaphor for our complex, interdependent, and, of necessity, highly disciplined society. The conductor functions as the leader, but he can only function in his role when all the players cooperate and accept his authority. Once they assert autonomy, the music becomes flawed, then discordant, and then completely chaotic. Even the opera house, under attack by unseen enemies, begins to fall down. Eventually, out of sheer discomfort, the orchestra reforms itself and returns to fulfilling its best potential.

An allegory like this helps to show how a band and bandmaster might be a rather potent metaphor for a political unit such as a tribe or a nation. In fact, by dealing with charisma and authority, our movie could quite easily become a parable about power and prevailing ideology.

Some readers from the social sciences may feel uneasy here and say, "But that's manipulation!" I would answer yes, it is. The documentary, because of film's subjectivity, cannot be an ideal tool of social science. It cannot credibly postulate, as one can in print, the existence of such and such a phenomenon and reinforce its arguments with objectively gathered evidence. Rather, its purpose is artistic, to share a way of seeing. At its best the documentary can take something apparently banal and unmeaningful, and give us a heightened, subtly argued vision charged with significance.

So what meaning, what thematic structure, can one find in the band situation? You have discovered what you never believed existed: a benevolent despot who is valued and valuable, even though all his "subjects" see themselves as rugged individualists. It's a wonderful allegory for a "free" society that consents to march in lockstep in order to achieve supremacy, one that enthusiastically submits to a form of leadership that is the very antithesis of its democratic and individualist ideals. This is the kernel of your idea—this paradox below the surface that you "see."

Now all your sequences—the activities, interviews, and discussions you ask the kids to have between themselves for the camera—must create the contradictory parts. It is a complex vision, and ultimately a nonjudgmental one that reflects nothing you expected to find, but rather what was there, existing in the face of all logic and belief.

I invented this example but myself experienced a similar conversion while making a film many years ago on a lordly estate in England. My film (*A Remnant of a Feudal Society*) reflected my inability to reconcile the contradictory nature of the estate, which operated in quite a feudal way until modern times. For some of the survivors, the estate was remembered nostalgically as a place of security and order—plenty of hard work but a great spirit of community. For others, the regime was to some degree imprisoning, demeaning, and overdemanding. Not one person had clear, simple feelings because all had differing experiences and had come to tentative, qualified conclusions, if they had come to conclusions at all. The only predictable element was that the people in the upper part of the social scale remembered the old days more pleasurably than did those at the bottom, although all valued the place's safety and continuity.

Before going to the estate, I had expected those who had served a feudal master to be united in their condemnation because this was the rather monolithic course of history I'd learned in school. The real thing turned out to be more human, more complex and interesting, and showed me why my school history books had seemed simplistic and dull.

THE WORKING HYPOTHESIS AS A NECESSITY

One never starts any journey without some direction and purpose. In documentary any kind of hypothetical explanation at the outset, even a prejudice, provides a better starting point than vacuity masquerading as scientific method. Had I not begun my feudal estate film with strongly felt opinions, no independent vision of the place would ever have developed. Instead, the film would have been a tedious exercise in nostalgia, with colorful rustics and their master remembering the old days.

From the moment you are first attracted to an idea, write out *the minimum your film must express*. This, modified during research, will ensure a minimum, or "bottom line," to be realized. Then you are freed during shooting from the gremlin whispering in your ear, "Do you really have a film here?" With thorough and focused preparation, the basic film is sure, barring accidents.

From this kind of solid base you will be able to see further and supplement or modify your original vision. Even with the pressures of shooting, you can easily keep the hypothesis in mind as the measure of everything you film. Nearly always, a working hypothesis is extended and enriched during the shooting into something far beyond the original minimum for an interesting film.

One gruesome fact about research must be stated emphatically: If you don't decide what your film's hypothesis is to be, you will *not* find it during shooting. The demands of shooting preclude contemplation, so we might say that *a documentary only becomes a true inquiry when it starts from having something to say.* If instead you go out with a crew expecting to find that "something to say," all your energies will be burnt up keeping the crew busy and trying to deceive them that you know what you're doing. Back in the editing room, you'll find that the material has no focus and no vision.

Research is useless unless you turn your findings into specific, practical, concrete resolutions.

THE NEED FOR DEVELOPMENT, CONFLICT, AND CONFRONTATION

One ingredient essential to any story is growth or change in the main character or situation. Here many documentaries fail by dwelling on what is essentially a static situation. You can avoid this, if logistics permit, by filming over a period of time so that change is inbuilt. A film that capitalizes magnificently on the passage of time is Michael Apted's *28 Up* (1986), which revisits a group of children at 7-year intervals from the ages of 7 through 28. Because so many eerily fulfill their earliest ideas about education, career, and marriage, the film is haunting and raises important questions about how, and even whether, people make the choices that so deeply affect personal destiny. By now there is a *35 Up,* but I prefer the scope of its predecessor.

Unfortunately most documentaries have to be shot in a restricted period, and many leave the viewer disgruntled because nothing of importance changed. The best way to ensure development in your film is to search out where change is happening. This may be *physical movement* (e.g., new house, new job, journey) or *movement in time* (change of season for farmer, growth in child, retrospective of painter's work), or it may be *psychological development* (ex-prisoner adjusts to freedom, teenager gets first paying job, adult illiterate learns to read).

Another way to give your film a feeling of development is to make sure that it deals with some kind of conflict and that this conflict is followed through sufficient stages to achieve a sense of movement. This conflict might be within one character (a mother takes her child for his first day at school), between two characters (two social scientists have conflicting theories of criminality), between a character and the environment (an African farmer survives a drought from day to day), or thousands of other combinations.

Showing change comes from a sensitivity to people and their issues. When you face the vital questions—*What is this person trying to get or do? What does he want?*—it means that you are defining that person in terms of movement and will. Volition cannot exist without opposition, so you arrive naturally at the next question: *What or who is keeping this person from getting what he wants?*

The elements of struggle, contest, and will are at the heart of drama in every medium, including documentary. A documentary without a struggle for movement is just a catalogue of episodes. You and I have yawned through a hundred such films.

During the shoot of your marching band film you might anticipate several kinds of development. One might be the development of a young contender from among those who audition to enter the band. Another might happen during a big competitive event that puts everyone under stress. Yet another might be after graduation, when a senior goes from being a big man at school to a nobody searching for a job. With these processes covered, you have metaphorically encompassed a cycle of birth, life, and death in the band's ongoing existence.

You may define a conflict in your head, but it remains an invisible abstraction unless you find how to show it in action on screen. Be sure, therefore, that you build the conflict's sides stage by stage, and be sure to arrange, if necessary, a *confrontation* between the opposing elements in your movie. If an instrumentalist has to pass a stringent test, be sure to shoot its key elements. If a young man must find a job, be sure to shoot him interviewing for one. It is always better to show struggle than to talk about it.

You may have to ensure that "the confrontation" happens; you might, for instance, arrange for two players with opposing views of the band to slug it out verbally in front of the camera. If the key issue in a film about a homeless people's shelter is whether strict rules are necessary, be sure to film clashes between inmates and those in charge. It may be necessary to ask either staff or inmates to initiate a typical episode if none happens spontaneously. Here you must employ artifice if you are to do justice to the spirit of your subject. This is the catalyst function that *cinéma vérité* directors employ and direct cinema exponents abhor.

THE DRAMATIC CURVE

What documentary materials will be like is never easy to forecast. Applying the traditional dramatic curve (Figure 9-1) to one's ideas, however, is useful during research and is outstandingly useful as an analytic tool during editing, which is really a second chance to direct.

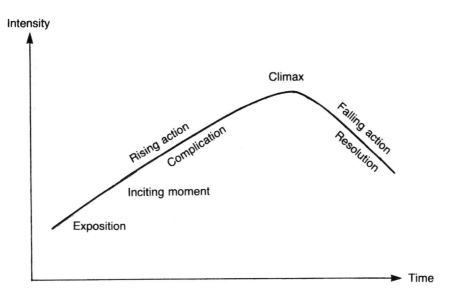

FIGURE 9-1

Dramatic curve. Variations of this apply to most narrative art, including documentary films. The same principle is also useful in analyzing a single scene.

The dramatic curve concept is derived from Greek drama and represents the way that most stories state their problem, and develop tension through scenes that show increasing complication and intensity, until the central conflict arrives at an apex or "crisis," after which there is change and resolution—though not, let me say quickly, necessarily a peaceful one.

In Broomfield's and Churchill's *Soldier Girls* (1981), the crisis is probably the point at which Private Johnson, after a series of increasingly stressful conflicts with authority, leaves the army dishonorably but in a spirit of relieved gaiety. The film's resolution after this major character leaves the stage is to examine more closely what training soldiers need to survive battle conditions.

In the Maysles brothers' *Salesman* (1969), most people pick as the apex the moment when Paul Brennan, the salesman who has been falling steadily behind the pack like a wounded animal, sabotages a colleague's sale. In the film's coda, his partners distance themselves as if deserting a dying man. The film leaves Paul staring offscreen into a void.

If one understands the idea of the apex or crisis, the rest of the dramatic convention arranges itself naturally in stages before and after the peak of the curve:

1. The *introduction or exposition* lays out some of the characters and their situation, and gives other necessary factual information about time, place, period, and so on. Since modern drama often lacks a captive audience, it cannot afford to delay major committing action, so the main conflict, or struggle between opposing forces, will probably be delineated early in what I think of as the documentarian's

"contract." Signaling the scope and focus of the film to come, it aims to secure the audience's interest for the duration.

2. The *inciting moment* is whatever sets in motion the opposition of interests. In the army, basic training is a battle between the homogenizing goals of the army and the individualism of the recruit. The army aims to break down individual identity and to replace it with a psyche trained to unthinkingly obey. In *Soldier Girls* the inciting moment is when Sergeant Abing sees Private Johnson smirking after he has rebuked her. This signals the onset of a long and unequal struggle between them. Because a white male is imposing his will on a black female, the situation has disquieting reverberations of slavery times.

3. *Rising action* or *complication* usually shows the basic conflicts being played out as variations having surprise, suspense, and escalating intensity. In *Soldier Girls,* the army's expression of will and the misfits' expression of cowed resistance are repeatedly raised a notch to more serious and offensive levels. Seeing protagonists and antagonists engaged in such a revealing struggle, we come to understand the motivations, goals, and background of each, and during this period we choose sides and, in the face of ambiguity, vacillate.

4. The *climax* or apex of the curve is where the final *confrontation* leads to irreversible change.

5. The *resolution* or *falling action* is what the piece establishes as the consequence. This includes not only what happens to the characters but also what interpretation for the whole is suggested by the last scene or scenes. In documentary, as in other story forms, one can change the after-effect of an entire film depending on how the audience last sees the characters.

Few documentaries fall neatly into this shape, but a number of memorable ones do. The formula is used with awful fervor in Hollywood. Many scriptwriting manuals go further and add alarmingly rigid prescriptions for "plot points" on particular pages. Documentary, thank goodness, is too wayward a form to attract this kind of control fever, but the need for documentary to be dramatically satisfying remains inescapable. It is also true for essay, montage, or other forms of documentary, not just the narrative variety. Indeed, this escalation of pressure, crisis, then lowering to resolution is also found in songs, symphonies, dance, mime, and traditional tales, because it is as basic to human life as breathing or sex.

What I find fascinating is that a successful scene is a drama in microcosm, following the same curve of pressures that build to a climax, then release into a new situation. During the shoot, the documentary director often sees a scene develop, spin its wheels, and refuse to go anywhere. Then, perhaps with some side coaching, the characters lock onto an issue and struggle over it until one gives in. This fulcrum point of change, called in the theater a *beat,* is the basic unit of any scene containing dramatic interchange. Even montages lacking foreground characters, such as those in Lorentz's *The River* (1937), follow the same expressive curve.

The dramatic unit's life cycle (initiating an issue, building its pressures, confrontation, change of consciousness in one character) may be repeated several times in a single scene. When you recognize it in life, or when shooting life that is really happening, you know when to shoot and what portions of a documentary scene to use. The existence of this progression contributes *dramatic tension.* Never be afraid to make your audience wait and guess. As Wilkie Collins, the father of the mystery novel, said, "Make them laugh, make them cry, but make them wait." The need for this kind of tension applies fully to the documentary.

It matters little whether you know dramatic terminology or whether by instinct you can spot the cycle as it happens. Having the capacity to recognize this dramatic breathing action as it takes place is really the preeminent directorial skill, for fiction or documentary.

FACTS AND NARRATION

Before shooting, you can often see the need for some expository narration to get your film rolling and to link successive blocks of material. Nobody wants to use a narrator if it can be avoided, so keep an ongoing list of facts vital to an audience's understanding of the material. These will include names, places, ages, dates, times, the sequence of main events, relationships, and so on. This information must emerge one way or another if the film is to make sense to a first-time audience. An important part of your directorial responsibility is to make sure this material is drawn out of the participants, and *in more than one version*. Cover all your bases, and you can probably avoid writing and recording narration. Images and characters may supply all vital information as it is needed.

RESEARCH PARTNERSHIP

An ideal way to research is in partnership with a second person, perhaps a key member of the crew. Film's strength lies in its collaborative nature, and you will appreciate how much richer your perceptions and ideas can become when you exchange them with a like-minded partner. Another benefit is having moral support when penetrating new places and confronting prejudicial attitudes. Together both partners can be relaxed, and the reassuring naturalness between you carries over into your participants' attitude to the camera.

A further benefit of partnership is being able to compare intuitions, particularly those of foreboding. One often detects what is significant only on the edge of one's consciousness, and is inclined to overlook an important early warning. If this seems negative, there is a positive: The edge of your consciousness may pick up clues and hints that lead to greater things. And in this area too, a partner can provide the vital endorsement.

SETTING UP THE SHOOT: LOGISTICS AND THE SCHEDULE

Estimating how long each scene will take to shoot only comes with experience. In general, careful work takes much longer than you imagine possible. You should probably only schedule two or at most three sequences in a day's work unless you are using available light and have good reason to anticipate that what you want is straightforward. Even a simple interview, lasting 20 minutes on tape, may take an 3 hours overall to accomplish. You should also allow plenty of time for transport between locations, because tearing down equipment in the old location and setting it up anew is time consuming. A new unit is usually a lot slower than the same unit 10 days later.

A 30-minute documentary can take between 3 and 8 working days to shoot, depending on (a) amount of travel, (b) amount of large lighting setups, and (c) the complexity and the amount of randomness inherent in the subject matter. For instance, if you are shooting in a school yard and want to film a scuffle between boys during break, you may have to hang around in a state of exhausting readiness for days. On the other hand, if you simply want to film the postman delivering a particular letter, you can organize things so it all gets done in 10 minutes.

Avoid the tendency to schedule optimistically by making best-case and worst-case estimates, and allotting something in between.

One luxury peculiar to the independent filmmaker (and there are few) is associated with the nature photographer—the freedom to shoot over a long period. Most documentaries have trouble showing any real development because the economics of filmmaking make it prohibitive to reassemble a crew at, say, 6-month intervals for a period of 2 years. Yet this kind of long observation is most likely to capture real changes in people's lives. Independents tend to work as a group and on more than one project at a time, so they do not have to reassemble the way a commercial crew does.

Whether you are shooting in a drawn-out or compact way, make up a model schedule in advance and show it to all concerned for comment. Well in advance, *make sure everyone has a copy of a typed schedule.* Time spent planning and time spent informing people of the plans is time, money, and morale saved later. Poorly informed people tend to wait passively for instructions and to take few initiatives.

In the schedule include a phone contact number for each location. Whenever several people are meant to converge in an arranged place at an arranged time, count on someone getting lost or having car trouble. It is maddening to be incapacitated for lack of information, and unless everyone has a mobile phone, this is a constant threat on location. A low-tech solution is to have a *prearranged contact number* (your sister, who works all day in an office, say, or a message service) so that any number of people in transit can make contact through a reliable third party.

A schedule should also list special equipment or special personnel required in particular locations and give clear navigational instructions to help get everything there. Photocopies of a map marked up with locations and phone numbers can save hours of precious time.

THE PERSONAL RELEASE FORM

The personal release form is a document in which the signatory releases to you the right to make public use of the material you have shot. You will not normally have to contend with legal problems unless you allow people to nurture the (not unknown) fantasy that you are going to make a lot of money selling their footage. No one ever got rich making documentaries, and you should lose no time correcting contrary notions.

Personal Release Form

For the $_____ consideration received, I give _____
Productions, its successors and assigns, my unrestricted permission to distrib-
ute and sell all still photographs, motion-picture film, video recordings and
sound recordings taken of me for the screen production tentatively titled ___.

Signed _____
Name (please print) _____
Address _____
_____

Date _____

Signature of parent or guardian _____
Witnessed by _____
Date _____

FIGURE 9-2 ————————————————————————

Typical personal release form.

Have personal release forms (Figure 9-2) ready for participants to sign immediately after their filming is complete. No signature is valid without the $1 mini-
mum legal payment, which you solemnly hand over as symbolic payment. The
signed release is a form of consent that gives you copyright over the image and
words of the participant. Since it is clearly impractical to get releases from, say, all
the people in a street shot, one usually gets signed releases from speaking participants. Naturally, judgment must be used here: The release is to prevent those you
have filmed from going back on a purely verbal agreement or deciding at the elev-
enth hour that they do not want to appear in your film. So forestall any problems
over getting permission to use the footage later by always obtaining the signed release. Minors cannot sign legal forms themselves and will need the clearance of a
parent or guardian.

PERMISSION TO FILM AT LOCATION FACILITIES

Conditions vary from country to country, but in general personal releases are
signed immediately *after* the performance has been given, while location permission must be secured in writing *before* you start shooting. Strictly speaking, you
should obtain permission to shoot inside private buildings and in public transportation, parks, stadiums, and so on. Anything unrestrictedly open to public view
(such as the street, markets, public meetings) may be filmed without asking anyone's permission. All events on private property must be cleared by the owner unless you care to risk being taken to court for invasion of privacy. This happens if

you or your company seem worth suing, or if someone wants a pretext for a court injunction to block a showing of your film. This is more a hazard of investigative journalism.

Most cities have restrictions on filming in the street. In practice this means you are supposed to get police permission and perhaps pay for a cop to wave away troublesome bystanders ("rubbernecks") or to control traffic. Technically if you abandon a handheld technique and put up the tripod, you have crossed over from news gathering to the big time, but there is seldom anyone around who cares as long as you don't tie up traffic. Some big cities such as Chicago are film friendly, but for others, such as Paris and New York, the honeymoon is long gone. Conditions are increasingly restrictive and usually you must work through a special division of the mayor's office to get permission to film at any given location. Tied in with this is a requirement to carry liability insurance to cover the many occasions when filming implies some risk to the public. In our litigious times, a creative lawyer can make a piece of chalk left on a sidewalk into a negligent threat to life and limb, so be careful—it's a jungle out there . . .

By tradition, documentary makers often shoot first and ask questions afterward, knowing that the combination of ideals and poverty will probably lead to an irritable dismissal if someone official starts asking questions. This solution can be risky in nondemocratic countries where cameras are often and correctly regarded as engines of subversion.

C H A P T E R   1 0

DEVELOPING A CREW

USING PEOPLE WITH EXPERIENCE

The title of this chapter speaks of "developing" rather than "choosing" a crew be-cause even when experienced crew members are available, you should still do some experimental shooting together. This verifies not only that equipment is functioning, but that you understand each other. It is quite usual to discover that one camera operator's close-up is another's medium shot. A brief and unambiguous language of communication will become especially important when you are "grab" shooting, that is, making camera-position changes in response to a sponta-neously changing situation. With no possibility for rehearsal or repeats, a wide margin exists for fatal misunderstandings.

Successful framing, composition, speed of camera movements, and micro-phone positioning all come about through mutual awareness and adaptation. This happens when people understand each other's values, signals, and terminology. While shooting exercise footage, expect to discover a wide variance of taste and skill levels, as well as variations in responses, technical vocabulary, and interpreta-tion of standard jargon.

DEVELOPING YOUR OWN CREW

Let us suppose that you live remote from centers of filmmaking, must start from scratch finding and training your crew, and need to work up your own standards. We will assume that you have access to a camcorder, microphone, and a video monitor. How many and what kinds of people will you need? What are their re-sponsibilities?

All the crew need to appreciate—or better yet share—your values. So before working together on anything so personal as a documentary, inquire into not only each person's technical expertise and experience, but also their feelings and ideas concerning documentary, books, plays, music, hobbies, and interests. Technical acumen is important, but a person's maturity and values are more so. Knowledge deficiencies can be remedied, but you won't change someone who dislikes your choice of subject or who disapproves of your approach.

CREW MEMBERS' TEMPERAMENTS ARE IMPORTANT!

A documentary crew is very small, two to six persons. A good crew is immensely supportive, not only of the project, but also of the individuals in front of the camera, who are usually being filmed for the first time. The crew's interest and implied approval becomes a vital supplement to that of the director. Conversely, anyone's detachment or disapproval will be felt personally, not only by you the director but also by participants, who are highly aware owing to the unfamiliar work you are asking them to do.

I was usually assigned wonderful crews when I worked for the BBC but occasionally got an individual with problems. Typically it was lapses in mental focus, but more than once I got someone actively subversive. Being under pressure and far from home unbalances some people or exacerbates insecurities and jealousies. This is hard to foresee, and an appalling liability in documentary, which hinges on good relationships.

If a potential crew member has done film or other team work, speak to colleagues. Filming is so intense that work partners quickly learn each other's temperamental strengths and weaknesses.

In each crew member look for

- realism
- reliability
- the ability to sustain effort and concentration for long periods
- a deep interest in the processes and purposes of making documentaries
- someone who knows and values films you particularly respect

In all film crew positions, beware of those who

- have only one working speed (it's usually medium slow, and when faced with a crisis these people usually slow up in confusion or go to pieces)
- forget or modify verbal commitments
- fail to deliver on promises
- habitually overestimate their own abilities
- let their attention expand detrimentally beyond their own field of responsibility
- see you only as a stepping stone toward something more desirable

CLEARLY DEFINE THE AREAS OF RESPONSIBILITY

No crew functions well without clear definition of roles and responsibilities. This should include plans to cope with emergencies such as a predictable absence. For example, the director of photography (DP) normally takes over when the director is absent or occupied. Crew should, in any case, be discouraged from taking any and every query to the director when the DP can handle the answers. A director should not have to decide whether someone should put another coin in a parking meter.

When first working together, maintain a formal working structure in which everyone takes care of their own responsibilities and refrains from comment or action in areas of responsibility of other crew members. As you come to know and trust each other, formality can be relaxed. If, on the other hand, you start out informal and then need a tight ship, the change will be mightily resented.

A small film crew—director, camera operator, sound recordist, grip, and production manager—also may consist of prophet, visionary, scribe, strongman, and fixer. Someone will always assume the role of jester or clown because every crew develops its own special dynamic and in-jokes. The pleasure that comes with working together well is the best intoxicant you can imagine and is strongest under pressure. And there is no hangover the morning after.

Careful selection of partners makes anything possible, because a team of determined friends is unstoppable.

CREW ROLES AND RESPONSIBILITIES

Here is an outline of each crew member's responsibilities and the strengths and weaknesses you might look for. Of course, in real life many of the best practitioners are the exceptions, so this list is fallible. To complete it I have also included a summary of the director's role.

DIRECTOR

The director is responsible for nothing less than the quality and meaning of the final film. He or she must conduct or supervise research, decide on content, assemble a crew, schedule shooting, lead the crew, and direct participants during shooting, and then supervise the editing and finalization of the project. Because profits are seldom in view, the documentary frequently has no producer, so the director must also assemble funding before shooting and hustle distribution afterwards.

A good director has a lively fascination with the cause and effect behind the way real people live; a mind that searches tirelessly for links and explanations, is social, and loves delving into other people's stories. Outwardly informal and easygoing, he or she is methodical and organized but quite able to throw away prior work when early assumptions become obsolete. A good director has endless patience in stalking the truth, and in doing it justice in cinematic terms; is articulate and succinct; knows his or her own mind without being dictatorial; can speak on terms of respectful equality with all film craftspeople; and is able to understand their problems and co-opt their efforts into realizing his or her authorial intentions.

This sounds impossibly idealistic, so here are some of the negative traits that make directors all too human. Many are obstinate, private, awkward beings who do not explain themselves well, who change their minds, and who are disorganized and visceral. Most can be intimidated by bellicose technicians, have difficulty in giving appropriate attention to both the crew and the participants, and tend to desert one for the other. During shooting, sensory overload catapults many into a Woody Allen condition of acute doubt and anxiety, in which all choice becomes a painful effort. Some cannot bear to deflect from their original intentions and appear to crew members like the captain who insists on sinking at the wheel of the ship.

Directing frequently changes perfectly normal people into manic-depressives who suffer extremes of hope and despair in pursuit of the Holy Grail. If that is not enough of a puzzle to crew members, the director's mental state often generates superhuman energy that tests crew members' patience to the limit.

The truth is that directing an improvisation intended to crystallize life itself is a heady business. It often means living existentially; that is, fully and completely in the present and as if each moment may be your last. The exigencies of directing often bring on this state, whether you like it or not, and particularly so after an initial success. Thereafter you confront failure and artistic/professional death every step of the way. But like mountaineers who feel most alive when dangling over a precipice, the director feels completely alive during the dread and exhilaration of the cinematic chase. Like stage fright for actors, this is a devil that never really goes away.

But aren't fear and excitement the portents to everything worthwhile?

CAMERA OPERATOR

In the minimal crew, the camera operator is responsible for ordering the camera equipment, for testing and adjusting where necessary, and for being thoroughly conversant with its working principles. (Never begin important work without first running tests to forestall Murphy's Law: "Anything that can go wrong will go wrong.") The camera operator is also responsible for lighting arrangements, for scouting locations to confirm electricity supplies, and for supervising the setting up of the lighting instruments.

The camera operator is responsible for the handling of the camera, which means taking an active role in deciding camera positioning (in collaboration with the director), and controlling all camera movements, such as panning, tilting, zooming in/out, and dollying.

A good operator is highly image conscious, and preferably has training in photography and fine art. You hope for a good sense of composition and design, and an eye for the sociologically telling details that show in people's surroundings. A good operator picks up the behavioral nuances that reveal so much about character. In "grab-shooting" only the operator can really decide what to shoot moment to moment. While the director sees *content* happening in front of (sometimes behind) the camera, only the operator sees the action in its framed, cinematic form. The director may redirect the camera to a different area, but must be able to place almost total reliance in the operator's discrimination.

For this reason a camera operator must be decisive and dexterous. Depending on the weight of the equipment, he may also need to be robust. Keeping a 20-pound camera on your shoulder for an 8-hour day or loading equipment boxes in and out of vehicles are not for the delicate or fastidious. The job is dirty, grueling, and at times intoxicatingly wonderful. The best camera people seem to be low-key individuals who don't ruffle easily in crises, practical and inventive people who like improvising solutions to intransigent logistical, lighting, or electrical problems. Look for the perfectionist who will cheerfully try for the best and simplest solution when time runs short.

Many experienced camera personnel have an alarming tendency to isolate themselves in the mechanics of their craft at the expense of the director's deeper quest for themes and meanings. One such replied to a question of mine with "I'm just here to make pretty pictures." He might have added, "and not get involved."

Having a crew of frustrated directors can be a problem, but worse is to have one of isolated operatives. The best crew members comprehend both the details and the totality of a project, and can see how to make the best contribution at any given moment. This is why a narrow "tech" education is never good enough.

GAFFER

The gaffer is an expert in rigging and maintaining lighting equipment, and knows how to split loads so lighting runs off light-duty household supplies without starting fires or plunging the whole street into darkness. Good gaffers carry a bewildering assortment of clamps, gadgets, and small tools. Resourceful by nature, they sometimes emerge as mainstays of the unit when others get discouraged. During a night shooting sequence in England, I once saw a boy stumble behind the lights and hurt his knee. Because he had been told he must be silent while we were shooting, he doubled over and clutched his knee in mute agony. The kindly electrician (as the gaffer is called in Britain) swooped silently out of the gloom and cradled him in his arms until the shot was finished.

Because the gaffer is usually the only person whose attention is free when the camera is running, he may be the only person with a whole and unobstructed view. Directors in doubt, therefore, sometimes discreetly ask how the gaffer felt about a certain piece of action.

Gaffers are usually chosen by the person responsible for lighting (the cinematographer or videographer), and the two will often work together regularly. An experienced gaffer gets to know a cinematographer's lighting style and preferences, and can even arrive ahead of a unit to prelight. Teams of long association even dispense with much spoken language.

SOUND RECORDIST

Among students, sound recording is considered easy and unglamorous, and is often left to anyone who says they can do it. But badly recorded sound disconnects the audience even more fatally than does a poor story. Most student films sound like studies of characters talking through mashed potatoes in a labyrinth of echoey bathrooms. Capturing clear, clean, and consistent sound is deceptively demanding and lacks the glamour to induce most people to try.

The recordist, who is responsible for checking equipment in advance and solving sound malfunctions as they arise, needs patience, a good ear, and the maturity to be low man on the totem pole. Lighting and camera position are determined first, so the sound recordist must hide mikes, cause no shadows, and still achieve first-rate sound quality. Shoots become a series of aggravating compromises that caring sound people tend to take personally. Many end up bitter that "good standards" are routinely trampled. But it's always the disconnected craftsperson rather than the whole filmmaker who gags on compromise.

Because the sound recordist should listen not to words but to *sound quality,* you need someone who can truly hear the buzz, rumble, or edginess that the novice will overlook. The art of recording has very little to do with recorders and everything to do with the selection and placement of mikes, and *being able to hear the difference.* No independent assessment is possible apart from the discerning ear. Only musical interests and, better still, musical training seem to instill this critical faculty.

The sound recordist, often kept inactive for long periods and then suddenly expected to "fix up the mike" in short order, needs to habitually make contingency plans. The least satisfactory is the person who only begins to think when setup time arrives and who then causes groans by asking for a lighting change.

When documentary work is mobile, the recordist must keep the mike on the edge of the camera's field of view and as close to the sound source as possible, without casting shadows or letting the mike creep into frame. With a camera handheld and on the move, this takes skill, awareness, and quietly agile footwork.

GRIP

A grip is responsible for fetching and carrying, and also has the highly skilled and coordinated job of moving the camera support to precisely worked-out positions when the camera takes mobile shots. Grips should therefore be strong, practical, organized, and willing. On the minimal crew, they will help to rig lighting or sound equipment. A skilled grip knows something about everyone's job and in an emergency can do limited duty for another crew member.

PRODUCTION MANAGER (PM)

The PM is probably a luxury on a minimal crew, but there are many whose business background equips them to do this important job surpassingly well. The PM takes care of all the arrangements for the shoot. These might include finding overnight accommodations, booking rented equipment at the best prices, securing location or other permissions, making up a shooting schedule (with the director), making travel arrangements, and locating food near the shoot. The PM monitors cash flow, has contingency plans when bad weather stymies exterior shooting, and chases progress. All this lightens the load on the director, for whom these things are a counterproductive burden.

It is hardly necessary to say that the good PM is organized, a compulsive list keeper, socially adept and businesslike, and able to scan and correlate a number of activities. She must be able to juggle priorities; make decisions involving time, effort, and money; and be unintimidated by officialdom.

EQUIPMENT SELECTION: DRAWING UP A WANT LIST

In this book, and at this time of technological revolution, I can give no equipment recommendations. If you own or are borrowing equipment, you will in any case have to work within its capacities. I can, however, make broad recommendations:

- Sit down as a group and brainstorm over what you think you need. Make lists and include basic tools. Invariably something will need corrective surgery on the job.
- Plan to shoot as simply as possible, aiming for straightforward solutions rather than elaborate ones.
- Any decisions about the style of the movie—how it looks, how it is shot, how it conveys its content to the audience—are best developed organically from the nature of the subject. The best solutions are usually elegantly simple.
- Insecure technicians sometimes try to forestall problems by insisting on a need for the "proper" equipment, which usually means the best and most expensive. This can be a costly gesture to neurosis because initially you face basic conceptual and control difficulties, and can seldom profit from the sophistications of advanced equipment.
- Learn all you can about the technical functions in the shoot so you and your PM can decide what outlay is truly justified. Some extra items will be lifesavers, but others cost money and are never used.
- Read all equipment manuals carefully; there is always vital and overlooked information there. At the end of this book, there is a bibliography of sources for detailed information on lighting, sound recording, and so on.

No film was ever made without equipment problems, so do not be discouraged at design defects. Remember it is human ingenuity more than equipment that makes good films. Film history, so rich in creative advances, was after all made with hand-cranked cameras made of wood and brass.

PREPRODUCTION CHECKLIST

During Preproduction, Remember
- Logistical and mental preparation is the key to coherent moviemaking.
- Find a subject in which you can make a personal, emotional, long-term investment.
- A documentary shares a way of seeing and evokes feelings. It is propaganda and not a documentary unless you invite the audience to weigh evidence and judge human values.
- Avoid situations where you are expected to give up editorial control.
- Make requests sound natural and rightful, and you will often get the moon.

- Know before shooting what you want to say through the film. No plans lead to no film; the pressures of shooting prevent radical inquiry.
- Generalization is the enemy of art. Research knowledge only communicates when focused into specific plans for shots, sequences, or questions.
- You need to find ways to bring conflicting values into on-screen confrontation with each other.
- Good documentary, like any good drama, shows people in some kind of struggle and undergoing some kind of change and development.
- Development is often missing in documentaries, making them static and pointless.
- Behavior, action, and interaction best show how people live.
- Most people blossom when given lights, camera, and a sympathetic hearing.
- Treat the lives you enter with care.
- Expect to face constant moral dilemmas. The greater good will often be in conflict with a sense of obligation you feel to an individual.
- Documentaries are only as good as the relationships that permit them to be made (this applies to the crew as well as participants).
- Be ready throughout to supplement or modify your vision.
- Documentary making is long and slow; be ready for enthusiasm to dim and to have to work on during its absence.

In Preproduction, Do Not

- Bite off more than you can chew.
- Set out to make a film that merely confirms what anyone would expect of the subject.
- Stretch your resources too thin or your subject too wide.
- Be put off by participants' initial reservations and hesitancy. Keep explaining, and see what happens.
- Force people into situations or attitudes that are not their own.
- Tell anyone you are filming anything until it is 100 percent sure.
- Promise to show footage if by so doing you lose editorial freedom.
- Allow yourself to act as if you are begging favors, especially with officials.

When Searching for a Subject

- Make a habit of maintaining several project ideas on the back burner.
- Read avidly about what is going on, and keep a subject notebook and clipping file.
- Reject the obvious subject and the obvious treatment. You can do better.
- Only take on something that matches your capabilities and budget.
- Make a conscious effort to discover and reveal the unexpected.
- Define what you want to avoid as well as what you want to show.

- Think small, think local, think short. Do something contained and in depth.

When Researching a Particular Subject
- Expect filmmaker's funk, that is, stage fright.
- Take a research partner with you, and exchange impressions afterward.
- Be tentative and general when you explain your project.
- Be friendly and respectful, and signify that you are there to learn.
- Make a prioritized shopping list of possible participants.
- Make a shopping list of sequences, and define what each might contribute.
- Keep your options open and make no impulsive commitments.

When You Have Found a Subject, Ask Yourself
- Do I *really* want to make a film about this subject?
- In what other subjects am I already knowledgeable and opinionated?
- Do I feel a strong and emotional connection to this subject, more so than any other practicable one?
- Am I equipped to do justice to this subject?
- Do I have a drive to learn more about this subject?
- What is this subject's *real* significance to me?
- What is unusual and interesting about it?
- Where is its specialness really visible?
- How narrowly and deeply can I focus my film's attention?
- What can I *show?*
- What recent films am I competing with?
- What can I reveal that will be novel to most of the audience?
- What are my prejudices that I must be careful to examine?
- What are the facts an audience must know in order to follow my film?
- Who is in possession of those facts? How can I get more than one version?
- What change and development can my film expect to show?

When Talking with Possible Participants
- Assume the right to be uncommonly curious and questioning.
- When they ask about your ideas, turn the conversation so that you learn about theirs.
- Go at the participant's speed, or you will damage trust and spontaneity.
- Use a "student of life" attitude that invites the participant into an instructional role.
- Use the "devil's advocate" role to tread in risky areas without implicating yourself.
- Watch, listen, and correlate what you take in with what you already know.

- Use networking: Ask to be passed on to the next person. It always helps to have been personally referred.
- Evoke each person's view of the others as a cross-check.
- Do some informal, nonaggressive audio interviews to see if being "on record" hinders participants' spontaneity.

When Deciding What and How to Shoot

- Define what each participant's function is in life.
- Define what each might represent or contribute as a character in your film.
- Give each character and situation a metaphorical role.
- Define what each sequence should contribute to the whole.
- Define what microcosm your subject is and what macrocosm it represents.
- Define what conflicts are at the heart of your drama and how to show them in confrontation on the screen.

When Defining the Working Hypothesis

- What is the minimum your film absolutely must be able to say?
- What are the conflicts you want to show?
- What are the contradictions in the people and their situations?
- What is each person's "unfinished business"?

When Scheduling

- Schedule loosely, especially to begin with. Other people need food and rest!
- Place the least demanding work first.
- Discuss scheduling in advance with those affected.
- List special equipment or special requirements on the schedule.
- Take travel time into account.
- Give a typed schedule to crew and participants ahead of time.
- Give clear navigational directions, plus photocopies of maps to drivers.
- Put phone contact numbers in schedule in case anyone gets lost or delayed.
- Obtain location clearances well in advance.
- Have personal release forms and fees ready for shoots.

P A R T 5

PRODUCTION

CHAPTER 11
Equipment Selection   155

Camera Body   155
Lens   155
Exposure Control   156
Color Balance, Picture Gain, and Automatic
     Controls   156
Power Supplies   157
Camera Support Systems   157
Sound Equipment   158
Camcorders and Sound   158
Monitors   159
Lighting Instruments   160
Power Calculation   162

CHAPTER 12
About Lighting   164

When You Need It   164
Contrast and Color-Temperature Problems   165
Working with Light Sources of Different
     Color Temperatures   165
Adding to a Base and Using a Key Light   166
Defining Shadows: Hard and Soft Light   166
Key Light Direction and Backlighting   167
Tests: How Much Is Enough Light?   167
Avoiding the Overbright Background   168
Reactions to Lighting   168

CHAPTER 13
Avoiding Problems   169

Logs and Budget Control   169
Where Videotape Differs   169
Shooting Ratio   170

Equipment Breakdowns   170
Human Breakdowns   171
Keep Alternatives Up Your Sleeve   172

CHAPTER 14
Interviewing   173

Why Interviewing Matters   173
Who Interviews   174
Types of Situations   175
Preparation and Basic Skills   176
Setting People at Ease   176
Framing Questions   177
Guidelines for Effective Interviewing   178
Preparations to Edit Out the Interviewer's
     Voice   179
The In-Depth Interview   180
Brevity   180
Pushing Boundaries   181
The Right Order for Questions   181
Believing in your Authority   182
Interviewer and Camera Placement   182
Audience Participation   184
Shooting for Ellipsis   184
Shoot Alternatives   185
Briefing the Camera Operator   186
Concluding the Interview   187

CHAPTER 15
Directing Participants   188

In Search of Naturalness   188
The Mind-Body Connection   189
Self-Image and Self-Consciousness   190
Why Your Motives for Filming Matter   191

Obstacles: Habits of Being   192
Compromises for the Camera   192
Maintaining Screen Direction   193
Motivation for Camera Positioning and
    Camera Movement   196
Chance . . . ?   196
Scene Breakdown and Crib Notes   197
Handheld or Tripod-Mounted Camera?   199
Special Photography   200
Using Social Times and Breaks   200
Wrapping   200
Limits to the Form   201

CHAPTER 16
Directing the Crew   **202**

Scheduling and Communication   202
Maintaining Communication   203
Monitoring and Instructing   203
Negative Attitudes in the Profession   204
Working Atmosphere   205
The Problem of Having Authority   206

CHAPTER 17
Authorship   **207**

Scripting   207
Defining and Fulfilling Your Intentions   208
Measuring Progress   209
Digging Below the Surface   209
Cover Important Aspects More than One
    Way   210
Concessions and Risk   211

CHAPTER 18
Production Projects   **212**

Direct or Observational Cinema (Tripod)   213
    Project 18-1: Dramatizing a Location   213
    Project 18-2 Three-Person Conversation
        (Interior)   215
Direct or Observational Cinema (Handheld)   216
    Project 18-3: Covering a Process for
        Ellipsis Editing   216
    Project 18-4: Covering a Conversation
        (Exterior)   216
    Project 18-5: Mobile Coverage of
        Complex Action   218
Cinéma Vérité or Catalyst Cinema (Tripod)   219
    Project 18-6: Interview in Depth   219
    Project 18-7: Two-Person Conversation
        with Conflict   221
Cinéma Vérité or Catalyst Cinema
    (Handheld)   223
    Project 18-8: Unbroken Five-Minute Story   223
    Project 18-9: A One-Shot, Catalyzed
        Event   224
    Project 18-10: Vox Populi Interviews and
        Metaphoric Counterpoint   224
Reflexive Cinema   227
    Project 18-11: Self-Portrait   227
    Project 18-12: Observing the Observer   228
    Project 18-13: Story, Question, and
        Suggestion   228
Compilation and Essay Cinema   230
    Project 18-14: Making History   230
    Project 18-15: National Anthem   231
    Project 18-16: Video Letter   232
Eclectic Cinema   233
    Project 18-17: The Final Project   233
Production Checklist   235

C H A P T E R 1 1

EQUIPMENT SELECTION

CAMERA BODY

Because you will often shoot handheld, the ideal camera has a viewfinder at the side and a body balanced to sit on the operator's shoulder (Figure 11-1). Film cameras are all like this but some video cameras, in particular the new generation of miniature digital ones, have the finder at the back of the camera, home movie camera style. These are uncongenial because you cannot steady the camera against your head and shoulder. Increasingly, camcorders incorporate image stabilization technology to compensate for unsteadiness during handheld shots.

LENS

Consider the lens specifications. The range of the zoom lens is expressed in millimeters from shortest to longest focal length; in 16mm photography for example, 15 to 60mm. If the lower number (or "wide-angle" end of the zoom lens) is lower

FIGURE 11-1

Typical camera layout. (Courtesy of Sony Electronics, Inc.)

than 15mm, you are in luck. Nine or 10mm is especially useful, because it gives your camera a wide angle of acceptance, which in turn allows you to cover a decent area in a small room. You are also, at this focal length, freed from making a lot of focus adjustments. But a wide-angle end greater than 15mm (say, 18 to 25mm) is going to present problems. You will be unable to shoot effectively in tight surroundings, will have problems achieving a steady handheld picture, and will find difficulty staying in focus in low-light situations. Test shoots will reveal what limitations you must work within to do acceptable work. Supplementary lenses are widely available to alter a zoom's entire range, but picture definition may suffer, particularly at the edges and in low-light situations.

Check to see if your camera has an interchangeable lens. Some will accept 35mm lenses or C-mount (standard 16mm) film lens. You can rent a 10mm lens quite reasonably; it is wide enough to provide a steady handheld image and to take in a reasonable-sized image in confined quarters, but not wide enough to introduce the fairground distortions inherent to wider lenses. It allows you to go anywhere at almost any time.

Some low-priced consumer camcorders have noisy tape transports, have only one zoom speed, and emit an enthusiastic whining noise every time you change image size. See if the zoom feature can be used manually and whether automatic focus can be disengaged so the camera doesn't hunt for focus every time the picture composition changes.

EXPOSURE CONTROL

Examine your camcorder's lens and controls to see if the *lens aperture* (or *f-stop*) can be manually controlled. Some have a manual exposure control, which is good, and a lock, which is even better because it means that the exposure will hold steady if a lady in a white dress walks across your frame during a street shot. Floating exposure happens because automatic exposure circuits react slavishly to brightness changes, with no regard for picture content. A manual control allows the user a degree of control vital to many kinds of lighting situations. Non-disengageable automated controls are to be avoided generally.

COLOR BALANCE, PICTURE GAIN, AND AUTOMATIC CONTROLS

Most camcorders now have a white balance control that allows electronic adjustment of color rendition so white is reproduced as white under different light sources. Daylight, tungsten-filament bulbs, fluorescent, and other light sources all have different *color temperatures*. A useful feature is a white balance memory, which retains the white balance setting when the camera is off or its battery is being changed. Some need rebalancing under these conditions, so check this too.

Manual *white balance* (done by framing up a piece of white paper under the relevant light source), is always preferable to the presets (daylight, tungsten light, and fluorescent light) that most camcorders offer because these are approximations only. The ultimate reference in all color work is that flesh tones should look natural. Auto white balance is valuable when you must track with a subject through different lighting zones in, for instance, an airport.

A useful feature found on some cameras is a picture gain control. It allows you to shoot an enhanced image in low-light situations but you pay with an increase in *picture noise* and graininess. A backlight control, if there is one, is supposed to compensate exposure for a subject whose major illumination is coming toward the camera and is thus backlit.

Other controls usually found only on semiprofessional or professional camcorders are black level control, and manual exposure, focusing, and sound level settings, all of which can be locked. Amateur equipment tends to be automated, and uncontrollable. Film equipment is invariably manual control with automation applied, if at all, to exposure and, in the case of sound recorders, to level control.

POWER SUPPLIES

Equipment intended for location shooting runs off batteries that can be recharged from 110 or 220 volt AC current, or even a car battery. The charger often doubles as a power converter so that you can run the whole outfit from an AC wall outlet. *Batteries* commonly do not run the equipment for very long, especially if they have been incorrectly charged after use. Be pessimistic about how many and what kind of batteries you need because manufacturers' literature tends toward optimism.

Rechargeable batteries are inclined to be slow chargers, with 6 to 10 hours being normal. Never allow rechargeable batteries to become completely exhausted, but work each nicad battery to the limit and then completely recharge, or you will shorten the battery's "memory." There are small, sealed lead-acid batteries that be charged and discharged as the car batteries they resemble, but being unvented they too must be trickle-charged.

A conclusive solution to the dying battery problem is to buy or rent a battery belt, which has a much larger capacity than a battery pack and may power a camcorder for a whole shooting day without the need to recharge.

CAMERA SUPPORT SYSTEMS

Here there is not much comfort for the underbudgeted filmmaker. The budget *tripod* and tilt head is a miserable piece of equipment indeed. For static shots it is adequate, but as soon as you try to pan or tilt, your wobbly movements will reveal why heavy tripods and hydraulically damped tilt heads are preferred. A wide-angle lens will minimize camera movement problems, and electronic or mechanical image stabilization in video camcorders helps smooth out handheld shooting.

For a *dolly,* an excellent solution is a wheelchair. For exteriors, shoot backwards out of the trunk of a car or station wagon. You can tie down a tripod inside a car and shoot out of a side window. For a forward shot, rope the camera securely to the hood. In all cases use a wide lens to minimize road vibration. For superlative tracking shots with sync sound (dialogue, for instance), use a light car with partially deflated tires as a dolly, and get several people to push it so engine noise doesn't drown your dialogue. A well-practiced, well-coordinated human being also makes an excellent camera support, especially with one of the low-cost Steadicam systems now available.

SOUND EQUIPMENT

Sound is the area of commonest neglect. Start by investing in a good pair of *head-phones* that enclose the whole ear and exclude outside noise. Shun camera-mounted mikes at all cost because they pick up camera motor sounds and handling noise transmitted through the camera body. Use the best mike you can afford in a rubber shock-absorbing mount on a short *fishpole* (a light, extendable aluminum boom). This allows the mike to be held forward of the camera but out of shot, either above, below, or to one side of the shot perimeter. One can impro-vise a fishpole using an extending aluminum paint-roller handle from a paint store. Be careful to buy one that will not rattle in use.

Good low-cost mikes of the *electret* family are small and perform well. You will need a foam plastic windscreen for outdoor work, where air currents will rat-tle the mike's diaphragm. An improvised solution that works perfectly well is to wind many layers of cheesecloth around the mike, and then hide this abomination under a black tube sock.

Though *omnidirectional mikes* give the most pleasing voice reproduction, they pick up unwanted sound being reflected by surrounding surfaces. A *direc-tional mike* (often called a *cardioid* because of its heart-shaped pickup pattern) helps cut down on reverberant sound and background noise but is not a magic so-lution. Using mikes intelligently is a highly specialized skill requiring some knowl-edge of sound theory and a lot of ability to hear differences (see Sound Theory in Chapter 7).

A useful type of mike for interviews or speech recording in noisy surroundings is the *lavalier* (or chest) mike, which is small and worn under a subject's upper clothing. One mike per speaker is required, and a small mixer is necessary unless your recorder has multiple inputs. Your subject's mobility is limited by the mike cable, hidden in clothing and emerging from a pants leg or skirt bottom. One of the funnier sights is seeing a subject who's forgotten he's wired arrive abruptly at the end of a cable.

Radio mikes are theoretically wonderful, but cheap ones frequently fade or pull in taxi and radio frequency (RF) interference in urban areas.

The mike operator should *at all times* wear headphones to monitor the effect of the current mike positioning. Make sure you have backup cables because breakdowns often occur in cables and connectors. Electret mikes need batteries: be sure to carry spares.

CAMCORDERS AND SOUND

There are now so many camcorder models that comment must be brief and gen-eral. Try to find one with manual sound-level control so pauses during speech don't get absurdly amplified when the automatic level control goes hunting for a signal. Professional machines use balanced line mike cables that have three-wire connectors instead of the two-wire (unbalanced) connections common in amateur equipment. If you must use long sound cables at, say, a concert or other event needing a complex sound setup, check all equipment ahead of time, and preferably in the location, because there may be RF interference (radio stations and other such noise).

MONITORS

Some kind of monitor on location is indispensable for playback. If you intend making do with a domestic television set, it must either have video and audio inputs, or your camcorder must be able to produce an RF (TV transmission frequency) output, with an adapter if need be. Better results, especially with regard to color and the edges of framing, are obtainable by using a proper field monitor linked at the video signal stage. This may be your only guarantee of color fidelity while shooting and the only check on the framing that shows in the camera viewfinder. All monitors and most television sets have abysmal sound quality. Camcorders and videocassette players normally have a sound output (line out) that on playback can be fed into any stereo set (line in or AUX input). The improvement in sound quality is dramatic.

FIGURE 11-2

A 2k softlight. The bulbs are recessed so that light is diffused by the white reflector. (Mole Richardson Co.)

LIGHTING INSTRUMENTS

This entire book could be written about lighting alone. A considerable amount of quite acceptable interior work can be done using only a 1000 to 2000-watt *softlight* (also expressed as 1 to 2 kW, with "kW" standing for kilowatts). You might use a *luminaire* (jargon for lighting fixture) with recessed bulbs and a very large, white-painted reflector (Figure 11-2). Or, since there needs to be 4 to 6 square feet of illuminating area, you might adapt a spotlight's output by diffusing it with silk or fiberglass. Light can also be diffused by throwing it into a reflecting aluminized umbrella or by bouncing it off a white wall or ceiling.

Whichever method is used, the effect is the same: light coming from a broad area throws very soft-edged shadows—shadows so soft that they are hardly noticeable. Hence the terms *hard light* and *soft light,* which refer to the hardness or softness of any shadows cast.

If you want to cast the kind of hard light associated with sunlight or any other source casting hard-edged shadows, you will need *focusing lamps* or *spotlights* (Figures 11-3 and 11-4).

Open-face quartz lamps (Figure 11-5) are light and inexpensive, but light tends to pour uncontrollably in every direction, making lighting a rather rudimentary exercise. Hardware and office supply stores sell cheap and serviceable quartz lights that even have stands, but without barndoors they are only useful as bounce light sources.

Warning: Never touch quartz bulbs when you change them, because the oil in your skin will bake into the quartz envelope and cause it to discolor, or even explode, when next turned on. For interior work, try to use *fresnel lights* (lensed stu-

FIGURE 11-3 ⎯⎯⎯⎯⎯⎯⎯

Handy small spot. The fresnel lens produces hard light. (Mole Richardson Co.)

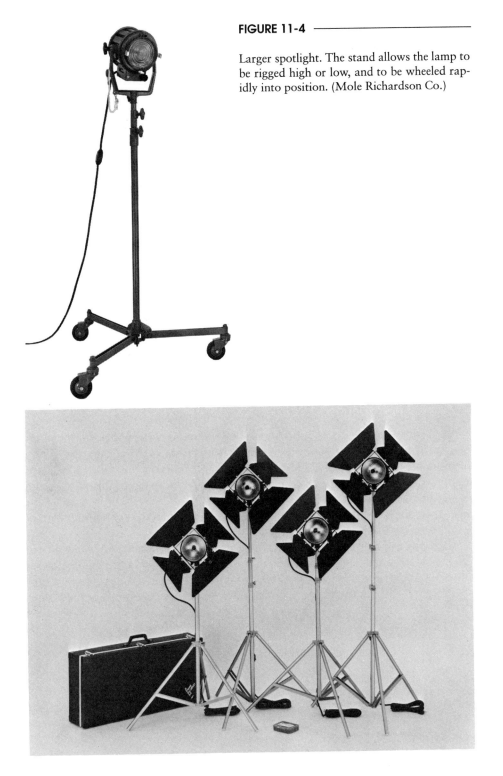

FIGURE 11-4 ————————————

Larger spotlight. The stand allows the lamp to be rigged high or low, and to be wheeled rapidly into position. (Mole Richardson Co.)

FIGURE 11-5 ————————————

Lightweight open-face quartz kit. Barndoors on lamps permit lighting spread to be restricted. (Lowel-Light Mfg.)

dio lamps with a directional light output) having a tungsten filament with a color temperature rating of 3200 degrees Kelvin scale (3200K). This will standardize color rendition. You will have flesh tone problems if you shoot under a mix of sources, such as daylight (approximately 5600K) and tungsten, or tungsten and other light sources, such as fluorescent lighting. Fluorescents have a broken spectrum and no set color temperature. To add insult to injury, they come in various modified colors to offset the hideous discomfort of working under them. An office or supermarket ceiling may contain a cocktail mix.

Movie lights are power-hungry, consuming 500 to 1000 watts each. A decent softlight will require 2 kW (2 kilowatts, or 2000 watts). Since 1000 watts is equivalent to 9.5 amps when run from 110 volts (or 4.5 amps when the supply is 220 volts), it follows that you cannot expect a 15A standard 110V household circuit to power a 2K lamp; you must search for a 20A power circuit.

POWER CALCULATION

To find power consumption in *amps* (rate of flow), add your total desired *watts* (amount of energy consumption) and divide it by the *volts* (pressure) of the supply voltage. We can represent the common calculations as formulas:

To calculate amperage (A): $A = W \div V$

To calculate wattage (W): $W = A \times V$

To calculate voltage (V): $V = W \div A$

Rather high current requirements must be kept in mind when you scout locations for electrical supply, and you must be careful not to tap into a 220V supply by mistake. Plan to bring heavy-load extension cables so you can take each light's supply from a differently fused source and thus spread the load. The amount and type of lighting you will need depends on such things as size and reflectivity of the space to be lit, how much available light there is, and what kind of lighting "look" you are aiming for.

Lighting is highly specialized, but there are simple and basic setups outlined in Chapter 12 that can get you through a lot. Lighting for black-and-white demands more skill if the viewer is to have a sense of dimension, space, and textures. Color often separates tones by hue so less elaborate lighting is necessary for an acceptable result.

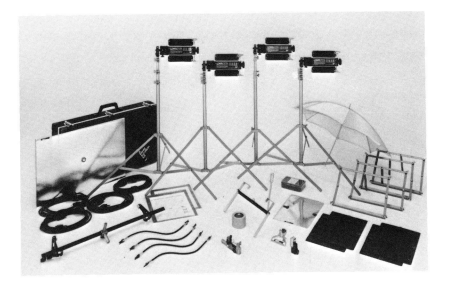

FIGURE 11-6

A lighting kit with great flexibility. The reflective silver umbrella converts an open-face (hard) light into a soft-light source. The frames carry diffusion material or gels. (Lowel-Light Mfg.)

ABOUT LIGHTING

Any comprehensive lighting instruction for film or videotape is far beyond the scope of this book, but here are a few useful basic points. Video has an immense advantage over film in that a lighting setup's failings are immediately apparent from the video monitor.

WHEN YOU NEED IT

Lighting is necessary when there is insufficient light to get an exposure. It is also necessary because neither film nor video renders images like the human eye, which effortlessly evens out illumination and color inequities. Image-recording systems simply record within their capacities all that can be perceived by the recording medium. The result may not look natural, that is, the way our eye is used to seeing things. Artifice is sometimes necessary to adjust lighting in an image so it looks natural.

Supplementary light becomes necessary when:

- It is too dark to shoot.
- Low available light forces you to use a very wide lens aperture. This, in turn, demands very precise focusing, which is especially difficult if subjects are moving. Adding light allows the camera to function at a smaller lens aperture, and thereby benefit from a greater depth of field and suffer fewer focusing problems.
- Available light is very contrasty, creating "hot" (overbright) highlights and deep shadows. Fill light in shadow areas reduces the shadow to highlight differential.
- You have mixed color-temperature sources, that is, light sources having different color biases (see later).

CONTRAST AND COLOR-TEMPERATURE PROBLEMS

Film and video image recording limitations often require raising shadow light levels to reduce the disparity between the highest and the lowest illumination levels in the picture. By using *fill light* to boost shadow areas, you can reduce the lighting ratio, that is, the all-important ratio of shadow to highlight illumination. Fill light may come from a lighting instrument or may be provided by a *bounce card* (a white cardboard reflector). When you bring the range of brightnesses in the image within the limited capacity of the recording medium, the screen reproduces the contrasty picture you wanted with detail in both the highlight and deep shadow areas. These would both have been lost had the picture been shot without lighting adjustments.

Currently film stocks reproduce detail over a wider brightness range than video, which tends to perform best in brightly lit, low-contrast situations and to do worst in contrasty low-key setups. This is particularly true of inexpensive analogue cameras. Digital cameras are a significant improvement.

Color-temperature mismatches are a big problem where daylight and artificial lighting are present together. Different light sources have different color biases, a problem that must be addressed if flesh is to look human rather than martian. The eye effortlessly compensates for the biases in light sources and sees a white object as white whether the light illuminating it is sunlight, tungsten-bulb light, or the light from a fluorescent tube. But film stock must either be specially chosen or the camera lens filtered to render white as white. Electronic cameras permit adjustment for an optimal color rendition. This is called *white balancing* and is a simple, routine operation.

WORKING WITH LIGHT SOURCES OF DIFFERENT COLOR TEMPERATURES

Any camera can be balanced for *one* color-temperature source, but it cannot handle mixed light sources. Imagine an interior setup lit by available daylight. You need to raise the exposure in the shadow, but color consistency problems arise if you boost blue-biased daylight by adding orange-biased tungsten light. For if the color camera is adjusted to render daylight (5400K) as "white" light, the light coming from a movie tungsten light (3200K) will, by comparison, cast a noticeably orange hue. A domestic bulb (approximately 2800K instead of 3200K), if there is one in the shot, will look even more orange because its color temperature is lower still.

If we try to solve the problem by filtering the camera for the 3200K movie lighting, the daylight-illuminated highlights will now look very blue. In close-ups, these unnatural lighting effects are particularly noticeable because we base our judgments on how natural flesh tones look. So when you have to mix light sources, use a color-conversion gel over one or more of the light sources in order to bring its color-temperature output in line with the majority lighting. This solves the color imbalance, but filtering lowers the light's output by as much as 50 percent, so you may need twice as much light.

Even an apparently simple interior lighting setup becomes a thicket of problems as the cinematographer faces contrasty, burnt-out walls, multiple shadows, and mike shadows, to mention just a few of the common difficulties. If you expect to encounter problems such as these, see the bibliography at the back of this book for specialized literature.

ADDING TO A BASE AND USING A KEY LIGHT

Luckily you can get away with a fairly simple and reliable solution to lit interiors. Called *adding to a base,* it means providing enough ambient light for an exposure, then adding to this base some modeling by way of a key light. The base can most easily be made by bouncing light off white walls and ceilings, thus casting a comparatively shadowless overall illumination. If there are no white walls, light can be bounced off a white card or diffused through spun glass or another diffusion material that won't discolor with heat.

The lighting from the bounce source alone will be flat and dull, especially in longer shots, so you must now add the key light. The key light should be "motivated," that is, it should appear to be coming from the scene's logical source. For a bedroom scene, position the key low and out of the frame so shadows are cast by an apparent bedside lamp. For a warehouse scene lit by a bare overhead bulb hanging into the frame, the key would have to come from above. In a laboratory scene where the source is a light table, the key would have to strike the subject from a low angle, and so on. You can cheat substantially on the angle of the key for artistic effect and to minimize shadow problems, provided you do not depart too blatantly from what seems likely and possible.

Any lamps that appear in the picture are called *practicals* but are seldom a functioning part of the lighting. They are adjusted for light output—enough to register as a light, but not enough to burn out that portion of the picture. If a practical looks too orange, use a photoflood, but be careful of the heat it generates. Cut a practical's output by putting a neutral-density filter or layers of paper around the inside of its shade.

DEFINING SHADOWS: HARD AND SOFT LIGHT

The key light not only provides highlights but also throws a shadow, and it is mainly by a scene's shadow pattern that the observer infers time of day, lighting mood, and so on. *Hard* and *soft* light are terms for light quality that are indispensable to discussions about lighting and lighting style. *Hard light,* you may recall, is light that creates *hard-edged shadows,* while *soft light* is light that creates soft-edged shadows or even no shadows at all.

Note that *hard* and *soft* have nothing to do with the strength of illumination. Thus, in spite of its dimness, a candle flame is a hard-light source because it creates hard shadows. Hard light comes from a small-area light source or from a source that is effectively small because it is distant (e.g., the sun) or because it is fitted with a lens (e.g., a spotlight). Light rays coming from effectively small sources are organized and parallel to each other, and thus project a shadow image of impeding objects.

Soft light tends to come from a large-area source that sends out disorganized rays of light incapable of projecting clean-cut shadows. A fluorescent tube is such a source, and is specially favored in everyday use as a "shadowless" working light. The most bountiful source of soft light when you are shooting exteriors is an overcast sky. This is why one sees huge lights being used on feature shoots during daylight shots; available light is too soft to produce adequate shadow patterns so it must be augmented with a local hard source.

KEY LIGHT DIRECTION AND BACKLIGHTING

Folklore about taking photos "with your back to the sun" might make us think that light must always fall on the subject from the camera direction. But because this ensures a minimum of shadow area, it tends to remove evidence of the subject's third dimension—depth. Actually some of the most interesting lighting effects are created when the angle of throw of the key is to the side of the subject or even relatively behind it (see Chapter 6 for pictorial examples and further discussion).

Backlighting creates a rim of light that helps to separate the subject from the background. Achieving this separation is important in black-and-white photography but less so in color, where the colors help to define and separate the different planes of the composition.

Key light can come from an open-face quartz lamp, suitably backed off, or, like the fill, it too can be somewhat diffused to soften unsuitably hard shadows. Using multiple key lights is a skilled business and without a lot of care can lead to that trademark of amateur lighting, ugly and unrealistic multiple shadows.

TESTS: HOW MUCH IS ENOUGH LIGHT?

For shooting interiors with film, you will need three or more lamps and each should be at least 750 W. For video, less power is necessary. Quartz bulbs have a relatively long life, are small enough to provide fairly hard light, and remain stable in color temperature throughout their life.

Be forewarned that 3 or 4 kW of lighting goes nowhere in a large space, or in a smaller room painted a dark tone. The only way to learn about lighting is to shoot tests. If you are hiring film camera equipment and want to know ahead of time what your lighting will look like, shoot 35mm color slides (tungsten balanced) on a fairly fast slide stock (say, 125 ASA at 1/50th of a second shutter time). You can then project them and study in depth what your deficiencies or triumphs look like. Many people use a Polaroid camera, which gives instant but somewhat misleading results because the color and light sensitivity of Polaroid film are very different from those of negative/positive film.

Avoid the costly embarrassment of lighting and electrical failures by having a lighting rehearsal beforehand. Long demoralizing delays are the penalty for taking chances. Check out where to find the location's fuses or breakers, which sockets belong on which circuit, and whether high-consumption, intermittent appliances, such as refrigerators and air conditioners, are going to kick in during shooting and cause a circuit overload. If you turn off a refrigerator during shooting, remember to turn it back on or else you may have to replace the family frozen food supplies.

AVOIDING THE OVERBRIGHT BACKGROUND

One truly aggravating problem when you shoot in small, light-colored or white spaces is the amount of light thrown back by the walls. The on-screen result is a set of humanoid outlines moving against a blinding white background. The video image is especially vulnerable because automatic exposure circuitry adjusts for the majority of the image, letting the actual subjects go relatively dark. Color quality and definition all suffer, and this is why family video often seems to document orange hominids living in a glacier.

Ideally one should try to shoot in spaces with dark or book-covered walls which absorb instead of reflecting your light. When this is impossible, the solution to "hot" walls is to angle and barndoor your sources to keep light off the background walls, and to raise the illumination of the foreground subject. It helps to keep participants away from walls by "cheating" chairs, tables, and sofas several feet forwards. This seldom looks unnatural on-screen and also helps with shadows. When light comes primarily from above and characters are separated from the walls, the actors' shadows are thrown lower and thus largely disappear from the camera's sightline. Moving participants away from sound-reflective surfaces also improves sound quality.

REACTIONS TO LIGHTING

The discomfort caused by injudicious lighting tends to inhibit the nervous. Give your participants a chance to get used to unusual amounts of light pouring down on them, particularly in their own homes. Lighting also creates heat, and when windows must be kept closed to reduce outside noise, interior shooting can become unpleasantly tropical. Participants whose faces sweat may need to be dulled down with a skin-tone powder. This is the only makeup ever used in documentary. Unless makeup is done in a highly skilled manner, it tends to look dreadful. Use a removable dulling spray (from an art supply store) for objects producing overbright reflections, such as chromium chairs or glass tables.

C H A P T E R   1 3

AVOIDING PROBLEMS

LOGS AND BUDGET CONTROL

When you shoot a documentary or a fiction project on film, keeping logs for picture and sound is imperative. Logs serve various functions. Should the lab or the cameraperson want to examine a particular film or video camera original after seeing a workprint, the log allows quick access. It also allows for tracing which piece of equipment was responsible for any anomalies, and, of course, it is invaluable in the cutting room for tracing material and for cross-referencing.

During the shoot, logs help you keep a running total of stock consumption and indicate the state of the production budget. Particularly when shooting film, a common mistake for beginners is to assess stock requirement for the total shooting and then to put it out of mind until dwindling reserves direct everyone's attention to the approaching famine. This results in liberal coverage for early material and insufficient coverage for later material.

Keeping a running total not just of stock used but of all vital expenditures helps the low-budget filmmaker to mobilize precious resources according to rational priorities. The production manager rather than the director is the best person to carry this out.

Budget monitoring,

- lets you compare your projected budget with the reality taking shape
- gives early warning of impending crises
- teaches you what to do differently next time around

WHERE VIDEOTAPE DIFFERS

Videotape stock is cheap compared with its film equivalent, but this encourages one to shoot promiscuously and without keeping track. This is a pity. Sound and picture are all on one tape, so a log is easily maintained. A contents description (tape roll number, date, location, activity, personnel, digital counter reading) is enough to assist a quick replay during the shooting period. Keep logs and records simple on location. The more elaborate your bureaucracy, the more likely it is to be abandoned when the pressure is on, leaving you with no records at all. You can make a detailed log in peace and comfort when you review the rushes (also called *dailies*) at the start of postproduction.

SHOOTING RATIO

Shooting ratio is a way of expressing the ratio of material shot to that used on the screen. It is quite usual for a half-hour film to emerge from 6 hours of shooting. This would be a ratio of 12:1. In preproduction add up what you expect to shoot and divide it by your intended screen time, and the result is an expected shooting ratio. If you are shooting on film negative, your film stock, processing, and work-print will blow a large hole in the budget, while videotape camera stock, being cheaper, is less of a concern.

A commonly asked question is, what's a normal ratio for a documentary? To this I usually answer, "How long is a piece of string?" It all depends on what you are tying up. A film of mine about Alexandra Tolstoy and her relationship with her parents (*Tolstoy Remembered by his Daughter*) was shot in only 3 hours. It consisted of one long interview, which I afterwards slugged with many still photos, 1910 news film, and shots of documents. The shooting ratio was about 5:1. It was this low because my subject was 86 and I had to limit my questioning. Madame Tolstoy being an accomplished writer, spoke in beautifully succinct paragraphs. Virtually everything we shot was usable.

At the other extreme are the observational films of Fred Wiseman, usually 90 minutes long, which are often culled from 70 hours of film (46:1). The high ratio results from aiming for a long screen time, with its need for large themes and plenty of action material to sustain development over such a long haul. It also stems from Wiseman's strict policy of nonintervention, which prevents him from polarizing or influencing the events he films or even from providing narrated guidance in the finished product.

The only way to predict an adequate shooting ratio is to rate each sequence for its expected contents. If you want to catch certain kinds of unusual but highly significant behavior in children, you might need a 60:1 ratio. An interview with their teacher might, on the other hand, come in at 3:1 because she is knowledgeable and concise about what she does.

A good practice when shooting film stock is to project the smallest and largest figures for each sequence so you can modify, as necessary, how you predict the ratio. During the shoot have someone monitor actual consumption and predict what needs to be done to come in on target.

EQUIPMENT BREAKDOWNS

Many equipment failures are traceable to inadequate checkout procedures in the first place. However "good" a rental house may be, no matter how "well" someone maintains a piece of rented equipment, nothing should leave its place of origin without a thorough inspection by the user and a *working test*. Batteries for cameras, recorders, and mikes are frequent culprits. Rechargeable batteries are picky about how much and how often they are put on a charge, and hire houses may unknowingly issue defective units. Conserve batteries by running off a power line via the AC power converter whenever possible.

Any parts that wear out, such as lamp elements, belts, and plugs, should have backup spares on hand. Wiring is especially vulnerable at its entry point to plugs and sockets. The crew should carry electrical and mechanical first-aid equipment to carry out spot repairs.

Equipment failures sometimes require replacements in double-quick time. Prepare for this situation by making an emergency aid list for the area (or country) in which you will be working. This cuts down time lost in getting information. Once I had a camera cable for a new Hitachi camera die on location in Baltimore. No cable existed in all of Baltimore, but with the cheap test meter and soldering equipment I usually carry, I was able to trace the problem to a wire lurking inside a particular plug and to reconnect it. Prepare for the worst and you will seldom be disappointed.

HUMAN BREAKDOWNS

Human breakdowns happen, but any healthy crew member who walks off a shoot will find out that the word goes around and no one will ever use him again. Voluntary workers, even those wanting to "break into the industry," sometimes imagine they are immune from this law, thinking "I'm doing you a favor, so I'll come if I feel like it." Volunteers need to be drawn from that rare breed who honor commitments to the letter. A more usual breakdown is error or omission as people get tired. A wise schedule and careful checklists help to minimize these (see summaries provided at end of the parts, Preproduction and Production). Sometimes when responsibility is poorly defined, a duty will be carried out by two people or, more dangerously, by neither.

A real disaster is when a participant withdraws or fails to appreciate how much is at stake when you plan a shoot. Sometimes people think it is nothing to put off shooting by a couple of days, offering only that maddeningly evasive explanation, "Something has come up." To avoid this, stress the importance of your scheduling from the outset.

Even then, people drop out. In Paris I once had a couple of artists cancel three days before shooting. In the plane from London I had read about a sculptor and was lucky enough to secure him as my subject just in time for the crew's scheduled arrival. I then discovered that he spent much of each day wandering under migratory instinct. He did not always remember where (or whether) he had promised to meet us. I was sure the film would be so awful that I would never get another to direct. This conviction is, I have since discovered, common to most directors most of the time—an occupational hazard like dogs to postmen.

KEEP ALTERNATIVES UP YOUR SLEEVE

Given the loyal presence of so many technical and human difficulties, it is prudent to always keep alternatives on hand. Exteriors that rely on a certain kind of weather should be scheduled early with interiors on standby as an alternative cover. Shoot crucial sequences—those that decide the viability of the film as a whole—early rather than late in the schedule, and so on.

When someone tells you something cannot be done, examine the explanation carefully. Filming always depends on the coordination of several aspects, and when one of them is unfavorable, some assume too readily that the intention cannot be carried out. Often by changing two of the other aspects, the original intention becomes viable again.

Assume that everything can be accomplished with good planning and inventiveness, and you will usually be right.

C H A P T E R 1 4

INTERVIEWING

WHY INTERVIEWING MATTERS

Interviewing is at the heart of documentary, even though your film will contain not a single "talking head." By *interviewing* I mean not only eliciting on-camera information, but the skills one needs to conduct person-to-person exchange at a deeper level. To face another human being while making documentaries is to probe, to listen, to reveal oneself by responding with further questioning. It means helping someone express the meanings of her life. Considered as an extended, trusting exchange, the research interview is plainly the foundation for most documentaries. Later, if the resulting film itself tells someone's story well, if it builds through exposition and specific emotional detail to a satisfying climax, then we have the sensation of seeing into a human soul. This is because a skilled and empathic director drew out what we see. Subtly or otherwise, the interviewer *directed* the participant, providing the necessary support, guidance, or encouragement to help make a soul emerge. Part of that process means providing resistance to the immediate and superficial when one senses there is something else beneath the surface.

Here we face the duality of documentary. Interviewing—indeed, documentary making in general—can create a liberating arena for discovery and growth, or can become intrusive and a form of exploitation. But this is true for all human relationships. A friendship, for example, can be kept safely limited or can be steered by mutual agreement into areas of risk. Some friendships are manipulative and extremely complex. The more there is at risk, the greater is the potential for growth, and for damage. No gain without pain, they say.

However, in making documentaries the relationship is seldom as equal as it is between friends. The director arrives with advantages and hoping to get access to another person's life. As such we always exploit other people because there can be no film without such access. So you have the obligation to give and not just take, to be sensitive yet also assertive in the positive sense. Often the documentarian aspires to set up a partnership, like the "poet as witness" Seamus Heaney describes in his discussion of World War I poets. To Heaney, Wilfrid Owen and others represent "poetry's solidarity with the doomed, the deprived, the victimized, the underprivileged." Heaney might be speaking of the documentarian when he says, "The witness is any figure in whom the truth-telling urge and the compulsion to identify with the oppressed becomes necessarily integral with the act of writing itself."[1]

Think of interviewing as a form of displaced authorship; it means midwifing others into eloquence, particularly those unused to speaking about their innermost lives. A good edited interview should have all the elements of a successful oral tale, so you can learn much about your directorial skills from doing them. Even when all the questions have been removed, the interviewer's power as a catalyst, selector, and organizer remains written all over the screen. By watching rushes critically, you can plainly see your strengths and weaknesses as a director. By groping for a level of interviewing that is truly your own, you come to see the blind spots and artificiality in your own behavior. There are spontaneous moments of humor, inspired questions, and well-judged pauses, but also persuasion tilting into manipulation, and timidity masquerading as respect—truly a rendezvous with oneself.

WHO INTERVIEWS

Some documentary units include a researcher, who digs up facts; locates, and even chooses, the participants; and thus contributes importantly to the film's identity. Some directors rely heavily on the experience and judgment of their researchers. This shared control usually arises out of having had a working relationship long enough to establish mutual trust.

It is important during the researcher's initial visits to refrain from pressing interesting questions to a conclusion if important and unexplored areas are to be opened up later on camera. When it's time to shoot, the question arises, Who is better equipped to conduct the interviewing, the researcher or the director? Each has possible advantages. If the researcher does the interviewing, he is continuing a relationship begun during the research period. This continuity might be crucial for putting a hesitant participant at ease. If instead the director conducts the questioning, the interview may be more spontaneous because the subject is addressing a fresh listener instead of repeating himself to the researcher.

A researcher/director team often decides who will interview according to which combination is most promising. Sometimes one must be more creative to put a subject at ease. I made a film with Dr. Benjamin Spock (*Dr. Spock: "We're Sliding Towards Destruction,"* "One Pair of Eyes" series, BBC) and found that, although I had done all the research with him, his to-camera manner was stiff and unnatural. We stopped the camera and talked about it. He realized that as a pediatrician he was used to talking to women, so I placed our production assistant, Rosalie Worthington, in my position under the camera lens. Although I was still asking the questions, Dr. Spock addressed himself to Rosalie and his manner became relaxed and spontaneous. Had reflexivity been allowable, this biographically revealing information could have been included.

---

[1]Heaney, Seamus. *The Government of the Tongue.* London: Faber, 1988, p. xvi.

TYPES OF SITUATIONS

Interviews can be shot in almost any surroundings, but you must consider the likely effect on the interviewee. In settings such as one's home, workplace, or the home of a friend, the interviewee is more at ease and will give you more intimate and individual responses. In public places, such as streets, parks, or the beach, the interviewee is more likely to feel like one of many. Depending on the individual subject, this may be important. Other settings, such as a battlefield or the scene of an accident or demonstration, will have a special aura because the speaker feels in dramatic juxtaposition to events that were beyond his control.

Each environment is likely to evoke a different "self" in the interviewee and make him resonate a little differently. This is never entirely predictable, but if you use common sense and imagination and take into account the significance the person probably attaches to being filmed, you can guess what contribution different settings are likely to make.

We are all—interviewers included—very much affected by our surroundings and tend to lower barriers (or erect them) according to our sense of circumstance. Filming may dignify a situation or render it embarrassingly public; it may offer a hot line to the world's ear, be the confessional box, or be good conversation with a friend. How the interviewee feels will depend on both the environment and the way you present your purpose. Remember that *a documentary film is the sum of relationships,* so the unseen relationships carried on with you and your crew are quite as influential as those visible on-screen.

Another practical factor when shooting is the effect of someone off camera. If you are interviewing a gentle older woman whose peppery husband is always correcting her, arrange to have the husband otherwise occupied so she can tell you her story. On the other hand, the relationship between the two may be an important and visible aspect of who they are or what they represent. I once shot an interview of a farm manager together with his wife (*A Remnant of a Feudal Society,* "Yesterday's Witness" series, BBC). She interrupted and modified everything he said, and this, apart from being funny, drew attention to a larger dimension of modification and idealization in her account.

Interviewing is not therefore only one-to-one. A married couple may separately be inarticulate through shyness yet prod each other into action and reaction very well. Friends or workmates can likewise provide mutual support. Inhibitions may just as easily be released through mutual antipathy: putting two people together who disagree and interviewing them together can be a highly productive strategy. You may even interview a whole group, which provides two options: One is to "recognize" each new speaker from among those who want to speak, and the other is to encourage them to begin speaking to each other. What matters here is to be less concerned with maintaining control than with eliciting people's thoughts and feelings. If this is taking place without you, you can remain happily silent because your role as catalyst has been accomplished.

Usually when you start talking to a few people in a public place, say, at a factory gate, others gather to listen and join in. Unless the interviewer asserts herself, it will turn into a spirited conversation or dispute among those present, depending, of course, on how controversial the topic was in the first place. The interviewer is now on the sidelines but may step in at any time with a question or even a request, such as, "Could the lady in the red jacket talk a bit about the union's attitude toward safety precautions?" And talk she will.

There is one very useful technique often used with street interviews. Called *vox pop* (short for *vox populi,* meaning "voice of the people"), it consists of asking a number of people the same few questions, and then stringing the replies together in a rapid sequence. It is entertaining and useful for demonstrating opinion in a range of people. The same technique can be used to show either diversity or homogeneity.

Sections of vox pop are favored as lively relief from something sober and intense, such as an expository section explaining a complicated political development. They can also function as a legitimate parallel action to which you can resort in times of need. In the film about Dr. Spock mentioned earlier, I had to compress the salient points of his 3-hour peace speeches into about 12 minutes. I did this by setting up a dialectical counterpoint between Spock at the podium and the ubiquitous man in the street. Because each gave piquancy to the other, a virtue came out of necessity.

PREPARATION AND BASIC SKILLS

No matter who does the interviewing, the same basic skills are needed. First and foremost, the interviewer must be prepared. This emphasizes how important it is to define a hypothetical focus for your entire film from the outset. With a fundamental *purpose* behind your directing, you should have a clear expectation of what each interviewee will contribute. I am not suggesting you prepare a script or even anticipate specific statements, because anything so confined would thrust a participant into an acting role. You see this in phone company and other commercials masquerading as documentary. They have a glib sincerity that reeks of manipulation. Some quite sincere documentary makers habitually intrude on their interviewees, perhaps because they are anxious to be in control. The interviewee tries to fulfill a sense of requirement, and the results are a pervasive staginess and self-consciousness that devalue the whole film.

During the interview, you should maintain eye contact with your subject, and give visual (NOT verbal!) feedback as the interviewee talks. Nodding, smiling, looking puzzled, and signifying agreement or doubt are all vital forms of feedback that sustain the interviewee in what might otherwise feel like an egocentric monologue. Erroll Morris claims to get his extraordinary interviews by keeping expectantly silent and letting the camera roll.

SETTING PEOPLE AT EASE

Research, I have argued, is to discover more or less what a person's potential contribution may be, while the interviewer's task is to catalyze it on film.

To put the interviewee at ease and yet guard against digression, it is a good practice to *say which subject areas you want to cover in the film, and which you don't.* Beginning directors are often too timid to set limits on the areas they can use, and allow their subjects to range far and wide. This ambiguity is ultimately unkind to the interviewee, who senses that he somehow isn't connecting. Remember, you have the right and the obligation to say what you want. If you let this be challenged, or even invite challenge, you can assure yourself that you aren't being unfairly restrictive.

You must also prepare the interviewee for the occasional interruption or redirection, so I usually say, "This is a documentary and we always shoot a lot more than we use. So don't worry if you get anything wrong because we can always edit it out. Also, if I feel we're getting away from the subject, I may suddenly interrupt, if that's all right with you." Nobody objects; indeed, people seem reassured that I take responsibility for the overall direction of our conversation. I augment this deliberate reduction of pressure on the interviewee by making my first question relaxed and even bumbling. I want to demonstrate that my shooting expectations are nothing like the manic brightness people usually see in television interviews. By example, I signal that no change of self-presentation is necessary just because a camera is rolling.

If you want spontaneity, you must be natural yourself. You set the tone for the interview; if you are formal or uptight, your interviewee will be more so. Because it is important not to bury one's face in a page of notes, I prepare a list of questions short enough to go on an index card. These I keep on my knee. Having them there is a "security blanket" that releases me simply to have a conversation. I'm free to really *listen,* knowing I can always glance down if my mind goes blank (which it sometimes does). The mere act of preparing the questions somehow ensures that I naturally and informally cover all my intended ground.

Before you conclude the interview, double-check that you covered everything you intended. With the camera running, I usually ask, "Is there anything else you want to say, anything we forgot to cover?" This hands the final word to the participant.

FRAMING QUESTIONS

Before an interview, formulate your questions to be direct and specific. Read each question aloud and listen to your own voice. See if it sounds direct and natural. See if you can interpret the question "wrongly." Sometimes certain wording allows another interpretation; alter it until the intended understanding alone is possible.

Focused questions are vital if you want to lead rather than follow your interviewee. Inexperienced interviewers often use general questions such as, "What is the most exciting experience you've ever had?" This signals that the interviewer is devoid of preparation or focus and is casting a big, shapeless net. Another common pitfall is the long, rambling question with so many qualifiers that it ends up as a shapeless catalogue of concerns. The confused interviewee only answers what she remembers, which is usually the last thing said.

Know what you want, use simple, conversational language, and deal with one issue at a time. A question such as, "You have some strong feelings about the fears suffered by latchkey kids?" will work well because it points the interviewee at a vital experience already mentioned during research and signals your interest in how he *feels*.

There is nothing unethical about signifying your interest in an exact area. Indeed, it gives clear and encouraging guidance. It should not, on the other hand, be confused with the leading question, which seeks to manipulate the interviewee into a particular response rather than to indicate a particular *area* of interest. "Did you feel angry coming home to an empty house?" is manipulative because it is fishing for a particular answer. The answer may come as a yes or no, which is useless. However, "Talk some more about the anger you mentioned when you came home to an empty house" is absolutely legitimate because it asks for amplification on something already mentioned.

GUIDELINES FOR EFFECTIVE INTERVIEWING

There are a number of straightforward techniques that will help you to maintain focus and intensity:

- Plan interview questions to produce responses covering specific areas.
- Don't be afraid to give direction to the interview.
- Maintain eye contact at all costs.
- Never think about your next question, it keeps you from listening.
- It's your film, so don't give undue control to the interviewee.
- Let the interviewee control the interview if by so doing he or she reveals something significant.
- Above all, listen for subtext, what lies behind the words being used.
- Act on your intuitions and instincts.

A subtle way to *steer* an interview is to summarize briefly what you have so far understood and ask the participant to continue. This has the effect for the interviewee of consolidating her progress so far and gives clear encouragement to go further.

A polite way to *redirect* someone is to say, "Can we return to . . . " and name the topic you would like to be amplified. Yet another way is to repeat particular words the interviewee has used in a questioning tone; this encourages further exploration. "Could we move to . . . (new subject)" is a courteous way of changing the subject.

The interviewer needs to *listen for leads,* that is, for hints of further material, especially when strong feelings may be involved, which need following up. You might say, "I was thinking you might have strong feelings about . . . " and then name what you have detected. Interviewees will be grateful for your discerning encouragement. If your interviewee goes silent, respect the silence and wait for him to go on. If he needs encouragement, try repeating his last words in a questioning tone.

Remember that your audience has no prior knowledge, so you must get comprehensive cover. Interviewing should be exploration that leads to understanding, so make your interviewee *stay with a significant subject* until you feel it is exhausted. Keep exploring until you reach complete understanding yourself—both factual and emotional.

Never settle for abstractions or generalities; press for an example or a story to illustrate every worthwhile point. If you don't know what the interviewee meant, your audience won't either, so press for clarification. You have to *listen as if hearing everything for the first time* so you can elicit whatever a first-time audience will need.

Do not be afraid of interviewing people in crisis. You will soon know if someone truly wants to be left alone, but you'll never find out if you're too timid to ask. For most, crises are the time when one needs to talk, and a truly satisfying exchange leads to a sense of release. If this is at all strong, you will feel it and so will your audience. Listening to testimony is itself a healing act, for all concerned.

Excellent examples of formal interviewing can be seen in Connie Field's *The Life and Times of Rosie the Riveter* (1980) and Erroll Morris' *The Thin Blue Line* (1988). Very informal interviewing can be found in Ira Wohl's *Best Boy* (1979), where it produces spontaneous conversation. Here Philly's family members, principally his mother, pour out their hearts.

When a person speaks from the heart, particularly for the first time, it can be magical. Here, speech is the action. Conversely, when an interviewee speaks routinely and without a sense of discovery, the result can sever our connection with the film. Talking head films must be intense and tell a good story, or they are hypnotically boring.

PREPARATIONS TO EDIT OUT THE INTERVIEWER'S VOICE

If the interviewer is offscreen and you intend to edit out all questions, you must prepare interviewees by telling them that the information in your questions needs to be included in the answer. Many people will look puzzled, so you will have to give an example: "Say I ask, 'When did you first arrive in America?,' you might answer '1959,' but the answer '1959' wouldn't stand on its own, so I'd be forced to include my question. However, if you said, 'I arrived in the United States in 1959,' that's a whole and complete statement."

In spite of such explanations, most people repeatedly forget to make a whole statement out of their answers. You will have to listen critically at the beginning of each answer. Sometimes one has to feed an interviewee the appropriate opening words to clarify by example what one needs. You would say, "Try beginning, 'I arrived in America . . .'"

Another interviewer's hazard is the monosyllabic answer.

Q: "I understand you weren't entirely satisfied when you moved into this apartment?"
A: "Yep."

This is the interviewer's nightmare—someone who can't or won't talk. Try pressing for specifics: "Would you tell me what you remember?" If the person doesn't respond to this kind of verbal prodding, it is probably wise to abandon your attempt. He may be stonewalling or may simply not be a talker.

THE IN-DEPTH INTERVIEW

There is a good general rule for interviewing: Start with factual questions and keep the more intimate or emotionally loaded material for later, when the interviewee has become more comfortable with the situation. If there is a delicate area you want to open up, there are a couple of ways it can be done. One approach is to use the devil's advocate approach; for instance, "Some people would say there's nothing special or frightening for a kid in getting home a couple of hours before his mother." The interviewee is being invited to discharge his feelings against all those too lacking in imagination or curiosity to have discovered what it's like, when you're young, to enter an empty house.

Another way to initiate a sensitive topic is first to invite generalized, impersonal comment. For instance, you are almost certain that the woman you are interviewing has a suppressed sorrow because she ended up nursing a chronically ill mother instead of getting married. You really want to ask, "Didn't you resent your mother when you saw your fiancé marry someone else?" Instinct warns that this is too brutally direct, so instead you start more generally and at a safe distance: "Our society seems to expect daughters more than sons to make sacrifices for their parents, doesn't it?" She has the choice of stopping at an impersonal opinion as an observer of life or of getting closer and closer to the injustice that has spoiled her life. When she ventures her opinions, simply ask for an example. By mutual and unspoken agreement, you steer toward the poignant testimony that both you and she want to put on record. You frame her situation as one of the sad injustices that overcome people who are not warned, rather than inviting her to display her sense of personal victimization.

The distinction is important: Many people who are too proud or too realistic to complain and will only break self-imposed restraints if doing so can save others from the same fate. Without this beautiful and generous human impulse, much documentary would be impossible.

The secret to good interviewing is to really *listen* and to press always for specifics and examples. Simple rejoinders, such as "How?," "Why was that?," and "How did that make you feel?," are the keys that unlock the sentient human being from the apparently detached observer. Occasionally it helps to ask the interviewee to take his time and only speak when he can see things in his mind's eye. Sometimes this elicits a new and better kind of telling.

BREVITY

People often recount the same events in more than one way. When you pose an unexpected question, your interviewee will search and struggle to explain. This can be attractively spontaneous. But when this battle is directed toward, say, getting a few facts in order, it is tiresome to watch. Sensing this, an interviewee will often spontaneously repeat the explanation in a more orderly and rapid form. When this does not happen, you might ask, "Maybe you'd just like to go over that last explanation again as there were one or two stumbles." People are usually grateful for assistance and you benefit from getting alternative versions. In editing later, you can choose and you may even be able to combine the best of both.

So don't be afraid to ask for a briefer version of events for which you only need a summary. Most people enjoy collaborating in the making of a movie, and in playing the role of themselves they are no less sincere when doing something a second or third time.

PUSHING BOUNDARIES

Experienced interviewers deal first with what is familiar and comfortable, and only then steer toward new territory. A memorable interview invites the interviewee to take new steps and cross new emotional thresholds—either large or small. This is seeing the change or development that all stories need, and for the audience to see it is part of the emotional shock I mentioned earlier—something we seek from dramatic art. It might come from facing someone with the contradictions in her account of her mother, and seeing her realize that she despises aspects of someone she believed she only loved. Or it might be a man admitting to himself that he was unequal to a job in which he suffered a humiliating demotion. In both examples, the interviewee *is living out something important for the very first time*. The suspense and sense of sharing a "privileged moment," as this major break takes place, is electrifying.

There are strange moments in interviewing when one senses there is more to tell but the person is unsure whether to risk telling it. A gentle "And?" or simply "Yes, go on" signals that you know there is more and that you support him in continuing. After this, do not be afraid to remain silent. *The expectant silence is the interviewer's most powerful encouragement to go deeper.* When used appropriately, it provides a memorable and telling moment on-screen, when the interviewee is visibly grappling with a vital issue. The inexperienced or insensitive interviewer fails to realize that a silence is full of action for the viewer, and construing it as failure to keep the interview going, comes crashing in with a new question, oblivious to the missed opportunities left dangling.

The real cause of the problem is *not listening properly*. If you use the "security blanket" trick of keeping written questions on hand, you will be released to really listen and maintain eye contact. Remember, the material is going to be edited, and you are taking no risks by using silence and waiting.

THE RIGHT ORDER FOR QUESTIONS

Do not worry about the order of questions in relation to your intended film. Later you can reorganize the replies any way you want. The only logical order for an interview is the order that makes sense to the interviewee. Facts are safe, while opinions or feelings require more trust and a more relaxed state of mind. Thus, keep the most demanding material for the end, when your subject has become used to the situation and is even enjoying it.

In a documentary I made with Alexandra Tolstoy, the twelfth and most controversial of Leo Tolstoy's children, I knew from research that she was unwanted and that she had stumbled on this knowledge in childhood. Particularly during the interview, I saw how this grievous knowledge had affected not just her youth but her whole life. Hoping I would be able to touch on it but nervous about offending or hurting her, I delayed my most vital questioning to the end of the interview. Her reply patently came from the heart.

In the film I placed this section early because her contradictory feelings about her parents illuminate everything she says subsequently about herself. In my naïveté, I hardly supposed that an elderly lady of 86 could still feel the anguish of childhood so deeply. What emerges about a person's private pain always leads to a deeper appreciation, particularly of their strengths. There would be no justification for intruding otherwise.

The most impressive points in an interview come as detonations of truth—what Jean Rouch calls "privileged moments"—when someone on camera suddenly confronts something unfamiliar and important to him. It is like watching a mountaineer climb a challenging rock face, and seeing not only the danger of the climb but also the climber's intensified commitment.

BELIEVING IN YOUR AUTHORITY

For the interviewer it takes observation and empathy, rather than any mystic powers, to spot areas of unfinished business in another person's life. Actually it is easier to see into another's life than to see into one's own. If you have ever read a good mystery novel, you already know how to gather and collate the clues to patterns, personality, and motives. But novice directors are often too hesitant to act on their impressions and intuitions for fear of rebuff. Remember that the role of making a record—as a writer or as a filmmaker—empowers you to be assertive and demanding in a way that is (wrongly perhaps) deemed invasive in normal life. Most will accept that you are a seeker after truth and will collaborate to a degree that is surprising, and on occasion very moving.

When you doubt your authority to enter another person's life, remember that the ordinary person doubts his own importance, and that your invitation to become part of a documentary record represents a confirmation that he exists, that he matters. This is what you give, and what you give entitles you to a partnership that is seldom denied.

Why is this? It may be that the filmmaker—for reasons I can only guess at—is vested with some of the confessional powers of the priest or doctor. In the name of record making, you are allowed, even *expected,* to make incursions into your subjects' lives. At first this is hard to believe and harder to act on. You ask favors with an almost grotesque sense of apology and obligation, only to find that you are welcomed and assisted open-heartedly. You will need to treat any such openness with great responsibility, but you must also resist having your editorial decisions forged by a multiplicity of obligations. Sometimes this is very hard.

INTERVIEWER AND CAMERA PLACEMENT

There are two approaches to camera placement when you are filming interviews, each reflecting a quite different philosophy of the interviewer's function. You can tell which is in use by examining the interviewee's eyeline on-screen. One approach (Figure 14-1) has the interviewee answering an interviewer who sits with

FIGURE 14-1

Placement of the interviewer affects the subject's eyeline: With the interviewer's head immediately under the camera lens, the subject talks directly to the viewer.

his head just below the camera lens. This makes the interviewee appear to be looking directly into the camera. In the other approach (Figure 14-2), the interviewer sits to one side of the camera and out of frame, which makes the interviewee look offcamera at an unseen interlocutor. These two approaches have different effects on the audience.

Audience in Direct Relationship to Interviewee: Because I prefer to edit out the interviewer altogether, I like to leave the audience in a face-to-face relationship with my interviewee. I organize shooting so that my subject speaks into the camera (as in Figure 14-1). I thus see my interviewing as asking questions that the audience would like to have answered. Thus, I interview on behalf of the audience and function as a catalyst. Once the interviewee is talking, my presence as the listening party is irrelevant to the audience and even a distraction.

In order to clear away traces of my input from the process, I sit on something low with my head just under the camera lens. Although the interviewee is talking to me, it looks as if he is talking directly to the camera (i.e., to the audience). Once my voice is edited out, the audience is left in direct relationship to the person on the screen.

Audience Witnessing Interviewee and Implied Interviewer: If, however, you sit to either side of the camera (as in Figure 14-2), your interviewee appears to be talking to an offscreen presence—whether the interviewer's voice survives in the finished film or not. The farther away the interviewer is from the camera-to-sub-

FIGURE 14-2

With the interviewer to the side of the camera, the subject is evidently talking to someone offscreen.

ject axis, the more acute is the impression. Some filmmakers like this because it acknowledges there is an interviewer even though her voice is no longer present. My private thought is that some people who make films really want to be in them. Television journalists have no such ambiguity; when they interview, they expect to be in picture. Appearing on-screen is their career and is sometimes thoroughly justified. But unless the interviewer is a really active participant rather than an incidental catalyst, it seems redundant to see the occasional question being asked or to cut away conveniently to a nodding listener.

The most justification for an on-camera questioner is when there is a confrontation of some sort. Here the questioner's pressure and reactions become a highly relevant component of the exchange. One has only to recall the Watergate hearings to remember that some situations demanded both questions and answers for their full significance to emerge.

If you must use off-axis interviewing (in vox populi interviews, for instance, it is virtually unavoidable), be careful to vary the side from which you interview, or else all of your interviewees will monotonously face the same direction.

AUDIENCE PARTICIPATION

The more indirect the spectator's relationship is to the characters on the screen, the more passive and detached he is allowed to feel. When I am a spectator, someone on-screen who speaks directly to me almost challenges me to respond with a dialogue in my mind. This is much less so when an interviewee is plainly in conversation with someone offscreen.

Because watching film is inherently passive, I think filmmakers need to mobilize the audience's active sense of involvement or else the viewer (particularly in television) won't watch in an emotionally active and critical frame of mind.

SHOOTING FOR ELLIPSIS

One problem that arises in any filmed interview is how best to shoot it for abbreviation in editing. Shooting the whole interview in a one-size shot and then bridging the different sections together leads to the jump cut (Figure 14-3). In practical terms, this means that our subject's face suddenly changes expression, and his head is suddenly in a slightly different position. Today this is acceptable evidence of ellipsis, but if the film is generally transparent, that is, if it hides evidence of the editorial processes under the guise of apparent continuity, then jump cuts will violate that technique. You could cut away to a reaction shot, but they usually make the interviewer look inane.

There may be something more relevant to which you can cut. For instance, if the interviewee is talking about the Dust Bowl era, you might cut to illustrative photographs, but this can be disappointingly literal. Another photo sequence might develop its own independent story in parallel. To do this, you would probably restructure the interview somewhat and resort to the speaker's face at moments of special animation. *Parallel storytelling,* as this is called, is immensely useful because it allows the restructuring and telescoping of not just one, but both, story elements. It transcends mere illustration by developing a counterpoint whose

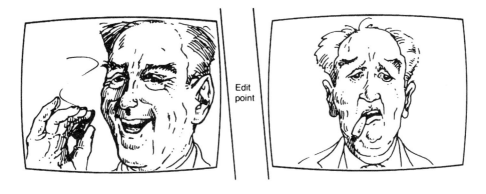

Edit
point

FIGURE 14-3 ——————————————————————————————————————

A jump cut: When footage is removed from a static camera angle, the image may jump at the cut.

meaning must be reconciled in the spectator's imagination. This is a big advance over the deadly show-and-tell of the classroom or of TV journalism.

SHOOT ALTERNATIVES

Documentarians therefore *always try to shoot each issue in several ways* to permit alternative narrative strategies. A political demonstration, for instance, would primarily be covered by footage showing the march beginning, close shots of faces and banners, the police lines, the arrests, and so on. But it might also be covered through photographs, a TV news show, participant interviews, and perhaps an interview with the police chief. This would produce a multiplicity of attitudes about the purpose of the march and a number of faces to intercut (and thus abbreviate) the stages of the march footage. Two vital purposes are thus served: multiple and conflicting viewpoints can be evoked, and the materials can be focused into a brief screen time.

Erroll Morris in *The Thin Blue Line* (1988) shoots his interviews in one unvarying shot size, but constantly cuts away to reconstructions that evoke the time, mood, or "facts" being recalled by the speaker. This heightens the subjective and even dreamlike quality of the account, drawing one into assessing each speaker's world of unreliable memory and perception.

Suppose you want to shoot an interview for which there is no valid cutaway yet still achieve abbreviation and still restructure without using the pernicious jump cut. How can it be done?

Try this yourself. During the interview have the camera operator use the zoom lens to unobtrusively change the image size; then the conventions of the screen allow you to subsequently edit segments together, provided that

- there is a bold change of image size, either larger or smaller.
- the subject is in the same attitude in the two shots

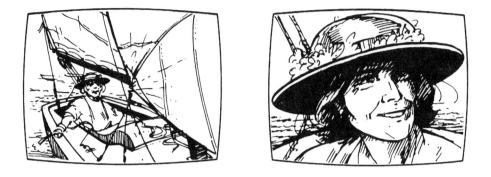

FIGURE 14-4

A match cut: By a bold change in image size, two shots can be edited together, if the images match.

- speech or other rhythms that flow across the cut are uninterrupted
- action flows across the cut uninterrupted

Because of the bold change of image size between the two frames in Figure 14-4, minor mismatches will go unnoticed by the audience, especially because *the eye does not register the first three frames of a new image.*

BRIEFING THE CAMERA OPERATOR

When I am going to interview, I first agree on three standard image sizes particular to the shot. As I interview I signal changes using unobtrusive touches on different parts of the operator's foot. Typically this will be a

- wide shot, used to cover each question
- medium shot, used after the answer has got under way
- close shot, used for anything particularly intense or revealing

During a lengthy answer I alternate between medium and close range until there is a change of topic, when I again signal for a wide shot. One place to change image size is when a speaker shows signs of repeating something (which in normal speech we do all the time). The repeat version is usually more succinct and can for ellipsis be intercut with the first version only if the image size is different or there are valid cut-ins or cutaways.

Image size-changing allows

- restructuring an interview and thus its abbreviation
- elimination of the interviewer's questions

- longer stretches of interview on the screen because the apparent camera movement, intensifying and relaxing scrutiny, answers the spectator's need for variation

More notes on camera placement appear in the next chapter, Directing Participants.

CONCLUDING THE INTERVIEW

At the end of an interview, after you have got what you want, give the participant the opportunity to add to or modify what has been recorded. After you cut the camera and thank the interviewee, make a point of acknowledging whatever was successful about the exchange. Keep everyone in place so the recordist can shoot a minute of quiet atmosphere (also called *buzz track, presence,* or *room tone*). Later the editor will use this vital substance to fill in any spaces in the track. Without authentic presence as filler, the background atmosphere would either change or go dead, signaling where each of many edits takes place.

When everyone rises to start dismantling equipment, give each participant a sum of money (often the minimum $1) and the *personal release form,* so you obtain for your records a signed permission form allowing you to use the material publicly. For the director this is always the most uncomfortable moment of all. I confess that I give the ghastly ritual to an assistant with instructions to carry it out as a necessary formality.

Very occasionally it happens that one wants to curtail an interview because the interviewee is, for whatever reason, hopelessly unsatisfactory. Every director has at some time run the camera without film in order to escape without hurting the participant's feelings. Then again, to satisfy the man in the street who wants you to "take a picture of my store," the crew will, upon a prearranged signal, solemnly go through the actions of taking a shot without actually turning the camera on. It is a small price to make a complete stranger happy.

C H A P T E R   1 5

DIRECTING PARTICIPANTS

IN SEARCH OF NATURALNESS

Documentarians are often asked, "How do you get people to look so natural?" Of course, one is tempted to shake one's head sagely and say something about many years spent learning professional secrets. Actually, naturalness is much easier to achieve than is, say, a satisfactory dramatic structure, but it still takes some directorial skill.

The key lies in the way you brief your participants. Interviewing is one way of giving direction in a documentary, but when overused it leads to a "talking head" film. In an oral history work, where nothing but survivors are left to photograph, this may be the only film possible. Most directors, however, take great pains to show people active in their own settings, doing what they normally do. In part, this is to spare the audience from the hypnotic intensity of being talked at for long periods, but there is another reason. We judge character and motivation less by what people say than by what they do, and how they do it. Film is inherently behavioral so actions speak louder than words.

So you might want to shoot the subject of your film in his family life, at work instructing an employee, and in the neighborhood bar playing pool with cronies. But each situation will be stereotypical unless it contributes behavioral revelation about either the subject or his milieu. There is also another slight hitch. For most people, normality only exists when one doesn't feel watched. I once filmed in a glass-door factory, and one of the workers, who had spent years passing frames through a machine, completely lost her facility as soon as we turned the camera on. To her embarrassment the frames began to jam or miss the jet of rubber sealer solution. Why? She was thinking about her actions instead of just doing them.

When a person feels under intense scrutiny, his whole sense of himself can fragment. The implications are critical in documentary because we aim to capture life as it really is. Sudden attacks of self-consciousness by our subjects wreck the process. The factory worker, feeling she must "act," lost automatic harmony with her machine, and there was nothing I could do except reassure her that this sometimes happens. So we waited until she managed a few rounds in her old rhythm. It was a striking example of the mind impeding the body's habitual function and illustrates that one must know how to help people stay inside their own normality.

THE MIND-BODY CONNECTION

The Russian actor and dramatic theorist, Konstantin Stanislavski, has important things to say about the mind's effect on the body. He maintains that every interior state has an outward and visible manifestation, and that when an actor becomes self-conscious instead of maintaining "focus" (experiencing the thoughts and emotions of the character), she visibly loses conviction in everything said and done. The ability to focus, to shut out the anxious and critical "other" self, is behind everyone's ability to function naturally. In everyday life we discharge our actions and relationships quite unthinkingly, but we depend on a wellspring of assumptions about what and who we are, and how we affect others. We only question these when, under exceptional circumstances, we become self-conscious. Then we cease to function harmoniously and normally.

Stanislavski stressed that an actor can only perform naturally and believably when his attention is fully occupied by the thoughts and actions of his character. To this end, both the director and actor are responsible for generating "work" natural to the actor's role, because any opportunity for unstructured thought lets the ever-anxious mind take over. Insecurity of all kinds, even fear of losing focus, leads to a loss of focus, so trained actors stay in character by remaining mentally and physically occupied. Paradoxically, it is mental and physical focus alone that lets a person be relaxed enough—whether acting or leading their personal life—to function emotionally and authentically. At such times of relaxation the person has the bodily, mental, and emotional unity that comes from pursuing goals important to him. While directing you learn to tell from a person's body language whether he is focused or in internal division.

The key to directing actors or people who are "only playing themselves" in a documentary is identical. Make sure they have plenty to do, so they aren't stultified by self-consciousness. If you ask a mother and daughter to let you film them washing the dishes at night, ask them to sustain a conversation as well. They start to discuss their plans for the next day, and now having so much familiar physical and mental activity to keep alive, they relax into obliviousness of the camera. The least helpful thing to say is, "Just be yourself." It seems to set people worrying: What did he really mean? How does he see me? And which me does he really want? Ask the participant to *do*, not *be*, something. If you are shooting a scene of two brothers making dinner, ask what they would usually be doing. If they say "Talking," ask what they usually talk about, and pick a topic that relates well to your intended film.

A contemporary solution to keeping a participant natural during the unnatural situation of being filmed is to use the technique of reflexivity. That is, to deliberately include his relationship with those behind the camera—his questions, jokes, and even uncertainty about filming—as part of the movie. This may or may not work because participants tend to deal with their unease by throwing the initiative back on the film crew. A director, invited to become a character in her own film, will usually follow the authorial tradition of giving only a modest and minimal response. Then a vacuum develops at the threshold that the director won't cross. In Nick Broomfield's hilarious *The Leader, The Driver, and the Driver's Wife* (1992), this threshold is justified. Broomfield uses boyish disingenuity to draw out the South African white supremacist Eugene Terreblanche (sic) and we know full well why Broomfield holds back. But in other films of this type, it is the director's manipulation that stands uncomfortably naked, even at times in Ross McElwee's sophisticated *Sherman's March* (1989).

When you use a nonreflexive, or "transparent" technique, tell participants that in documentary we shoot far more than we use, so they shouldn't worry about mistakes or silences because you expect to edit. Also, ask participants to ignore the crew's presence and *not look at the camera*. This prevents them from falling into the trap of "playing to the audience." The crew can help by concentrating on their jobs, avoiding eye contact, and giving no facial or verbal feedback.

Should participants feel that you are trying to manipulate or misrepresent them, they become uncomfortable or even uncooperative. But if you establish justifiable and trustworthy reasons for making the film, participants usually take part with touching composure. With good will, common sense, and some ingenuity, naturalness and spontaneity on the documentary screen are the norm. This can be very revealing when an oppressive middle-aged couple, for example, fall into a recurring argument about what food the dog should have tomorrow.

Not infrequently people reveal their abiding passions. I once filmed old miners describing the bitter days of the 1926 General Strike in England. We filmed overlooking the mine in question, and the camera went within 2 feet of their faces as they relived the greatest events of their lives. They had lost all awareness of being filmed because they were reliving events that embodied the deepest and most divisive issues in their community. Our camera's attention lent the moment a special gravity and meaning, so their involvement was deeply emotional and left no attention to spare for how they might appear to us or the world beyond our camera.

I saw the same thing during a drama improvisation when Aiden Quinn and a partner afterward had no memory of our roving camera's presence. They had been too involved in the improv to even notice it. Drama and life being lived in the imagination can be one and the same thing—consuming.

SELF-IMAGE AND SELF-CONSCIOUSNESS

The easiest people to work with are those oblivious to their effect on others. Old people and small children are natural because there is no ego, no internal censor at work. Knowing this, you can predict who is going to present difficulties; those compulsively careful of their appearance or with many nervous mannerisms are least likely to be at peace in front of a camera. During a street interview I once had a lady completely lose focus. I was puzzled as to what had happened until, in midsentence, she began to remove the hair net she realized she was still wearing. The more "proper" someone feels they must look for the record, the less flexible, impulsive, and openly communicative that person is likely to be.

But care and circumspection were this lady's stamp, so the action was also wonderfully representative. Her friends, seeing the film, would smile in recognition. It's fascinating that the camera still did not make her behave uncharacteristically.

People often say, "But the presence of the camera *must* change people." I answer that it only changes the aspect or degree of a person's response. Neither the camera nor any other form of observation can make anyone act out of character because it cannot change their underlying nature. Indeed, the camera sometimes catalyzes an honesty and depth of feeling seldom seen by a participant's closest friends. When the human craving for recognition is fulfilled, the floodgates may open wide.

There is one further observation that you should find liberating: Because you film something doesn't mean you have to use it, so there's no need to be unduly protective while shooting. Later in the cutting room, you will have time and advisers to help you thoroughly consider the implications of your footage. Documentarians often decide, for one reason or another, not to use material. In rare cases, filmmakers have destroyed footage (shot in repressive or totalitarian countries, say, or implicating gangsters) when they realize that its very existence endangers someone's life. One exception here is when you shoot for a program or series, and someone else has editorial control of your material. If you can lose complete editorial control, never shoot anything that may injure your participants or yourself.

WHY YOUR MOTIVES FOR FILMING MATTER

You and your camera will only plumb the depths of someone's life if she senses that you and your crew personally accept, like, and value her. A documentary is a record of relationships, so success depends on what takes place before the camera is ever switched on. For this reason I avoid topics or participants for which I feel little interest or empathy. I once embarked with very mixed feelings on a film about Sir Oswald Mosley and his 1930s British Union of Fascists (*The Battle of Cable Street*). We set about tracing people who would admit to being followers, and in the end I interviewed Mosley himself. I was apprehensive not only about the violence that surrounded those people but also about the disgust I felt for their values. I was afraid of their reputation for evil. As it happened, Hannah Arendt's phrase about the banality of evil fitted the situation better than any of my imaginings. The British upholders of the ideology that exterminated 11 million people were shockingly ordinary; no horns or cloven feet to be seen. They were anxious to present their case and even made a specious kind of sense. The only stance that researcher Jane Oliver and I needed to take was that of younger people wishing to learn history from its protagonists.

During the lengthy editing period, I found myself both fascinated and repelled by Mosley. An urbane, upper-class member of the establishment, he had egocentrically distorted everything connected with himself. I wanted to relay his version of the 1936 events, yet show what a self-delusion his version was. The film contrived to satisfy the Left (who opposed the freedom Mosley was given to organize racial hatred), and even Mosley himself, because he had expected to have his account distorted.

Part of creating trust is explaining plausibly why you want to shoot a particular scene or topic. You can get a taxi driver to chat to the camera while he cruises looking for a fare because it is his reality and he enjoys sharing it. You may discreetly film a woman in her morning bath because it was in this very bath that she took the momentous decision to visit Egypt. You can film an old man feeding his dog and talking to it because he believes you too feel this is a special part of a special life. Organizations, especially those on the political left, are much more likely to be paranoid than are individuals. At any moment you may need to make explanations of why you are filming this topic or this scene, and you should make it as simple and uncontroversial as you can. Your explanations should be consistent because participants often exchange notes, but they should not be so specific that you box yourself into a corner.

OBSTACLES: HABITS OF BEING

Particular jobs attract particular kinds of people, and some employment seems to generate mannerisms and self-awarenesses that are a liability in filmmaking, unless, of course, it is these very characteristics you want to show. Many officials, afraid of alienating superiors and unused to public statement, make excruciatingly boring and self-conscious contributions. Lecturers and politicians on camera will address invisible multitudes instead of talking one-on-one as they did so nicely during research.

Pressured or misunderstood circumstances cause people to fall back on custom, and many ingrained habits of behavior are hard or even impossible to change. Before you try to alter a participant's idea of how one should relate to the camera, estimate what is habit and what is only a misperception about filming. The latter you may be able to alter. For instance, the person who seems to be addressing a large audience can sometimes be redirected by simply saying, "There is only one person, me, listening to you. Talk only to me." Another mistaken notion that has horrendous consequences is the idea that one must project the voice. If the person cannot respond to direction, a little playback may do the trick. Because people are often shocked when first seeing or hearing themselves, exposing an unsatisfactory "performance" should be a last resort, to be done privately and supportively.

Sometimes you will get someone whose concept of a film appearance is taken from commercials and who valiantly tries to project *personality*. This is still true to an aspect of the individual's character and assumptions: If you are making a film about stage mothers who want their children to learn acting for commercials, you could hardly ask for anything more revealing.

A person's response to being filmed may or may not be appropriate, but some thought beforehand can prepare you for what's likely. Choosing participants is "casting" as much as it would be for a fiction film. Documentaries are not truth itself but dramatic constructs made from found or catalyzed life materials. Who you use affects what you end up saying.

COMPROMISES FOR THE CAMERA

When shooting action sequences, you may need to ask people to slow down or control their movements because movement in general, once it has a frame round it, looks perhaps 20 to 30 percent faster. Then again, the operator's fanciest foot-work cannot keep a hand nicely framed and in focus if its owner moves too fast.

How willing are you to intrude to get a result that is visually and choreo-graphically accomplished? The ethnographer will want to intrude as little as pos-sible into the life being documented, and the most intrusive documentarians still have a lot of the ethnographer in them. But as Godard perceived, if you start out making a documentary, you are driven toward fictional techniques, and if you make fiction, you will be compelled toward documentary. Even in the most mechanized Hollywood drama shoot, there is always an element of improvisation and inventiveness that leaves the camera documenting a "happening."

If you are shooting outdoors, especially in a public place or where there are crowds, do not be afraid to penetrate areas you would normally not enter. The camera is your license, so use it to cross police lines, go to the front of a crowd, or squeeze between people looking in a shop window. In western countries, the cam-era's right to do this is accepted as part of the freedom of the press. Of course, this is a cultural assumption not made everywhere. A colleague went to film in Nigeria and learned (through being stoned) that taking a person's image without asking first is regarded as theft.

MAINTAINING SCREEN DIRECTION

Camera placement is one of the few areas where a little ignorance can produce catastrophic results. Some theoretical knowledge can avoid all this. Because film presents the pieces of an artfully fragmented world, the audience is mentally as-sembling an image of the whole for each succeeding location. In film, four partial angles of individuals in a room are enough for the audience to conjure up an idea of the entire room and its occupants. To avoid confounding this useful process, the director should know the rules that maintain a sense of geographical consis-tency.

Let us imagine you are shooting a parade. You must decide ahead of time (based on background or lighting factors) from which side of the parade you in-tend to shoot. By shooting from only one side, everyone in every shot will march across the screen in the same direction, say, screen left to screen right. If you were to hop through the parade halfway and film from the other side, your parade on-screen would start marching in the reverse direction, screen right to screen left. Intercutting this material will cause the viewer to wonder: Is this a counterdemon-stration marching from another direction? Is this another wing, marching away toward another destination?

To maintain screen directions, the camera must *stay to one side of a scene axis or invisible line*. You can draw an axis between two people having a conversation, as illustrated in Figure 15-1. As long as your camera stays to *one side of that line,* the character in black will always look left to right, and the character in white will always be looking right to left across the screen. Three different camera angles are shown in Figure 15-1: B is a two shot, and A and C are over-the-shoulder shots. Look at the resulting frames. You can intercut any one with the others.

Should you take up position D, however, the camera has "crossed the line," and we have a problem. Compare frame D with its complementary shots. The

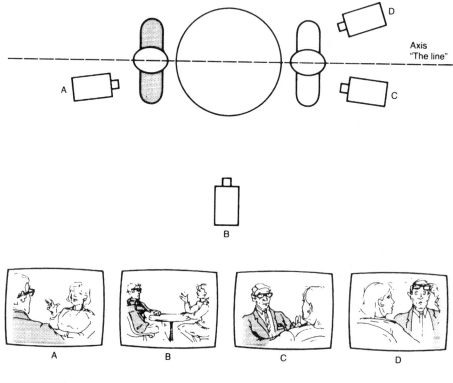

FIGURE 15-1 ——

"Crossing the line": The three images produced from camera positions A, B, and C all intercut because the characters maintain their screen directions. Position D, however, produces a composition that reverses the characters' eyelines and would not intercut with the other angles. Position D has crossed the invisible line between the characters.

character in black is now facing in the same screen direction as the character in white. This makes no sense! This is the cardinal filmmaking transgression called *crossing the line*. Of course, there is no sin without redemption, so in fact you *can* cross the line halfway through the conversation, but you would have to dolly the camera sideways during the shot from position B to position D so the audience sees the camera *moving to the new position*. From here onward, all new angles must be shot from the new side of the line to preserve the revised logic of screen direction.

In a situation like a parade, where you have people and objects on the move, you can cover yourself by taking safety shots that show a change of direction on-screen. Figure 15-2 shows how the parade, after marching right to left, turns a corner and now marches left to right. By including several direction-change shots in a day's shooting, you can shoot from either side of the parade and rest assured that it should all cut together in a logical flow.

FIGURE 15-2

Changing screen direction: The procession starting right to left changes to left to right all in the one shot. This is a useful shot to keep in reserve because, in showing a change of direction, it allows you to shoot from both sides of the axis and still cut shots together in a logical flow.

When you shoot people at a garden party or in a museum, where they are free to move around, they will regroup and face in new screen directions during the scene. This means that early and late material won't intercut and editing a scene to give it a more logical development may be hard or impossible. Shooting cutaway reaction shots will help, especially if the subject's moving eyeline indicates someone moving offscreen. Remember to shoot these to cover all likely directions of movement. You may need to manufacture these shots by asking a bystander to follow someone on the move with their eyes.

MOTIVATION FOR CAMERA POSITIONING
AND CAMERA MOVEMENT

Recommending camera positioning is difficult because every scene has its nature to be revealed and the inherent limitations of its environment. These are usually physical: windows or pillars in an interior that restrict shooting to one direction or an incongruity to be avoided in an exterior. A genuine settler's log cabin might have to be framed low in order to avoid seeing, above the ancient trees, an ominous revolving sausage proclaiming the neighborhood hot-dog emporium.

CHANCE . . . ?

Making films, and especially making documentaries, is serendipitous and plans must often be jettisoned to accommodate the unforeseen. Such limitations shape film art to a degree undreamed of by film critics. You will often feel challenged by the magnetic pull of roads not taken, or not yet. Suddenly your beliefs, values, and preparation are all under siege from the gods of chance.

Sometimes serendipity participates in eerie ways. The British miners mentioned earlier sabotaged a scab coal train in the 1926 General Strike, and while I was in their area making the film, an express train derailed close to the original site. It happened during the night prior to interviewing a doctor who had participated in the 1926 incident. He knew we were coming the next day, and thought he must be dreaming when summoned to a train crash in the small hours. After some soul-searching about voyeurism, I altered our plans to film the wreckage, because

FIGURE 15-3

Be ready to adapt to the unexpected: an unplanned train wreck that occurred at the site while filming *The Cramlington Train-Wreckers*.

it brought home like nothing else the destruction the saboteurs risked by their demonstration (Figure 15-3).

For some, adapting to the unexpected is frustrating, while for others it is the soul of existence and represents a challenge to their inventiveness and insight. The temptation is not to make plans. But one must, and sometimes plans even work out.

SCENE BREAKDOWN AND CRIB NOTES

The first step in filming any scene is to determine what it must establish and goals for what it should contribute to the planned film. As always, list these so nothing gets overlooked in the heat of battle. If, for instance, you are shooting in a laboratory, you might make a reminder, or crib note on an index card as shown in Figure 15-4.

Less tangibly, you also might also want to show that the lab workers are dedicated and even heroic. This is your bottom line; you cannot leave without getting shots that establish these things.

Then, treating the camera as an observing consciousness, you must imagine in detail *how you want the scene to be experienced*. If you were shooting a boozy wedding, it would make no sense to use carefully placed tripod shots. It's better for the camera to adopt a guest's point of view; by going handheld and peering into circles of chattering people, it can legitimately bump into raucous revelers, quiz the principals, and even join in the dancing.

LAB SEQUENCE

Remember to show:

lab's general layout

that six people work there

three kinds of equipment

four experiments going on

one experiment is dangerous

FIGURE 15-4 ———————————————————

Crib note: goals for a laboratory sequence written on an index card.

If, however, you were to shoot in a courtroom with its elaborate ritualized performances, the placing and amount of coverage by the camera would be quite different and certainly should not be unsteady and mobile.

Whatever the shooting situation, ask yourself:

- Whose point of view is the audience mostly sharing?
- Where does the majority of the telling action lie? (In the courtroom, e.g., does it lie with judge, plaintiff, prosecutor, or the jury?)
- When is point of view likely to change, and to whom?
- What factual or physical details are essential to imply the whole?
- What will be each essential stage of development that I must cover?
- What signals the start and end of each developmental stage?

Camera positioning can change a piece of an action's statement. Isolating two people in two separate close shots, for instance, and intercutting them, will have a very different feel than cutting between two over-the-shoulder shots. In the single shots, the observer is always alone with one of the contenders, but in the over-the-shoulder shots their relationship in space and time is shown, not manufactured through editing, so the viewer constantly sees one in relation to the other.

There is no mystery here; your guide to how an audience will respond always lies with the common experience and the common sense that makes you and I alike, that makes us react and understand similarly when sharing an unfolding situation. Where we are, what we see, in what order things unfold, affect us similarly; if not, cinema would not be the universal language that it is. *Knowledge of cinema, therefore, comes from growing self-perception.* If this is too slow or too ambiguous for you, you can always "audition" different fiction and documentary approaches to situations similar to yours to see how others have done it. Remember that whenever you get sucked into imitating the practice of others, you risk losing yourself in theoretical abstraction. This is the negative side of film schooling; in teaching the range of film language, it tends to inhibit the very instincts that lead to an individual voice.

Another camera positioning issue lies in deciding how the background is to comment on the foreground. If a participant is in a wheelchair, and the shot contains a window with a vista of people in the street, the composition will unobtrusively juxtapose her with what she is so poignantly denied.

Looking down on the subject, looking up at the subject, or looking at it between the bars of a railing can all suggest different ways of seeing—and, therefore, ways of experiencing—the action that makes the scene. Don't leave the camera to be a passive recorder; make it into a instrument of ironic juxtaposition or disclosure. True, revelation can be manufactured through editing, but so much more is accomplished by observation and juxtaposition that is built into the shooting.

Exploit the location fully for its own signs and revelation, and make your camera respond to how participants' movements and actions convey the scene's subtext. The difference is between sharing the consciousness of someone intelligent and intuitive, who picks up the event's underlying tensions, and sharing the consciousness of an eye that swivels dully toward whatever moves.

How best to shoot one's movie is answered by asking how one might inhabit its events at a very high level of consciousness. Transfer this inhabiting to the screen, and you are on your way.

HANDHELD OR TRIPOD-MOUNTED CAMERA?

A tripod-mounted camera can zoom in to hold a steady close shot without crowding whoever is being filmed, but it cannot suddenly move to a better vantage should the action call for it. The handheld camera gives this mobility, but at the price of unsteadiness. Going handheld may be the only solution when you cannot predict the action or know only that it will take place somewhere in a given area. New camcorders are equipped with image stabilizers that compensate (sometimes rather successfully) for the kind of operator unsteadiness that comes from the occasional need to breathe.

The two kinds of camera-presence—one studied, composed, and controlled and the other mobile, spontaneous, and physically reactive to change—contribute a quite different sense of involvement, imply quite different relationships to the action, and alter the film's storytelling "voice."

The *tripod-mounted camera* always "sees" from the same point in space, no matter which direction the camera pans or tilts. Even when zooming in, the perspective remains the same, reiterating how much the observation is rooted in an assigned place. This feeling would be appropriate for a courtroom, because the positions of judge, jury, witness box, and audience are all symbolic and preordained by seating. Because no court would tolerate a wandering audience member, it is logical that the camera/observer also be fixed.

The *handheld camera* is an intelligence on legs. Because the close end of the zoom is impractical, the lens must be kept at wide angle, and the camera must be moved through space if a long shot is to become a close shot. Changes in perspective alone make this dynamic relocation apparent. During a handheld conversation, the camera may reframe, reposition itself, and change image size many times to produce all the shots one would expect in an edited version: a long shot, medium two-shots, complementary over-the-shoulder shots, and big close-ups. Covering a spontaneous event with a well-balanced succession of such shots is a rare skill that calls for the sensibility of an editor, director, and camera operator in one person. Because human life generates much redundancy, these shots can often be edited to approximate the feature film's elegant freedom of access to its characters. However, if the cutting is too elegant, it will throw doubt on the spontaneity of the edited material.

Successful handheld work conveys something twofold: the feeling of a spontaneous, uncut event unfolding, and simultaneously that it is being assessed by a discriminating intelligence. This astute, comprehensive view is formal and relatively invisible in fiction filmmaking, but in handheld documentary it is manifestly a daring improvisation, something unfolding on the run. Good camerawork is therefore a matter of acute concentration and acute sensitivity to underlying issues. Why else would the Hollywood veteran Haskell Wexler call documentary "real filmmaking"?

SPECIAL PHOTOGRAPHY

Documentaries sometimes include material that must be shot under special conditions, such as graphics on a rostrum camera, mountaineering on a sheer rock face, underwater, from a helicopter, or, if the subject includes insect life, through a high-power lens. At such times the director is in the hands of a specialist. The relationship may be pleasantly instructional or it may be uncomfortable and confusing. Experts can be wonderful or (as everyone knows who's gone shopping for a hardware widget with an infinitely forgettable name) they can use their knowledge to intimidate. Research the process and the personnel beforehand so you remain in control of your filming. Bullying, subtle or blatant, is apt to take place whenever the pecking order is upset. A young director can expect some flak from older crew members, a woman's authority may be challenged by male subordinates, and a foreigner may feel pressure from the indigenous. All are tiresomely human, so be on guard.

USING SOCIAL TIMES AND BREAKS

During production spend time outside shooting with your participants. It is a mistake to retreat to the understanding company of the crew, however exhausted you may be. Without imposing, try to keep the crew and participants together during meals or rest periods. Frequently, while lunching or downing a beer together, you will make discoveries that help your ideas evolve. Being engaged in filmmaking generates a higher consciousness in everyone, and shakes out many memories and associations. It also develops a shared intensity of purpose and adventure, which binds everyone together. Conserved and encouraged, this excitement makes a more profound fellowship and communication inevitable.

This energizes even a jaded crew, and an aware and involved crew act as an antenna, alerting you to things said or done beyond your knowledge. While we were making a film about Dr. Spock during his anti-Vietnam War rallies, the sound recordist Roger Turner picked up a radio broadcast calling for demonstrators at a Christian prowar rally. As a result, we changed our plans and went to Trenton, New Jersey, where we filmed proponents of the Vietnam War in full cry. This came at a time when I was overwhelmed with fatigue and was low on ideas. Crew initiatives can sometimes be gold.

WRAPPING

At the end of a day's shoot, make a point of thanking both the crew and participants personally. Be especially careful that all possessions and furniture have been replaced exactly as found. Attention to the details of someone else's home signifies your concern and appreciation, and helps ensure that you will be welcome if you want to return. Initial reluctance to accept a film crew's presence often comes because people have heard a horror story about another crew that was inconsiderate.

LIMITS TO THE FORM

A predictable topic when documentary makers get together over a beer is always what is or is not documentary. Allegiance to fact is fundamental, but Grierson's "the creative treatment of actuality" is pretty good, and Zola's "A work of art is a corner of nature seen through a temperament" is even better. There are no rules in this young art form, only decisions about where to draw lines and how to remain consistent to the contract you will set up with your audience.

Documentary film can include: acted reconstructions of events long before living memory, docudrama (a form of re-enactment mixing actors and real people), and re-enactment of previous events by the protagonists themselves. Ruth First, formerly imprisoned in South Africa, acted her own story in reconstructed surroundings and with actors playing the parts of guards and interrogators. Is this documentary? I think it can be, depending on its authorial goals and the fidelity to what was actual. If First's experience had included hallucinations from hunger or torture, these should be recreated in the spirit of the truth. Her art must have done its job powerfully enough, for the racist oligarchy she unmasked made sure she was assassinated.

C H A P T E R   1 6

DIRECTING THE CREW

Some aspects to directing a crew are:

- communicating the schedule and purpose before the shoot
- making sure everyone knows (and keeps to) their areas of responsibility
- moment-to-moment communications during the shoot
- encouraging the crew to act supportively towards the participants
- encouraging solidarity and maintaining professionalism when there are internal disagreements
- keeping the crew attuned to the project's larger dimensions so they can make creative contributions beyond the confines of their own specialty

SCHEDULING AND COMMUNICATION

Day-to-day direction should begin from a comprehensive printed schedule with timely updates in cases of change. Include travel directions and a location contact phone number in case of emergency. *Everything of possible importance should be written down* since shooting is no time to test people's powers of recall. If you want professional reliability from your crew, you must first be a model of professionalism yourself. Be formal about the chain of responsibility at first. After incontestable proof of a person's trustworthiness, you can relax the traditional structure as appropriate. Starting informal and then trying to tighten up is a recipe for mutiny.

Once everyone is present at the location, reiterate the immediate goals. You might want a store to look shadowy and fusty, or to emphasize a child's view of the squalor of a trailer park. Confirm the first setup, so the crew can get the equipment ready. A clear working relationship with your DP will relieve you from deciding a myriad of details that might detract from your main responsibility, which is toward authorial coherence. Now get busy preparing the participants.

Beginning directors usually try to shoot too much in a given time. After a few grueling days, work gets sloppy and the crew resentful and hypercritical. Err on the light side, because a crew in good shape is always ready to shorten a given schedule by working longer, while a crew suffering from terminal fatigue may rebel at the idea of an extra 2 hours. Treat your crew reasonably and they will rise to crises selflessly.

Here's something else to remember: Because the director is fully involved, you tend to overlook mere bodily inconveniences, such as hunger, cold, and fatigue. If you want a happy crew, keep to an 8-hour working day, and have meals and coffee breaks built predictably into the schedule. A flask of coffee and packets of sandwiches produced at the right moment will work miracles on a weary crew's morale. On long shoots, crews need time off. When I first directed abroad, Brian Lewis, my producer, advised that I allow time for sightseeing and shopping for presents to take home. As with all of his advice, it proved excellent.

MAINTAINING COMMUNICATION

The director must first outline intended filming for the crew, and during the shoot should keep them abreast of developments—something it's fatally easy to forget when the pressure is on. During breaks encourage discussion of the production. One can learn much from mainly listening. At first you may be shocked by the lack of all-around observation by key crew members. The reason is simple: A good camera operator concentrates wholly on composition, lighting, shadows, framing, and camera movements. Only to a minor degree can he or she be aware of content. Likewise for the diligent sound recordist, words are less important than voice quality, unwanted noise or echo, and the balance of sound levels.

Crew members monitor a restricted area of *quality*, each tending a particular vegetable patch, oblivious to the garden as a whole unless the director periodically invests time and energy in connecting them to the project as a conceptual entity. Some crew members will not appreciate your efforts. But if you want a farsighted crew, take pains to share your thinking on both local and global terms. It takes special and sometimes unfamiliar effort for a crew member to consider the work in hand from an authorial standpoint, so crew feedback should never go unacknowledged even when embarrassingly off target. Make mental adjustment for any skewed valuations and be diplomatic with advice you can't use. Above all, encourage involvement.

MONITORING AND INSTRUCTING

Each time you start shooting, allow a minimum of 10 seconds of equipment runup time before you say "Action" to your participants. Good action immediately after a camera start may be unusable because the editing runup requirements cannot be met. Another good reason for runup is that you may have color and picture instability problems until mechanical and electronic coordinations in the equipment have stabilized.

Before and after shooting, always look through the camera to see if what you expect is really there. This is of paramount importance when you use film; it is too late to correct misunderstandings as you watch rushes days or weeks later.

Always stand right next to the camera so you see as nearly as possible what it sees. Relay minimal camera directions by whispering into the operator's ear, making sure, of course, that your voice will not spoil a recording. Be brief and specific: "Go to John in medium shot," "Pull back to a wide shot of all three," or "If he goes into the kitchen again, walk with him and follow what he does."

Your sound recordist adapts to the action and to what the camera does, but will probably shoot you meaningful glances now and then. Listening for quality, she will grow agitated at the approach of a plane or the rumble of a refrigerator that has turned itself on in the next room. Wearing headphones, she will have no idea which direction the interference is coming from and will look around in alarm. She may draw her finger across her throat (industry sign for "cut") so that you find yourself being wordlessly beseeched to call "cut!"

You have to make a decision and your head pounds from stress. You are supposed to be keenly aware of ongoing content and yet resolve through glances and hand signals all sorts of problems—problems of sound, of shadows, of people who have done the unexpected, or of pets who have escaped temporary bondage. At such times the director is blinded by sensory overload.

Before allowing the crew to wrap, cast your mind back over the events you have filmed and itemize cutaway shots or inserts (sometimes called *cut-ins*) to shoot in case you later need to shorten or cross-cut segments. For instance, during an interview with a carpenter in his workshop, I noticed that he folded and unfolded his rule below frame as he spoke. The close shot we took enabled me to bridge together two separate sections of the interview and also to visually explain the strange clicking noises coming from offscreen. Many times you will use eyeline shifts to "motivate" cutaways. For instance, if someone says it is getting late and looks up, you would shoot an insert of the clock. If he looks moodily out of a window, you would do a cutaway of his point of view. Frequently a person will show a picture, refer to an object in the room, or look offscreen at someone, and in each case he directs our attention to a legitimate cutaway.

The difference between a cutaway and a cut-in is that a cutaway is beyond the frame, while a cut-in is a magnification of something already in frame. Sometimes a cutaway or cut-in will reflect an authorial attitude. For example, in the kitchen of a neglected elderly man, the tap drips incessantly. You film a close shot of it and of the dusty, yellowing photographs on his shelf in the background because it speaks volumes about long-standing disregard. Such shots, drawing the viewer's eye to significant detail, are narrative rather than action motivated, and express an authorial point.

When shooting two or more people, shoot listening or reaction close-up shots of each individual. These are worth their weight in gold to the editor. Never leave a scene, interior or exterior, without shooting a *presence track,* that is, an audio background filler shot with the same mike position, same recording level, and with everyone keeping silent and still for 2 minutes (also called a *buzz track* or *room tone*).

NEGATIVE ATTITUDES IN THE PROFESSION

Interestingly, the situation for the film crew is opposite that of the participants. While participants need a sense of purpose and work on which to focus, the crew has ready-made work, which can insulate them from responsibility to a larger purpose. Too often, seasoned crew members bury themselves in technical or "company" concerns and signify disconnection by their attitudes, remarks, or lack of involvement.

This is not malice, but an exigency of the job. Unfortunately, working under pressure for large concerns turns many a good person into a production-line operative. Because corporations are steered by competition and the profit motive, the crew member feels like a foot soldier shunted cynically from pillar to post. Even the excitement of going to distant places wears off. Seriously jaded crews begin to rate the production solely by the level of hotels and restaurants to which they are taken. The terminally institutionalized know both company and union rules backwards, and care not at all about filmmaking. They will lay down tools on the stroke of the clock and compute their overtime to the penny.

I do not mean to detract from the achievements of the craft unions in protecting their members from the gross exploitation that has bedeviled film technicians since the dawn of our industry. There were, and still are, huge profits to be made in entertainment, and it is absolutely right that those who create the product should share in the rewards. However, rules and restrictions become the refuge for the third-rate worker, whose presence is adverse in any small, tight-knit operation.

The problem begins with the aptitudes and education (in the broadest sense) of the individual.

Many working in film and television are inadequately or narrowly educated, and as a result have built defenses around themselves. Directors disassociate themselves from the technical problems of their sound and camera people, and draw ill-informed and emotional conclusions; sound and camera personnel remain within tightly drawn compartments of technical operation and avoid acknowledging the conceptual problems inherent in directing.

If you are sympathetic toward the crew's problems, they will be generous when you want their help solving one of yours.

WORKING ATMOSPHERE

The transition into shooting should hide the excitement and tension you may feel and instead be a time of serious, focused attention. Shooting should take place in as calm an atmosphere as possible, and the crew should convey warnings or questions discreetly through signs. For instance, the recordist or camcorder operator may hold up three fingers to discreetly indicate that only 3 minutes of tape are left. It is important that, in potentially divisive situations, only the director gives out information or makes decisions. Any disagreement or dissent among the crew should be kept scrupulously away from the participants. For them, a calm, respectful atmosphere is a necessity. The crew should preserve outward unity at all costs and should, as a matter of professionalism, make no comment or observation that might undermine the authority of the director.

Filmmaking, although collaborative, is seldom democratic. A crew used to each other can be very informal, but there must be lines of responsibility respected on all sides if the unit is not to look foolish and discordant. The prime reason behind student film breakdowns is that each crew member considers himself more competent to lead than the person actually directing. As difficulties arise, well meant but contradictory advice showers down on the director. Such disunity of purpose soon generates alarm and despondency in the participants and crew.

THE PROBLEM OF HAVING AUTHORITY

The major anxiety for the beginning director is of lacking competency and authority. Authoritativeness is not something a person can just assume, especially under what one imagines is hostile scrutiny. Therefore, choose colleagues carefully and, once you have started a collaborative relationship, work to reduce the misunderstandings and compartmentalizations that grow like barnacles on any enterprise. Take time to understand your crew's concerns and problems, and make every effort to include them in the conceptual considerations of the film. This, in turn, invites suggestions that may not be practical or desirable. Unless everyone understands from the outset that only a director can decide ultimately what goes into a film, the director's openness may be misconstrued as an invitation to make the film by committee.

The balances involved in respectful collaboration are delicate, but won't be a problem for the person who finds his function in the unit fulfilling. Not all groups of people behave so maturely and responsibly. Sometimes there are odd chemistries, and one must be alert to the fact that groups react to the pressure and intensity of filmmaking in unpredictable though always revealing ways. The director, though at the center of all this, cannot necessarily control what goes on. Simultaneously the information center and parental figure, the director is usually found wanting somewhere, so reconcile yourself to sometimes having to tough it out, and to being unpopular. It goes with the territory.

That said, most who choose to work in documentary are fine, dedicated people. It is unwise to try to fool them or to make claims beyond your knowledge. Having authority really means being respected; it means having the humility to ask for help or advice when you genuinely need it.

A good way to develop mutual understanding is to see and discuss films together and to analyze rushes of your own project. Television crews seldom see their own material, except on the air after editing, and are thus routinely denied the chance to learn from their own mistakes. Ideally, the crew should be present at salient points during postproduction, when the growth and internal complexity of the film come under intense scrutiny. It is here, if anywhere, that the comprehensiveness of the director's work begins to show, and that crew members understand the contribution they have (or haven't) made.

AUTHORSHIP

SCRIPTING

Some readers may be looking in perplexity for information on how to write a script. But a modern documentary is an improvisation fashioned from real-life materials, so trying to write a very detailed script would rob the result of spontaneity by forcing participants into the role of actors. However, there are several nonfiction genres that each have some degree of preplanned relationship between words and images, such as the:

- *compilation* film, made up from library or other available footage and achieving its continuity and meaning through narration, voice-over, and music
- *nature* film
- *science* or *medical* film
- *travelogue*
- *educational* film
- *historical* or *social science* film
- *biographical* film
- *informational* film

Because the function of so much factual film is to convey information, scripting can be useful and timesaving. Many of the categories just listed can be planned by using the split page script format shown in Figure 6-2 of Chapter 6. Much favored by news, scientific, corporate, industrial, and educational sponsors, who have little use for the more organic creative process, the script gives a highly detailed, if misleadingly final, idea of what a film will be. The weakness is that it shows didactic goals and not what the material's idiosyncrasies support. Any good editor will confirm that one discovers the true potential of screen materials only after experimenting with the sound and picture materials themselves.

Whenever an emotional significance arises from the interplay of words and images, as in Ken Burns' *Civil War* series (1990), which was made entirely from 1860s words and images, you will always need to be guided in the editing room by the actual impact from the screen, and be ready to make a myriad of significant adjustments.

In live-action documentary, scripting is limited to making a proposal and planning a structure to contain the materials you expect to get. You may even write a treatment. But you should list intended sequences and assign to each the contribution you hope it will make.

DEFINING AND FULFILLING YOUR INTENTIONS

The toughest demand on the director during shooting is to determine whether you are fulfilling your intentions and to know "if you have a film." I want to stress that without the working hypothesis mentioned earlier to guide all aspects of your direction, you will surely be rudderless during the shoot. That carefully wrought definition of intent is *vital!*

Here is a sample of intentions for an imaginary film about Hans, a likable, impulsive engineer I knew who lost the battle against cancer. An overall statement would say, "These scenes must establish this German immigrant engineer's decision to sell all he has worked for and to jettison his whole life in order to try to buy back his health and future."

Hans lived above his Chicago electric-motor shop. In the back was a workshop of staggering size and untidiness, containing many large metalworking and electrical machines. After looking at all this, a documentary director would make up, in her head or on paper, a shopping list of shots and sequences annotated with their intended meaning:

Scene	Intended Meaning
Hans at shop counter, afternoon.	Last normal day of business.
Hans descending stairs from apartment, morning.	Morning, a new day.
Hans in greasy-spoon restaurant eating breakfast.	Listless, sad, unresponsive to friends.
He arrives at shop, walks through.	Change of routine, ominous.
Stands high above his silent workshop; begins to tour the metal shop, picks up one or two items.	Making his last rites.
Drawer with photographs emptied.	Collecting, sifting through his past.
Other clearing out, ending shots.	Collecting, sifting through his past.
Shock cut to auction: Hans stands impassively as machine after machine is auctioned.	Hans stoic, numb, betrays no feeling.
Check being signed.	The price of his life's work.

Torn papers in waste bin.	Break with the past.
Subjective shot, walking into building with "Mayo Clinic" sign.	Feeling what it is like to enter as a frightened, sick person.
Voice-over: Receptionist greeting him, telling him his room is ready, etc.	

These are based on what Hans is expected to do. The list shows not just expected shots but what feeling and information are desired from each, and what impact the various brief scenes should have on the audience, both factually and emotionally, as the story builds. My example for the Hans film, treated as a script, looks rigid and too locked down. But it's only a safety net, something to remind me what to look for, what to expect, how to get a decent range of material. It is a resource, not a straitjacket.

MEASURING PROGRESS

Keep your intentions clear and handy so you can make running checks. Keep nothing in your head that can be dumped onto a piece of paper. During the shoot, you generally suffer a gnawing doubt just when you are supposed to be feeling "creative." This, of course, is nothing you dare share with anybody. When you define what story points must be made, and have nailed down what you need from each sequence, you are directing from a plan of campaign. You can now, at any juncture, assess whether you have won or lost the individual battles. This is made hard only because you are usually *under*whelmed by what takes place before the camera. Later, in the rushes, you usually find a great deal more than you imagined.

DIGGING BELOW THE SURFACE

It is important when directing to delegate everything you can. If you micromanage your crew you will be too busy to see "subtext" in each situation—the real meaning lying below the surface and hidden from all but the dedicated observer. Often, if not always, there are hints of something else imminent, some other unacknowledged truth just under the surface. Be alert and ready to back your instincts. Just leaving the camera running may tip the balance and make it emerge. A few words of side-coaching from you might steer the scene toward the confrontation you strongly sense wants to happen. *Side-coaching* means you interpolate, at a static moment in the scene, a verbal suggestion or instruction, such as "Richard, try asking her what she really means."

If your instinct is right, the real magic happens, and the genie comes out of the bottle. You can best grasp after him by asking yourself:

- What life roles are these people playing?
- What dramatic characters do they remind me of?

- What human truth is being played out?
- What metaphor sums up what is happening?

Metaphysical questions make you search for the more universal but invisible event in progress. In my Hans film one sees him selling his life's collection of tools and getting rid of memorabilia before entering a hospital. Sad but necessary, one thinks. But to stop there is to miss the point. What he is really doing is daring and desperate: Betting everything in one last convulsive gamble. By destroying his past, he is saying to the gods, "If I let go of everything I've ever loved, will you let me live a little longer?"

Here a man refuses the inevitable, and bargains with the devil clutching at his coat tails. He is a latter-day Faust. As soon as one realizes he is Faust, then you know what mood you want to create throughout, and how you will shoot his workshop machinery to show a kind of power that he abandons.

The director's enemy is the passive, uncritical habit of accepting life's surfaces as "what is." What distinguishes the artist from the common person is the habit of treating life's superficialities as a cunning deception, a mask to be peeled away in search of deeper meanings. You can practice this in everyday life by treating each new event as a scene hiding a profoundly significant meaning that you must extract. It takes great effort to wrest meaning in this way, but anyone who has ever buried a loved one has realized how much of life passes unexamined and un-lived.

Making films is a discipline to help you live consciously. It forces you to think in terms of juxtaposition, irony, and comparison. This is creating as you go, in-stead of just being a lazy bystander. Because you are working in a highly allusive medium, your audience is attuned by decades of film history to expect metaphori-cal and metaphysical overtones, so someone is waiting to see what you can do. You must work overtime with your imagination to find the poetry behind the raw material of life, most particularly because the camera itself deals with externals and surface banality.

How do you get beyond recorded realism? As in poetry, by juxtaposing mate-rials to make a provocative antiphony. Look for the contradictions in your subject and make sure its dialectics are well evidenced. By dialectics, I mean the opposing polarities of action, opinion, and will that set person against person, movement against movement, idea against idea, and the parts of a person against himself. These are the spars—the pressures and tensions, often insoluble and irresolv-able—that stand like bridge construction in a fog of banality.

COVER IMPORTANT ASPECTS MORE THAN ONE WAY

Be doubting, and cover yourself. Make sure that vital points are made several ways so you can choose the best. I once filmed conscientious objectors from World War I (*Prisoners of Conscience*), thinking I could find one man whose story could stand as an analogue for all of them. But it was a leaderless movement that downplayed its own heroism. I found no one person with more than fragments of the total experience. So I ended up doing detailed interviews with some twenty men and women to profile the movement and its underground support. In the rushes, no individual prevailed so I gave equal voice to all, as Robert Altman did with the characters in *Nashville* (1975). Because I shot several accounts of many incidents, I was able to choose the best, as well as to combine them. It was a gamble that came off because the texture of voices, faces, and photographs was simple and appropriate for a leaderless, self-effacing movement.

CONCESSIONS AND RISK

Authorship requires ceding control of the piece at certain points to an amorphous but vibrant sense of what is true. This happens regularly during editing. One feels a certain awe when an assembled piece begins insistently making its own demands, telling you, its creator, how it wants to be. Parents will recognize this situation. Like your maturing children, your films each turn out to have their own nature, idiosyncrasies, and integrity. Each will want to make its own decisions and to exist autonomously. It is a shock and a delight to see them take wing, each differently.

During shooting you will sometimes find yourself in similar wonderment, making a similar capitulation. A different truth is emerging about a certain character or a certain situation, and you must either ignore it or let it guide you into the unknown. For this reason, Marcel Ophuls limits his preparation so he "will be surprised." He wants to shoot something open and developing, rather than to fulfill a blueprint of conclusions. Thus filmmaking can embrace the spiritual mystery of existence. You put authority, identity, and career in jeopardy. If you do not respond to those emerging, elusive truths, the crew at least will realize it and respect you less.

Committing to this search for deeper truth makes you a sort of Everyman undergoing a spiritual journey. What is present may always be the devil in disguise, throwing a seductive irrelevancy to trip you up, or it may be the angel of truth, challenging you to follow its footsteps to unknown destinations. As a documentarian, you search the world for the freestanding counterparts to your own experience. Finding them, you can communicate your vision without the need for self-portraiture.

C H A P T E R   1 8

PRODUCTION PROJECTS

Carrying out the projects in this chapter will give you excellent experience. Only a few basic categories cover practically all of the documentary techniques used to probe the human condition. Most filmmakers use mixed forms according to purpose, taste, and the situation in hand; however, these projects confine you to relatively pure examples so you can experiment with the nature of each separately. Use them to further your own authorial interests, not just as technical exercises. Throughout, aim to use your material not only for what it shows (denotation) but also for the hidden, poetic meanings (connotation) that emerge through artistic compression and ironic juxtaposition. The projects are grouped as follows.

DIRECT OR OBSERVATIONAL CINEMA

Sometimes called the fly on the wall approach, the camera intrudes as little as possible. Aiming to give us transparent access to people and situations, direct cinema tries to make us feel we are watching life uninterrupted and unmanipulated.

A. Tripod

Project 18-1: Dramatizing a Location

Project 18-2: Three-Person Conversation (Interior)

B. Handheld

Project 18-3: Covering a Process for Ellipsis Editing

Project 18-4: Covering a Conversation (Exterior)

Project 18-5: Mobile Coverage of Complex Action

CINÉMA VÉRITÉ OR CATALYST CINEMA

Also known as intercessional cinema, the filmmakers acknowledge that their presence is part of the subjects' reality, and may question, challenge, and seek information or a response in a number of ways.

A. Tripod

Project 18-6: Interview in Depth

Project 18-7: Two-Person Conversation with Conflict

B. Handheld

Project 18-8: Unbroken Five-Minute Story

Project 18-9: A One-Shot Catalyzed Event

Project 18-10: Vox Populi Interviews and Metaphoric Counterpoint

REFLEXIVE CINEMA

This approach acknowledges the filmmaking process in the film, and may even make the autobiographical experience of the filmmaker(s) central to its purview. Either observational or catalytic modes may be used during the acquisition stage.

Project 18-11: Self-Portrait

Project 18-12: Observing the Observer

Project 18-13: Story, Question, and Suggestion

COMPILATION AND ESSAY CINEMA

These highly interpretational forms, virtually unavoidable in historical filmmaking, often make films from existing records, or use original footage in highly plastic ways.

Project 18-14: Making History

Project 18-15: National Anthem

Project 18-16: Video Letter

ECLECTIC CINEMA

Because most films are a mix of techniques, the final classification is reserved for the "final" or ultimate film in your course, and permits you to mix and match.

Project 18-17: The Final Project

The projects that follow will be potentially a richer experience if you first read Chapters 26 to 30 in Part 7, Aesthetics and Authorship.

DIRECT OR OBSERVATIONAL CINEMA (TRIPOD)

PROJECT 18-1: DRAMATIZING A LOCATION
(Courtesy of NFTVA, Amsterdam)[1]

This 5-minute screen time project is shot silent but uses music and optional non-sync sound effects. Using a silent camera focuses one usefully on the narrative, symbolic, or metaphoric possibilities of image and action.

---

[1]This and other exercises attributed to European film schools can be found in Stanjek, Klaus and Renate Gompper, Eds. *Teaching Documentary in Europe.* Berlin: Vistas, 1995. The book contains the same text in both English and German, and can be ordered by mail for $25 (including postage) from Vistas Verlag GmbH, Bismarkstrasse 84, D-10627 Berlin, Germany. Much of the book is about Project VISIONS, the first European documentary student workshop.

You learn how to combine research observation, "scripting" from notes, and careful shooting to develop powers of documentary expression; how to condense a lengthy physical process; how to use music; and practice unintrusive coverage of uncontrollable events.

Suggested subjects: Any locale with a cyclical life can be a good subject (train or bus station, restaurant kitchen, street market, construction site, market, café, plaza, hairdresser's shop)

Action: Using camerawork, lighting, and sound indigenous to your location, shoot materials for a 5-minute film that compresses into shorthand form the feel and mood of a location over a time span of at least 4 hours.

Film example: John Schlesinger's classic short *Terminus* (1961), a day in the life of London's Waterloo Station, or street scenes in Martin Bell's the study of Seattle street children, *Streetwise* (1985).

Steps:

1. Pick a visually interesting public location that has a strong cyclical life.

2. Spend at least a day just observing and listening; you will be amazed by the number of evocative sounds there are to choose from. Keep notes of everything that strikes you. You might want to zero in on a single character who is associated with the place, or to depict several.

3. Work your notes up into a script that uses images and actions to show the life, people, and spirit of your location. From your notes write a detailed shot list "script" that implies a structure and a dramatic curve. Pay special attention to depicting the beginning, middle, and end of each cycle in the location's life.

4. Show your instructor or peer the script and discuss the music you have chosen as well as any intended sound effects. Aim to make the cyclical events of a period (usually a day) into a narrative that economically and wittily depicts character, time, and place. Do *not* use a song because it will act as a narration and short-circuit the test of your narrative skills.

5. Shoot your scripted shots plus any "gifts" that come your way.

Editing: For tips see Project 25-4. Edit according to the script and the opportunities or limitations of your rushes. Show the rough cut to a trial audience for feedback, and make your fine cut exactly 5 minutes long.

Criteria

Location's geography is well shown.

Camerawork is controlled appropriately.

Engaging characters with dimension emerge.

Shows typical life cycles of the place.

Shows unexpected detail.

Visually imaginative shooting is used.

Sets a strong mood.

Passage of time is shown well.

Music enhances mood.

Choice of music is fresh and interesting.

Form in the music echoed in the form of the film.

Visuals make use of transitions and accents in the music.

Sound effects and atmospheres (where used) stimulate imagination.

Piece has impact and makes a statement.

Piece has wit.

Piece is exactly 5 minutes in duration.

PROJECT 18-2: THREE-PERSON CONVERSATION (INTERIOR)

You learn to cover a group interaction from a single camera position, with camerawork that does not draw attention to the filmmaking process.

Action: Here the camera must pan, recompose, and choose the appropriate shot size, which may include one, two, or three persons. How you set up the group will affect how natural they feel and look.

Coverage: Shoot around 8 minutes in preparation for a 4-minute final screen length. Shoot *plenty* of safety cutaways on each person listening to both of the others. To get these, let the conversation run past completion and signal the camera operator to shoot prearranged types of cutaway close-ups.

Lighting: Because this is such a controlled environment, try for a distinct lighting mood. Make lighting look "motivated," that is, natural to the setting.

Sound: Find a mike position out of frame that will cover all three speakers equally, or use a fishpole that can pan the mike just above or below the frame (watch out for telltale mike shadows).

Film example: The interior union discussions in Barbara Kopple's *Harlan County, USA* (1976) or the motel group scenes in the Maysles Brothers' *Salesman* (1968).

Suggested subjects:

The rewards and difficulties of artistic collaboration

I thought I was unshockable until . . .

The hardest thing about learning to make documentaries is . . .

Edit using Project 25-2 guidelines.

Criteria

Sound is good and no mike is visible.

Composition proportions are appropriate from shot to shot.

Zooming and recomposing happen simultaneously and smoothly.

Cuts maintain rhythm of speaker's speech patterns.

Cutaways used successfully to eliminate some camera transitions.

Interviewer's voice successfully eliminated.

Conversation successfully restructured to develop meaningfully.

Tends to use wide shot for new subject matter.

Tends to cover moments of intensity in big close-up (BCU).

Participants are at ease.

Conversation has impact and intensity throughout.

DIRECT OR OBSERVATIONAL CINEMA (HANDHELD)

PROJECT 18-3: COVERING A PROCESS FOR ELLIPSIS EDITING

You learn how to cover a course of action so that it can be shortened in editing. This is absolutely fundamental because in documentary Life, often long and boring, is supposed to become short, fascinating Art.

Action option 1: A car drives up and stops and the driver gets out to inspect the tires. One is soft, so he/she changes the wheel. Driver gets back in and drives away. During the whole action, the driver does not look at or talk to the camera, and must carry out actions as though nobody were present. The crew may not direct the driver in any way. This is a catch-as-catch-can exercise in which no one has control over the action.

Action option 2: A game of skill and visible change such as Jenga®, in which two people build a tower of wood blocks, with the loser being the unfortunate one to make the move that brings the tower toppling. Lots of skill and tension.

Planning: Walk through the likely actions, then draw a ground plan showing the anticipated camera positions. Plan framings that reveal what is significant through relatedness, that is, *by juxtaposing major aspects of the situation* rather than framings that separate and isolate.

Coverage: Cover in *one unbroken take,* and shoot with editing in mind because this will be the material for a vital editing exercise. While shooting on the fly, make sure to get plenty of close-ups, cut-ins, and motivated cutaways.

Film example: Most of Ira Wohl's *Best Boy* (1979) is shot with long, unbroken takes because of the unpredictable nature of the subject, as is Joe Berlinger and Bruce Sinofsky's *Brother's Keeper* (1992).

Editing: Aim for a 2-minute edited result. See Project 25-3 for instructions and editing criteria.

Criteria (to be applied to rushes)

Whole action is adequately covered.

All major steps of the action are clearly shown.

Interesting framings and compositions are used.

Compositions integrate and juxtapose elements of the action.

Camera is absolutely steady between necessary movements.

Camera movements are positive and controlled.

Camera movements are motivated by the subject.

Camera movements are in rhythm with the subject's movements.

There is good balance between close-ups and longer shots.

Transitions between stages are clearly shown.

PROJECT 18-4: COVERING A CONVERSATION (EXTERIOR)

Two people waiting for public transportation discuss something that interests them intensely. Once the interchange begins, your continuously running camera must cover all aspects of the conversation and respond to its changing focus and implications. Using a handheld camera and wide-angle lens only, keep the audience at the conversation's psychological center.

To create material that will edit well together, you will need to pan from composition to composition, and to relocate the camera position physically near or far from the subject to create sufficiently different shots and image sizes.

When you move the camera, know where you want to go, and go there in a nicely executed movement. This creates positive movements from shot to shot, with an appropriate period of static "hold" on each new composition. The alternative to this kind of deliberation is a drifting, wandering series of movements called "firehosing" that communicate insecurity to the audience.

Be sure to shoot an all-purpose "any sync" shot (an establishing shot, where mouth movements are either hidden or too distant to be properly seen). This will help you get around any unforeseen cutting difficulties.

The raw footage rushes should present an "edited" look that shows reactions, follows eyelines, and implies the conversation's subtext.

It is helpful during preparation to sketch a ground plan. This will help you figure out what angles are necessary and what cutaways might be legitimized by points of view (POVs) and eyeline shifts. Remember that your people are waiting for something, and that it should be visually (not just verbally) established. Try to shoot

- 8 to 10 minutes of continuous-take rushes
- BCU single shots
- two angles of over-the-shoulder (OS) two-shots, both well framed
- low angle shot for practice
- smooth, usable transitions between all shots
- transitions that respond to the speed and rhythm of exchanges
- camera movements motivated by subjects' movements and eyeline changes
- cutaways and/or reaction shots to help editing
- sound according to mike operator's different priorities as he/she keeps out of frame

Film example: any well-shot action documentary, such as Barbara Kopple's *Harlan County, USA* (1976), *American Dream* (1990), or any Fred Wiseman or Maysles Brothers film.

Edit into a smooth 4-minute sequence using Project 25-3 for editing guidelines.

Criteria

Visuals set interesting mood.

Participants look spontaneous and natural.

Camera movements are properly motivated.

Compositions are well framed.

Compositions create depth.

Close-ups come when speakers are most intense.

OS shots are well composed, complementary.

Low angle shot(s) are motivated.

Cutaways and reactions are motivated and good.

Eyeline shifts are exploited in cutting.

Camera moves in rhythm with conversation.

Why they are waiting is visually explained.

Recording yields good sound.

Extra cut-ins and cutaways are shot and used.

Distant shots ("any-sync") are included to aid editing.

Length requirement (4-minute max) is observed.

Sound is checkerboarded and mixed.

Film has high overall impact.

PROJECT 18-5: MOBILE COVERAGE OF COMPLEX ACTION

This challenging assignment needs practice but will be a rewarding demonstration of your coordination.

You learn how to operate while navigating doors, steps, and interior/exterior lighting changes. Open your nonviewfinder eye occasionally to see where you are going (or expect to fall over something . . .). Using both eyes for different purposes is a chameleon skill that one can acquire, but expect nausea at the beginning. To make it more interesting, ask your subject to talk throughout. Suggested conversation subjects include: an interesting accident, a worst moment, a relationship that had to be abandoned (fits metaphorically with action).

Action: Start inside building, the camera static with your subject walking past you. Pan around then follow your subject through the door out into the open air. Overtake the subject so we see his/her face while walking toward a car. Then let the subject overtake you so that you are again following as the subject moves toward the driver's side of a four-door car. Keeping the driver framed, open the rear-passenger side door with your free hand, and slide into the car as the driver gets in. By shooting over the car roof and sinking the camera as you both get in, you can completely avoid showing your own door opening and closing. Hold onto the driver as the car starts, then pan forward to show the road ahead. Hold for 15 seconds. Use onboard video camera mike, or if you want real choreographic fun, use a mike operator.

Coverage: If the action allows, shoot feet walking, point of view of door knob opening—anything in addition to the specified camera angle changes that will facilitate ellipsis editing later.

Film example: The beginning motorcycle sequence of Peter Watkins' classic *The War Game* (1965) or the long mobile coverage of prison routines in Frederick Wiseman's *Titicut Follies* (1967).

Edit using Project 25-3 guidelines.

Criteria

Good framing is used throughout shot.

Solves getting out of house door.

Shows person's face as he/she walks.

Solves getting into car.

Camera is on driver as car gathers speed.

Pans to straight ahead.

Camera is steady throughout.

Camera moves in sync with events.

Compositions are appropriate.

Subject informally tells entertaining tale.

Sound is OK (no expletives, bumps, crashes, etc.).

CINÉMA VÉRITÉ OR CATALYST CINEMA (TRIPOD)

PROJECT 18-6: INTERVIEW IN DEPTH

This exercise is for honing on-camera interviewing skills, but it is also excellent for eliciting an informal, natural-sounding narration or voice-over.

You learn to direct an interview that will

- stand alone in an edited version without the interviewer's questions
- be well recorded with minimal ambience so it could be used without picture as voice-over or interior monologue
- evoke memories and feelings in an interviewee
- provoke the interviewee into self-examination
- take the interviewee over some personal threshold of realization that requires effort and courage on both of your parts
- be shot in different image sizes, allowing flexible editing later with minimal cutaways

Preparation: Tell your interviewee in advance only that you want to ask about an event that has been pivotal in his life. Preinterview so you have a sense of what is involved and what is at stake. Concentrate on listening for the underlying issues, and be sure not to ask any probing questions until the interview proper. Brief the camera operator on three basic shot sizes and compositions, and agree on a signal system so you can direct camera changes.

Environment: Try to set up the interview in one of the person's own environments, such as a place of work, kitchen, study, or whatever else seems appropriate. Try to make the setting comment on the individual. Perhaps you can revisit the site of the event itself, and this will trigger feelings and memories for your participant.

Interviewing: Be sure to elicit whole statements; you will want to cut out your own voice later. Respond facially but not vocally, or you will interject your voice into the interview and make it very hard to edit. Before you begin, tell the interviewee

- not to worry about the recording, as anything can be edited out
- that you may interrupt if he gets away from the subject or if you want more information
- that you want information in your question included in the answer so you can edit out questions

As the interviewer, listen for freestanding sentence beginnings. No overlaps are permissible between your voice and the response because they would force you to keep the interviewer's voice, which is usually unnecessary and intrusive. Most interviewees will need repeated reminders to include the question's substance in their answer.

Most missed opportunities occur when the interviewer uncritically accepts generalizations instead of pressing for illustrative stories, examples, and specifics. Listen not only for what you expect, but also for the unexpected hiding out among the subtexts.

After the interview and before you leave, prepare the ground for a return visit in case you later discover this is necessary.

Film example: Connie Field's *Rosie the Riveter* (1980), Michael Apted's *28 Up* (1984), or most films that rely on interviews.

Edit using Project 25-1 guidelines.

Criteria

Interviewee was at ease, spoke interestingly and freely.

Relevant facts about the event are supplied.

Relevant facts about the interviewee are supplied.

Gave a personal, emotional perspective of the event.

Interviewee revealed his own change and development.

Interviewee faced a substantial issue or implication for the very first time.

No questions or narration are necessary to make sense of the answers.

Interview structured like a story, with beginning, middle, and end.

Climactic moments are well placed.

Different image sizes edit well together compositionally.

Interviewer nowhere overlapped the interviewee.

The sound quality is clear and intimate in quality.

Film was high overall impact.

PROJECT 18-7: TWO-PERSON CONVERSATION WITH CONFLICT

There are several objectives in this exercise:

- To find, manage, and present a human interaction.
- To use ingenuity to film a conversation with conflicting viewpoints that, nevertheless, looks spontaneous.
- To make the material elegantly lit, composed, and shot.
- To have faultless sound.
- To portray a topic through an interaction with opposing and subjective viewpoints.

Locate and preinterview two people who know each other well, then:

- Be nondirective so you don't catalyze the best interaction to happen before the camera is present.
- Pick a shared event in their lives about which each feels very differently.
- Find visual documentation (photos, movie or video footage, etc.) on which they can concentrate.
- Note in advance what their cutaway pictures might support so that you can direct their attention to particular subject matter for which visuals exist.

After research and before shooting:

- Write up a working hypothesis.
- Get feedback about it from someone reasonably objective and critical.
- Use it to determine what expository information and what conflict your piece must make evident.
- Determine how to direct them so that you best exploit the visual documentation.

When you've got the best, clearest statement of intention, shoot. Because this is *cinéma vérité*, not observational cinema, you must be ready to catalyze without violating credibility or your own code of ethics. Prepare the subjects to *focus on what they disagree about* and be ready to intercede and redirect them if they move away from what you want. Make sure they cover everything you thought significant during research. Aim to shoot a 15-minute interaction. You should:

- Do/say whatever is necessary to make their interchange become natural.
- Make sure the known differences of emotion and perception emerge strongly, and be ready to intercede with side-coaching if they do not.
- Get them to *talk to each other* rather than to the camera.
- Contrive the setting so the frame is "packed" and interesting, and so subject placement does not force awkward camera movements.
- Light the set both interestingly and credibly.

- Shoot from *one camera position only.*
- Use the zoom to shoot different-sized images on each person.
- Direct the camera to follow the scene's psychological focus throughout.
- Shoot enough natural-looking reaction shots on each person.
- Cover any motivated cut-ins or cutaways after the main shooting.
- Make videotape of any pictures, 8mm film, graphics, or family video that would legitimately expand your interview's purview.
- Take care to get good, clean sound.
- Shoot sound presence to fill sound gaps during editing.

Film example: The doctor's office sequence in Ira Wohl's *Best Boy* (1979), or any of the group scenes in Joan Churchill and Nick Broomfield's *Soldier Girls* (1981).

Edit down to a 5- to 6-minute piece, using reaction shots and cutaways to help restructure and condense their interaction. For editing guidelines, use Project 25-2. Aim to checkerboard their tracks, if necessary, for a seamlessly clean sound mix with no bumps in level or quality.

Criteria

Pair are interesting, well chosen.

Event is well defined.

Sharply differing perceptions are recorded.

Sequence builds to a climax.

Climax is well placed in sequence.

Resolution is interesting.

Sequence has natural end.

Length of sequence is appropriate.

People creatively placed, not just arranged on a couch.

Setting creates a mood.

Lighting augments mood.

Compositions create depth and perspective.

Camera movements are smooth and unobtrusive.

Camera follows psychological center of the action and reveals subtext.

Compositions are well framed.

Framings cut together well.

Imaginative, well shot cut-ins and cutaways are present.

These used in motivated, creative way.

Listener reactions used effectively.

Good sound heard throughout.

Editing rhythm is smooth.

Sound is checkerboarded onto two tracks.

Mix is good for level and equalization.

Film has high overall impact.

CINÉMA VÉRITÉ OR CATALYST CINEMA (HANDHELD)

PROJECT 18-8: UNBROKEN FIVE-MINUTE STORY
(Courtesy of VGIK, Moscow)

You learn to plan an approach and cover a storyteller in one unbroken take, with no recourse to editing. This is also an exercise in exploiting all the possibilities of a location in relation to the story, all within a given time. Although the story must be true, the project leans toward fiction because there is considerable possibility for an artful dramatization—and equally, a danger that it will look phony!

Research/preparation: Pick an articulate, interesting person with a story he/she can tell engagingly but don't allow the story to be told in any depth until you shoot. Do a preinterview and view the storyteller's choice of space where you are going to shoot. Discuss what he/she could be doing while talking (laundry, making a meal, servicing a bike, laying out a dead body . . .)

Plan: Make notes of:

- your working hypothesis
- likely special areas you want to highlight
- how much time you will allot for each intended stage
- likely image size changes, camera angles, and movements
- what you want to accomplish overall
- special signals to be worked out with crew to cover exigencies

Shoot the story in one, unbroken 5-minute take, using an offscreen prompt to signal the 5-minute countdown to the participant. Shoot more than one take to see what happens in different versions.

Film examples are difficult to come up with, although parts of Ross McElwee's *Sherman's March* (1989), Claude Lanzmann's *Shoah* (1985), and Terry Zwigoff's *Crumb* (1994) qualify.

Show the best take to a trial audience, and be ready to summarize the nature of the others.

Criteria

Story comes out at exactly 5 minutes.

Film is well structured for information and development.

Storyteller produces an interesting story.

Film is emotionally engaging.

Content seems natural, spontaneous, and unrehearsed.

Time allotment is used in good proportions.

Story is told naturally and without forced or slack moments.

Story has a natural, well-situated climax.

Camera moves inventively with or around storyteller.

Good framing and compositions are found throughout.

Camera movements are smooth and motivated.

Sound is good and consistent.

PROJECT 18-9: A ONE-SHOT CATALYZED EVENT

You learn how to plan and direct a complete event in a single take, and how to think on your feet so you make good use of the unexpected.

Action: Using a mobile camera record events in an unbroken 7- to 10-minute take. The director (or a surrogate) must make things happen. For instance, during Project VISIONS (the European documentary workshop), a camera crew followed a woman into a Berlin male-only Turkish café and shot what happened. To carry this assignment off, you will need a strong idea and then plans for foreseeable contingencies. It requires both the abilities to improvise and to bring events to a conclusion in the allotted time span.

Film examples: Jean Rouch's seminal *Chronicle of a Summer* (1961) and Werner Herzog's shattering and inspiring piece about the deaf blind, *Land of Silence and Darkness* (1971).

Criteria

Film covers its ground in 7 to 10 minutes.

There is an interesting build and denouement.

The protagonist keeps events moving.

There are no flat spots.

There are no unduly forced moments.

The camera is where it should be throughout.

The camera handles the unexpected with aplomb.

Sound is well recorded throughout.

The premise to the film was original.

The film makes a socially critical point.

The film has a strong impact.

PROJECT 18-10: VOX POPULI INTERVIEWS AND METAPHORIC COUNTERPOINT

This is a *cinéma vérité* project that requires you to think on your feet and to have a good grasp of both technical and authorial skills. *Vox populi* (voice of the people) is a montage technique for creating a "Greek chorus" of faces and voices. By using it you can

- broaden the cast of a film narrowly focused on few people
- demonstrate where a main character belongs in relation to mass opinion

- remind your audience of the diverse character and opinion of the common person
- demonstrate norms, received wisdom, or dissident voices just as you please
- remind us how the individual exists fallibly within a web of prejudices and transient, societally influenced norms

Topic: Pick a subject area in which you think public awareness is likely to be searching, divided, or prejudiced. Avoid overexposed topics, such as AIDS, abortion, and racism, unless you feel you can shoot something that both exposes and critiques commonplace wisdom.

Counterpoint: Plan to shoot a separate activity (not just cutaways) that, when intercut with vox populi footage, will act as a metaphoric counterpoint. Make sure your counterpoint story is visual and develops through a beginning, middle, and end. An example is the eviction sequence in *Roger and Me* intercut with General Motors' celebration of Christmas, and elsewhere in the same film, the killing of the rabbit ("Pets or meat?").

Hypothesis: Decide the main conflict you expect to emerge, then write a hypothesis by filling in the gaps:

> *"In life I believe that . . . To demonstrate this in action I will show that . . . The main conflict is between . . . and . . . I want my audience to understand . . . and to feel . . . "*

Conflicts may exist between people, within the individual, or between the individual and some other force, such as Nature.

Interviewing: What one asks and how one asks it will exert a great influence on the replies you get. Confusing, unfocussed, or unchallenging questions do not give the interviewee much to push against, but live issues presented from a provocative, devil's-advocate position can release a tirade.

Using *only four major questions,* be ready to probe the interviewee to get a satisfactory response to each. The key questions must be brief, directive, in the vernacular, and hard to misinterpret—even for the occasional person of limited intelligence. Your object is not to produce "balanced reporting" or to elicit a body of data by neutral questioning. It is, first, to tap into public feeling and opinion and, second, through responsible editing *to make an overall statement of your own* about the issues at stake.

Posing the same few questions often yields usefully predictable results, but sometimes you meet unusual and original responses, or learn that your assumptions have been wrong. This project raises questions about ethical and representation issues, how general truths can be represented, and to whom they will be ascribed by the audience.

Through your questioning, you will need to elicit from your interviewees any necessary factual framework that the audience will need to understand the issue at hand, especially because you will be editing out your questions.

Shoot your interviews in at least two locations. One person armed with clipboard acts as "catcher," stopping passersby to ask if they will participate. You will need an interviewer/mike handler and a cameraperson. When you interview:

- Stay informal.
- Use only four questions.
- Listen for the subtext of the response.
- Capitalize on the idiosyncrasies of the interviewee by probing with further questioning.
- The name of the game is finding ways to get people to open up.
- Address at least two distinct socioeconomic groups.
- Shoot without showing interviewer or microphone.
- Unobtrusively use backgrounds that highlight the person's identity, if possible.
- Vary backgrounds and compositions.
- Using a wide-angle lens alone, move the camera to produce varying shot sizes within the interview.
- Interview equally from either side of the camera to give on-screen variety.
- Rotate crew members through all roles.

During the shoot, review how your hypothesis is working, and change it to match reality. Refine and rephrase your questions as you need, or even reformulate them to evoke sharper responses. Because the street interview is immediate rather than built on a lengthy two-way relationship, it can be unfairly manipulated either during the interview or later in editing.

Film example: Michael Moore's *Roger and Me* (1989) uses many street interviews, while Erroll Morris' *The Thin Blue Line* (1988) makes an entire film out of interviews.

Editing: Use Project 25-4 for editing guidelines. If each group member does his/her own edit, you will see quite wonderfully different sequences emerge out of a shared experience, each expressing something of the editor. "Art," Jay Ruby has said, "contains and espouses the ideology of the artist." And, "Image makers show us their view of the world whether they mean to or not."[2] Here you can see for yourself.

Criteria

Good vox populi topic is used.

Genuine differences of opinion are expressed.

Visual metaphor is organic to vox populi's world.

Is truly metaphoric and not just illustration or visual diversion.

Good vox populi hypothesis is used, evident on screen.

Sequence makes socially critical statement.

Conflicting views are well exploited.

---

[2]Ruby, Jay. "The Ethics of Imagemaking," in *New Challenges for Documentary,* Alan Rosenthal, Ed. Berkeley, CA: University of California Press, 1988.

Participants are stimulated and at ease.

Different types and socioeconomic groups are represented.

Compositional backgrounds are interesting, pertinent.

Good framing, composition, steadiness are seen.

Variety of image sizes and angles are shown.

Depth created in compositions.

Film is entertaining, lively in pace.

Good developmental arc of ideas is presented.

Good sound is heard.

Work is crisply and intelligently edited.

Length is well judged.

Delivers emotional impact.

Leaves one thinking.

REFLEXIVE CINEMA

PROJECT 18-11: SELF-PORTRAIT

Using a written narration and family records of your growing up, such as photos, film, or video, make a 5- to 8-minute self-portrait that

- includes necessary facts concerning your growing up
- reveals what is unusual about you and your family
- ponders how you feel about your memories and the images of yourself
- considers the value of this self-presentation

As with any documentary, however short, write and rewrite a working hypothesis. Be prepared to be very selective indeed, because you are confined to the records that your family happened to make. Records reveal the recorder as well as the person recorded, so be ready to explore the how and the why, as well as what was left out.

Film example: Autobiographical section in Michael Moore's *Roger and Me* (1989), much of Deborah Hoffman's *Complaints of a Dutiful Daughter* (1995).

Edit using Project 25-4 guidelines.

Criteria

Factually coherent autobiographical portrait is given.

Gives insight into at least one formative event.

Portrays some credible family tensions.

Avoids self-indulgence.

Is bearably self-critical.

Avoids self-censure.

Is not overprotective of self or family.

Considers some difficulties of autobiography.

Seems trustworthy.

Is entertaining and memorable.

Has acquitted him/herself well in this very difficult form.

PROJECT 18-12: OBSERVING THE OBSERVER

Take one of your street interviews, or any human process you've filmed (preferably one where your subjects avoid looking at the camera), and make a short film that questions how the camera is affecting the situation. Freeze the action, run it in slow motion, and rerun salient moments to recreate the way a viewer can probe a screen record for cinematic insight. Instead of writing a commentary, have someone perceptive interview you to evoke your spontaneous reactions, thoughts, etc. Use this either as voice-over or as a to-camera interview. The resulting footage and verbal speculation should last 5 to 8 minutes on-screen.

Film examples: Michael Rubbo's *Sad Song of Yellow Skin* (1970) and Mark Wexler's *Me and My Matchmaker* (1996).

Edit using Project 25-4 guidelines.

Criteria

Material to analyze is well chosen.

Method of examination feels motivated and unforced.

Speculative comments are informal and un-self-conscious.

Analysis yields insights into specific moments.

Film reveals genuine ethical dilemma.

Avoids self-congratulation.

Avoids self-mortification.

Avoids being overearnest.

Avoids avoidance humor.

Critique neither belittles nor aggrandizes human subjects.

Shows empathy and insight into at least one participant.

Film is gripping.

Acquits him/herself well in this difficult form.

PROJECT 18-13: STORY, QUESTION, AND SUGGESTION

This project explores the initiation of a story from a participant, how the questioner inwardly reacts, and questions aspects of it, then how the storyteller handles these questions, comments, and reactions.

Action: Because you probably don't have a couple of decades to try Apted's process (see film example below), here's a small, fast version. It should be a gold mine for connoisseurs of conceptualist humor:

- Get someone to agree to answer a non-embarrassing question that, for spontaneity, you will only reveal once the camera is running.
- Set up equipment and participant, and ask for a true autobiographical story, 2 or 3 minutes long, that is somewhat testing of the participant's candor; for example, you might ask for a story about an occasion when the participant had to confront an undesirable aspect of his/her own personality.
- View the resulting tape alone several times, develop your thoughts, then videorecord your questions, doubts, speculations in 2 or 3 minutes.
- Show both tapes to the participant, and elicit his/her reactions (making sure your voice can be edited out). Have a list of points so you can prompt whatever significant material the participant forgets or avoids.

Film example: Jean Rouch and Edgar Morin's seminal *Chronicle of a Summer* (1961), in which Parisians were asked if they were happy. Rouch and his subjects debate the making of the film as it is being made. Michael Apted's masterful study of a dozen people's values, beginning when they are all 7 years old and continuing longitudinally through adulthood. The most famous version is *28 Up* (1984); in the next, *35 Up* (1991), participants are intensively revisiting their own and Apted's earlier comments in a clear pattern of self-reflexivity.

Editing: Use Project 25-4 for guidelines. This film will collapse into a hall of mirrors unless you manage to keep the unfolding layers clear and consistent. It could also be hilariously funny. A suggested assembly is:

- 1st layer: Show your setup question, then the participant thinking of and telling the story, either in complete or abridged form. Cut to
- 2nd layer: Reprise salient portions of the story, interpolating your comments and questions, perhaps using voice-over played on freeze frames. Cut to
- 3rd layer: Show participant's explanations, justifications, comments interpolated in abridged version of 2nd layer.

Criteria

Participant "casting" is good.

Good story is evoked by astute choice of question.

Story provokes reflection on its implied values, dilemmas.

Director has spotted all the ambiguities in 2nd layer "thoughts tape."

Final layer shows multiple reflexivity.

Final layer provokes thought about first impressions.

Final layer provokes thought about afterthoughts and follow-ups.

Two people's adjustments to each other are visible.

Layers are distinct and experiencing them is not confusing.

Each added layer earns its presence in the film.

Each layer is well judged in length.

Subsequent layers are increasingly complex but not alienatingly so.

Some wit and irony show through.

Participant does not emerge exploited.

Film emerges as a worthwhile dialogue.

Developmental arc is consistent and satisfying.

COMPILATION AND ESSAY CINEMA

PROJECT 18-14: MAKING HISTORY

This is practice in exploring the didactic and expository power of film. The aim is to take visual records, such as a series of photographs and/or news film from another era, and to put them together with a first-person reading of a contemporary letter, diary, or account. Pictures and words should work together to make us imaginatively enter the spirit of the speaker and his or her time.

Shooting: Check that your camera shoots what its viewfinder shows. Many don't and there's no margin for error when shooting graphics. Out of one photograph you can often find several more within it. Movements between these subsidiary compositions are hard but not impossible to do smoothly, and panning the camera on small subjects is too clumsy. Try shooting vertically onto a table and improvise a sliding platen so a photograph can be guided between prearranged stops in any direction relative to the camera.

Narration: Directing a non-actor to read like everyday speech is a challenge. Usually the obstacle lies in the person's sense of occasion; he will project his voice, or use "period" mannerisms. Sometimes you can help him focus by placing a listener 3 feet away, or by having the reader imagine he's telling something to an intimate nearby. If you can figure out what's stopping naturalness, you can probably invent a strategy to unstop it. We become natural when no longer self-conscious or trying to be special.

Tip: Most screen history, like school history, is tedious stuff because television, which finances it, is obsessed with panoramic overviews. Concerning itself with so many facts and exposition, instead of the questions of interpretation or present-day relevance, television makes history seem dull when it's really a vibrant and mysterious source of human drama. See if you can bring human tensions and dilemmas alive, even if only briefly. As in any drama, the trick is to show someone go through change, however small and symbolic.

Film examples: Any television history, such as Ken Burns' *Civil War* (1990) series, that uses primary accounts; Alain Renais' trauma-inducing holocaust classic *Night and Fog* (1955), which has one of the most masterful narrations ever; and Pare Lorentz's classics *The Plow That Broke the Plains* (1936) and *The River* (1937).

Criteria

Interesting historical episode was chosen.

Imagery is inherently interesting.

Text is inherently interesting.

Text and images go together well.

Tells a story with characters and situations.

Develops some narrative tension.

Somebody learns something and is changed by experience.

Developmental arc of the piece is well judged.

Sets a compelling mood (using music and effects, perhaps).

Holds the viewer's interest throughout.

Pacing is appropriate, nothing rushed or dragging.

Words and images counterpointed interestingly.

Speech rhythms used to pace the cutting.

Text is acted convincingly so it sounds authentic.

At the end you wished there was more.

PROJECT 18-15: NATIONAL ANTHEM[3]

Using the national anthem for your sound track, find or shoot images that contrast its lofty ideals with the reality you think people should be aware of.

You learn how to use conventional, familiar music and through visuals make it yield an unconventional point of view. This project is ripe for cheerfully subversive personalities, but please don't try it anywhere in the world where critics end up in prison.

Steps:

- Plan your film using split-page format scripting, with anthem words written out, and cutting points and counterpointed images indicated on the picture side.

- If you wish, use up to one third "found" images (newsreel, archive, stills, etc.) but make the rest original footage.

- Shoot and edit, placing cuts to any musical rhythm 3 or 4 frames *before* music beat point so our perceptual lag makes us think you are cutting exactly in time with the music.

Film example: See how ironically and effectively Michael Moore uses songs in *Roger and Me* (1989). Virgil Thompson's score in Pare Lorentz's *The Plow That Broke the Plains* (1936) makes ironical and highly atmospheric use of American folk songs, popular songs, and hymns in its orchestral score.

Criteria

Images make their own narrative.

Piece has beginning, middle, and end.

Makes ironic use of anthem's words.

Is keyed to musical rhythm and transitions.

Is imaginatively shot.

---

[3]I believe I heard this exercise from György Kárpáti, Academy of Drama and Film, Budapest. Apologies if I've attributed it wrongly.

Camerawork is controlled and well composed.

Has something memorable to say about your country today.

Works on our emotions.

Has a sense of humor or irony.

Leaves us thinking.

PROJECT 18-16: VIDEO LETTER

Conceive and shoot a video letter that you send to documentary students in a film school abroad. Foreign exchanges, where they can be arranged, are immensely exciting and invigorating, and sometimes begin from "correspondence" like this. As schools acquire nonlinear video editing, tape compilation becomes immensely easier.

You learn how to correspond with people of like interests in another country using documentary video techniques as the medium of communication. You also learn how to shape a piece for a particular audience.

Starting: Consider whether you already have contacts in a particular country. If not, pick out one or two places that interest you from the list of foreign film schools at the end of this book and fax them a letter of inquiry. In your letter of inquiry you could seek to find out:

- whether they have a documentary program, and who runs it
- whether their documentary students are interested in a video letter exchange
- if they can play your VHS video standard (NTSC, PAL, SECAM) and say what video formats your institution can play and record
- what they'd be interested in hearing about

Sending your video letter: The people you will be addressing probably live and learn in a rather different environment, so you'll need to explain yours. In your tape you might:

- Introduce the concepts, personalities, and contents of your courses.
- Explain what kind of place your institution is and how the education system works (they are incredibly different from country to country).
- Outline how particular personalities in your group came to be interested in documentary.
- Discuss the projects, mix of theory and practical work, texts, etc. in your coursework.
- Share what you most disagree about.
- Include clips of the work you have been doing.
- Talk about what particularly interests you.
- Show what your homes are like and perhaps a typical day.
- Show what kind of economic juggling act you have to perform to actually go to school, and how you have to wait tables, drive a cab, etc.

Criteria

The video letter's narrative method was effective.

Facts and necessary information were included.

It gave voice to more than one person.

It accurately reflected a part of our reality.

It showed some of our activities as "newsreel" material.

Some of the letter directly addresses the other group.

Some of our satisfactions were well addressed.

Some of our frustrations and difficulties were outlined.

We included some of our philosophy and belief—why we make documentaries.

We showed where we study, our equipment, and facilities.

We asked good questions and can expect an interesting response.

We had fun putting this together and learned something about ourselves.

ECLECTIC CINEMA

PROJECT 18-17: THE FINAL PROJECT

This project should only be done after you have built some solid experience in documentary language by doing the earlier projects. If you are in a degree program requiring a thesis film or diploma film, this project could be a rehearsal using an allied or analogous subject.

This project lets you mix forms according to the needs of your subject, just as most real-world documentaries do. You direct a documentary that is between 12 and 15 minutes long. To avoid depending on interviews, make your film *no more than one-third sync interview*. It would be better to avoid talking heads completely, if you can.

You learn whether you know the foundations, and whether you do better than your first time around!

Write a proposal: Writing a documentary proposal (see Chapter 8) should raise the organization and thematic content developed during research to its ultimate clarity, and it should make a persuasive statement of your intentions to those whose support you need. Bear in mind that good documentaries:

- tell a good story
- change us more by our emotions than by facts
- usually take a passionate and critical view of the human condition
- dramatize human truths, both large and small
- need the traditional dramatic ingredients—characters, exposition, building tension between opposed forces, confrontation, climax, and resolution

1. Write a subject description and working hypothesis (or "premise") by filling in the gaps: "In life I believe that . . . To demonstrate this in action I will

show that . . . The main conflict is between . . . and . . . I want my audience to understand . . . and to feel . . . "

2. From your research, write an analytical draft under capitalized headings (see Chapter 8, Proposal Helper), organizing your material to demonstrate your research and analysis. Eliminate any repetition in subsequent drafts by deciding under which heading particular ideas and observations truly belong. Your writing, here and in the treatment later, should convince the reader you can make a film of impact and significance. Quoting participants' own words from your preinterview session is often a highly effective way to present them on paper.

3. Write a treatment by reworking material from the analytical draft. Write in the present tense, using a new paragraph for each sequence, describing only what could be seen and heard from the screen. Write evocatively, where necessary imagining what will happen so the reader "sees" the attractive film that you hope and expect to make.

4. Make a shooting schedule to show your shooting dates and arrangements.

5. Make a provisional budget covering all phases to indicate how you will fund your film.

6. Obtain the permissions you need to shoot (location clearances, agreement with participants, etc.).

7. Shoot.

8. Edit first assembly.

9. Fine cut.

10. Finalize sound by mixing and equalizing tracks.

11. Show for evaluation.

Film examples: You choose!
Editing: Use Project 25-4 guidelines.

Criteria

Film's "corner of nature" is successfully shown "through a temperament."

Successfully exploits visually interesting situations.

Camerawork controlled and interesting.

Demonstrates mastery in cinéma vérité of director's catalyst function.

Demonstrates masterful use of observational cinema techniques.

Demonstrates mastery of reflexive techniques.

Demonstrates mastery of tripod camerawork.

Demonstrates mastery of handheld camerawork.

Demonstrates use of words and images together in mastery of essay form.

Demonstrates mastery of controlled filming situations.

Demonstrates mastery of uncontrollable filming situations.

Sound composition is aurally rich.

Sound mix is well judged.

Editing feels secure and well judged.

Structure of film works well.

Theme of film is discernibly original.

Thematic development is well paced.

Film handles conflicting forces.

Film brings conflicting forces into confrontation.

Film shows something or someone changed, and achieves a meaningful outcome.

Overall length feels right.

Film has high overall impact.

Authorship shows authority and evidence of passion.

PRODUCTION CHECKLIST

Before Interviewing

- Rehearse questions aloud and listen to see if there is room for misunderstanding.
- Decide who is best equipped (director or researcher) to interview.
- Consider putting people together to talk: people in couples or in groups sometimes give you more.
- Remember that antipathies and disagreements often stimulate good "talking" situations between people.
- Have a clear expectation of what each interviewee can contribute to your film through prior research.
- Decide the audience's relationship to interviewees, and plan on- or off-axis interviews as appropriate.
- Decide if the interviewer or her voice should ever be in the film.
- Focus questions carefully on issues you want discussed.
- Decide what setting will most productively affect the interviewee.
- Remember that you must know in advance the minimum your film must say.

When Interviewing

- Carry questions on index cards as a "security blanket."
- Make sure you have properly explained to participants *why* you are filming.
- Warn interviewees that you may interrupt or redirect conversation.
- Coach interviewees to include the question's information in the answer.
- Review who is present and what effect they might have on interviewee(s).
- Be natural and unaffected when you interview.
- Listen to the beginning of each answer to be sure it stands alone without your question.
- Be ready to jump in and ask for a new start.

- Maintain eye contact with the interviewee.
- Listen not only for what you want, but for what she is *really* saying.
- Give facial, but never verbal, feedback while the interviewee is talking.
- Use the devil's advocate role to represent negative attitudes in questioning.
- Ask factual, nonthreatening questions first, hold back difficult or intimate matters until interviewee becomes comfortable.
- Ask *always* for specifics, examples, or stories to back up any assertion that is interesting.
- Get a second version if the first, though spontaneous, was clumsy or too long.
- Remain silent whenever you suspect there is something yet to be said.
- Remember the camera empowers you to go further and deeper than in everyday life.
- Make sure you have filmed the necessary confrontations inherent in your movie's system of issues.

When Interviewing, Do Not

- Forget to allow the camera at least 10 seconds of runup before letting action begin.
- Worry about the order of the interview—it will all be cut and reorganized.
- Use vague, general questions.
- Ask more than one question at a time.
- Overlap your voice on that of an interviewee.
- Make sounds of encouragement or agreement—use facial expressions only.
- Hurry on to the next question or you risk quashing a "moment of truth."
- Allow correct editorial decisions to be swayed by a sense of obligation.
- Be surprised by mannerisms accompanying certain lifelong roles held by participants.
- Forget to a shoot presence track for each interview location.

Preparation to Get Proper Coverage and to Ensure Variety

- Make shopping list of sequences and shots, and *what feeling each must convey.*
- Ask participants not to look at the camera.
- Do not forget inserts, cutaways, and reaction shots.
- Remember that vox populis are a great resource (the "person in the street" speaks).
- Show people active in their own surroundings.
- Each situation must be credible but also must reveal something special about the participants through their behavior.
- Make sure each participant has plenty to do to avoid self-consciousness.
- Expect people in unfamiliar circumstances to fall back on habit.

Shooting in General

- Decide with camera operator the size and framing of each shot.
- Stand next to camera so you see more or less what it is seeing.
- Whisper directions into operator's ear, or use touch signals (if the camera is on a tripod).
- Try to make the camera into a conscious instrument of revelation and story-telling, rather than just a passive observer.
- Look through the camera often to check framing, composition, and image size.
- Choose between a steady, immobile camera (tripod), and a subjective and mobile but unsteady camera (handheld) for each sequence.
- Decide whose point of view the camera should sympathize with moment to moment.
- Decide where the center of significant action lies.
- Exploit location as a meaningful environment rather than as a mere container.
- Try, wherever possible, to create a sense of depth in the frame.
- Be responsive to participants' changes of eyeline, and be ready to follow them.
- After the main shooting, use participants' eyelines as guides for shooting all possible safety cutaways.

Social Skills

- Give individualized positive reinforcement to participants and crew as you go.
- Keep the group together during rest periods and meals so the process of relationship continues informally.
- Keep to meal breaks; do not overwork people.
- Thank everyone personally at the end of each day.
- Replace locations exactly as you found them.
- Insist that the director alone speak for the unit.
- Keep dissent from the ears of participants.
- Let your crew know when you need advice or help, and when not.

Crew and Scheduling

- Make sure there is a clear structure of responsibility for everything that may happen.
- Provide the crew with a clear schedule that includes map details and phone contact numbers.
- Underschedule when in doubt.
- When everyone is in transit, make sure there is a phone number all can call in the event of separation or breakdown.
- Be tolerant of the crew's incomplete grasp of subject development.

- Keep the crew involved and aware of developments in the picture's content and themes.

Authorship

- Look for subtext in each situation, and try to make its existence evident.
- Use side-coaching to impel something nascent into being.
- Be aware of life roles people fall into.
- Think of the dramatic characterizations each seems to have.
- Create a private metaphor for each situation and activity.
- Look for the dialectics in everything, and therefore where confrontations are called for.
- Make sure facts and vital points are covered in more than one way so you have options later.
- Check your shopping lists as you go to make sure you have not overlooked anything important.

PART 6

POSTPRODUCTION

CHAPTER 19
A Postproduction Overview   241

Editing Theory   241
The Editor's Role and Responsibilities   242
The Editing Process Begins: Viewing the
     Rushes   243
The Case for Making Transcripts   244
Logging the Rushes   244
Selecting Sections for the First Assembly   245

CHAPTER 20
The Paper Edit: Designing a Structure   249

Why a Structure Matters   249
Time and Structural Alternatives   250
Story Structures Need to Show Change   251
Assembling the Paper Edit   253

CHAPTER 21
Editing: The First Assembly   255

Finding Equipment   255
Changing Editing Technology   256
Time Code: Off-Line to On-Line Editing   259
Video: From Tape to Digital Production   261
Digitizing for Nonlinear Editing   261
The First Assembly   262
Return to Innocence   262
After the First Viewing: Deciding on an
     Ideal Length   263
Diagnostic Questioning   264
Dealing with Material that Doesn't Work   264
The Documentary Maker as Dramatist   265
Making the Visible Significant   266
After the Dust Settles, What Next?   266

CHAPTER 22
Editing: The Process of Refinement   268

The Problem of Achieving a Flow   268
How Editing Mimics Consciousness   268
Looking At and Looking Through   269
Editing Rhythms: An Analogy in Music   269
Counterpoint in Practice: Unifying Material
     into a Flow   270
The Audience as Active Participants   272
The Overlap Cut: Dialogue Sequences   272
The Overlap Cut: Sequence Transitions   274
Help! I Can't Understand!   275

CHAPTER 23
Narration   276

Narration as an Option   276
Drawbacks and Associations of Narration   276
Positive Aspects of Narration   277
Two Approaches to Narration   278
The Scripted Narration   278
     Writing   278
     The Tryout   279
     Adjusting Syntax   279
     Accommodating Sound Features   280
     The Power in Each First Word   280
     Operative Words   281
     Complement, Don't Duplicate   282
     Trying it Out: The Scratch Recording   282
     A Script for the Narrator   282
     Narration: Auditioning and Recording   283
     Voice Auditions   283
     Recording and Directing the Narrator   283
Creating the Improvised Narration   284
Recording the Presence Track   285

Fitting the Narration	285
Using Music	236

CHAPTER 24
Editing: The End Game   **288**

Diagnosis: Making a Flow Chart	288
A First Showing	290
Surviving Your Critics and Making Use of	
What They Say	291
The Uses of Procrastination	292
Try, Try Again	292
The Fine Cut	293
The Sound Mix	293
Preparation	294

Track Hierarchy	295
Mix Chart	296
Sound-Mix Strategy	298
Titles and Acknowledgments	300
Getting Titles Made Commercially	302

CHAPTER 25
Postproduction Projects   **303**

Project 25-1 Interview, Varying Image Sizes	303
Project 25-2 Conversation, Two or More	
Persons	304
Project 25-3 Editing for Ellipsis	305
Project 25-4 Complex Editing Project	306
Postproduction Checklist	307

A POSTPRODUCTION OVERVIEW

Postproduction is the phase of filmmaking or videomaking that transforms the shot material, or rushes, into the film that the audience sees. Mainly handled by the editor and sound editing crew (if there is a full editing crew), these stages include:

- Screening rushes (also known as *dailies*) for the director's choices and comments.
- Getting dialogue transcripts made.
- Logging.
- Making a "paper edit" (a way of planning the intended film on paper).
- Editing a first assembly or rough cut.
- Editing to a fine cut.
- Narration recording (if there is any).
- Music recording (if there is any).
- Cleaning and checkerboarding dialogue tracks for equalization.
- Laying component parts (effects, music, atmospheres) in preparation for the mix.
- Mixdown of these tracks into one smooth final track.

Other processes follow, also supervised by the editor. In film it is laboratory work to produce projection prints, while for video an online, or computer-assisted, postproduction process creates a final sound track and a clean, stable image suitable for broadcasting.

EDITING THEORY

Unless you have just read through Chapter 5, Screen Grammar, I recommend you revisit it. You should find much there to help you think creatively while editing (and yes, this book is written by a former editor, who really loved the whole process).

THE EDITOR'S ROLE AND RESPONSIBILITIES

The documentary editor's task list demonstrates how vital he or she is to the creative evolution of the film. It is well recognized that someone of imagination and judgment supplies a strongly co-authorial input. Because so much of the documentary's structure and authorial voice develop in postproduction, the documentary editor has been rightly characterized as the second director.

In a low-budget movie, the editor and director are sometimes the same person, especially if the director is afraid to share control. This is a mistake, because an independent and creative collaborator is a huge asset at this stage. The director knows all the situations that produced the film, while the editor faces the material with an unobligated and unprejudiced eye, and can see its potential more realistically.

The editor receives the director at a time of considerable anxiety and uncertainty; the film is shot, but has yet to prove itself. Most directors, however confident they appear, are acutely aware of their film's failures, and often experience something similar to postnatal depression. If the editor and director do not know each other well, they will usually be formal and cautious because both are aware that the editor is taking over the director's baby. The editor must be understanding, patient, organized, willing to experiment extensively, and diplomatic about trying to get her own way.

At this point the director might present the editor with a paper edit (an edit plan on paper) to carry out. Another might discuss what the intentions were at the time of shooting and let the editor find the best way to implement them. Yet another will be intensely interested in what the editor thought was strongest among the materials, what feeling each sequence carried, which had the most interesting situations and impact, and so on, and base a game plan on shared reactions and ideas. With good will, any of these working relationships can work well.

The editor sets to work, assembling a first, raw version of the film. Wise directors now leave the cutting room to ensure that they return with a fresh eye for what the editor produces. The obsessive director, however, will camp in the cutting room to monitor the editor's every action. Whether this arrangement is amenable depends on the editor. Some enjoy debating their way through cutting, but the more private thinker prefers being left alone to work out the film's problems in bouts of intense concentration over logs and equipment. Digital or nonlinear editing has made the experimental aspect of editing immeasurably faster. Doing this in film required much sweated labor, with splicing, filing, and reconstructing both sound and picture prints. Linear video editing made every change a job of reconstruction. Nonlinear video gets the best of both worlds.

Whatever the road taken, very little escapes discussion; every scene and every cut is eventually scrutinized, questioned, weighed, and balanced. The relationship is intense, and the editor is often using delicate but sustained leverage against the prejudices and obsessions that every director develops about the material. Ralph

Rosenblum's *When the Shooting Stops ... the Cutting Begins* shows just how varied and crazy editor/director relationships can be.[1]

However the association gets worked out, the professionally minded director comes to depend on the partnership of a good editor. The scrutiny of the emerging work by an equal, and the advocacy of alternative views, help produce a tougher and better balanced film than one person can generate alone.

THE EDITING PROCESS BEGINS: VIEWING THE RUSHES

Even though rushes have probably been viewed piecemeal by the end of shooting, the crew should see their work in its entirety in order to do better next time. You may need to break screening into more than one session because 4 hours of unedited footage is usually the longest that even the most dedicated can maintain concentration. Because the crew viewing will probably include much post-mortem discussion, viewing with the editor is better handled as a separate event.

The editor needs an atmosphere of quiet and concentration while internalizing the material and thinking about the film's construction. It may help to pause after each sequence's rushes to discuss the possibilities of the material. You are interested in what information and facts emerge, but are also on the lookout for telling juxtapositions.

A marathon viewing of rushes highlights the utter relativity of all the sequences and the issues that each raises. Note down as you go all new thoughts about ways the material could be used. These spontaneous ideas will be useful later, but they are apt to evaporate unless you commit them to paper on the spot.

Note any particular mood or feeling evoked by a sequence or interviewee. If, during the rushes viewing, you find yourself thinking, "Funny, but I don't trust him," write this down because, far from being personal and isolated, the feeling is almost certainly latent in the material, a sabotaging force in whatever film you go on to make. Many gut feelings seem so logically unfounded that one is inclined to ignore or forget them, yet what triggered them remains present and potent as an experience for any first-time audience.

It is useful to have someone present who can take dictated notes. Failing this, dictate them into a cassette recorder. But try never to take your attention from the screen, as you can easily miss important points. There will probably be debates over the meaning or importance of different parts of the rushes, and crew members and the editor may have opposing feelings about what they see. Encourage this dialogue and listen closely, because it anticipates something of a general audience's reactions, and may lead you usefully to modify your assumptions.

There is a spiritual discipline to documentary making. One must set aside all the intentions one held so dear, purify one's heart of all the passions connected with the shooting, and confront the materials in a spirit of open-minded inventiveness. For nothing outside the rushes is relevant to the film you are going to make; *you must find your film in the given materials,* yet remain loyal to your central vision.

---

[1]Rosenblum, Ralph. *When the Shooting Stops ... the Cutting Begins.* New York: Penguin, 1980.

THE CASE FOR MAKING TRANSCRIPTS

Tedious though it may seem, transcribing every word your characters say is of great value in fully understanding your participants and in editing. It is not, however, everything. As those who examined the Nixon White House tape transcripts discovered, transcripts are still not a foolproof method of determining total meanings, because *how* something is said is quite as important as *what* is said.

Transcription is not as laborious as people fear: it saves work later and it also helps ensure that you miss few creative opportunities once the long editing process is done. If you cannot endure the idea of typing a transcript of everything of any importance said in your film, there is an alternative method that is less arduous. Instead of writing down actual words, you summarize the topics covered at each stage of a discussion, filmed scene, or interview. This gives you *topic categories* and quick access to any given subject. You now make decisions during editing by running whole sections and deciding which parts are best. Avoiding transcripts is a "buy now, pay later" situation, because making content and choice comparisons without a transcript is hard labor of a different stripe.

Aids, lists, and filing systems that make the material more accessible are the lazy person's shortcut to creative excellence. Putting it all in a computer allows you to use the search function of a word processor, which immeasurably speeds up locating remembered words and phrases.

LOGGING THE RUSHES

In filming, every new camera start receives a new clapperboard number. The clapper bar allows the editor to synchronize separately recorded picture and sound. With video, picture and sound are recorded alongside each other on the same magnetic recording medium, so scene numbers (and clapperboards) are not strictly necessary. Any log, however, must later facilitate easy access to the material. A log of rushes should be cumulative, giving the new timing (or time code) for each new scene or for each important action or event. Descriptions should be brief and serve only to remind someone who has seen the material what to expect. For example,

01:00:00	WS man at tall loom.
01:00:30	MS same man seen through strings.
01:00:49	CS man's hands with shuttle.
01:01:07	MCS face as he works, stops, rubs eyes.
01:01:41	His POV of his hands & shuttle.
01:02:09	CS feet on treadles (MOS).

The figures are hours: minutes: seconds, and there are the usual shot abbreviations (see Glossary). Draw a heavy line between sequences and give each a heading in bold type. Thus if I am looking for the loom sequence, I will look first for "Handicrafts," knowing the loom material was shot as part of a block of handicraft coverage that also contains Blacksmith's Shop, Pottery, Broom making, and Basketry.

Logs exist to help you locate material quickly, so any divisions, indexes, or color codes you can devise will help the eye in its work, and save time and energy, especially when a production has many hours of rushes. Hasty and short-cut filing exacts its own revenge because Murphy (of Murphy's Law) loves to lurk in filing systems. When you are tempted to take a short cut, be sure that this will be the very shot you absolutely must find. Of course, it will be late at night, the shot will be buried in 5 hours of material, and you will gnash your teeth and rend your garments.

SELECTING SECTIONS FOR THE FIRST ASSEMBLY

Your first assembly should be constructed from long, loosely selected sections, so let us look at a methodology for narrowing one's choices into a workable form. Figure 19-1 is a flow chart to illustrate this.

Step A: You have made transcripts (1) and from them a photocopy. Place the transcripts in a binder titled *Original Transcripts,* and keep them somewhere safe. You are going to work with the photocopy (2).

Step B: Run the material on a VCR or editing machine, and follow each speaker's words in the transcript photocopy (2). When you are struck by an effective section—for whatever reason—put a vertical "preference mark" in the margin as in (3). You are leaving a record of your responses. Some will be to a story graphically told; others to some well-presented factual information; still others will be in response to an intimate or emotional moment, be it humor, warmth, anger, or regret. At this stage just *respond* and don't stop to analyze your reactions. There will be a time for that later.

Step C: Once you have preference marks against all striking sections in the photocopy, study each and find a logical in-point and out-point, using two kinds of "L" brackets to show the preferred start and finish of the section (4).

In Figure 19-2, a chosen section has been bracketed at an in-point and out-point. However, only by returning to the recorded material can one determine whether verbal warm-ups (so common when people begin a statement) can be edited out as intended. Similarly, our intended out-point might need modifying if it forced us to cut away from Ted on a rising voice inflection that sounded strange and unfinished.

In the section's margin is the cryptic identification "6/Ted/3." This decoded means "Tape cassette 6, Ted Williams, section 3." These section IDs will later prove vital because they allow you to find the section in the full text and to locate the film section in its parent cassette. There is no set format for section identity codes, but as with all filing systems, *stick with one system for the duration of the project,* and build improvements into the next project when you can start clean.

Returning to Figure 19-1, you now have photocopies (4) with selected sections marked, their in-points, out-points, and IDs, any or all of which might go

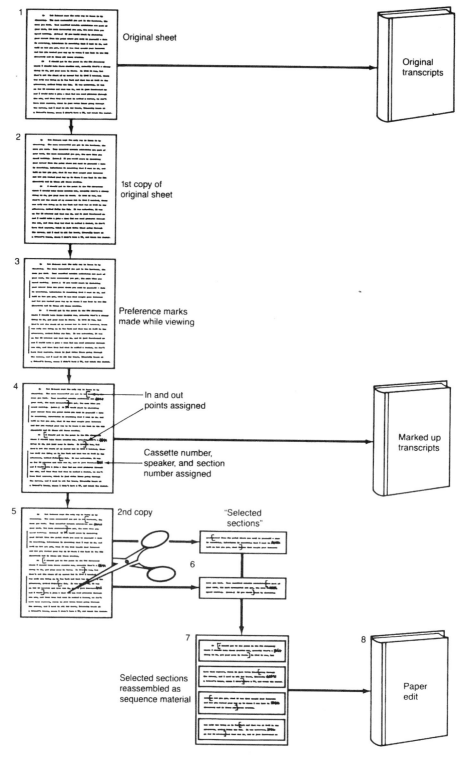

FIGURE 19-1

A flow chart showing how to use transcripts to make a paper edit.

```
Q:  What do you remember about the farmer?

Ted:  What do I....?  Oh, well, you know, [he          6/Ted/3
was all right if you kept your place.  But if
you got smart, or asked too many questions,         Ted's descript. of
he'd be after you.  "Where's that wagon load of     Farmer Wills.
straw?  Why ain't them cattle fed yet?"  And
then he'd say there were plenty of men walking
the streets looking for work if I didn't want
to work.  The only thing you could do was be
silent, 'cos he meant what he said.]  Now his
wife was different.  She was a nice soul, you
know what I mean?  Couldn't see how she came
to marry him in the first place....
```

FIGURE 19-2

A section of an interview transcript marked with in-point and out-point brackets, cassette/speaker/section ID, and margin description.

into a finished film. You need to assign each section a description of its function, such as "Ted's descript. of Farmer Wills," as shown in Figure 19-2.

Step D: Now make a photocopy (5) of these marked sheets. The parent marked transcript photocopy (4) can now be set aside. File its sheets in cassette order in a binder titled *Marked-Up Transcripts,* with an index at the front so you can quickly locate each character. Later, during editing, this file will be an important resource.

Step E: The photocopy of the marked-up transcripts (5) is cut up with scissors into selected sections (6), ready for sorting and grouping in pursuit of the paper edit. Because each slip is identified by subject or intended use, and because it carries an ID, you know at a glance what it is, what it can do, and what its context is in the parent sheets, the *Marked-Up Transcripts.*

Now you are ready to go to the next chapter, which tells you how to construct a *paper edit*—really a detailed sketch for the first assembly. The selected sections (6) will eventually be stapled to sheets of paper (7) as sequences, and the sequences will be assembled into a binder (8) holding the paper edit or plan for the first assembly of your movie.

This procedure may sound unnecessarily complicated, but, believe me, time spent organizing at the outset (indexes, graphics, guides, color coding, and so on) is rewarded by disproportionate time saved later, especially when the project is complex. I learned this when I was hired to edit the final game in a soccer World Cup documentary. There were 70,000 feet of 35mm film (nearly 13 hours) shot from 17 camera positions. The only coordination was a shot of a clock at the beginning of each 1000-foot roll. I spent a week with my assistant, Robert Giles, up to our armpits in film, making a diagram of the stadium and coding each major event as it appeared in all the various angles. The game had gone into overtime due to a foul, and it was my luck to eventually establish that *not one* of the 17 cameras was running at this decisive moment! From sports reports and with Robert's far superior grasp of the game, I set about manufacturing a facsimile of the foul using an assortment of appropriate close shots. No one ever guessed we'd had to fake it.

The project was an editor's nightmare. Had we not first taken the time to invent a decent retrieval system, the men in white coats would have taken us away later in the legendary rubber bus.

C H A P T E R   2 0

THE PAPER EDIT: DESIGNING A STRUCTURE

Now that the select materials of your film are thoroughly accessible, you can make the paper edit. This phase makes use of shot descriptions and transcripts to design an effective first assembly. There is a special value to manipulating ideas on paper rather than editing footage at this stage. Handling descriptions enables one to consider content and subtext from a bird's-eye view and to concentrate on how each segment might function. If you try to do it from hours of footage, you get submerged in moment-to-moment action. Work on a paper edit is therefore a focused search for the *underlying structure and factual logic* that any film needs to be successful.

WHY A STRUCTURE MATTERS

This book belabors the necessity of an imaginative thematic structure, no matter what genre of documentary you are making. It takes unusual imagination, energy, and spirit to make something direct from life into a gripping story. The occasional film does this well and, by evoking a large public response, dramatizes how the rest of us fail to ignite public imagination.

The Achilles' heel of documentary is that it too seldom rises above the banality of recorded realism. Of course, there are reasons for this. We depend on the spontaneity and "performance" of people who are not actors and who have no script. But too many films fail to take an authorial grip on the meanings reverberating in their subject. They drift by loose association rather than advancing with a definitive purpose. Few contemporary viewers will stay long with any story unless it reveals a larger direction and purpose behind its telling.

The best way I know to overcome this is by inventing a good working hypothesis, or thematic organizing principle. This helps clarify how to select and prime participants, to know what to evoke, what to shoot, and how to shoot it.

If you were able to do this and keep to your goals during the shoot, then structuring the assembly may now be straightforward. Usually it isn't. Usually one's goals were frustrated or had to change, so there's all the more need for a first assembly planning process that can reconnect you with what you really filmed, and that will make something imaginative out of it. Editing is your second chance.

TIME AND STRUCTURAL ALTERNATIVES

Structure and the "Contract" with the Audience: Planning a structure means, first of all, deciding how to handle time, because progression through time is the all-important organizing feature of any narrative. You must decide in what order cause and effect will be shown, and what dramatic advantages lie in altering the natural or actual sequence of events. All this is arguably the most important aspect of the contract you will strike with your audience.

Yes, consciously or otherwise, *your audience looks for a contract,* the manifestation of your film's premise, goals, and route. The contract may be spelled out in a narration, or be implied in the logic of the film's development. It may also be implicit in the film's title or in something said or done at the outset. Your audience needs a *sense of direction and an implied destination* in order to embrace the pleasurable prospect of a journey.

Here are a few structural types with film examples to help you decide what limitations, and therefore what potential, lie in your rushes.

Chronological Time Structuring: Countless films mark out a time span in order to show the evolution between the bookends, so to speak. I assisted on a BBC series called "All in a Day," which chronicled, from multiple viewpoints, a large event taking place in a single day. My unit followed the gamekeeper (at a shambling, gasping run) during a pheasant shoot on a lordly estate.

Time is no less significant in structuring fiction. Agnes Varda's *Cleo from Five Till Seven* (1961) could well be a direct cinema documentary, because it is a 2-hour film that follows a woman for 2 hours after learning she has cancer. Pierre Schoendoerffer's documentary, *Anderson Platoon* (1966), follows an American platoon in Vietnam for 2 weeks, and logs the events that befall them. I once made a film showing the development of an amateur dramatic production from casting through to the last performance.

Nonchronological Structures: There are countless organizing devices in screen stories, and here a few examples must suffice to remind you of the diversity. One artifice is to show an event and then backtrack in time to analyze the events and interplay of forces that led up to it, as in Heinrich Böll's novel, *The Lost Honor of Katharina Blum* (1975), made into a feature film by Volker Schlöndorff and Margarethe Von Trotta. The novel deals with the murder and the murderer first, and then doubles back to show the concatenation of events that impel the blameless, gentle young woman to shoot the newspaper reporter. The film, however, shows the events more conservatively in their natural sequence.

Subjective POV Structuring: Other kinds of structure reflect how the film was made. Michael Rubbo's reflexive *Sad Song of Yellow Skin* (1970) investigates the impact of the American occupation on the Vietnamese. It documents a journey through the prism of personal impressions, rather like Louis Malle in his 1968

Phantom India series. The film is driven more by the logic of Rubbo's contemplation than by considerations of space and time.

Inventory Structuring: Rather different are Les Blank's films about Americana, such as *Garlic Is as Good as Ten Mothers* (1980), *In Heaven There Is No Beer* (1984), and *Gap-Toothed Women* (1987). They reflect Blank's anthropological leanings and are like pleasurably leafing through catalogues offering many versions of the same item.

Metaphoric Journey Structuring: At first sight, the organization of Ross McElwee's *Sherman's March* (1986) seems determined by the chronological succession of failing encounters he has with southern U.S. women. But lightly paralleling these are segments of McElwee's discourse on the equally fatal swathe cut by his doppelganger General Sherman during the Civil War. The filmmaker and his benighted ghost cross the country arm in arm, and at the film's conclusion their journeys end—in death for Sherman and in ominous rebirth for McElwee in the shape of another feminine attraction.

When No Time Structure Predominates: There may initially be no obvious time structure. For instance, a film about stained glass windows may have no discernible time structure in the actual footage. It could be arranged by historical dating of stained glass windows, by technical developments in glass, or by the regional origin and idiosyncrasies of the glassmakers. You decide which option to take by deciding what you want to say, and what your material best supports.

STORY STRUCTURES NEED TO SHOW CHANGE

A huge problem for documentary is that, unless one can shoot intermittently over months or years, human change and development may have to be implied because it is not always possible to show it in an affordable shooting schedule. Here Michael Apted's *28 Up* (1986) is spectacularly successful because it logs the same children's progress over three decades, repeatedly exploring each individual's sense of goals and destiny. Similar longitudinal studies have since been started in several countries.

Sometimes a subject is large and diffuse, and the macrocosm must be dealt with through microcosmic examples. I worked on a series that attempted to show the contrasting values of Britain's nearest neighbors as Britain was reluctantly joining the European Common Market. Called "Faces of Paris," it showed aspects of the French capital by profiling some interesting citizens.

Here one confronts a familiar paradox, which goes something like this: In order to show France, I want to show Paris; but because this is too diffuse, I will concentrate on a representative Parisian so my film will have some unity and progression. But how to choose a "typical" Parisian? To represent the universal, one looks for an example of the particular. But particularizing on behalf of the general tends to demonstrate how triumphantly atypical all examples turn out to be, and thus how absurdly stereotypical are one's ideas about Parisians. (Conundrums like this are responsible, no doubt, for the apocryphal story of the Oozlum bird, which is said to fly in ever diminishing circles under the hot desert sun until, vanishing up its own rear end, another Oozlum bird is born.)

The camera is relentlessly literal to its surroundings: It can only ever approach the abstract or metaphysical through the physical. Thus the ideas it conveys most readily arise from what is visible and therefore superficial, rather than from what is underlying and much more significant. Compared with literature, film authorship is handicapped when it wants to convey compact generalizations or to deal with abstract ideas. Making generalizations in film without resorting to the literary overview form of narration can be a real problem, and this may be a signal that you should bite the bullet and consider narration.

Writers faced, and solved, similar problems in previous centuries. One answer is to find a naturalistic subject that carries strongly metaphorical overtones. On the literal level, Bunyan's *Pilgrim's Progress* is a journey of adventure, but it functions also as an allegory for the human spiritual voyage. The Maysles brothers' superb *Salesman* (1969) is like this—a journey film about a group of bible salesmen on a sales drive in Florida. During it we see the eclipse of Paul, once a star salesman, according to the measure by which he and his company determine success. Not only does the film show every phase of door-to-door selling—something the Maysles brothers had done themselves at one time—but it establishes how much moral compromise and humiliation may be the price of competing as a salesman for the American dream.

Another famous documentary maker repeatedly uses an allegorical "container" structure. Fred Wiseman will take an institution and treat it as a walled city, a complete and functioning microcosm of the larger society housing it. Through the emergency-room doors in *Hospital* (1970), for example, come the hurt, the frightened, the wounded, the overdosed, and the dying in search of succor. It conveys an apocalyptic vision of self-destructiveness stalking American cities. As a mirror of a society, or as a metaphor, the movie is terrifyingly effective. Yet the same "institution as walled city" idea applied in *High School* (1968) seems diffuse and directionless; the relationship between teachers and taught that Wiseman wants us to notice is too low key and too repetitive to build a sense of development. Because of his nonintercessional approach, because he rejects narration and interviews, his technique fails to develop and intensify what I presume is the key issue: whether an unexceptional American high school can possibly prepare children to participate in a democracy.

So to summarize:

- A documentarian must be a good storyteller, so you must look for the best story in your rushes and the best way to tell it.
- Your approach to and structure for a particular subject must reach beyond the material world of cause and effect to also lay bare a thematic development and interpretive stance.
- All satisfying stories deal with change, or the need for it. An interesting subject but insufficient development in its characters, theme, or emotion will not make a film that fulfills its potential.

Do not be fooled by the sophistication of today's technology into thinking that a storyteller's apprenticeship has changed. Your masters are in all the arts; you belong with both Bunyan and Buñuel, and with Brecht, Bergman, Brueghel, and Bartók too. Take a keen interest in how fellow artists solve the problems you face, and you will learn fast.

ASSEMBLING THE PAPER EDIT

The paper edit is the first large-scale conceptual blueprint. To avoid a film that is wall-to-wall speech, first deal with action sequences, that is, sequences that show a human process with a beginning, middle, and end. Make a list of these sequences and design an overall structure that moves them logically through time. Eventually you will bring speech to these behavioral sequences. If, on the other hand, you start from transcripts, you will end up making a wordplay, to which you apply the film's stock of behavioral illustration. This makes for a less cinematic use of the material.

Be conservative with your first structure. If you have a film about a rural girl going to the big city to become a college student, stay true at first to the chronology of events (as opposed to the events unfolding according to their importance, say). Afterward, when you can better see how the material plays, you might intercut her high school graduation, conversations with a teacher, discussions with her father, and leaving home with the development of her first semester as a college drama student. You would now have two parallel stories to tell, one in the "present" and one in the "past." It could be a serious mistake to assume you can do this in one giant step.

First view the action or behavioral material in time sequence so its narrative possibilities are firmly established in your mind. Now you can go on to plan a safe, linear version, beginning from a paper edit that includes speech.

To do this, take your chosen transcript sections, as discussed in Chapter 19 (see Figures 19-1 and 19-2). These slips of paper, coded ("Jane" for Jane's sequences) so you can rapidly turn to parent copies in the marked-up transcripts, might look something like this:

1/Jane/1	Graduation speech
1/Jane/2	Dinner with boyfriend's family
1/Jane/3	Conversation with English teacher
2/Jane/1	Conversation with Dad

Additionally, you have the many pieces of action made into a preliminary assembly, ready to accommodate the dialogue sections of the film. These are best represented as sequences rather than as individual shots, which would be too detailed and cumbersome. Three sequences would go on separate slips of paper, each with a cassette location (cassette number, minutes, and seconds):

1/5:30	Exterior school, cars arriving
2/9:11	Preparations at podium, Jane rehearses alone
4/17:38	Airport, Jane looking for bus

On the floor, or a large table if you have one, move the slips of paper around to try different orders and juxtapositions. Certain pieces of interview or conversational exchange belong with certain pieces of action, either because the location is the same or because one comments on the other. This "comment" may be literally a spoken comment, or better, it might be implied by an ironic juxtaposition (of action or speech) that makes its own point in the viewer's mind.

An example would be a scene in which our student Jane has to make a graduation speech before the whole school, an obligation that scares her. To make a literal comment, one would simply intercut the scene with the interview shot later in which she confesses how nervous she feels. A nonliteral comment might take the same rehearsal and intercut her mother saying how calm and confident she usually is. A visual comment might show during the rehearsal that she is flustered when the microphone is the wrong height and that her hands shake when she turns the pages of her speech.

What is the difference here? The literal comment is show and tell because it merely illustrates what Jane's thoughts and feelings already give us. The nonliteral comment is more interesting because it supplies us with conflicting information. Her mother rather enviously thinks she can handle anything, but we see the girl is under a lot of strain. Either the mother is overrating the girl's confidence or she is out of touch with her child's inner life. This alerts us to scrutinize the family dynamics more carefully. The purely visual comment gives us behavioral evidence that all is not well, that the girl is suffering. It is a privileged insight discreetly shared with the audience.

The order and juxtaposition of material, therefore, have potent consequences. The way you eventually present and use the material signals your ideas about the people and the subject you are profiling and reveals how you intend to relate to your audience. In essence, you are like a lawyer juxtaposing *pieces of evidence* in order to stimulate the interest and involvement of the jury, your audience. Good evidentiary juxtaposition provides sharp impressions and removes the need to do much arguing.

However, don't aim for too much refined control in the paper edit. Much of the final effect depends on the nuances of the material and can only be judged from how it plays on the screen. But the mobility and flexibility of the paper edit system will reveal initial possibilities and get you thinking about what design these individual materials could make.

Do not be disturbed if your paper edit is vastly too long and includes repetitious subject matter. This is normal, because your more refined decisions can only be made from experimentally intercutting and screening the material.

Your slips of paper have been moved about like the raw materials for a mosaic. Once a reasonably logical order for the chosen materials has been found, you can staple the slips of paper to whole, consecutively numbered sheets, which you then bind into a file called the *Paper Edit*. Now you have a rudimentary story; you can rule lines between sequences and group the sequences into scenes and acts. From this master plan you begin making a loose, exploratory assembly on the editing machine.

CHAPTER 21

EDITING: THE FIRST ASSEMBLY

Probably during the first assembly, and certainly after it, your material will start telling you where and how to cut. This signals a welcome and slightly mysterious change in your role from proactive to reactive. Formerly you had to apply energy to get anything done, and now the energy starts to come from the film itself. Soon, all you have to do is to run the film, comprehend as an audience member, and act on what you understand. As your creation comes to life, this will be profoundly exciting.

FINDING EQUIPMENT

Video and digital editing equipment is being developed and marketed so rapidly that it would be imprudent to make specific recommendations in this book. There is, however, some general information that will be useful.

Impoverished independent filmmakers seldom edit on their own equipment because it is too expensive to purchase. Instead one either rents editing time or talks one's way into being allowed access to free facilities. Quite sophisticated and underutilized equipment may be found at small television stations or audiovisual departments in hospitals, police departments, universities, and high schools. You can also rent time from a production house (expensive!) or from a cooperative. Cooperatives are good because they hold prices down and provide a center of activities for like-minded people.

If you can find none of the above, do not despair. It is not unusual for the owner of a commercial operation to allow someone dedicated and impoverished to use the equipment during down-time—either free or for a very modest sum. A surprising number of hard-bitten media types have a soft spot for the committed novice, and many an unlikely partnership has developed from such an initial relationship. This, by the way, is even true of Hollywood.

CHANGING EDITING TECHNOLOGY

Film: At one time all film editing was done using one of the range of film-editing machines—Moviola, KEM, Steenbeck, or other. Film editing machines, whether upright Moviola or flatbed type, like the once ubiquitous Steenbeck (Figure 21-1), are all variations on the same theme. They run picture alongside one or more separate sound tracks so you can both see and hear your movie. You mark up changes, execute them, then build them into the intake side of the machine, and make further decisions from viewing the result.

Film editing is labor intensive. Finding trims, keeping sound and picture in sync, then filing trims so they can be retrieved at a moment's notice take method and patience. Now both film and video are being edited in the digital domain, where any frame from among hours of material can be pulled up, viewed, edited, and reviewed in seconds.

Editing aesthetics have not changed a jot, but the technology that editors use to get there has undergone a revolution. A brief overview of recent editing history is necessary, especially because economics may place you, the low-budget filmmaker, somewhere to the rear of the cutting edge. By the way, you are in good company. The renowned Spike Lee won't use an Avid and prefers to edit film on a flatbed, and there are plenty of others like him. There is, in fact, a quiet bonanza for the traditionalist—a buyers' market in used flatbeds that nobody much wants any more. Almost any Steenbeck will grind away for decades more with little attention.

Machine-to-Machine Tape Editing: The common format for off-line editing (i.e., editing from a workprint prior to a computerized final from the camera original tapes) used to be the 3/4-inch U-Matic (Figure 21-1). But then cheaper and smaller 1/2-inch VHS machines became common. After this came time-code-controlled, frame-accurate U-Matic, followed by high-band 8mm or Hi8, also time-code-controlled and frame accurate. Those in affluent surroundings still use Betacam origination, the industry standard for quality and durability. Nowadays it is digital Betacam. But many people shoot on highly portable, 3-chip Hi8 or 6mm digital video (DV) format and then dump to the more durable Betacam format by simply dubbing (electronically transferring) from one format to another.

The player-to-recorder editing machines used in linear video editing are uncomplicated to operate and do not take long to master. Essentially they work by transferring chosen sections from the source machine across to another that records. You pick an out-point at the end of material already assembled and then select in- and out-points for the "new" section in a source tape. The rig will let you preview your intended cut. If you are satisfied, you hit the record button and the machine will back up, stop, roll forward for 5 to 10 seconds of preroll, and go into record mode at the prearranged cutting point. On the monitor you see the last seconds of previously compiled material and then the new segment cut onto the old.

Sound is handled similarly, and Figure 21-2 shows in diagrammatic form how sound is transferred from the source deck to the recorder. I have assumed that the original tape was a two-microphone setup with each mike's output appearing on

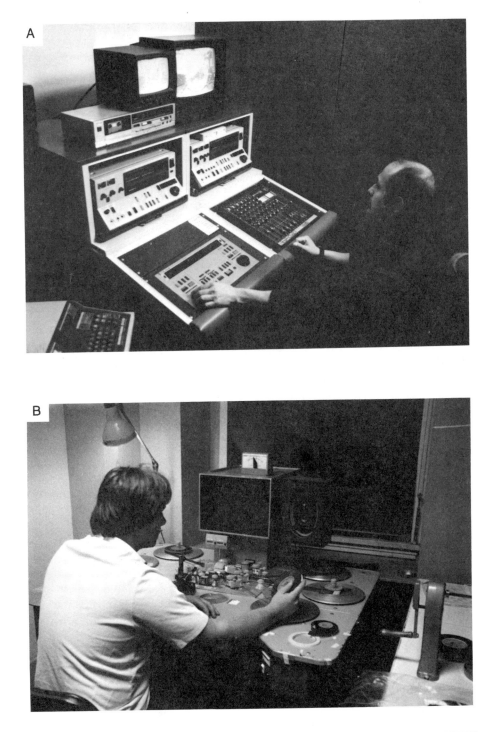

FIGURE 21-1

A typical off-line (noncomputerized) video editing setup (A), and a typical film editing machine (Steenbeck flatbed) (B).

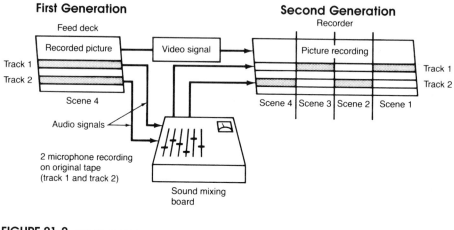

FIGURE 21-2

Assembling scenes from rushes with sound checkerboarded to facilitate sound mixing later.

a separate track. The two tracks are adjusted for level (or volume) at the mixing board, and the mixed result is routed to the recorder. At the mixing board you send the mixed track alternately to track 1 and track 2, scene by scene, in what is called *checkerboard fashion.* At a later stage (Figure 21-3), these individual scenes' tracks can be further mixed down, equalized (made consistent through adjustment of individual tone controls), and adjusted for level, resulting in a smooth, seamless sound mix. Figure 21-3 includes a cassette player that is feeding in a non-sync atmosphere, such as wind, traffic, or sound, from a television set in an adjacent motel room.

You can see from Figure 21-3 how in each stage two tracks get combined into one. This leaves an unused track on which you can, as a separate step, record additional materials for a further mix. Each stage prior to the final mix is called a *premix.* In analogue audio, but not digital to digital, repeated mixdowns lead to a generational deterioration audible as an increased hiss level, but by using time code and a multitrack recorder, you can keep degeneration to a minimum.

Generational losses in analogue video picture are disturbingly evident as increasing *noise* (picture breakup) and deterioration in both color fidelity and overall sharpness. You can, however, place a sixth- (or any other) generation sound track on a second-generation picture. The last stage is risky because it involves wiping an audio track from the second-generation video (combined picture and sound) cassette and replacing it with the sixth-generation audio mix, starting from a common sync start mark. *Practice with unimportant copy tapes before you take risks with vital materials!*

Sophisticated on-line equipment is needed to make picture dissolves and other electronic effects because a minimum of two source and one record machines are needed, and they must be capable of genlock synchronization. Also required is a video switcher to handle superimpositions. This raises the cost of equipment by perhaps 10 times over that of a basic off-line rig.

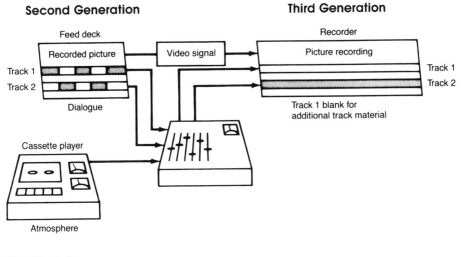

FIGURE 21-3

Premixing tracks 1 and 2 down to one leaves an unused track on the new recording, where track 3 may now be laid. A cassette player is contributing a nonsync atmosphere track.

Graphics and titling equipment are coming within reach, especially if you already own an up-to-date home computer. A *character generator* (CG) is a useful addition to the basic off-line editing rig because it allows one to create titles on black, gray, or colored backgrounds quickly or to superimpose them on live action. Not only can one put a person's identity as a title under her image at the beginning of an interview, but also linguistic barriers disappear when foreign language footage can easily be subtitled.

It is nevertheless quite possible to make a professional film with none of these optical embellishments. Having access to basic editing alone need not constrain your creative development.

TIME CODE: OFF-LINE TO ON-LINE EDITING

Time coding is a process that assigns every frame of film or video its own time identification—an invisible version of the bar code familiar from groceries. Once only available in professional video equipment, it is now common in consumer/professional, or "prosumer," equipment too. Time code enables postproduction equipment to locate a single frame with total accuracy, and provides a reference system for running several video and audio machines in interlock sync.

Time code in video is either laid down in a special *address track* while you are recording or is retrospectively applied in postproduction, in older machines in an unused sound track. From the invisibly time-coded camera original is made a *window dub*. This copy has a burned-in window displaying each frame's coding (Figure 21-4). A linear edit is made from window dubs, partly to protect the camera original from heavy use and partly because all generations from the window dub,

FIGURE 21-4 ——————————————————————————————————————

A video image displaying time code with cassette number, hours, minutes, seconds, and frame counter.

no matter how degraded their image, will carry the time code display. Regardless of how complicated the editing process becomes, the time code—like the legendary ball of string—allows one to return safely to the point of origin, the camera original.

Film too is now time coded. *Bar code* (called *Keycode*™) is printed on the edge of the negative so there are reference numbers by which digital editing systems can digitize, retrieve, and display an electronic version of sound and picture. Time code also allows the film laboratory to conform the negative to a computer-generated *edit decision list* (EDL).

Because on-line editing is expensive and complicated, a simplified setup, called an *off-line rig,* which is little more than a programmable transfer setup, is widely used for the creative part of editing. Because older machines do not read time code, their edits are only accurate to within a few frames. If you preview a cut before making it, accuracy deteriorates further, which is maddening if you are trying to cut between two words in a sentence. Newer equipment, including Hi 8 editing machines, operate from time code and are frame accurate every time.

Once a fine cut is achieved, a clean copy of the entire edit will be reconstructed from the camera original. The process works much like a film lab conforming the negative to the workprint by film edge numbers.

Video postproduction consists of taking an off-line fine cut, the log or EDL, and camera original cassettes to a postproduction house. Here, using a computerized rig and working from a log of time code in- and out-points, specialists make a pristine replica of your bleary and battered workprint fine cut. The process entails audio sweetening, adjusting the video signal components to broadcast standards, and making color corrections. Most importantly, it includes electronic restabilization of an image made jittery through mechanical replay and rerecording. This is done using a *time-base corrector* (TBC), a device that takes in each frame as it emerges in time, whether slightly ahead or behind schedule, and releases it to the recorder with phenomenal time accuracy. Such precision, unnecessary in tolerant video replay equipment, becomes vital when a signal must be dispersed over a nationwide system of interlocked transmitters.

VIDEO: FROM TAPE TO DIGITAL PRODUCTION

Video production allows a high shooting ratio at little extra cost, but because electronic postproduction is labor and equipment intensive, broadcast quality is often as expensive per screen minute as it would be shooting good old low-tech film on a tight ratio. Few real documentaries allow one to work with the tight control possible in fiction filmmaking, so the ability to shoot speculatively and at length usually forces the independent with an eye to national-level visibility to work in video. The new digital camcorder formats, such as Sony's DV, approach Betacam specifications and permit both perfect copying and transfer direct into computer hard disk, with the necessary video compression being done as the camcorder records on to its tiny (6mm wide) tape.

If you expect your work to be replayed locally on videocassette only, a careful off-line edited version may be more than adequate. Even quite elaborate documentaries that were edited off-line have been taken by cable or network television, and electronically "straightened out" by the reluctant engineering department. If your documentary goes that route, stay away from the engineers while they are doing it. They may tell you what they are thinking.

DIGITIZING FOR NONLINEAR EDITING

Material to be edited has to be loaded from the digital camera original into the computer storage system. If the original was shot in a digital format, it will already have a degree of compression, which is to say, it has already been processed by an algorithm to strip out the repetitive, redundant information that occurs when many frames are similar. This is a solution to the problem of reducing huge quantities of video and sound information so that a quart can fit into the proverbial pint pot. Compressed information can go straight onto hard drive, but uncompressed, such as analogue audio or video must go through a JPEG, MPEG, or other compressor card according to the system in use.

Here documentary has a special problem owing to its high shooting ratios. It means you face hard choices—whether to digitize all of your material at an astonishingly awful resolution, or to digitize selects only at one more watchable. Whichever way you intend to go, see rushes in the best resolution possible, so hidden flaws don't show up in the show copy just before your premiere.

Most software allows you to start in one resolution, then to use the EDL to automatically redigitize your selected material at a higher resolution. This, however, could subject the precious camera original to extra handling, so it's wise to do all off-line work from jam sync copies. *Jam sync* means that the working copy is made from the camera original using equipment that will transfer, frame for frame, the original's time code as well as everything else. Be aware that an EDL derived from anything other than a jam-sync copy of the camera original is useless when you get to the on-line stage.

This discussion is important here because if the first assembly stage requires that you work from a limited storage capacity, you must discard source material at a rather early stage. The paper edit helps but may not completely solve this problem, depending on your hard drive's capacity. The rule of thumb is that about 50 minutes of original material can be digitized at medium resolution on every gigabyte of hard drive available. If you have a 9 gig drive, you have few worries. If you are working from only 1 gig, you must either work in sections or be ready to view all the rushes again at a late stage to retrieve any gold that shows up late. You should do this anyway. But your most pressing problem will be deciding what to digitize and how to work.

THE FIRST ASSEMBLY

Putting the material together for the first time is the most exciting part of editing. You should not worry at this stage about length or balance. In the film's paper edit, you have attempted to plan its themes and capitalize on your material. You can now put the material together roughly as planned without agonizing over the consequences of what you are doing. Leave everything long and do not worry about repetitiveness. You may need to see both men tell how the dam broke before you really know which to use or which to use most. Keep in mind that you cannot totally premeditate a film from knowledge of rushes any more than you can plan a journey to shore on a surfboard.

I think it is important to *see the whole film as soon as possible in some long, loose form before doing any detailed work on any sections.* Once you have seen the whole ungainly epic, you can make far-reaching resolutions about its future development. Of course, you will be longing to go to work on a favorite sequence, but fixing details would be avoiding the need to first assess the film's overall identity and purpose.

RETURN TO INNOCENCE

The discipline of filmmaking requires that one regularly return to a state of innocence. When you are about to see a first assembly of the film, you must deliberately set aside all foreknowledge or you will be unable to see the film with the eyes of a first-time viewer. This is never easy. But seeing as your audience sees is central to working effectively in an audience medium. Only by acquiring that insight can you construct a film that speaks satisfyingly to someone of your own intelligence who is seeing the film for the first time.

The same unobstructed, audience-like viewing is necessary *every* time you run your film. Though you use your familiarity with the source material to solve problems, this is only one of your identities. You must change hats every time you assess the film and *see it for itself, as a first-time audience would.* It helps to have one or two people present who have not seen the movie before. Although they may not utter a word, somehow their mere presence enables the makers to see the film from a fresh perspective.

If, on seeing your editor's new version, you experience a resistance in yourself because it is not what you expected, screen the new version again in order to see it more acceptingly, as an audience sees it, before you make any negative pronouncements.

AFTER THE FIRST VIEWING: DECIDING ON AN IDEAL LENGTH

That first viewing will yield some important realizations about the character, dramatic shape, and best length of the film. It may be that you have a particular length in mind. Television, for instance, usually has quite rigid specifications, with a 30-minute PBS or BBC "slot" requiring a film (including titles) of about 28 minutes 30 seconds to allow for announcements at either end. Almost all television documentaries are shown as part of a series, because audiences only learn to watch, seemingly, once a time in the week becomes associated with a particular kind of film. This is why professional films are more often funded as packages and as coproductions.

If your movie is to be shown on commercial television, it will have to be broken up into segments of perhaps 5 minutes with so-called natural breaks to allow for commercials. Thus, the outlet for your film determines both length and structure. Classroom films are normally 10 to 20 minutes, while television uses 30-, 40- (in Europe), 60-, and 90-minute slots. Short films that say a lot have an immeasurably better chance of acceptance everywhere.

Look to the content of your film itself for guidance. Films have a natural span according to the richness and significance of their content, but the hardest achievement in any art form is the confidence and ability to say a lot through a little. Most beginners' films are agonizingly long and slow; if you recognize early that your film should be, say, 40 minutes at the very most, you can get tough with that 75-minute assembly and make some basic decisions. Most of all, you need a structure to make the movie as interesting and assimilatable as any well-told tale. Bear in mind that a good plan does not guarantee a satisfying experience for an audience. Other criteria will come into play, arising from the emotional changes and development an audience will actually experience.

DIAGNOSTIC QUESTIONING

You are dealing with the film in its crudest form so you want to elicit your own dominant reactions. To assess a likely audience response, question yourself after the first viewing:

- *Does the film feel dramatically balanced?* For instance, if you have a very moving and exciting sequence in the middle of the film, the rest of the film may seem anticlimactic. Or you may have a film that seems to circle around for a long while before it really starts moving.
- *When did you have the definite feeling of a story unfolding, and when not?* This helps locate impediments in the film's development, and sets you analyzing why the film stumbles.
- *Which parts of the film seem to work, which drag, and why?*
- *Which participants held your attention the most, and which the least?* Some may be more congenial or just better on camera than others.
- *Was there a satisfying alternation of types of material?* Or was similar material clumped indigestibly together? Where did you get effective contrasts and juxtapositions? Are there more to be made? Variety is as important in storytelling as it is in dining.
- *Does the audience get too much or too little expository information?* Sometimes a sequence "does not work" because the ground has not been properly prepared or because there is insufficient contrast in mood with the previous sequence.
- *Could exposition be delayed?* Exposition that is too much or too early reduces the will to concentrate by removing all anticipatory tension in the viewer.
- *What kinds of metaphorical allusions does your material make?* Could it make more? This underlying statement is the way you imply your values and beliefs. That your tale carries a metaphorical charge is as important as the water table is to pasture.

DEALING WITH MATERIAL THAT DOESN'T WORK

After seeing an assembly, scribble a list of memorable material. Then, by referring to the paper edit sequence list, see what you *didn't* recall. Quite purposefully, the human memory discards what it doesn't find meaningful. You forgot all that good stuff because it failed to work, however great it looked on paper. This does not mean that it can *never* work, only that it is not doing so at present.

Here are a few common reasons why material misfires:

- *Two or more sequences are making the same point.* Repetition does not advance a film argument unless there is escalation. Make choices, ditch the redundant.

- *A climax is in the wrong place.* You are using your strongest material too early, and the film becomes anticlimactic.
- *Tension builds then slackens.* Think of your movie as having a rising or falling emotional temperature; see if it is raising the temperature then inadvertently cooling it before an intended peak. If so, the viewer's response is seriously impaired. Sometimes transposing sequences will work wonders.
- *The film raises false expectations.* A film, or part thereof, will fail if the viewer is set up to expect something that never gets delivered.
- *Good material is somehow lost on the audience.* We read into film according to the context, and if this gives misleading signals or fails to focus the right awareness, the material itself falls flat.
- *Multiple endings.* Decide what your film is really about and get out the pruning shears.

THE DOCUMENTARY MAKER AS DRAMATIST

The previous discussion looks like traditional dramatic analysis because it is. Like a playwright watching a first performance, you are using your instinct for drama to sniff out faults and weaknesses. It is hard because no objective measurements are possible. All you can do is dig for your own instincts through *feeling* the dramatic outcome of your material. If you called in some people whose reactions and tastes you respect, you will probably find some unanimity in their responses.

Where does the instinct for drama come from? It seems to be a human constant that resides in our collective unconsciousness, a human drive present since antiquity. We have both a compulsion to tell stories and a hunger to hear them. Think of the variations on the Arthurian legends that exist. They come from the Middle Ages, yet are still being adapted and updated, and are still giving pleasure after a thousand years!

The documentary probably carries on the oral tradition; it is history personally felt and relayed. To be successful, it too must connect with the emotional and imaginative life of a contemporary audience. As a filmmaker, you need to be concerned not just with self-expression, which is too often a narcissistic display of conscience or feelings, but also with entertaining and therefore serving your society.

Like all entertainers, the filmmaker has a precarious economic existence and either fulfills the audience or goes hungry. In *Literature and Film*,[1] Robert Richardson argues that the vitality and optimism of the cinema, compared with other twentieth-century art forms, is due to its collaborative authorship and its dependency on public response. Of course, it would be absurd and cynical to claim that only the appreciation of the masses matters, but the enduring presence of folk art—plays, poetry, music, architecture, and traditional tales—should alert us to how much we share with the untutored tastes of our forebears.

---

[1]Richardson, Robert. *Literature and Film*. Bloomington, IN: Indiana University Press, 1969, pp. 3–16.

The simple fact is that the "ordinary" person's tastes and instincts—yours and mine—are highly acculturated. But because in ordinary life we never have to discuss them in depth or use them to make art statements, we lack confidence when it comes time to live by them. Making a documentary is exciting because you have to lay your perceptions and judgments on the line.

MAKING THE VISIBLE SIGNIFICANT

In Chapter 5 of *Literature and Film,* Richardson goes to the heart of the problem filmmakers face compared with writers: "Literature often has the problem of making the significant somehow visible, while film often finds itself trying to make the visible significant."[2]

It is difficult, as we have said before, to drive the audience's awareness deeper than what is literally and materially in front of the camera. For instance, we may accept a scene in which a mother makes lunch for her children as simply that. So what? you ask. Mothers make lunch for kids all the time. But there are nuances: One child has persistent difficulty choosing what she wants. The mother is trying to suppress her irritation. Looking closely, you see that the child is manipulating the situation. Food and eating has become their battleground, their frontier in a struggle for control. The mother's moral authority comes from telling her daughter she must eat right to stay healthy, while the child asserts her authority over her own body by a maddening noncompliance.

What we have here (as so often in film) is the problem of showing how a meal is more than food, of showing it as a battleground with a deadly serious subtext. If we first see child and mother in some other, more overt conflict over control, we would probably read the scene correctly. There may be other ways, of course, in which attention could be channeled. But without the proper structural support, the significance and universality of such a scene could easily pass unappreciated. Naturally, what you the filmmaker can see happening will not necessarily strike even the most perceptive of first-time viewers because they lack your commitment, your behind-the-scenes knowledge, and your repeated exposure to the situation, with its deepening insights. However you evolved, you must now evolve your audience to the same point, but in 30 minutes instead of 30 weeks.

AFTER THE DUST SETTLES, WHAT NEXT?

After seeing the first assembly, fundamental issues really begin to emerge. You may see your worst fears: Your film has no less than three endings—two false and one intended. Your favorite character makes no impact at all beside others who seem more spontaneous and alive. You have to concede that a sequence in a dance hall, which was hell to shoot, has only one really good minute in it or that a woman you interviewed for a minor opinion actually says some striking things and is upstaging an "important" contributor.

---

[2]Ibid, p. 68.

The first assembly auditions the best material and becomes the launching pad for a denser and more complex film. As a show, it is woefully inadequate because it is so long and crude, yet because of its very artlessness it can be both affecting and exciting.

In the coming stages avoid trying to fix everything in one grandiose swipe. Wait a few days and think things over. Then tackle only the major needs of the film. Forswear the pleasures of fine-tuning or you won't see the forest for the trees.

C H A P T E R 2 2

EDITING: THE PROCESS OF REFINEMENT

THE PROBLEM OF ACHIEVING A FLOW

After you have run your first assembly two or three times, it will increasingly strike you as clunky blocks of material having a dreadful lack of flow. First you may have some illustrative stuff, then several blocks of interview, then a montage of shots, then another block of something else, and so on. Sequences go by like a series of floats in a parade, each quite separate from its fellows. How does one achieve the effortless flow seen in other people's films? Let's return to the way human perception functions and how it affects eyeline shifts.

HOW EDITING MIMICS CONSCIOUSNESS

Take the commonly dramatized situation of two people having a conversation. When inexperienced players act such a scene, they invariably lock eyes as they speak. This is the stereotyped idea of how people converse, but reality is more subtle and interesting. Observe yourself during a normal conversation, and see how neither you nor the other person makes eye contact more than fleetingly. The intensity of eye-to-eye contact is reserved for special moments.

During any interaction—whether we know it or not—we are either *acting* on the other person, or *being acted on*. At crucial points in either mode, we glance into the other person's face to see what she means, or to judge what effect we have just had. The rest of the time our gaze may rest on some object or jump around the surroundings. Special junctures in our inner process send our eye back to the other person. A feel for how this works helps greatly in deciding camerawork and editing.

Now become the observer of two people talking and decide what makes your eyeline shift back and forth between them. Notice how often your eyeline shifts are triggered by shifts in their eyelines. Your consciousness is alerted by the significance of their shifts. As you watch, you will become conscious not only of a rhythm and motivation to their shifts of eyeline (controlled by the shifting contours of the conversation itself), but also that *moment to moment your eyes make their own judgment as to where to look.* Much of the time your center of attention independently switches back and forth, following the pair's action and reaction, and their changes of eyeline.

Notice that you often leave a speaker in midsentence to monitor the effect on the listener. Instinctively, from a lifetime's practice, we *"edit" according to our developing insight, trying to extract the most subtextual information from the scene.* This exercise explains how and why editing developed as we know it.

LOOKING AT AND LOOKING THROUGH

In my example above, a film would have to relay three different points of view (POVs): one for each of the participants and a third for the observer. The observer's POV is outside the enclosed consciousness of the two speakers and tends to look at them from a more detached, authorial vantage. According to choices made in editing, the audience can therefore identify with either one of the characters or with the more removed perspective of the invisible observer who in film is really the storyteller. While character A talks, for instance, the observer (through whose eyes and mind we see) might look at either A or B in search of ideas that A has of B or vice versa. Or the film might allow the audience to look at both of them in long shot. This flexibility of viewpoint allows the director to structure not only geographically privileged viewpoints but to share what the observer sees (and therefore feels) at any particular moment. This probing, analytic way of seeing is, of course, modeled on the way we unconsciously delve into any event that interests us. *The film process thus mimics the interpretive quest that both accompanies and directs human observation.*

To write about this is to make it sound complicated. Film and human consciousness may run under complex and similar rules, but the best teacher is always going to be the movement of your own consciousness, that is, what you see, what you hear, what acts on your feelings, and what these make you think. Human beings are similar to each other (otherwise, there could be no cinema) and there are many nonverbal signs—in body language, eyeline shifts, voice inflections, and particular actions—to which we all ascribe similar meanings. The great benefit of documentary is that it's an excellent instructor in all of this.

EDITING RHYTHMS: AN ANALOGY IN MUSIC

Music makes a useful analogy if we examine an edited version of a conversation between two people. We have two different but interlocked rhythms going: First, there is the rhythmic pattern of their voices in a series of sentences that ebb and flow, speed up, slow down, halt, restart, fade, and so on. Set against this, and often taking a rhythmic cue from speech rhythms, is the visual tempo set up by the interplay of cutting, image compositions, and camera movement. The two streams, visual and aural, proceed independently yet are rhythmically related, like the music and physical movements in a dance concert.

When you hear a speaker and you see his face as he talks, sound and vision are in an alliance, like musical harmony. We could, however, break the literalness of always hearing and seeing the same thing *(harmony)* by making the transition from scene to scene into a temporary puzzle.

Here is an example: We are going to cut from a man talking about unemployment to a somber cityscape. We start with the speaker in picture and then cut to the cityscape while he is still speaking, letting his remaining words play out over the cityscape. The effect is as follows: While our subject was talking to us about growing unemployment, we glanced out of the window to see all the houses spread out below us, and the empty parking lots and cold chimneys of closed factories. The film version mimics the instinctual glance of someone sitting there listening; the speaker's words are powerfully counterpointed by the image, and the image lets loose our imagination as we ponder the magnitude of the disruption, of what it is like to live in one of those houses.

This *counterpoint,* of a sound against an unlike image, has its variations. One usage is simply to illustrate the actuality of what words can only describe. We might cut from a bakery worker talking about fatigue to shots taken through shimmering heat of workers in a bread factory moving about their repetitive tasks like zombies.

Another usage exploits discrepancies. For instance, we hear a teacher describing an enlightened and attractive philosophy of teaching, but see the same man lecturing in a monotone, drowning his yawning students in a wash of irrelevant facts and stifling their discussion. This discrepancy, if we pursue the musical allusion, is a *dissonance,* spurring the viewer to crave a resolution. Comparing the man's beliefs with his practice, the viewer resolves the discrepancy by deciding that here is a man who does not know himself.

COUNTERPOINT IN PRACTICE:
UNIFYING MATERIAL INTO A FLOW

Once a reasonable order for the material has been found, you will want to combine sound and action in a form that takes advantage of counterpoint techniques. In practice this means, as we have said, bringing together the sound from one shot with the image from another. To develop the previous example, in which the teacher with a superb teaching theory proves to have a poor performance, one could show this on the screen by shooting two sets of materials, one of relevantly structured interview, the other of the teacher droning away in class.

In editing, we bring these materials into juxtaposition. The conservative, first-assembly method would alternate segments as in Figure 22-1A: a block of interview in which the man begins explaining his ideas, then a block of teaching, then another block of explanation, then another of teaching, and so on until the point is made. This is a common, though clumsy, way to accomplish the objective in the assembly stage. After a little back-and-forth cutting, the technique and the message are both predictable. I think of it as boxcar cutting because each chunk goes by like boxcars on a railroad.

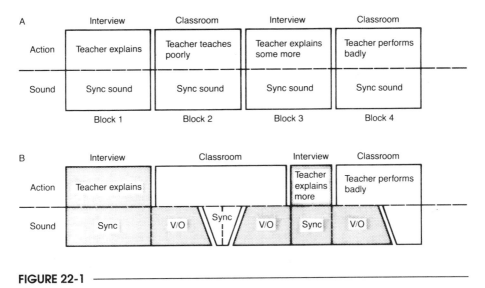

FIGURE 22-1

(A) First assembly of material through a block or "boxcar" approach compared with (B), an overlap edit, which allows a simultaneous counterpoint of idea and actuality.

Instead of alternating the two sets of materials, it would be better to integrate them as in Figure 22-1B. Start with the teacher explaining his philosophy of teaching and then cut to the classroom sequence, with the classroom sound low and the teacher's explanation continuing over it (this is called *voice-over*). When the voice has finished its sentence, we bring up the sound of the classroom sequence and play the classroom at full level. Then we lower the classroom atmosphere and bring in the teacher's interview voice again. At the end of the classroom action, as the teacher gets interesting, we cut to him in sync (now including his picture to go with his voice). At the end of what was Block 3 in Figure 22-1A, we continue his voice but cut—in picture only—back to the classroom, where we see the bored and mystified kids of Block 4. Now, instead of having description and practice dealt with in separate blocks of material, description is laid against practice, and ideas against reality, in a much harder hitting counterpoint.

The benefits are multiple. The total sequence is shorter and more sprightly. Talking-head material is kept to an interesting minimum, while the behavioral material, the classroom evidence against which we measure the teacher's ideas, is now in the majority. The counterpointing of essentials allows an interview to be pared down, giving what is presented a muscular, spare quality, usually lacking in unedited reminiscence. There is a much closer and more telling juxtaposition between vocalized theory and actual teaching behavior. The audience is challenged right away to reconcile the man's ideas with what he is actually doing.

Counterpoint editing cannot be worked out in the paper edit, but one can usually decide quite confidently which materials could effectively be intercut. The specifics can then be worked out from the materials themselves.

THE AUDIENCE AS ACTIVE PARTICIPANTS

Significantly, this more demanding texture of word and image puts the spectator in a different relationship to the "evidence" presented. It encourages an active rather than passive participation. The contract is no longer just to absorb and be instructed. Instead, the invitation is to *interpret and weigh what is seen and heard.* The film now sometimes uses action to illustrate, and other times to contradict, what has been set up and what has seemed true. The viewer's independent judgment was invoked in the earlier example of the teacher and the classroom because the teacher's ideas were an unreliable narration instead of conventionally bland guidance.

But there are other ways for juxtaposition and counterpoint to stimulate imagination when the conventional coupling of sound and picture is changed. For instance, one might show a street shot in which a young couple go into a café. We presume they are lovers. They sit at a table in the window. We who remain outside are near an elderly couple discussing the price of fish, but the camera moves in close to the window, so that we can see through the glass how the couple talk affectionately and energetically to each other, while what we hear is the old couple arguing over the price of fish. The effect is an ironic contrast between two states of intimacy; we see courtship but we hear the concerns of later life. With great economy of means, and not a little humor, a cynical idea about marriage is set afloat—one that the rest of the film might ultimately dispel with hopeful alternatives.

By creating juxtapositions that require interpretation, film is able to counterpoint antithetical ideas and moods with great economy. At the same time it can kindle the audience's involvement with the dialectical nature of life. If we are to interest people who normally turn away from the pedestrian nature of so much documentary, we must find ways be as funny, earthy, and poignant as life itself. In no other way can we draw audiences into willing contemplation of the darker aspects of life.

Counterpointing the visual and the aural is only an extension of what has been called *montage* from early in film's history. In editing, the juxtaposition of two dissimilar shots implies relatedness and continuity, and the audience's imagination is meant to supply the linkage between them or between sequences. The use of contrapuntal sound as a dialectical medium came relatively late and was, I believe, developed by documentary makers. In fiction filmmaking, Robert Altman's films from *M*A*S*H* (1970) onward show the most inventiveness in producing a dense, layered counterpoint in their sound tracks. Altman's sound recordist even built a special 16-track location sound recorder, which could make individual recordings from up to 15 radio microphones.

THE OVERLAP CUT: DIALOGUE SEQUENCES

Another contrapuntal editing device useful to hide the telltale seams between shots is called the *overlap cut.* It brings sound in earlier than picture, or picture in earlier than sound, and thus avoids the jarring level cut, which results in boxcar editing.

Figure 22-2 shows a straight-cut version of a conversation between A and B. Whoever speaks is shown on the screen. This gets predictable and boring after a while. You can alleviate this problem by slugging in some reaction shots (not shown).

Now look at the same conversation using overlap cutting. A starts speaking, but when we hear B's voice, we wait a sentence before cutting to him. B is interrupted by A, and this time we hold on B's frustrated expression before cutting to A driving his point home. Before A has finished and because we are now interested in B's rising anger, we cut back to him shaking his head. When A has finished, B caps the discussion, and we make a level cut to the next sequence. The three sections of integrated reaction are marked in Figure 22-2 as X, Y, and Z.

How do you decide when to make overlap cuts? It is often done at a later stage of cutting, but we need a guiding theory. Let's return for a moment to that reliable model for editing, human consciousness. Imagine you are witnessing a conversation between two people; you have to turn from one to the other. Seldom will you turn your head at the right moment to catch the next speaker beginning— only an omniscient being could be so accurate. Inexperienced or bad editors often make neat, level cuts between speakers, and the results have a packaged, premeditated look that destroys the illusion of watching a spontaneous event.

In real life one can seldom predict when someone will speak next, or even who it will be. So a new voice, after it has started, tells us where to look. If an editor is to convince us that a conversation is spontaneous, the observer/storyteller should mostly follow shifts, not anticipate them. The editor must replicate the disjunctive shifts we unconsciously make as our eyes follow our hearing, or our hearing focuses in late on something just seen.

Effective cutting always reproduces the needs and reactions of an involved observer, as if we were there ourselves. Listening to a speaker as she begins making

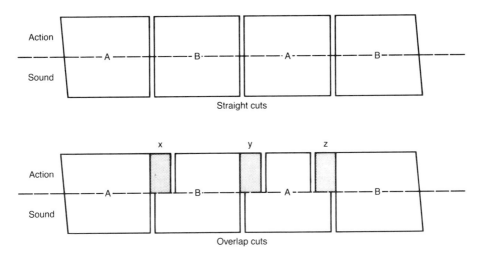

FIGURE 22-2 —————————————————————————————

Intercutting two speakers to make use of overlap cutting. Overlaps X, Y, and Z function as listening, reacting shots. Use this technique to reduce the sound gaps between speakers with no apparent speedup in pacing.

her point, we often switch to consider the point's effect on her listener. Even as we ponder, that listener begins to reply. A moment of forcefulness causes us to switch attention to the listener, so without ceremony we glance away from her. The line of her mouth hardens, and we know she is disturbed.

Here we are receiving two complementary impressions—the speaker through our hearing and the listener through our vision, hearing the person who acts but looking at the person on whom she acts. When that situation reverses and our listener has begun his reply, we glance back to see how the original speaker is reacting. Unconsciously we are searching for visual clues—in facial expressions or body language—to the protagonists' inner lives.

This type of cutting allows the spectator to be engaged not just in hearing and seeing each speaker as he speaks (which would be boring), but also in *interpreting what is going on inside each protagonist* through seeing key moments of action, reaction, or subjective vision. In dramatic terms, this is the *search for subtext*.

For the aspiring editor the message is clear: Be true to life and implant the developing sensations of the critical observer in the audience. Do this, and sound and picture changeover points are seldom level cuts. Overlap cuts achieve this important disjunction, allowing the film to cut from shot to shot independently of the "his turn, her turn, his turn" speech alternations in the sound track.

THE OVERLAP CUT: SEQUENCE TRANSITIONS

In the same way, a transition from one sequence to another may also be a staggered cut. Imagine a scene where a boy and girl are talking about going out together. The boy says he is worried that her mother will try to stop them. The girl says, "Oh don't worry about her, I can convince her." The next scene is of the mother closing the refrigerator with a bang and saying firmly, "Absolutely not!" to the aggrieved daughter.

A level cut would mimic a fast theatrical scene change. More interesting would be to cut from the boy/girl scene to the mother at the refrigerator while the girl is still saying " . . . I can convince her." While she is still finishing her sentence, the picture cuts forward in time to show the mother slamming the fridge door. Then she says her line, "Absolutely not!"

Another way to merge one scene into the next rather than make a staccato level cut would be to hold on the boy and girl, have the mother's angry voice say "Absolutely not!" over the tail end of their scene, and use the surprise of the new voice to motivate cutting to the mother's picture as the scene continues.

Either of these devices serves to make the "joints" between one sequence and the next less theatrical and noticeable. Sometimes one wants to bring a scene to a slow closure, perhaps with a fade-out, and then gently and slowly begin another, this time perhaps with a fade-in. More often, one simply wants to cut from one scene to the next and keep up the momentum. A level cut will often seem to jerk the viewer rudely into a new place and time, and a dissolve can instead integrate the two scenes. But dissolves insert a rest period between scenes, and may dissipate the desired carryover of momentum.

The overlap cut is the answer. It keeps the track alive and draws the viewer after it, so the transition seems natural rather than forced. You have surely seen this done with sound effects. It might look like this: The factory worker rolls reluctantly out of bed, then as he shaves and dresses, we hear the increasingly loud sound of machinery until we cut to him at work on the production line. Here *anticipatory sound* drags our attention forward to the next sequence. Because our curiosity demands an answer to the riddle of machine sounds in a bedroom, we do not feel the location switch is arbitrary.

Another overlap cutting technique would be to make sound work the other way; we cut from the man working on the assembly line to him getting some food out of his home refrigerator. *Holdover sound* of factory uproar subsides slowly as he exhaustedly eats some leftovers.

In the first example, the aggressive factory sound draws him forward out of his bedroom; in the second, it lingers even after he has got home. In both cases, a psychological narrative is implied, because both sound devices suggest that the sound exists in his head as an awareness of how unpleasant his workplace is. At home he thinks of it and is sucked up by it; after work the din continues to haunt him.

By using overlap cuts (also known as *lap cuts,* or *L cuts*) we can not only soften transitions between locations, but also suggest subtext and point of view through implying the inner consciousness of a central character. We could play it the other way, and let the silence of the home trail out into the workplace, so that he is seen at work, and the bedroom radio continues to play softly before being swamped by the rising uproar of the factory. At the end of the day, the sounds of laughter on the television set could displace the factory noise and make us cut to him sitting at home, relaxing with a sitcom.

By using sound and picture transitions creatively, you can transport the viewer forward without the cumbersome (and in film, expensive) device of using optical effects, such as dissolves, fades, and wipes. You can also give important clues about your characters' inner lives and imaginations.

These cutting techniques are hard to grasp from a book. Look for them in the films you watch, and work out how they reproduce the habitual way our eyes, ears, and intelligence work together as they dig for subtextual meanings.

In summary, we have established through these examples that in real life our consciousness can probe our surroundings either monodirectionally (eyes and ears on the same information source) or bidirectionally (eyes and ears on different sources). Our attention also moves in time, either forward (anticipation and imagination) or backward (memory). Film language can recreate all these aspects of consciousness, and by so doing helps the audience to share the sensations of a shifting consciousness, either that of characters or that of the storyteller, or both.

HELP! I CAN'T UNDERSTAND!

If this is getting beyond you, don't worry. The best way to understand editing is to take a complex and interesting fiction sequence and, by running a shot or two at a time on a VCR, make a split-page log of the relationship between the track elements and the visuals. In Chapter 6, Project 6-2, Editing Analysis, is an editing self-education program with a list of editing techniques for you to track down and analyze. Try returning to this section, and with examples in hand it should make a lot more sense.

C H A P T E R   2 3

NARRATION

Today, and for good reason, it is unfashionable to use the disembodied, authoritative narration. However, you may have planned to use narration all along, having directed a personal or anthropological film that quite properly needs your voice to provide links or to supply context. Or you may be forced into using narration because expositional material or an adequate story line is lacking, and the film's development needs help. Narration is always available as a recourse and is often neither a dishonorable nor detrimental one at that.

NARRATION AS AN OPTION

If during shooting you remembered to elicit all relevant information from participants, you can assemble the movie and see if it stands on its own feet. A common problem is getting one's film started (its exposition, in the language of drama). Establishing the necessary factual background, so the audience can enter the movie, need not be complicated, but sometimes only narration can handle it succinctly.

Another problem may not be in beginning the film but in keeping it moving or keeping it comprehensible. Perhaps you have good stories and good action, but getting from one sequence to the next takes too much explaining by the participants, explaining that could be accomplished in a fraction of the time with a few well-chosen words of narration.

Maybe your best efforts still produce a lack of resolution because the evidence never achieves a satisfying focus. Sure proof is when a trial audience expresses disappointment with the film's impact and then becomes enthusiastic when you add comments on the material. Obviously, a film cannot rely on its maker's presence to be effective. Whatever you said in person must now be built into the film.

DRAWBACKS AND ASSOCIATIONS OF NARRATION

Narration can get you out of tight spots, but it becomes one more element to shape and control. Narration is so intrusive that if it's not first rate, it will hamper rather than advance your movie. The very existence of a narrator poses problems because the disembodied voice becomes a mediating presence standing between audience and the film's "evidence." This, of course, is the voice of *authority,* with all its connotations of condescension and paternalism. Television audiences wait wearily to find out what product or ideology it is preparing to sell. Such a film makes us essentially passive, because it insists that we either accept authority or tune out. The intelligent documentary aims to involve the viewer's values and discrimination, not just to invade his memory or colonize his subconscious.

Viewers take the narrator's voice as *the voice of the film itself,* and base judgments about the film's intelligence and biases not only on what narration says, but also on the quality and associations of the voice. For this reason, finding a suitable voice is very hard. In effect, the search is for one that, by words and quality, can act as a surrogate for one's own attitude toward the subject.

POSITIVE ASPECTS OF NARRATION

In spite of narration's inauspicious associations, it need be neither condescending nor intrusive. It can also be a lifesaver, rapidly and effectively introducing a new character, summarizing intervening developments, or concisely supplying a few vital facts. Especially when a film must fit a lot into a short duration, time saved is time won for additional "evidence" footage.

Usually acceptable narration:

- Is limited to useful factual information.
- Is nonmanipulative emotionally.
- Avoids value judgments, unless first established by evidence in the footage.
- Avoids predisposing the viewer in any direction, but may justifiably draw our attention to those aspects of the evidence—visual or verbal—whose significance might otherwise be overlooked.
- Lets the audience draw its own conclusions from the evidence you show.

A narration can also, drawing on traditions in literature, ballad, and poetry, adopt a stylized "voice." Many films adopt special narrative strategies, such as:

- A historical view, as in countless films about immigration, war, or slavery.
- Artful simplicity, as in the naive reporter persona that Michael Moore adopts in *Roger and Me* (1989).
- A what-if suppositional voice, as in Alain Resnais' *Night and Fog* (1955).
- Poetic/musical identification with the subject, as in Basil Wright's *Night Mail.*
- Angry irony, as in Luis Buñuel's *Land Without Bread* (1932).
- A first-person writer voice addressing a particular reader, as in the war letters used in Ken Burns' *Civil War* series.
- A diary voice, as fabricated for Humphrey Jennings' *A Diary for Timothy* (1946).

TWO APPROACHES TO NARRATION

Any writing for film, whether documentary narration or dialogue for actors, must use the direct language of everyday speech or it will fail. Because film moves relentlessly in time, an audience either gets the narration or chokes on the obstacles. Following are two ways to create a narration:

Method 1: Read from a Script.   This is the traditional method and it can work well if your film acknowledges that it is based on letters, a diary, or other bona fide text. Then the formality of a reading makes sense. But when you want spontaneity or a one-to-one tone of intimacy, written narration nearly always fails. Think how often narration is the single element that makes a film unacceptably dull or dated. Some common faults are:

- verbosity
- heavy or literary writing
- something distracting in the narrator's voice (it may be dull, condescending, egotistic, projecting, trying to entertain, trying to be liked, or have distracting associations)

Recording a read narration is inherently risky. Do it well in advance and to picture (described later). Don't assume it will be all right on opening night.

Method 2: Use Some Degree of Improvisation.   Improvised narration can strike an attractively informal, "one-on-one" relationship with the audience. Examples include:

- When a participant serves as narrator.
- When you must use your own voice in a "diary" film that must sound spontaneous and not scripted.
- When you want to create a composite poetic voice, say, of a Japanese woman carrying out a tea ceremony (a highly questionable "speaking for" ploy but formerly more acceptable).

Let's now look in detail at what's involved with each method.

THE SCRIPTED NARRATION

WRITING

First and foremost, a narrator must have a good text. Be prepared to write and rewrite upward of twenty drafts. A test of quality for any piece of writing, particularly narration, is whether you can effectively read it aloud to a group of listeners.
Bad narration uses:

- the passive voice (where the subject is acted upon—fatal in a genre already replete with victims anyway!)

- sonorous, ready-made phrases and clichés
- long sentences
- the syntax of writing or literary discourse
- windy ornamentation
- jargon or other language designed to impress
- over-information that robs the audience of time to imagine or guess (regularly inflicted in children's films)
- description of what is already evident
- assumed voices or condescending humor

Good narration uses:

- the direct language of speech
- the right word for the job
- fresh language, not stale
- the fewest words—as if writing poetry, pack the most meaning in the fewest syllables
- language that is balanced and potent to the ear
- the active, not passive, voice (e.g., "Here immigrants *drive* the taxis" not "Here taxis *are driven* by immigrants." You wouldn't believe how much writing of all kinds falls into the latter, passive voice.)

As you edit and re-edit your film, hone your writing in search of the power of simplicity. Exult when you find a way to reduce a sentence by even one syllable.

THE TRYOUT

As you write, examine each film section and write what you think is necessary. Then read your words for each section aloud. Your narration should rhythmically match those of the outgoing and incoming sequences. What you write must sound right in relation to both old and new speakers (if there are ones), and it must be the right length so you don't have to speed up or slow down to fill the space. Ends and beginnings of scenes sometimes need adjusting to accommodate narration.

ADJUSTING SYNTAX

Sometimes it helps to invert the syntax so the narration follows the audience's order of perception in a sequence or shot. For instance, if you have a shot of a big, rising sun with a small figure toiling across the landscape, the viewer notices the sun long before noticing the human being. You might first write, "She goes out before anyone else is about." But this immediately sets the viewer looking for the "she." The rest of the sentence won't be assimilated because the viewer is busy searching for the subject. Reconfigure the syntax to accommodate perceptions (sun, landscape, woman) and you would get: "Before anyone else is up, she goes out." This complements the viewer's perceptions instead of swimming against the tide.

ACCOMMODATING SOUND FEATURES

Another reason to alter phrasing or to break sentences apart is to open up spaces for featured sound effects, such as a car door closing or a phone beginning to ring. Effects frequently create a powerful mood and drive the narrative forward, so don't obscure them with talking. Effects also help to mask the bane of the documentary—too much talk, or, to put it in the vernacular, verbal diarrhea.

THE POWER IN EACH FIRST WORD

Here's a fact not widely appreciated: The first word to fall on each new image exerts a major influence on how the audience interprets the whole shot. For instance, we have two shots cut together as in Figure 23-1; the outgoing is of a photo in which we see an artist at work at his easel, and the incoming shot shows a painting of a woman. The narration says, "Spencer used as a model first his wife and later the daughter of a friend."

Different juxtapositions of words and images actually yield quite different meanings, and the crux lies in which word hits the incoming shot, as illustrated in the diagram. There is a single, unchanging section of narration, but depending on

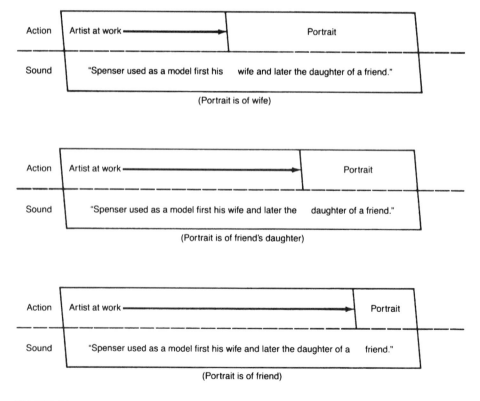

FIGURE 23-1

Three cutting points can convey three different meanings.

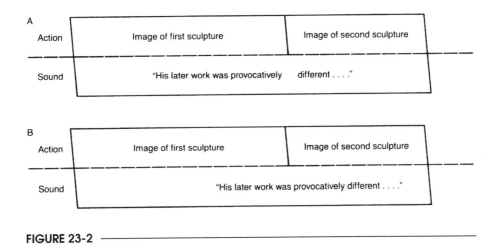

FIGURE 23-2

Shifting word position against image can shade meaning. In (A) the second sculpture will be seen as an example of departure in the artist's work, while in (B) it is suggested more that the second sculpture (the "later work") elicited an excited critical reaction.

how it sits against the three images, it can identify the person in the portrait in three different ways!

In another situation, illustrated in Figure 23-2, a simple shift in word positioning may alter only the emotional shading attached to an image rather than its basic identity. For instance, you see two shots, each of a piece of sculpture, and you hear the narrator say, "His later work was provocatively different."

By altering the relationship of narration to incoming image by a single word, the second sculpture can be made either just "different" or "*provocatively* different." Thus writing skill and sensitivity to word positioning gives you a potent tool of communication.

OPERATIVE WORDS

I have talked here about writing to images, but often you face the reverse situation. Pictures must be edited to a preset narration or dialogue. There is a little known key to doing this well: In any section of speech, there are strong places and weak places against which to make a picture cut. To decide this, examine the sentence. The speaker usually indicates dominant intentions by stressing certain syllables. Take something a mother might say to a recalcitrant teenager, "I want you to wait right here and don't move. I'll talk to you later."

Several readings each suggesting a different subtext are possible, but a likely one is: "I want you to *wait* right here and *don't* move. I'll *talk* to you later."

Each of the stressed words represents an operative intention on the part of the speaker, so I think of such words as *operative words*. If we were to design how images would cut to this piece of dialogue, the split-page script would look like this:

Picture	*Sound*
Wide shot, woman and son.	"I want you to . . .
Close shot, boy's mutinous face.	wait right here and . . .
Close shot, her hand on his shoulder.	don't move. (pause) I'll . . .
Close shot, mother's determined face.	talk to you later."

On each operative word this script cuts to a new image: the mother's determination and the boy's stubborn resistance are reinforced by these placements, each time a new shot against a strong operative word.

This dialogue principle pervades intelligent editing in both feature and documentary films. If you come across a sequence you like, study it in depth on your VCR and decide what the thinking is behind the editing. This kind of work can greatly clarify how to direct and edit in documentary, though you may not want your documentary work to look so openly controlled, or your audience may feel that you are manipulating them.

COMPLEMENT, DON'T DUPLICATE

When writing, avoid the temptation to describe what we can already see. Narration should add to the image, never describe the image's content. For example, one should never say that the child in the shot is wearing a red raincoat (blatantly obvious) nor that she is hesitant (subtly evident), but one might, however, say she has just celebrated her sixth birthday. This is information outside what we can see or infer.

TRYING IT OUT: THE SCRATCH RECORDING

Once you have written your narration, record a scratch (quick trial) narration using any handy reader or your own voice. Lay in the scratch narration and watch it as dispassionately as you can three or four times. You will see improvements in the wording and will know better what kind of voice you need. You will also be able to assess the pacing and emotional coloration (if any) that will work best. In some places, you see that the narrator has to hurry, so here you must thin the narration out; elsewhere the narration may seem too brief and perfunctory, and in need of developing. Now you are ready to think about auditioning and recording the final narrator.

A SCRIPT FOR THE NARRATOR

The script prepared for the narrator should be a simple, double-spaced typescript, containing only what the narrator will read. Blocks of narration should be set apart and numbered for easy location. Try not to split a block across two pages, because this may lead to the narrator turning pages audibly during the recording. Where it is unavoidable, lay both flat so no handling is required.

NARRATION: AUDITIONING AND RECORDING

Writing well is one art, and finding someone to speak it effectively is another. Even professional actors can seldom read a commentary without making it sound canned. The fact is, speech and reading aloud are utterly different. When speaking to a listener, one's mind is occupied finding words to act on him with an idea, while reading from a script makes one into an audience for one's own voice. Documentary participants are going to have even more difficulty speaking from a script than trained actors, even when the words or ideas are their own.

Because choosing a narrator is choosing a voice for the film, you will find yourself rejecting many types of voice due to their associations alone. The convention has been to use the deep, authoritative male voice, but today that signals either a sales pitch or a deeply tainted paternalism. For any number of reasons, most of the voices available simply will not fit. Other voices you will want to audition. As with any choice, you should record several, even when you believe you have stumbled on perfection.

VOICE AUDITIONS

To test native ability, give each person something representative to read. Then ask for a different reading of the same material, to see how well the narrator responds to direction. Sometimes the reader focuses effectively with the new interpretation but is unable to hold on to something deemed successful in the previous reading. Another reader may be anxious to please, can carry out instructions, but lacks a grasp of the larger picture. This is common with actors whose only experience is commercials.

After you make audition recordings, thank each person and give a date by which you will get back in contact. Even when you think someone is just right, do not confirm until you first listen carefully to the others. Listening to a disembodied, recorded voice is often a lesser or different experience than you felt at the time.

Your final choice must be independent of personal liking or obligation toward anyone who auditioned but, rather, made solely on what makes the best narration voice. Show your chosen narrator the film and discuss what it is all about.

RECORDING AND DIRECTING THE NARRATOR

Try to record in a professional fashion, that is, with the picture running so the narrator is keyed into the rhythms and intonation of other voices in the film. The narrator should neither watch the picture (that is the job of the editor and director) nor be able to hear the accompanying track in- and out-points, which would be distracting. If you don't have access to a custom-designed studio, setting up your own equipment will be a pain but more than worth the trouble. To record *wild* (i.e., not shot to picture or without an immediate regard for synchronization) is extremely risky because you can't be sure anything works until the artist has been dismissed.

A good voice recording will probably be made with the artist about 1 to 2 feet from the microphone. Surroundings should be acoustically dead (not enclosed or echoey), and there should be no distracting background noise. Listen through *good* headphones or through a speaker in another room. It is critically important to get the best out of your narrator's voice. Watch out for the voice trailing away at ends of sentences, for "popping" on certain sounds, or distortion from overloading. Mike positioning and monitoring of sound decibel (dB) levels all help.

The narrator should read each block of narration and wait for a cue (a gentle tap on the shoulder or a cue light flash) before beginning the next. Rehearse and give directions, which should be phrased positively and practically, giving instructions on how to say something rather than why. Stick to essentials, such as "Make the last part a little warmer" or "I'd like to hear that said a bit more formally." Try to name the quality you are after. After rehearsing, record that block and move on to rehearsing the next.

Sometimes you will want to alter the word stressed in a sentence or change the amount of projection the speaker is using ("Could you give me the same intensity but use less voice?" or "Use more voice and keep it up at the ends of sentences"). Occasionally a narrator will have some insurmountable problem with phrasing. Invite her to reword it while retaining the sense, but be on guard if this starts happening a lot. Your narrator may be taking over the writing.

When all narration has been recorded, play everything back against the film to check that everything really works. If there are one or two doubtful readings, cover yourself by making several wild versions incorporating a variety of readings before letting the narrator go. These can be tried later and the best one chosen.

CREATING THE IMPROVISED NARRATION

A spontaneous and informal narration that sounds like one-on-one conversation, so difficult to create through writing, can be achieved quite easily through interviewing. Under these circumstances the speaker's mind is naturally engaged in finding words to act back on the interviewer—a familiar situation that elicits normal speech. Here are some ways to create an improvised narration:

1. *Improvising from a rough script.* In this relatively structured method, briefly show your narrator a rough script or a list of ideas just before recording. You ask interview questions, and he or she then replies in character, paraphrasing because you have not allowed any learning of lines. Finding the words to express the narration's content reflects what happens in life; we know what we want to say, but have to find the words on the spot.

2. *Improvising from an identity.* This method develops a character or type of person for the narrator to "become." Together you go over who the narrator is and what that character wants the audience to know. Then you "interview" that character, perhaps by taking a character role yourself, asking pertinent and leading questions. Replying from a defined role helps the narrator lock into a focused relationship. This method might be used to create a historical character's voice-over.

3. *Simple interview.* In this, the most common method, the director interviews the documentary's "point of view" character carefully and extensively. It's probably done audio-only during shooting when the chase is on. From this you

can extract a highly spontaneous-sounding narration afterward in the cutting room. A variation is to shoot an extensive sync interview (i.e., sound and picture) so you can cut to the speaker at critical moments. If you want to narrate your own film, get a trusted and demanding friend to interview you.

All three methods produce a narration that can be edited down, restructured, and purged of the interviewer's voice. The results will be fresh and strike a consistent relationship with the audience. Of course, this means more editing than would a written narration, but the results more than justify the labor.

My film on baby expert Dr. Benjamin Spock (*Dr. Spock,* "One Pair of Eyes" series) was covered by method 3. As the central, "point of view" character in a television essay, Dr. Spock was expressing his vision of human aggression and its contribution to the American political scene during the turbulent 1960s. Shot all over the eastern United States, the film was due to be edited in England with no chance of return. In one day-long session, we interviewed him widely to ensure narration that would cover every eventuality.

Recording and then fitting the improvised narration to picture are editing procedures similar to those for the scripted narration, so read the next section carefully.

RECORDING THE PRESENCE TRACK

Whether you are recording a scripted or an improvised narration, you will need to record some of the recording studio or location atmosphere. Later you will have the right quality of "silence" should the editor want to extend a pause or add to the head of a narration block. Presence track is also called *buzz track* or *room tone,* and no two are ever exactly alike, even in the same recording studio and using the same mike. Make it an automatic act after recording a scene, an interview, or a narration to ask everyone to remain where they are and to record a couple minutes of silence *at the same sound level setting.* When this little ritual is overlooked, it causes the editor endless grief.

FITTING THE NARRATION

Track-laying narration should be done carefully so that operative words hit each new image to maximum effect. Small picture-cutting changes are often needed to accomplish this, though adding to or reducing the natural pauses in the narration can sometimes stretch or compress a section that is of unsuitable length. Be very careful, however, not to disrupt the natural rhythms of the speaker. Pay attention to operative words and their potential, and you will find that pictures and word patterns become responsive to each other, that the two fall into mutually responsive patterns that are magically effective, driving the film along with an exhilarating sense of inevitability. Good editing is the art that disguises art.

USING MUSIC

Use music discriminatingly because it is can be misused as a dramatic crutch. Too often filmmakers reach for music as a reliable means of stirring emotion that should, but doesn't, arise out of content. Music should not substitute for anything but should complement action and give us access to the inner, invisible lives of the characters and their situations.

Good music can initiate the emotional level at which the audience should investigate what is being shown. An example is how Errol Morris uses Philip Glass' minimalistic score in his masterly *The Thin Blue Line* (1989). In his film (which Morris describes as a documentary noir) the bleakly beautiful repetitiousness of Glass' music underlines the nightmarish conundrum in which a man is caught on death row for a crime he didn't do.

Films provide their own clues about whether music is needed, and where. It often seems natural during journeys and other bridging sequences—a montage of a character driving to a new home, for instance. Transitional sequences of any kind can benefit from music, especially if it lifts the film out of a prevailing mood. Music can highlight an emotional change when, for instance, an aspiring football player learns he can join the team, or when someone newly homeless lies down for the first night in a doorway. Music is being used more freely as documentaries dare to become more subjective and lyrical again.

Another use for music is to foreshadow an event and to inject tension—a favorite function in B movies but seldom legitimate in documentaries, which can seldom afford such an intrusive storytelling "voice." Music can make a film modulate from realism to a more abstract point of view, as Godfrey Reggio does in his long and bombastic parable about the human rape of the natural world, *Koyaanisqatsi* (1983). It can also supply its own ironic comment or suggest alternative worlds, as Hans Eisler's score does for Resnais' unforgettable Holocaust documentary, *Night and Fog* (1955). Instead of picture-pointing the deportation trains or the captured human artifacts with a tragic or poignant accompaniment, Eisler's score often plays against the obvious by using a delicate, ghoulish dance or sustaining a tense, unresolved interrogation between woodwind instruments.

In the best circumstances, music doesn't merely illustrate, it seems to give voice to a point of view, that of either a character or the storyteller. It can function like a storyteller's aside that expresses an opinion or alternative idea, imply what cannot be seen, or comment on what can.

Be aware that film music, like debt, is easier to start than stop. Music is addictive and we value it keenly just when it is removed. Ending a music section painlessly can therefore be a real problem. The panacea is to give something in its place. This can either be a commanding effects track (a rich train-station atmosphere, for example, really a composition in its own right) or a new scene's dialogue or inciting moment of action that lugs the spectator's attention elsewhere.

When using music not designed to fit your film, section ends can either be faded out or, better, come to a natural finish. In the latter mode, one would lay the music backward from the picture finish point and either fade up at the picture start or adjust the scene length to make the picture fit the music from composer's start to composer's finish. With music that is too long, you can frequently cut out a repeated phrase. Composers like to milk good musical ideas, so most pieces are replete with repeated segments.

If you are searching for, say, something that will work among commercially recorded classical music, enlist the advice of a knowledgeable enthusiast. You won't know whether a piece really works until you play it against the sequence in question. An informal arrangement using a cassette recorder can often solve this dilemma.

The copyright situation for music is complicated and may consist of fees and clearances from any or all of the following: composer, artist(s), publishers, and record company. Students can often get written clearance for a manageable fee but only for use in festivals and competitions. If you then sell your film or receive rentals for showings, you may find yourself being sued. The alternative is to use original music, although many a low-budget film has been rendered lifeless by the meanderings of a friend on a bad piano. It's better to use no music than bad music; well-orchestrated sound effects and atmospheres can be a composition in their own right and can have great impact.

C H A P T E R   2 4

EDITING: THE END GAME

After considerable editing, a debilitating familiarity sets in. You lose objectivity and feel your ability to make judgments departing. Every alternative version looks similar, and all seem too long. This is most likely to hit director-editors, who have lived with both the intentions and the footage since their inception.

Two steps are necessary. One is to make a flow chart, or block diagram, of your film to gain an overview of its ideas and intentions, and the other is to show the working cut to a chosen few.

DIAGNOSIS: MAKING A FLOW CHART

Whenever one needs to better understand something, it helps to translate it into another form. Statisticians, for instance, know that the full implications of their figures are not evident until expressed as a graph, pie chart, or other proportional image.

In our case, we are dealing with the mesmerizing actuality of film, which, as we view it, embraces us within its unfolding present to the exclusion of much sense of overview. Luckily, a block diagram can give one a fresh and a more objective perspective of one's work.

The Editing Diagnostic Form in Figure 24-1 makes a radical analysis of your film easy.

To use it:

- Stop your film after each sequence.
- Write a brief description of the sequence's content in the box. A sequence might contribute,

  factual information

  information on or introduction to a new character

  a new situation and a new thematic strand

  a location or a relationship that will be developed later in the film

  a special mood or feeling

  almost anything else!

EDITING DIAGNOSTIC FORM

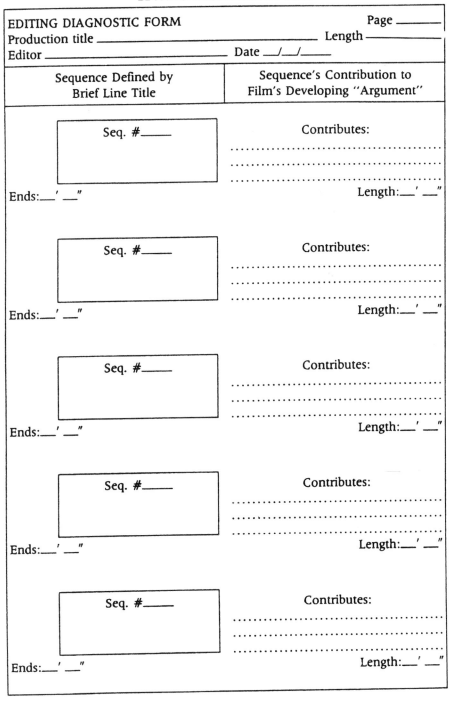

EDITING DIAGNOSTIC FORM   Page _____
Production title _____ Length _____
Editor _____ Date ___/___/_____

Sequence Defined by Brief Line Title	Sequence's Contribution to Film's Developing "Argument"
Seq. #_____ Ends:___' __"	Contributes: .... Length:___' __"
Seq. #_____ Ends:___' __"	Contributes: .... Length:___' __"
Seq. #_____ Ends:___' __"	Contributes: .... Length:___' __"
Seq. #_____ Ends:___' __"	Contributes: .... Length:___' __"
Seq. #_____ Ends:___' __"	Contributes: .... Length:___' __"

FIGURE 24-1 ——————————————————————————————

An editing diagnostic form that helps turn a film into the working parts of a block diagram.

- Next to the box write what the sequence contributes to the development of the film as a whole.
- Add timings (optional, and helpful only if you have to make length decisions).
- Give each sequence an impact rating of, say, one to five stars (also optional, but helpful in prioritizing).

Soon you will have a flow chart for your film that can help you see, dispassionately and functionally, what is subconsciously present for an audience.

What does the progression of contributions add up to? As with the first assembly, you will probably find many of the following:

- Lack of early impact or an unnecessarily pedestrian opening, so the film is a late starter (fatal on television).
- Duplication or redundancy of expository information.
- Inconsistent supply of necessary information.
- Holes or backtracking apparent in progression.
- Type and frequency of impact poorly distributed over the film's length (resulting in uneven dramatic progression).
- Similar thematic contributions made several ways; choose the best and dump (or reposition) the rest.
- A sequence or sequence group that does not contribute to the thrust of the film. Be brave and dump it. You have to kill your darlings.
- The film's conclusion emerges early, leaving the rest of the film as an unnecessary recapitulation.
- The film has more than one ending. Three is not uncommon.

Each ailment, as it emerges from the analysis, suggests its own cure. Put these into effect, and you will feel the degree of improvement rather than be able to exactly account for it.

I cannot overstress the seductions film practices on its makers. After radical changes expect new problems to creep in during housecleaning. It is smart to make a new flow chart, even though you think it's unnecessary. It will certainly turn up more anomalies.

Eventually much of what emerges in this formal process will become second nature to you and will occur in the earlier stages of the cut. Even so, filmmakers of long standing invariably profit from subjecting their work to this formal scrutiny.

A FIRST SHOWING

Preparing a flow chart now makes one more big contribution. Knowing what every brick in your movie's edifice must accomplish, you are excellently prepared to test your intentions on a small audience in a trial showing. This audience should be half a dozen or so, people whose tastes and interests you respect. The less they know about your film and your aims, the better. Warn them that this is a work in progress and still technically raw. Itemize what may be missing, such as music, sound effects, and titles. Incidentally, it is a good idea to cut in a working title because this helps focus the film's purpose or identity for the audience.

Whenever you show the film, the editor should *control the sound levels*. Even experienced producers drastically misjudge a film when it is made inaudible or overbearing through sound inequities. Take pains to present your film at its best, or risk getting misleadingly negative responses.

SURVIVING YOUR CRITICS
AND MAKING USE OF WHAT THEY SAY

After the viewing, ask for impressions of the film as a whole. Don't be afraid to focus and direct your viewers' attention, or someone will lead off a discussion that is superfluous to your needs. Soliciting feedback needs to be handled carefully, or it can be pointless. On the one hand, listen carefully, but on the other, retain your fundamental bearings toward the piece as a whole. Speak as little as possible, and at all cost don't *explain* the film or *explain* what you intended. Explanations at this stage are irrelevant and only serve to confuse and compromise the audience's own perceptions. A film must stand alone without explication from its authors, so concentrate on getting what your critics are really saying.

It takes all the self-discipline one can muster to sit immobile and take notes. For many, listening to reactions and criticism of their work is an emotionally draining experience. Expect to feel threatened, slighted, misunderstood, and unappreciated, and to come out with a raging headache.

Following is a suggested order of inquiry that moves from large issues toward component parts:

- What are the film's themes?
- What are the major issues in the film?
- Did the film feel the right length or was it too long?
- Which parts were unclear or puzzling?
- Which parts felt slow?
- Which parts were moving or otherwise successful?
- What did they feel about . . . (name of character)?
- What did they end up knowing about . . . (situation or issue)?

You are, in fact, testing what you wrote next to each sequence in the "what it contributes" description, and testing your working hypothesis for the film. Depending on your trial audience's patience, you may be able to get feedback on most of your film's parts and intentions. If your audience begins squirming, you may only get to test the dubious areas.

Write anything and everything down, or make an audio recording for study later. Subsequently, you can look at your film with the eyes of, say, the three audience members who missed that the boy was the woman's son. You see that it is implied twice, but find a way to put in an extra line where he calls her "Mom." Problem solved.

An irritation the director must often endure, and especially in film schools, is the critic who insists on talking about the film he would have made and not the film you have just shown. When this happens, diplomatically redirect the discussion.

Dealing with audience critics means absorbing other points of view, and when the dust settles, looking to see how such varying impressions are possible. As far as you can, allow for the biases and subjectivity of some of your critics. Take notice when several people report the same difficulty, but otherwise don't rush to fix anything. Where comments cancel each other out, no action may be called for. Make no changes without careful reflection. Remember that when you ask people to give criticism, they look for possible changes—if only to make a contributory mark on your work. *You will never, under any circumstances, be able to please everyone.* Nor should you be tempted to try.

Most importantly, hold on to your central intentions. You should never revise these unless you find there are strong and positive reasons to do so. You should meanwhile *only act upon suggestions that support and further your central intentions.*

This is a dangerous time for the filmmaker, or indeed for any artist. It is fatally easy to let go of your work's underlying identity and to lose your sense of direction. Keep listening and don't be tempted by strong emotions to carve into your film precipitously.

It is quite normal by now to feel that you have failed, that you have a piece of junk on your hands, that all is vanity. If so, take heart. You might have felt this during shooting, which is worse. Anyway, the film as a workprint is at its worst. Audiences are disproportionately alienated by a wrong sound balance here, a missed sound dissolve there, a shot or two that needs clipping, or a sequence that belongs earlier. These imbalances and rhythmic ineptitudes massively downgrade a film's impact to the nonspecialist viewer. The polish you can yet apply has considerable influence on the film's reception.

THE USES OF PROCRASTINATION

Whether you are pleased or depressed about your film, it is always a good thing to stop working on it for a while and do something else. If this anxiety is new to you, take comfort: You are deep in the throes of the artist's experience. This is the long and painful labor before giving birth. When you pick up the film again after a lapse of days or months, its problems and their solutions won't seem so overwhelming.

TRY, TRY AGAIN

With a film of some substance requiring a long evolution in the editing room, you should expect to try the film out on several new trial audiences. You may want to show the last cut to the original trial audience to find out what progress they think you made.

As a director with a lot of editing in my background, I am convinced that a film is really created in the editing process. It is here that magic and miracles are wrought from the footage. Few know what really happens in the cutting room, not even crew members. It is an alchemy unknown and unguessed by those who have not lived through it.

THE FINE CUT

The evolutionary process described earlier leads to the fine cut. With typical caution, it is called *fine* and not *final,* because there always seem to be further minor changes and accommodations. Some of these arise out of laying sound tracks and music for the sound mix.

THE SOUND MIX

You are ready to make a mixdown of sound tracks into one master track when you have

- finalized your film's content
- fitted music
- split dialogue tracks to facilitate level and EQ adjustments
- recorded and laid any narration
- laid sound effects and atmospheres
- made a mix chart

A whole book could be written on this subject alone, so what follows is no more than a list of essentials along with a few tips. The mix procedure determines:

- *Sound level relativities:* say, between a foreground track of an interview voice and a noisy bus station scene it is played over.
- *Level changes:* fade up, fade down, sound dissolves, level adjustments to accommodate new track elements, such as narration, music, or dialogue.
- *Equalization:* the filtering and profiling of individual tracks, either to match others or to create maximum intelligibility, listener appeal, or "ear comfort." A voice track with a rumbly traffic background can, for instance, be much improved by "rolling off" the lower frequencies, leaving the voice range intact.
- *Sound processing:* adding echo, reverberation, "telephone effect," and so forth.
- *Adjusting dynamic range:* a compressor squeezes the broad dynamic range of a movie into the narrow range favored in television transmission; a limiter leaves the main range alone but caps peaks to a preset level.

- *Sound perspective:* to some degree, equalization and level manipulation can mimic perspective changes, thus helping to create a sense of audio space and dimensionality.
- *Stereo channel distribution:* if a stereo or surround-sound track is being compiled, different elements go to different channels in order to create a sense of spatial "spread."
- *Noise reduction:* Dolby and other noise reduction systems help minimize the system hiss that would intrude on quiet passages.

The audience's intense, almost dreamlike concentration on a good film is easily sabotaged by clumsy changes in sound level, quality, or content. Except for moments of legitimate shock, a film's sound should lead the audience's attention seamlessly from one plane of attention to the next.

The only way to make this technically possible is to alternate sound sections, checkerboard fashion, between two or more tracks, as diagrammed in Figure 21-2. In film or video, unless you split tracks you cannot make a sound segue (sound dissolve) or effectively match sound from one track to another. The reason is simple: manual changes at the mixer board take time and cannot be done instantaneously at a juncture between two tracks.

An example in Figure 24-3 is the cut in Paul's dialogue scene between long and close shots at 1:36 (1 minute, 36 seconds). The 15-second silence beforehand in track 1 allows the sound mix supervisor to reset that channel's level and equalization before the next track section rides in. Each channel's blank sections are really adjustment periods and are particularly vital to dialogue sequences, as explained later. Computerized mixing boards, or tracks laid and mixed in the digital domain, do not have the same restrictions. One can preset and rehearse each section, at the expense of some spontaneity of feeling that happens in a mix theater when the film is being mixed "live."

PREPARATION

Film tracks are easier to handle than video because they follow a logic visible to the eye. Each track section is of brown magnetic stock, interspersed with different-colored spacing, and your conception is aided by physically handling what you are cutting. Fine control is easy because you can cut to the frame (1/24 second). Videotape tracklaying, accomplished by a transfer process, is more abstract but the working principles remain identical. When sound tracklaying is done digitally, your computer screen shows a left-to-right timeline, so track organization is highly graphic and logical. All level changes and even EQ can be programmed, so that real-time mixing promises to become a thing of the past.

Things to remember when cutting and laying sound tracks:

- *Inadvertent cutting:* Be careful not to cut off the barely audible tail of a decaying sound or to clip the attack. Do sound cutting at high volume so you hear everything you are cutting.
- *Awkward atmosphere changes:* Bury a nasty sound cut behind a distracting foreground sound (e.g., behind a line of dialogue or a doorbell ringing).

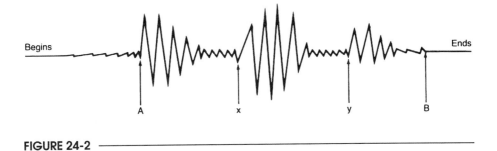

FIGURE 24-2 ————————————————————————————————————

Diagram of sound attack and decay for a recording of footsteps: Points A and B are ideal in- and out-cutting points. Points X and Y are alternative in-points.

- *Sound ellipsis:* Shorten cyclical sounds by cutting one or more cycles. Figure 24-2 profiles typical transient sounds, such as footsteps, with an attack and decay for each footfall. Alternative in and out cutting points are shown.
- *Unwelcome ambience:* With music or any sound effects (SFX) track that brings its own ambience, cut immediately before the attack and after the decay, so the alien ambience has the least time to intrude itself.
- *Strident ambiences:* Ease them in and out by unobtrusively fading rather than letting them ride in or out. Bear in mind that *the ear registers a sound cut-in or cut-out much more acutely than a graduated change.*
- *Sound logic:* Consider making level changes or perspective changes when point of view characters move (e.g., opening a door to the street).
- *Sound dissolves:* Remember to lay in the requisite amounts of overlap.

TRACK HIERARCHY

Sound track elements, presented later in the conventional hierarchy of importance, may vary. Music, for instance, might be faded up to the foreground and dialogue played almost inaudibly low.

Narration: How to lay narration has already been described in detail. If blocks of narration are laid against a silent (or MOS) sequence, you will need to build up the gaps between narration sections with presence so the track remains live.

Dialogue Tracks and the Problem of Inconsistencies: Dialogue tracks should be checkerboarded during tracklaying in the editing stage. With two-track video, each succeeding section is alternated between the recorder's two available tracks. Checkerboarding allows prior mixing-board adjustments during sections of silent or blank track. This allows the mixer to balance:

> *Inconsistent ambiences:* A ragged, truncated ambience is the badge of a poorly edited film, drawing attention away from the content to inadequacies of technique. Frequently when you cut between two speakers in the same lo-

cation, the ambience accompanying each is different in level or quality because the mike was angled differently. Because one angle was recorded subsequent to the other, there may be a different amount of background activity. Location presence tracks can add to and *augment the lighter track to match its heavier counterpart.* You cannot subtract ambience.

Inconsistent voice qualities: Varying location acoustical environments, different mikes, and mike working distances all play havoc with the consistency of location voice recordings. Intelligent "doctoring" with sound filtering (equalization) at the mix stage can massively decrease the sense of strain and irritation arising when your ear has to make constant adjustments to unmotivated, irrational changes.

Music: Easy to lay in, but start track immediately before its attack so you don't hear telltale studio atmosphere or recording system hiss. Take music out just before or under a new track or picture element, something commanding attention that weans audience attention away from the music.

Spot Sound Effects: These sync with action on-screen, such as a door closing, a coin placed on a table, or a phone ringing. Some general pointers include:

- Never assume that *anything* in a sound library is remotely practical until you have tried it against the picture.
- Library, CD, or other effects often come with noisy ambiences of their own. As mentioned earlier, minimize the amount of ambience played in the clear by cutting in immediately before the attack and immediately after its decay.
- You can shorten cyclical effects (such as footsteps or someone cutting wood) by shortening each cycle, and make them fit. But without digital wizardry that can slow sound without lowering its pitch, you cannot stretch cycles that are too short.
- The key to fitting some FX lies in whether you can find sufficient atmosphere to build up a gap.

Atmospheres and Ambience Sound: Lay atmosphere tracks to:

- Create a mood (e.g., bird song over a morning shot of a forest, wood-saw effects over the exterior of a carpenter's shop).
- Mask inconsistencies by using something relevant and distracting.
- Cover the entire sequence, not just a part of it, unless logic dictates otherwise.

MIX CHART

Once tracks are laid to picture, you will need to make a mix chart. Figure 24-3 shows how each column represents an individual track, and how track starts and finishes are marked with timings (or footages for a film mix). By reading down the

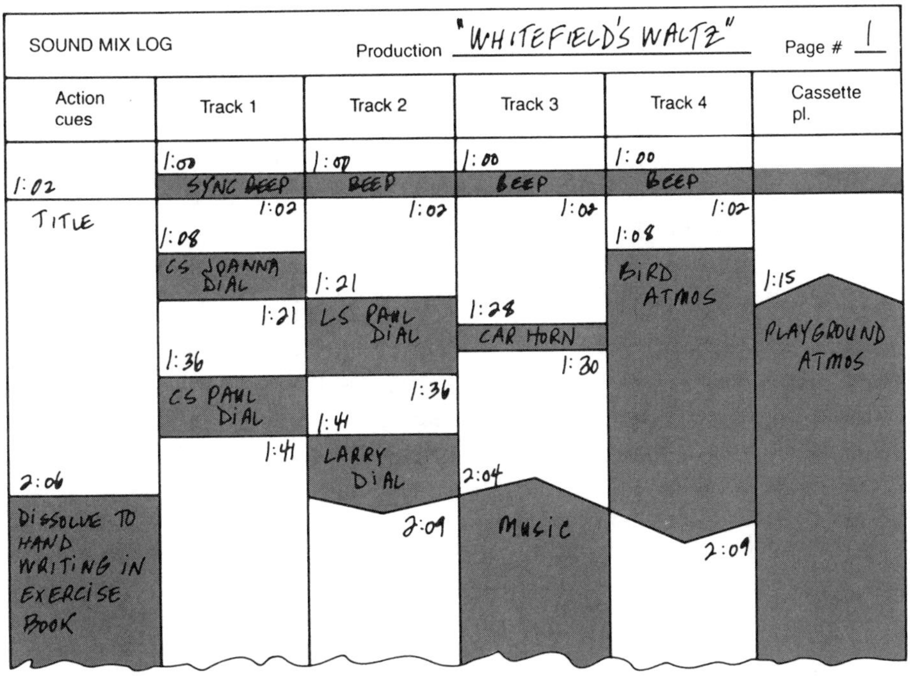

SOUND MIX LOG		Production _"WHITEFIELD'S WALTZ"_		Page # _1_	
Action cues	Track 1	Track 2	Track 3	Track 4	Cassette pl.
	1:00	1:00	1:00	1:00	
1:02	SYNC BEEP	BEEP	BEEP	BEEP	
TITLE	1:02	1:02	1:02	1:02	
	1:08			1:08	
	CS JOANNA DIAL			BIRD ATMOS	1:15
	1:21	1:21	1:28		
		LS PAUL DIAL	CAR HORN		PLAYGROUND ATMOS
	1:36		1:30		
	CS PAUL DIAL	1:36			
		1:41			
	1:41	LARRY DIAL	2:04		
2:06					
DISSOLVE TO HAND WRITING IN EXERCISE BOOK		2:09	MUSIC	2:09	

FIGURE 24-3

Part of a typical sound-mix chart.

chart, you can see how individual tracks are playing against each other like instruments in a music score:

- A straight-line start or finish represents a cut (as at 1:21 and 1:41).
- A caret represents a fade-in (track 3 at 2:04).
- A chevron represents a fade-out (tracks 2 and 4 at 2:09).
- Fade timings refer to the *beginning* of a fade-in, or the *end* of a fade-out.
- A sound dissolve or cross-fade (between 2:04 and 2:09) is where one track fades up while another is fading down.

Vertical space on the chart is seldom a proportional representation of time because you might have 7 minutes of talk with a very simple chart, then half a minute of industrial machinery montage with a profusion of individual tracks for each machine. To avoid either unwieldy or unduly crowded mix charts, allow no more vertical space than is necessary for clarity to the eye.

SOUND-MIX STRATEGY

Premixing: One reel of a feature film may mixdown from 40 or more tracks. Because one to four mixers work a manual board, it requires a sequence of premixes. The same is even true for the humble documentary, with its four- to eight-track mix, especially if the medium is the least sophisticated videotape, where only two tracks at a time can be played off tape.

Remember the golden rule: *premix in an order that keeps control over the most important elements to the last.* If you were to premix dialogue and effects right away, a subsequent addition of more effects or music would uncontrollably augment and "thicken" the competition to the dialogue. Because intelligibility depends on dialogue being heard, you must retain level control over dialogue above all else through the very last stage of mixing.

Although dialogue is not invariably the primary element, the order of premixes for the simplest situation (two-track capability video) might be:

1. Make dialogue premix from sync dialogue tracks.
2. Make FX premix of SFX and atmospheres.
3. Premix dialogue premix and music.
4. Amalgamate premixes 2 and 3, so you have dialogue, FX, and music.
5. Make final mix, narration (if there is one) with premix 4.

With nondigital recording, each generation of sound transfer introduces an additional level of noise, or system hiss. This can be distressingly audible in quiet tracks, such as a slow-speaking voice in a silent room or a very spare music track. The premix hierarchy may therefore be influenced by which tracks must be protected from repeated retransferring.

Rehearse, Then Record: Mixing is best accomplished through familiarizing oneself with the problems of a manageable section, mixing that, and moving on sequence by sequence from convenient stopping points. Check your work as you go.

Tailoring: Many tracks played as laid will enter and exit abruptly, giving an unpleasingly ragged impression to the listener's ear. This impairs an audience's appreciation of your subject matter, so aim for a seamless effect whenever you don't intend to deliberately disrupt attention. The trouble comes when you cut from a quiet to a noisy track or vice versa, and this can be greatly minimized by making a very quick fade-up or fade-down of the noisy track to meet the quiet track on its own terms. The effect on-screen is still of a cut, but one that no longer assaults the ear (Figure 24-4).

Comparative Levels, Err on the Side of Caution: Mix studios use misleadingly excellent speakers, and because most documentaries are seen on TV sets with small, cheap speakers, the home audience loses frequency and dynamic ranges. This blurs the separation between loud and soft, and foregrounds become swamped by ambiences. If you are mixing a narration section with traffic ambi-

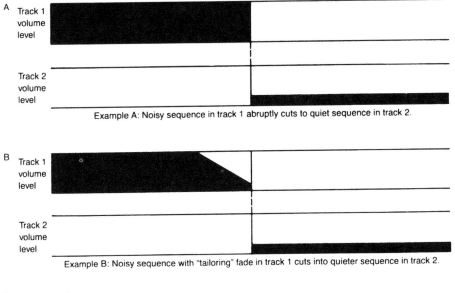

Example A: Noisy sequence in track 1 abruptly cuts to quiet sequence in track 2.

Example B: Noisy sequence with "tailoring" fade in track 1 cuts into quieter sequence in track 2.

FIGURE 24-4

A sound cut can be a jarring transition (A), or it can be tailored during the sound mix to be a smooth transition (B).

ence for a street scene, be conservative and make a deliberately high separation by keeping the traffic lower than maximum. Many mix suites keep a "Granny's TV" speaker on hand so the client an check how mix levels render on a home TV.

Mix Completion: At the end, *check the whole mix without stopping.*

Film Mixing to Final: The final mix will be transferred by a film laboratory onto an optical (photographic) track and photographically combined with the picture to produce a composite projection print. Oftentimes television will transmit "double system"; that is, the picture and the magnetic mix will be loaded onto separate but interlocked machines, and sound will be transmitted from the high-quality magnetic original instead of from dismal quality 16mm photographic track.

Video Mix to Final: Provided there are unbroken video control tracks, it is possible to transfer in absolute sync (using a sync start mark) from one tape to another (Figure 24-5). In practice this means that video mixing is done using copies made from the master edit, and subsequently the master mix is dubbed back onto the master cut, which is only a second-generation picture. CAUTION: Because this means erasing original tracks to make way for the mix, always first experiment with copies to verify the procedure.

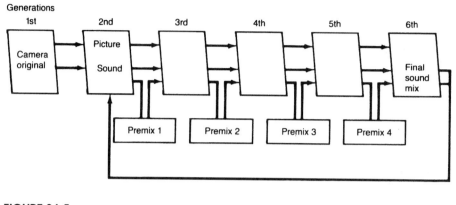

FIGURE 24-5

You can place a later-generation sound track (e.g., a sixth generation) against an earlier generation picture recording by wiping an audio track from the earlier generation video (combined picture and sound) tape and replacing it with the sixth-generation sound mix, starting from a common sync point.

Keep a Safety Copy of the Master Mix: Because a mix is a long, painstaking procedure, it is professional practice to immediately make a safety or backup copy. This is stored safely away from the original "just in case." Copies are made from the master mix.

TITLES AND ACKNOWLEDGMENTS

Every film has a working title, but the final title may be the last thing decided. Often this is difficult because it must epitomize the film's concerns and intentions. Bear in mind that your film's title may be the only advertising copy your audience ever sees, so the title must pique interest. Television listings and festival programs rarely have space to describe their offerings, so the title is your particular label in the tray of hors d'oeuvres.

A sure sign of amateurism is a film accompanied by a grateful welter of credit titles. One 4-minute film I once saw had titles almost as long as the film itself, an indulgence greeted by the audience with sardonic clapping. Keep titles few in words and short in duration. The same name should not crop up egocentrically in multiple capacities, and acknowledgments should be elegantly brief. Examples on television can serve as models, but here is a set of titles ready for an imaginary film:

Title card #	Title Wording	Seconds on screen
	(front title)	
1	HOW ARE YOU GOING TO KEEP THEM DOWN ON THE FARM? (end titles)	7
	(end titles)	
2	Narration—Robin Ragg	4
3	Music—Graham Collier	4
4	Research—Maggie Hall	13
	Camera—Tony Cummings	
	Sound—Rosalyn Mann	
	Sound mix—Daniel Richelet	
	Editing—Jacqueline Guinebault	
5	Written and directed by Avril Lemoine	5

6	Thanks to:
	  National Endowment for the Arts
	  Illinois Humanities Council
	  Agriculture Research Dept.,
	    Smith University, Illinois
	  Mr. and Mrs. Mike Roy
	  Joe and Lin Locker
		10

7	Copyright Avril Lemoine © (1997)	3

Assess timings by reading the contents of each card (which represents one screen of titling) *one-and-a-half times out loud*. When you shoot the titles, be sure to shoot at least three times as much as you need. This allows not only for a title to be extended if needed, but also for the on-line editing preroll.

Many favors are granted during filming merely for an acknowledgment in the titles, so carry out your promises meticulously. Funding often comes with a contractual obligation to acknowledge the grant in a prescribed wording, so this and all such obligations should be carefully double-checked before locking titles down. Spelling should be carefully checked by at least two literate people, and the spelling of people's names should receive special care.

With a character generator (CG) video titling is straightforward, but film titling has to be done very carefully because even small inequities of proportion and straightness show up badly, making titles look amateurish. White titles in film are easy to overexpose, leading to a loss of definition that looks like a focus problem.

Never assume that film titles will be "all right on the night." They are often tricky, especially if you are at all ambitious and want fancy effects. Titles, like troubles, are sent to try us, so give yourself plenty of time in case you must re-shoot.

GETTING TITLES MADE COMMERCIALLY

Large cities have companies that specialize in making up and shooting titles. Good titles are a wise investment for a good film. Because the bulk of "optical house" work is computerized and for commercials, you should check prices carefully in advance, because titling can be vastly expensive. Be sure to meet with the person who will be making them up, and check what reshooting charges you face should you be dissatisfied.

C H A P T E R   2 5

POSTPRODUCTION PROJECTS

Each project highlights particular aspects of editing and can be well explored using material from the projects in Chapter 18, Production Projects. However, the notes and criteria that come with the projects here are widely applicable, and you can use them to help accomplish almost any relevant film editing task.

PROJECT 25-1: INTERVIEW, VARYING IMAGE SIZES

Materials for this project can come from Project 18-6.

Goal: To shorten and restructure interview material shot with a single camera and using three different image sizes. Some recommendations include:

1. First restructure the interview. Like any story, long or short, you must find a storytelling structure that has a beginning, a middle, and an end. Use transcripts and the paper edit method if the interview is extensive.

2. Try to eliminate the interviewer's voice so the interview stands alone.

3. Try to avoid jump cuts or action mismatches.

4. When editing, play sound loud so you don't inadvertently cut into the middle of any low breathing sounds—they are part of normal speech and should be left intact.

5. Be careful to maintain the natural rhythms of the speaker's voice, and watch out that rising or falling inflections sound natural at the cutting points between shots.

6. Sometimes the least noticeable cut is one made after a sentence has begun. Using the null points between sentences, though logical, is often clumsy because it draws attention to the cut instead of burying it in a flow of words and movement.

7. Be careful that the speaker's head and body positions match as you cut from one image size to another. When this is a problem, remember that the more radical the change of image size, the less the audience will notice.

Criteria

Interview is well structured.

Head and body positions are well matched at cutting points.

Speaker's rhythms sound natural.

Sound track is cleanly cut, no clipped breaths or sounds.

Sound levels are consistent throughout.

Interview is a "transparent," smooth, uninterrupted monologue.

There is no evidence of the interviewer.

The film has high overall impact as a piece of editing.

PROJECT 25-2: CONVERSATION, TWO OR MORE PERSONS

Materials for this assignment could come from Projects 18-2 or 18-7.

Goal: To edit coverage of a multiperson conversation so that it is shorter and more compact; to restructure it as necessary; and, by using the different angles, cutaways, and inserts, to create a natural tempo and development; to turn what is usually lengthy material of uneven intensity into a sequence of appropriate length and development.

All the comments in the previous editing project apply concerning rhythms and matching the action, but depending on coverage and the cutaways supplied, you can develop the reactions and inner life of the participant who is being acted upon as well as, or in place of, the one who is speaking. You can also use motivated cut-ins or cutaways to give more feeling of what the characters are seeing or thinking. (A cut-in or insert is a magnified detail in an existing frame, while a cutaway is something beyond that frame.)

Criteria

Conversation is well structured.

Head and body positions are well matched at cutting points.

Speakers' rhythms sound natural.

Listeners' reactions are indicated through cutaways.

Additional detail is supplied in motivated cut-ins.

Visual rhythm feels balanced throughout.

Sound track is cleanly cut, no clipped breaths or sounds.

Sound levels are consistent throughout.

Film has high overall impact as a piece of editing.

PROJECT 25-3: EDITING FOR ELLIPSIS

Materials for this assignment can come from Projects 18-3, 18-4, or 18-5.

Goal: To reduce screen time when the camera has had to cover a long process in real time.

Often an editor, faced with an unbroken shot of a lengthy conversation or a process such as changing a car tire or planting a tree, must drastically shorten it. An alert camera operator will have shot reactions, cut-ins, and cutaways that can patch over ugly jump cuts. Even better, that operator will have covered the event from a number of logical angles. The editor can now compress essentials into a fraction of the original running time and has many options for maintaining "transparency," that is, keeping up the illusion that one is seeing real life rather than an edited film.

However, the unaware operator's rushes present difficulties. The hapless editor, starved of sufficient angle changes or cutaways, must use ingenuity or end up with a bumpy cut. Some comments:

- The odd jump cut in an otherwise transparent sequence disrupts attention by intruding an inconsistent narrative style, but several bold jump cuts can be a tasteful way of signaling time shifts.

- If you cannot create dissolves and have no parallel storyline as a cutaway strand, there is another saving resource—sound. You can create the effect of an optical fade-out/fade-in by fading the outgoing scene to silence, then fading up the incoming one from the cut.

- Likewise, if the two scenes have contrasting sound tracks, you can create the illusion of an optical dissolve by overlapping them and making one dissolve (or segue) into the other. These sound strategies are classically simple and effective.

Criteria

Solves the problem of compressing real time.

Begins and ends appropriately.

Each necessary stage of the action is shown or indicated.

Those that can be inferred are left out.

Each stage of the process is on-screen for an appropriate time.

Rhythms of actions and speech look natural.

Process/conversation develops comprehensibly.

Sequence uses narratively consistent screen language.

Uses sound and sound transitions creatively.

Uses available angles effectively.

Makes cutaways and cut-ins look motivated.

Length is appropriate.

Has high overall impact as a piece of editing.

PROJECT 25-4: COMPLEX EDITING PROJECT

Materials for this assignment might come from Projects 18-1, 18-10, 18-11, 18-13, 18-17, or from any film that uses a combination of materials and techniques.
Goals: You would expect to see in such a film:

- Action match cutting
- Montage principles to render a mood, compress action, or create a sense of lyricism
- Cuts making use of movement by either the subject or camera
- Intercutting between complementary shots
- Overlap cutting where sound precedes its accompanying picture
- Overlap cutting where sound continues over the next shot
- A sensitivity to inherent verbal, visual, and musical rhythms
- Use of cut-ins or cutaways as legitimate, motivated POV shots
- Development of subtextual hints and information
- Meaningful tension and counterpoint between words and images
- Use of figurative sound or visual devices to create foreshadowing, analogy, irony, metaphor, repetition
- Music

Some of these points require explanation. Sound overlaps using simple video equipment often require that you transfer the overlap as a separate sound-only pass, either before transferring the sync segment or after it. So make the sync cut at a null point between words or sounds, or else you will encounter sound-level difficulties when you add the sound overlap "tail."

Creating tension between words and images usually means looking at the available visuals for their figurative (as opposed to merely illustrative) content. A young man's voice saying it was a pleasure to leave home can take on different meanings: playing the voice over a shot of a cat looking through a window at the street carries different implications than playing it over a saucepan in a sink filling with water then overflowing. There is unlimited poetic force at your fingertips when you start placing ideas against the unexpected image, always providing that the image is organic to the world under scrutiny.

Criteria

Successfully details facts and situations.

Successfully uses action match cuts.

Uses subject motion to motivate cuts.

Cuts make use of camera movement.

Uses eyeline shifts or verbal cues to motivate cutaways.

Successful use of overlap cuts, sound precedes its sync picture.

Successful use of overlap cuts, track overhangs into next shot.

Has feeling for verbal rhythms.

Has feeling for visual rhythms.

Has feeling for musical rhythms.

Creates factual and emotional perspectives of characters.

Uses visuals well to create mood.

Counterpoint and tension seen between words and images.

Dialogue cutting and pacing make sound natural.

Choice of music for mood is original and effective.

Length is well judged.

Premix sound is checkerboarded.

Sound mix is well balanced and effective.

Has high overall impact as a piece of editing.

If you have access to digital nonlinear editing, you will be able to incorporate what in film are called *opticals*. That is, you can freeze a frame, slow or speed up motion, apply color or optical filtering, dissolve between shots, or fade to black or white. This armory of special effects can be gratuitous and annoying if overused, or it can tastefully move footage away from pedestrian realism toward a more subjective, contemplative mood that draws the viewer into a trancelike state.

Along with the ability to integrate text comes a full palette of techniques allowing full poetic freedom in the editing room. This freedom is not new—film has always been able to do these things, but expensively and with a huge investment of time and energy in planning. Now they can be tried at will on your desktop. The sky is the limit.

POSTPRODUCTION CHECKLIST

Editing

- Film recreates aspects of consciousness to help the audience share a character's (or storyteller's) shifting consciousness.
- Interesting discrepancies urge the audience into an active, problem-solving relationship with the film.
- Every call to imagination or judgment is an acknowledgment of equality with the audience and an invitation to participate in discovery.
- The film's structure and authorial voice are developed during editing.
- The editor needs to be patient, organized, experimental, and diplomatic.
- A first-rate documentary editor is really a second director and should be willing to make subjective judgments.
- To preserve some objectivity, the director is best advised to stay away from the cutting room while each new cut is evolving.

Transcripts

- Transcripts take no account of voice inflections, so don't assume that anything written will stand alone on screen.
- Summarize topics and their location as an index to finding important material quickly.
- Not making transcripts is "buy now, pay later."

Logging

- Time spent making a consistent, intelligent log is time liberated for creativity later.
- Do not change systems in midfilm.

Selecting Sections

- Make a photocopy of transcripts to use as follows:
    During a viewing, draw a line against any good transcribed section.
    Later bracket in- and out-points.
    Put ID (cassette, character/scene, section number) in margin.
    Also put a brief functional description in margin.

Preparing for a Paper Cut

- Make a photocopy of above marked transcript sheets to use as follows:
    Cut selected transcript sections into slips.
    Put name and origin of each action sequence on the slip of paper.

Paper Cut Structural Considerations

- How is your film to be structured in time?
- What basic factual information must be passed over to the audience in order to make the unfolding film intelligible?
- What other organizing features does it have that help you group material together?
- How will your film reveal its purpose? (The "contract" must not be long delayed.)
- Are there dramatic advantages to disrupting the subject's natural advance in time?
- Cross-cutting between two stories allows time to be telescoped or stretched.
- Cross-cutting allows juxtaposition and aids comparison and irony.
- How can you show development (which is so important)?
- Above all, try to tell a good story.

Assembling the Paper Edit

- Do your best, but remember a paper cut is only marks on paper representing film.

- To avoid word-driven documentary, give priority to action and behavior. Make an action-only paper cut first and bring speech in later.
- Exclude nothing workable if you are in doubt—leave choice of alternatives for later.
- Make a simple blueprint, let complexities develop from film, not on paper or in your head first.

First Assembly

- Put a loose version of whole film together without working on any detail.
- Don't deal with embellishment until you know the film's entire identity and purpose.
- The order and juxtaposition of material has very potent consequences.
- You are presenting pieces of evidence, one at a time, to build a case in the audience's mind.
- Let your film begin telling you what it wants you to do.

Rough Cut

- Deal only with the film's major needs at this stage (there will be many stages).
- An early decision about maximum length helps face the inevitability of jettisoning certain material.
- It is easier to shorten a long film than to pump substance back into one prematurely tightened.
- Try to see each new cut as an audience does, without prior conceptions or special knowledge.
- If a cut is different from what you expected, see it again before commenting.
- Where is the film dramatically unbalanced?
- Does the graph of "dramatic temperature" make sense?
- Where does the film drag?
- What remains in your memory, and what has left no trace?
- Have you made the most of revealing contrasts?

Narration

- Try to make your film tell its own story without narration.
- If narration is unavoidable, decide whether scripted or improvised narration will be best.
- Narration must be assimilated by the audience the first time or not at all.
- Narration must be in the simple, direct language of speech, not that of written discourse.
- Never describe what can be seen in the shot. Add to the image with words; do not duplicate.
- Be ready to invert syntax to fit the sequence of the viewer's perceptions.
- Leave spaces for featured sound effects.

- The first (or "operative") word to fall on each new shot has a major consequence for how the audience interprets the shot.
- Altering the juxtaposition of words and shots can imply different meanings.
- Use narration primarily to relay facts.
- Avoid predisposing your audience to any particular attitude with narration; they may resent it.
- The intelligent narration helps audience members make their own value judgments.
- Narration can accelerate your film's exposition and make brief, agile links between sequences.
- Any narration, especially that badly written or poorly delivered, is an intrusion into the audience's relationship with the subject.
- Narration can focus your audience on aspects of the material you want them to notice.
- The audience looks upon the narrator as the voice of the film.
- The narrator's voice quality and delivery must act as a surrogate for your own attitude to the subject.
- Try a scratch narration before recording to be sure that it works and that you have covered all your bases.
- Audition narrators cautiously, giving directions to see how the candidate responds.
- Show the chosen narrator the film, and explain what characteristics must be embodied in the narration.
- Give brief, positive, qualitative directions to a narrator.
- The narrator studies the script, the director watches the picture while recording and listens through a speaker or headphones to ensure that delivery is appropriate and tempo is correct.
- Remember to record 2 minutes of narration studio presence track.

Music

- Music should not inject false emotion.
- Choice of music should give access to the inner life of a character or the subject.
- Music can signal the emotional level at which audience should investigate what is being shown.
- You cannot know if music choice really works until you try it against the picture.
- Better to use no music than bad music.

Fine Cut

- Use overlap cuts to smooth transitions and to create interesting disjunctions between what is seen and what is heard.

- Know the preset lengths for likely distribution so you can choose one.
- Aim to say a lot through a little.
- Good short films are welcome everywhere.
- Most people are prejudiced against the long, well-meaning film unless it has a very high thematic density to repay the investment of time it demands.

Evoking a Trial Audience Response

- Remember, you can't please everyone!
- Use sample audiences and careful, open-ended questioning to see whether your film is functioning as intended.
- In a trial showing, exert maximum control over sound—it affects audience responses disproportionately.
- Direct audience attention to issues on which you need information, but remember to ask open, nondirective questions, listening carefully for what people are really saying.
- Is your audience getting the main underlying meanings? If not, why not?
- Hang on to your fundamental intentions; let go of them only with very good reason.

Diagnostic Method

- Make a block diagram of the movie to spot invisible anomalies (see text for common ones).
- After re-editing to cure the latest round of difficulties, make another block diagram to see what problems the housecleaning introduced by the back door.
- Put the film aside for a week or two, and view it again before deciding if the fine cut is final.

Track Laying and Mix Chart

- Alternate ("checkerboard") dialogue tracks to facilitate equalization and level adjustments.
- Use correct presence track to fill holes in dialogue, narration, or scene.
- When presences are mismatched, lay in extra to bring the quieter up to balance the louder.
- Plan featured sound effects to go in dialogue gaps (or vice versa).
- Sync spot FX carefully.
- Mask unavoidable inconsistencies with a logical atmosphere track.
- Cut into music or FX just before attack and just after complete decay to avoid hearing ambience.
- Sound dissolves require an appropriate track overlap.
- Make a fair-copy mix chart that the eye can easily follow.

Sound Mix

- Premix so you retain control over the most important elements until last.

- Rehearse each section before recording.

- Soften ragged sound cuts by tailoring the louder to the quieter in a rapid fade up or fade down.

- When mixing foreground speech with background sound (music, FX, atmosphere, and so on), err on the side of caution and separate foreground well from background.

- Make a safety copy of the mix, and store it somewhere separate and safe.

Titles and Acknowledgments

- Use a working title until the film is fully edited.

- Double-check contractual obligations for special wording.

- Double-check spelling, particularly that of people's names (they notice, and remember . . .).

- Shoot plenty of title, just in case.

- Keep title lengths on-screen short and sweet.

- Hold each title card on-screen for one-and-a-half times as long as it takes to read it out loud.

- Never assume titles can be done quickly and accurately. They are Murphy's last refuge.

P A R T 7

AESTHETICS AND AUTHORSHIP

CHAPTER 26
Documentary Theory and the
Issue of Representation 315

History 316
Documentary Issues 316
Film and Documentary Theory 318
It Comes Down to Point of View 319

CHAPTER 27
Elements of the Documentary 321

Sizing Up the Ingredients 321
  Picture 321
  Sound 322
Point of View 322
  Observation and Intercession 323
  Single Point of View (Character in the
    Film) 324
  Multiple Characters within the Film 326
  Omniscient 328
  Personal 331
  Reflexive 333
Time, Development, and Structure 336
  The Event-Centered Film 336
  The Process Film 337
  The Journey Film 337
  The Walled-City Film 339
  The Historical Film 340

CHAPTER 28
Form, Control, and Identity 344

Content Influences Form 344
Fiction and Documentary: Authorial Control 345
Common Limits on the Range of Subjects 345
Participants' Cooperation 346
Resistance to the Personal Viewpoint 346
Documentary Language 347
Documentary, Fiction Films, and the Future 349

CHAPTER 29
Re-enactment, Reconstruction,
and Docudrama 351

The Docudrama 352
Subjective Reconstruction 353
Fake Documentaries or Mockumentaries 354

CHAPTER 30
Ethics, Authorship, and
Documentary Mission 356

Participants Have to Live with the Film's
  Consequences 357
Approaching Participants 358
Directing and Reflexivity 358
Truth Claims 359
Shooting Process 359
Editing Process 361
Integrity of the Evidence 362
Public Showing 362
Philosophy and Mission 363
Documentary as Exposure to Life 363
Mission and Identity 364

CHAPTER 26

DOCUMENTARY THEORY AND THE ISSUE OF REPRESENTATION

This chapter is meant to be a resource guide to available theoretical writing rather than a discussion in depth. A theory according to the *Oxford English Dictionary* is "a hypothesis that has been confirmed or established by observation or experiment," and there is nothing so practical as a good one. It is a curious fact that film theorists come from history, psychology, sociology, anthropology, linguistics, philosophy—everywhere, it seems, except filmmaking. Their work is generally aimed not at making better or different films but at identifying the patterns and meaning in those already made. Together, filmmakers, film theorists, critics, and historians have acknowledged that some intractable and possibly unanswerable questions lie at the heart of documentary practice:

- What constitutes true documentary, during its history and now?
- What work is the documentary meant to do?
- Are documentary's means (intrusions on and exploitation of ordinary people) justified by its ends (doing good, making a difference, etc.)?
- What is the underlying relationship between filmmakers and those on whose behalf we make our films?
- When can a filmmaker truthfully represent another person or group?
- On what grounds do we make truth claims?

These questions are not easy to answer, but if you reread the above and substitute the words *religion* for documentary and *priest* for filmmaker, you see what large parts are played by ideology and belief. Crudely speaking, nonfiction films have mostly been made by those with power aiming to instruct and pacify, or those without power aiming to get it. Documentarians have often tried to occupy a middle ground, aiming to mediate by representing those without a voice—a noble but often delusional role. The history of religion (not to mention colonialism) shows how the beliefs of those with power tend to insulate the believers and guarantee neither morality nor justice. It is not enough to believe you are right and doing good in the world—you must be willing to examine your motives and practices.

For beginning filmmakers the fear of making "mistakes" or repeating history can be paralyzing. This is a pity, because the world badly needs the voice of passionate principle. Critics are important, but committed artists are more so. To become one means first exploring the traditions that best serve your needs. It is better to be clumsily energetic than exquisitely correct, which is to say, silent.

I suggest that you first experiment in your chosen field to verify your commitment and to build its substance. Once you have a personal stake in the art form, its history, and present-day issues will come alive as the context to your own work.

HISTORY

There are two standard texts, both very readable and recently updated. Richard Meran Barsam's *Nonfiction Film: A Critical History,* 2nd ed. (Bloomington, IN: Indiana University Press, 1992) on the earliest motion pictures is particularly good and surveys the genre's development by periods and geographical areas. Erik Barnouw's *Documentary: A History of Non-Fiction Film,* 3rd ed., (New York: Oxford University Press, 1993) is more concerned with the changing role of the documentarian, and has chapter headings such as Prophet, Explorer, Reporter, Painter, Advocate, Bugler, Prosecutor, and so on.

Both books contain stimulating portraits of the founders of the art form, including Shub, Flaherty, Dovzhenko, Vertov, Grierson, Rotha, Cavalcanti, Wright, Watt, Storck, Lorentz, Riefenstahl, Ivens, and Jennings, to name but a few. An interesting aspect of the early practitioners, particularly in the Grierson stable, is the great debates they pursued over documentary's identity, aesthetics, and function as a tool of social change. Little has ever been settled; the documentary remains a minefield of possibilities and tensions, just as in the early days. Some of the most active figures either wrote autobiographies or were written about, most notably Grierson, who was never in doubt that the documentary could and should change the world.

DOCUMENTARY ISSUES

There are many anthologies and they often focus on a particular film, filmmaker, issue, or historical movement. The sheer difficulty of seeing older films, or films that come from outside one's own culture, often makes these books seem like very specialized reading.

A filmmaker whose production experience, clear writing, and long commitment to documentary makes his works especially valuable is Alan Rosenthal. His mission has been to interview key critics and filmmakers. *The New Documentary in Action* (1971), *The Documentary Conscience* (1980), and *New Challenges for Documentary* (1988)—all published by the University of California Press—are a superb compendium of thought and documentary experience. *New Challenges for*

Documentary is the most stimulating and provocative collection imaginable for anyone engaged in production. In upward of 600 pages its 35 writers grapple with the following issues:

- vérité and the public's right to know
- protecting one's subjects from themselves
- drama documentaries and the dispute about how material is presented
- documentary conventions that need to be abandoned
- how "changes in documentary strategy bear a complex relation to history"
- reflexivity as "created, structured articulations of the filmmaker and not authentic, truthful, objective records"
- feminist documentary's theories and strategies
- women's documentary and raising consciousness
- films dealing with gay issues
- documentary's truth claims based on arguments and evidence
- legitimacy of the drama documentary
- the filmmaker's own voice, and presenting one's own opinions rather than being a conduit for others'
- the Canadian Film Board
- Ivens and filming the Chinese cultural revolution
- the compilation film and leftist history
- Wiseman as an analyst of American society
- traps and troubles in making the controversial series, *An American Family*
- ethnographic filmmaking practices
- how impassioned, politically motivated films can fail through poor craft
- documentary ethics, the right of privacy, the prevalence of victimhood, and "using human beings to make a point"
- the technologically produced image as a construct "of someone who has a culture, and often a conscious point of view"
- the conflict between the actuality of lives and the aesthetic needs of the portraying artist
- how "the western world created image-producing technologies . . . to control reality by capturing it on film"
- television's power to imply that a subject is guilty and then to manipulate the viewer for entertainment purposes
- exploitative cinéma vérité and audience voyeurism
- TV's "balance" within established structures, legitimizing prevailing interests and neutralizing conflict
- TV's inability to provide context and passion in covering war
- McCarthy, censorship, and blacklisting
- documentary, history, and the need to entertain

- poetic documentary as opposed to talking-head loquacity
- political myths: how life and "politics" are inseparable
- media research

FILM AND DOCUMENTARY THEORY

For an introduction to the (often arcane) language of film theory and for an overview of the evolving issues that have been debated throughout film's development, Dudley Andrew's *Concepts in Film Theory* (New York: Oxford University Press, 1984) is excellent. The following list of the book's headings shows how comprehensive it is:

- The State of Film Theory
- Perception
- Representation
- Signification
- Narrative Structure
- Adaptation
- Valuation (of Genres and Auteurs)
- Identification
- Figuration
- Interpretation

Though documentary receives little mention, it shares much with the world of fiction. At the end of the book is a classified bibliography.

Helpful and up to date is *Theorizing Documentary* (New York: Routledge, 1993), edited by Michael Renov. With a good bibliography and filmography, the book is a valuable anthology of critical essays. In his piece on the poetics of documentary, Renov proposes and then expands on the proposition that the genre has four basic tendencies:

- To record, reveal, or preserve
- To persuade or promote
- To analyze or interrogate
- To express

In other essays:

- Brian Winston argues that the idea of documentary evidence, sustained thus far on a highly questionable "naturalistic illusion," is deeply at risk as technology hands us ever more control over imagery.
- Philip Rosen, in examining what a documentary is or is not, places Grierson in the stormy waters of historiographical debate and demonstrates how documentary representation, in trying to control mass perception of truth, is really

a bid for political influence. He argues that the notion of "an organizing gaze as exterior to its objects" is untenable.

- Trinh T. Minh-ha, in a review of stunning breadth and penetration, covers the arena of documentary assumptions and shows how inadequate, contradictory, or downright colonial most of them are, including the "scientific" ones dear to anthropology.

- Paul Arthur discusses how documentarians have implied truth claims, and that in spite of postmodernism and new technology, these have not fundamentally changed.

- Ana M. López argues that in the Brazilian series, *America,* it is the Brazilian outsiders whose "methods of post-modernism itself—pastiche, simulacra, images, gloss, and nostalgia" produce a critique that becomes a "fetishization of the image . . . [which] ultimately reduces the historical past invoked to a collection, the equivalent of a vast multimedia photo album with witty captions. And the affect produced is . . . curiously flat while simultaneously aesthetically sublime."

- Bill Nichols' essay on history, representation, and claims for truth is an authoritative survey of the boggy foundations on which so much of documentary's claims to representation rest. He suggests that "disembodied knowledge and abstract conceptualization" are inherently less trustworthy because they do not bring "the power of the universal, of the mythic and fetishistic, down to the level of immediate experience and individual subjectivity."

None of these writers makes easy reading, though Nichols, widely considered the guru of documentary theory, is easier going here than elsewhere. His *Representing Reality* (Bloomington, IN: Indiana University Press, 1991) is considered the theorist's bible.

IT COMES DOWN TO POINT OF VIEW

These works put forward fascinating ideas about how politicized the documentary is, and how much it is class and culturally determined, both as a tool for social expression and as an art form. Much of the discussion revolves around the fissure that Brecht characterized when he distinguished between art as a mirror held up to society and art as a hammer acting on society to change it. Where you stand in this debate will rest on your temperament, your background, and how you intend to work for change. In this, the issue of representation—who can speak for another—looms large. This is natural at a time when the West is moving tortuously toward a form of democracy that includes a multiplicity rather than a hierarchy of voices.

Speaking on behalf of others is almost a disease among documentarians, and (as I learned through Henry Breitrose, a fine writer on the documentary) they have earned a special word: *behalfers.* Behalfers make it their work to represent those without a voice, which in the end is everyone who cannot make films themselves. This is reminiscent of the charitable activities of the privileged in another age and should alert us to the complex motives underlying all charity, and the dangers of thinking one is primarily serving someone else's interests.

Documentaries are, after all, a construct. They reveal as much about their makers as they do about their ostensible subject. Like it or not, it is our own assumptions that we put on the screen, so making films intelligently means examining and evolving who we are and what we believe, which has been this book's contention all along. In a just and open society, every group should be able to represent itself rather than hiring an "expert." Once the frontier was literacy (still is, in too many places); the next frontier is democratic representation on the screen. We—whoever "we" means—have to become our own experts.

CHAPTER 27

ELEMENTS OF THE DOCUMENTARY

SIZING UP THE INGREDIENTS

Impossible though it is to come up with formulations that fit all documentaries, there are a number of generalities we can look at, beginning with techniques and construction methods central to a documentary's aesthetic contours. It is interesting to realize how few are the ingredients from which all documentaries are made.

PICTURE

- **Action footage**

    people or creatures doing things, carrying on their everyday activities, work, play, and so on

    shots of landscapes and inanimate things

- **People talking**

    to each other with camera presence unobtrusive, perhaps even hidden

    to each other, consciously contributing to the camera's portrait of themselves

    in interviews—one or more people answering formal, structured questions (interviewer may be off camera and questions edited out)

- **Re-enactments,** factually accurate,

    of situations already past or that cannot be filmed for other valid reasons

    of suppositional or hypothetical situations that are indicated as such

- **Library footage**—can be uncut archive material or sequences recycled from other films

- **Graphics,** such as

  still photos, often shot by a camera that moves toward, away from, or across, the still photo to enliven it

  documents, titles, headlines

  line art, cartoons, or other graphics

- **Blank screen**—causes us to reflect on what we have already seen or to give heightened attention to existing sound

SOUND

- **Voice-over,** which can be

  audio-only interview

  constructed from the track of a picture-and-sound interview with occasional segments of sync picture at salient points

- **Narration,** which can be

  a narrator

  the voice of the author (e.g., director Louis Malle in his *Phantom India* series)

  the voice of one of the participants

- **Synchronous sound,** that is, diegetic accompanying sound shot while filming
- **Sound effects**—can be spot (sync) sound effects or atmospheres
- **Music**
- **Silence**—the temporary absence of sound can create a powerful change of mood or cause us to look with a heightened awareness at the picture

All documentaries are permutations of these ingredients, and it is the structure and point of view imposed on them that bring shape and purpose.

POINT OF VIEW

The phrase *point of view* suggests a bias, such as a Marxist or libertarian viewpoint, taken as a lens on a subject under scrutiny. Of course, filmmakers' cultural and ideological biases intrude everywhere, but here I refer to the impression one gets, when reading a story or watching a film, of the human vantage from which the story is being told. A documentary is a story and, as in literature, its effectiveness and "voice" emerge from having a coherent point of view. This is difficult to detect objectively and even as a concept is difficult to explain.

A story's point of view (POV) exists because the storyteller has a purpose for telling the tale and is clear about his or her relationship to the story and its characters. As with any art work, this can never be more than partially planned but evolves during a journey of discovery throughout the process of ideation and creation (hence this book's insistence on self-exploration as the foundation of creative identity, and creative identity as a springboard to effective storytelling).

There are, however, some quite discernible point of view categories, which follow with film examples. Most are not pure because they incorporate other, minor points of view. In fact, the uniqueness and force of a major viewpoint usually depend on its contrast with secondary ones.

For each named category there is a diagram to symbolize how a point of view works, but you will realize from viewing any of the films that this is necessarily simplified. The camera shape indicates the purview of an observing camera presence, which must be visualized as a camera, recording ear, and the human intelligences guiding their attention.

OBSERVATION AND INTERCESSION

As a preliminary we should again acknowledge in passing the philosophic division of documentary into two branches: intercessional and non-intercessional, or cinéma vérité and direct (or observational) cinema. This division has an entirely pragmatic imperative. At a scene where fifteen fire engines are hard at work, you won't need to intercede. Just shoot coverage. But at a scene where a man has chained himself to railings outside the Ministry of Agriculture, you will want to ask questions so the filming can go beyond a single enigmatic setup. Figures 27-1 and 27-2 represent the two approaches to recording actuality. In the diagrams that follow, the lines connecting characters represent their awareness of and relationship with each other. In Figure 27-2 the camera and the director (if they are indeed

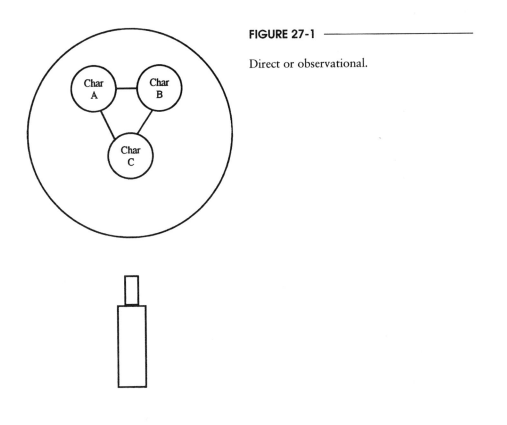

FIGURE 27-1 ——————————————

Direct or observational.

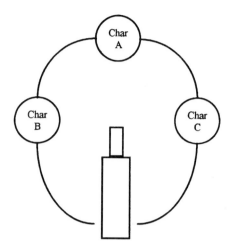

FIGURE 27-2

Cinéma vérité or intercessional cinema, in which the camera and crew cinema are discreet onlookers; they catalyze responses and situations.

separate people) are a part of this web of relationships, while in Figure 27-1 the camera stands deliberately outside and looking on.

Figure 27-1 represents rather symbolically how in direct cinema the camera does its best to remain an outside onlooker, minimizing its own effect on the proceedings. Figure 27-2 represents cinéma vérité, in which the camera and its crew is avowedly present and inquiring, ready to catalyze, if necessary, an interaction between participants or between participants and themselves.

SINGLE POINT OF VIEW (CHARACTER IN THE FILM)

As you can see from Figure 27-3, the film is being channeled through, and perhaps even narrated by, a main character. This person may be a bystander or major protagonist, and he or she is either observing, recounting, or enacting events. This kind of film may be biography or, if talking in the first person, an autobiography.

The seminal work is Robert Flaherty's *Nanook of the North* (1922), which takes as its central figure an Eskimo hunter struggling to survive in the ultimate of hostile environments. Though usually seen with a musical accompaniment, it still creates a strong sense of intimacy with the hunter/gatherer Eskimo and his family, even when shown silent. Many scenes were re-enacted for the camera's benefit, so we might classify the film as re-enacted observational cinema, if that isn't too contradictory. Yet the movie seems true to life and in such good faith that complaining about any artifice seems ungrateful. Though not true to the letter of Nanook's life, it is true to its spirit, or rather to his grandfather's spirit, because the tools and methods of hunting were archaic, even in Nanook's day. In later work, particularly *Louisiana Story* (1948), the passion in Flaherty's storytelling has become sentimentality and his dramatizing manipulative.

The Maysles Brothers' direct cinema classic, *Salesman* (1969), shows Paul Brennan competing with colleagues at selling bibles to unwilling Floridians, and stalks the mystery of his inner life. Audiences, usually invited to identify with winners, here identify with the loser. Consequently, we marvel at salesmen's values and the poignant human need to perform, even in such an exploitative race. Either

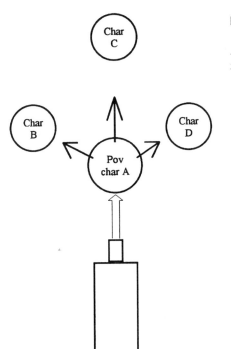

FIGURE 27-3

A single point of view (a character in the film).

Brennan's lack of perspective or denial keep him running, but failure may ultimately be self-inflicted by conscience.

Werner Herzog's *Land of Silence and Darkness* (1971) has such a strange and fascinating subject that it can use non-intercession most of the time. It shows the life of Fini Straubinger, a deaf-blind woman who lay in an institution for 30 years until taught the deaf-blind tactile language. We accompany her on a journey to locate others as isolated and despairing as she once was herself. As the film progresses, her eerie, prophetic simplicity stresses how elemental is the need for human contact, and how devastating its absence or loss. Fini emerges as a gauche angel personifying the love and nobility latent in the human spirit (Figure 27-4). Because the film includes interviews, it uses cinéma vérité elements.

Single character point of view may limit a film's scope to what its main character can legitimately know or understand. Another hazard is that too much thematic freight may pivot on what one person represents. In showing man against nature, for instance, Nanook carries the burden of portraying his race as an endangered species. Awareness of this forces Flaherty to reconstruct Nanook as an Eskimo archetype. Nanook, having a strong historical sense of his own people, collaborated willingly in this—a sharing of authorship that declined in Flaherty's later work.

The focus on a central character means that one can seldom avoid nominating a hero (or antihero). The emphasis on individualism implies that because destiny is experienced individually, it can also be challenged and thwarted individually. The corollary, equally disturbing, is that "society" always victimizes the dissenting individual. Flaherty's romantic idealization, already uncomfortably visible in *Man*

FIGURE 27-4

Land of Silence and Darkness, Werner Herzog. This documentary, through its character-within-the-film point of view, shows that for the deaf-blind, contact with the rest of the world is by touch alone. (New Yorker Films)

of Aran (1934), comes under sympathetic examination in George Stoney and Jim Brown's *How the Myth Was Made* (1978). By questioning surviving participants the film highlights the contradictions in Flaherty's outlook. As earlier critics charged, he chose to ignore how much of the islanders' point of view was due to an absentee landlord rather than a hostile Mother Nature.

A partisan viewpoint routed through a central character does not lead automatically to the distortions of sentimentality. Just be careful that your sympathies do not preclude broader insights, and that these are reflected in the movie. This will make for a stronger film anyway.

MULTIPLE CHARACTERS WITHIN THE FILM

The viewpoint represented in Figure 27-5 is of multiple characters, in which none tends to predominate. The camera and editing may look at them, or through them (implying information about the seer as well as what he or she sees). This mode, which can be observational or intercessional, is well suited to revealing cause and effect within an interdependent group, whether of a family, team, or class of society. When each character represents a different constituency in the social tapestry,

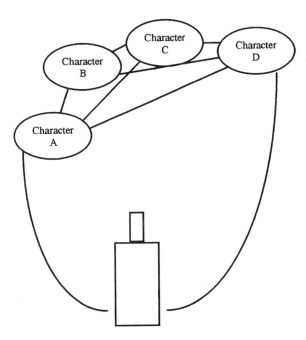

FIGURE 27-5 ───────

Diagram representing the multiple point of view. We may "see" anyone by way of anyone else's perspective.

one can build a texture of different, often counterbalancing, viewpoints, and thus demonstrate a social process, its actors, and its outcome.

Basil Wright and Harry Watt's *Night Mail* (1936) challenged the derisive image the British middle classes held of working people by showing the teamwork and camaraderie on an overnight mail run from London to Scotland. The film exalts the postal workers' pride and confidence in performing their intricately phased operation, and it poetically dramatizes how letters, that is, intimate communication, are oxygen for ordinary lives. If there is any central character it is the train itself. Though the movie has the look of poetic observation, it still comes from the Flaherty school of recreating reality, and is artfully contrived at every level.

Barbara Kopple's *Harlan County, USA* (1976) covers a strike by impoverished Kentucky coal miners (Figure 27-6). While there are prominent characters, there is no central point of view, because the conflict is class conflict, between workers and big business. Some of the narrative is carried forward by ironic protest songs, and a powerful aura of folktale and folk ballad makes the film live on afterward in one's memory. Shot mostly as direct cinema, there are moments—principally when the crew were shot at—when the filmmakers become participants in the events.

Michael Apted's *28 Up* (1986) shows a cross section of British children and concentrates on monitoring each individual's view of her- or himself. Beginning with 7-year-olds, Apted returns every 7 years until his subjects are in their late 20s, sometimes pressing the same issues. The questioning—empathic, cool, and incisive—challenges even his wariest subjects to a deeper scrutiny of their life's hidden meanings. The film relays a poignant vision of young men and women struggling with their beliefs and their demons, each believing that destiny was

FIGURE 27-6

Harlan County, USA, Barbara Kopple. Music as an expression of suffering and protest adds to the many facets of the *multiple characters'* point of view. (Krypton International Corporation)

freely chosen, yet each in conflict with some dimly perceived pattern no less constraining than the spider's web. A *35 Up* has been made but is somehow less embracing.

Terry Zwigoff's *Crumb* (1995) chronicles the life of Robert Crumb the cartoonist, and that of his family, the most dysfunctional imaginable. *Crumb* would seem a single point of view narrative, but its central character has little interest in introspection and even less in self-analysis. Instead his art pours out of him, like urgent and frightening messages from an urban nightmare. The real image of Crumb, shy and withdrawn, emerges from those around him and through the unblinkingly candid eye of his cartoon art.

OMNISCIENT

The limitations of diagramming (Figure 27-7) something so complex as the omniscient point of view could led the reader to suppose that omniscience simply means free camera movement. It means more than being unfettered by one character's consciousness or position in space, because the eye of the omniscient story, in literature and in film, moves freely around in time and space to suggest an unfettered, all-knowing consciousness. It is the eye of God, who sees all and knows all, and if this sounds apocalyptic, just look at a few familiar nursery stories or

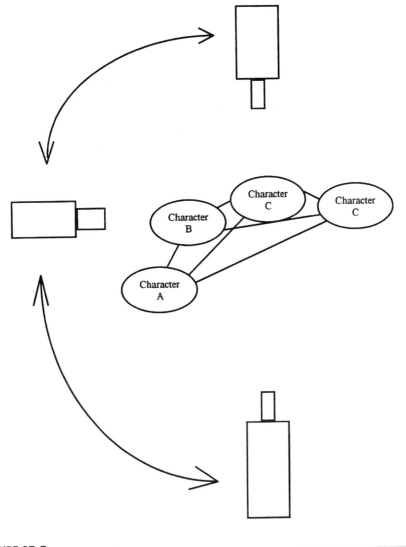

FIGURE 27-7

Diagram representing the omniscient point of view, in which the camera can move freely in time and space. The point of view isn't vested in any particular character and isn't fettered by anyone's limitations or insight.

folktales. They usually take an omniscient storytelling voice, one so familiar that we don't even notice it.

Typically narrated in the third person, it will express a collective rather than personal vision. Narration in film can, however, be implied, or it can be supplanted by subtitles and documents to get around the imprimatur of a narrator's voice. The central organizing vision may simply be that of the filmmaker, who makes no apology or explanation on-screen.

Many well-known films take an omniscient position. Joris Ivens' classic, *Rain* (1929), documents the timeless cycles of human behavior in a big city before, during, and after a rainstorm in Amsterdam. The movie documents a number of locations, cross-cutting between them to create a mood of melancholy reminiscent of childhood solitude. Jean Vigo's *A Propos de Nice* (1930), is the revolutionary director's satirical montage of a privileged society so degenerate that it seems to beckon its own overthrow. This film and *Rain* are both silent movies whose palpably musical atmospheres come from their strong visual rhythms.

Leni Riefenstahl's *Triumph of the Will* (1937) and *Olympiad* (1938) use objective-seeming film language to present an intensely partisan view of Hitler and his Germany. Riefenstahl's masterly use of narrationless documentary seems to ascribe power and inevitability to her subject, but this should be taken as a warning of what "art for art's sake" can mask. All film seeks to persuade, but films that suppress their subjectivity and gloss over the paradoxes and conflicts in the world they reflect are attempting more to condition than communicate.

Pare Lorentz's *The Plow That Broke the Plains* (1936) and *The River* (1937) use poetic narrations that turn each film into a long elegiac ballad, a folk form that underwrites the films' omniscient eye and seemingly egoless atmospheres. Their powerfully aesthetized imagery (Figure 27-8) and ironic montage set up a

FIGURE 27-8

The Plow That Broke the Plains, Pare Lorentz. Stark imagery and ironic montage are used to set up a haunting vision with an omniscient point of view. (Museum of Modern Art)

haunting vision of a land plundered through ignorance and political opportunism—propaganda at its best.

Peter Watkins' *The War Game* (1966) appropriates a news program style to posit the nuclear bombing of London. With grim impartiality, it constructs an infernal, incontestable vision of nuclear war and holds us mesmerized by its air of veracity. It too passionately seeks to persuade, but by refusing heroics it avoids the personalizing found so often in screen treatments of disaster. We are forced to put ourselves and our loved ones among the doomed.

The omniscient point of view can signify an author's modest wish not to stand between the viewer and the subject. Omniscience is a natural stance when a subject is as complex and far reaching as war or race relations, where an individualized point of view would seem parochial or egocentric. However, the unconfirmable nature of what may be so authoritatively asserted, and the undisclosed credentials of one's guides, should recommend caution.

This limitation is seen in most television history series, which usually cover vast thematic and factual territory. The excellent PBS series from Blackside, *Eyes on the Prize* (1990), which chronicled the development of civil rights in America, trod a fine line between omniscience and passionate commitment.

Powered from the resources of large corporations, and using an army of production workers, history series gravitate toward omniscience as naturally as royalty to saying "we." Thames Television's *The World at War* in the 1970s, WGBH's *Vietnam: A Television History* in the 1980s, and even Ken Burns' 1990 *The Civil War* all echo the textbook emphasis on facts. The ambitiousness, authorial impersonality, and apparent finality of such ventures makes them suffocate historical curiosity rather than awaken it. Who is speaking to whom, for whom, or representing whom? And why assume the voice of God?

Not all screen history fails: An openly critical film such as Peter Davis' *Hearts and Minds* (1974) argues that strands in American sports culture led inevitably to the tragically mistaken U.S. involvement in southeast Asia. The viewer is on a clear footing and can engage with the film's propositions rather than go numb under a deluge of information. More recently, the superb PBS eight-part series, *The Great War* (1996), overturned the TV history curse by making masterful use of a succession of poetically rendered subjective viewpoints.

PERSONAL

Here the point of view is unashamedly and subjectively that of the director, who may narrate the film himself or herself. A director's surrogate may still be in front of the camera as a "reporter" or catalyst, or the film may present its views in the form of a third-person or first-person cinematic essay. There are no limits to the personal point of view beyond what the author/storyteller can see and know. In Figure 27-9 the director is behind the camera, but he or she can step forward into the visible world of the film.

Pierre Schoendoerffer's little known *Anderson Platoon* (1966) is the work of a French army cinematographer returning to Vietnam, where he finds Americans now fighting the unwinnable war. Schoendoerffer's laconic commentary and compassionate eye reveal what moral bankruptcy lies at the heart of this, and most, warfare. Movingly evident is the desperate companionship between soldiers and

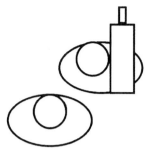

FIGURE 27-9

In the personal point of view, it is the author/storyteller who is the point of view character.

the starkness of the human desire to hold onto life. This insight, one feels, is very much a product of Schoendoerffer's austere but compassionate character.

Louis Malle's *Phantom India* series (1968) is conventional travelogue, except that Malle narrates his thoughts and feelings as he tries to penetrate the surface of a disturbingly alien and yet fascinating succession of cultures (Figure 27-10). The result—more revealing of Malle than of his subject—is of a privileged, intellectual mandarin failing to connect at any level with the natives. By default, the series exoticizes and contributes to the long tradition of colonial separatism.

FIGURE 27-10

Louis Malle's *Phantom India,* a personal view that reveals more about Malle than India. (New Yorker Films)

Peter Watkins' *Munch* (1978) is an excellent and imaginative biography of the beleaguered painter, but the omniscient point of view cannot hide the intensity of Watkins' identification with his subject. Ultimately the profile has an eerie feeling of displaced autobiography, and unintentionally perhaps, the film is intensely personal.

REFLEXIVE

"To be reflexive," says Jay Ruby, "is to structure a product in such a way that the audience assumes that the producer, the process of making, and the product are a coherent whole. Not only is the audience made aware of these relationships, but it is made to realize the necessity of that knowledge."[1] By sabotaging the traditional illusion that we are watching unmediated life, reflexivity signals that films are "created, structured articulations of the filmmaker and not authentic, truthful, objective records."[2]

---

[1]Ruby, Jay. "The Image Mirrored: Reflexivity and the Documentary Film," in *New Challenges for Documentary,* Alan Rosenthal, Ed. Berkeley: University of California Press, 1988, p. 65.
[2]Ibid, pp. 74–75.

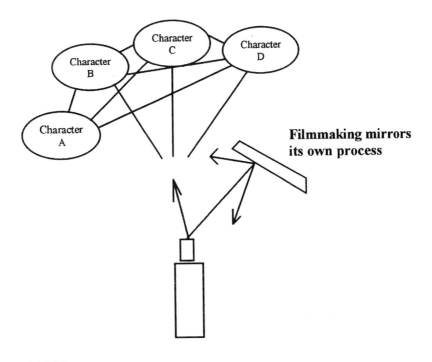

FIGURE 27-11 ——————————————————————————————

The film with a reflexive point of view can share salient points of its own filmmaking process with the audience.

Figure 27-11 shows that the filming process is not only taking in the complex relationships between our friends, A, B, C, and D, but the combination of directing, shooting, and editing will also permit incidents in the filmmaking process itself to reach the audience. This I have symbolized, not too confusingly, I hope, by a mirror.

Dziga Vertov, poet and film editor in 1920s Russia, is credited with the first radical investigation of documentary language. By seeking to show "life as it is," his *Kino Eye* was the precursor of the *cinéma vérité* movement 40 years later. *The Man with the Movie Camera* (1929) presents Moscow as a teeming spectacle of dialectical opposites. The exuberant camera, seemingly independent of human agency, embraces the constants and contradictions of human life. Sometimes we see the camera and cameraman, sometimes we see them literally in a mirror, as in Figure 27-11.

Vertov thought that the dynamic of camera and montage transcended human agency, and though we often see shots of the cameraman at work, he seems—like the dancer in *The Red Shoes*—less the camera's operator than its puppet. For ideological reasons, Vertov denied personal authorship by claiming that film truth was vested in the apparatus itself—an ebullient mystification that he doesn't quite pull off.

Buñuel's *Land Without Bread* (1932) has an unintentionally reflexive moment when a crew member steps into frame to examine the ulcerated throat of a dying child. Commendably humane sympathies sometimes turn observers into participants. Incidental reflexivity like this was sometimes used deliberately from the 1960s onward to signify to the audience that it was watching a film—rather a patronizing gesture in most contexts.

However, it is quite another matter when a film exposes, or even analyzes, the paradoxes of documentary exploration itself. This admits that major questions hang over every documentary, indeed over documentary itself. For instance, how often are we seeing not spontaneous life captured by the camera, but something instigated by filmmaking itself?

Reflexivity allows the filmmaker to open windows on the conditions and paradoxes encountered during production and to publicly contemplate whatever ethical or other ambiguities have become part of the experience. Ethnographic filmmaking, in which the culture under study is supposed to be uncontaminated by the filmmaker's own cultural assumptions, is a prime candidate for such scrutiny, but one is liable to make unconscious cultural impositions in any and every area, not just in ethnography. Making an ethnographic translation of one culture for the benefit of another is inherently hazardous (if not ultimately impossible), but has interesting lessons for all of documentary filmmaking.

Aside from issues of distortion and misinformation, there are fascinating and more abstract issues concerning the medium's boundaries. What may or may not be ethical? How, when, and why do we suspend disbelief? What deceptions does the medium practice on its makers? and so on. Such questions properly assume that film is an emerging and imperfectly understood medium, rather than a finished tool whose only use is as an informational or advocacy vehicle for a "subject."

The ethnographer Jean Rouch's seminal *Chronicle of a Summer* (1961) poses the people of Paris with a fundamental question, "Are you happy?" By showing participants their own footage, he initiates a moving self-examination and a desire to go deeper. The results show Rouch's radical curiosity, his sympathy with the ordinary person's need to find meaning in life, and his willingness to question the medium itself.

The ultimate in reflexivity is self-reflexivity, in which the film reflects not only its own process, but its author's thoughts, perceptions, and self-examination as well (Figure 27-12). This is by no means a modern pursuit, as a certain Narcissus of antiquity managed to drown himself while admiring his own image overmuch in a pool. The self-reflexive form performs the same service for the self-involved with great reliability, which is a way of saying that it's a difficult genre to pull off, though wonderful when it works.

Michael Rubbo's *Sad Song of Yellow Skin* (1970) is a Canadian filmmaker's search to define Vietnam amid the flux of that country's impossible contradictions. By mostly confining his attention to city street people and the young American dissidents working with them, Rubbo exposes us to paradoxical impressions of a peasant civilization rent asunder by a wealthy and technocratic occupying savior. Rubbo's ironic view of the world and of himself saves his films from sentimentality. Ross McElwee's output, from the highly influential *Sherman's March* (1989) till his most recent *The Six O'Clock News* (1997), solves the always tricky

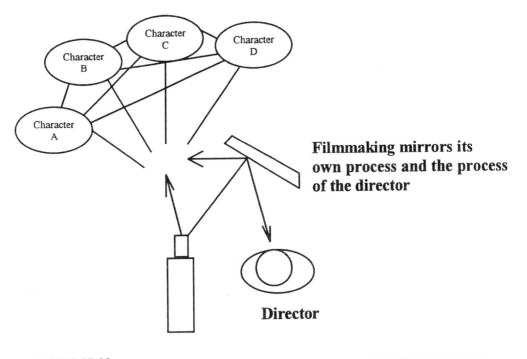

Filmmaking mirrors its own process and the process of the director

Director

FIGURE 27-12

The self-reflexive point of view allows examination of both its own process and its maker(s). However, treat this one carefully, for little separates self-reflexivity from self-indulgence.

problems of autobiography by portraying himself as a sort of antihero Everyman. His gentle amazement at the way of the world is beginning to seem cocooned because of all the disasters he films and the large journeys he takes.

TIME, DEVELOPMENT, AND STRUCTURE

Many possible elements influence a film's structure, but how time is handled is paramount. Documentaries often have trouble giving an adequate sense of development, so the power to abridge, and to make comparisons between past and present, may be vital to showing that change is indeed taking place. In a BBC series in which I participated, we preempted this problem by building change and development into the series formula itself, which by focusing on individuals making a major change in their lives, avoided the frustrating and familiar situation in which *nothing really happens.*

Following are some common documentary genres, each implying a different handling of time as an aspect of narrative. The examples, generally taken from well-known films, do not represent any rigorous or complete classification system, but are included to help you spot genres and to inspire you to see the films that epitomize them.

THE EVENT-CENTERED FILM

Here the event is the backbone of the film. It might be the launching of a ship, a dairy show, or the capture of a notorious criminal. The event has its stages, and plugged into its forward movement may be sections of interview, pieces of relevant past, or even pieces of future, such as a criminal telling what it would be like to be surrounded by armed police. The event film may be one of the rare occasions when more than one camera may be necessary. It often has its development and dynamics pegged out in advance by the shape of the event itself. Shooting it with multiple, mobile cameras takes the kind of organization and timing usually reserved for military operations if the cameras are not to end up shooting each other.

Leni Riefenstahl's dark classic, *Olympia* (1936), follows the process of the Olympic Games in Berlin. With extraordinary, seductive virtuosity, it places Adolf Hitler, godlike, at the center.

Werner Herzog's *La Soufrière* (1976) centers on a volcano about to erupt and how the islanders handle the imminent destruction of their home. Herzog and crew risked their lives to be there, but because the volcano elected not to explode, the film switches without batting an eyelid into meditating on the importance of taking risks, and ends up making capital out of the documentarian's nightmare—the nonevent.

George Stoney, Judy Helfand, and Suzanne Rostock's *The Uprising of '34* (1995) reconstructs an abortive 1934 cotton workers' strike through archive footage and the memory of survivors. The arc of the event and its failure as industrial action become the structure through which to contemplate how and why labor history has so often been suppressed in the United States. The film shows that it is the traumatized workers themselves who chose to forget, and not only official repression. The making and showing of the film was a memorably healing act that brought a local tragedy out of obscurity and properly reinstated a piece of America's class struggle history.

Juan Francisco Urrusti's *A Long Journey to Guadalupe* (1996) centers on the yearly phenomenon of the mass migration to worship at the shrine of the Virgin of Guadalupe in Mexico City. First the pilgrimage is examined conceptually from a historical and cultural perspective, and then, charged up with ideas, we watch the mass migration itself, a spontaneous enactment by a poor and deeply religious people of their suffering, history, and faith. The latter part of the film concentrates, as only film can, on the actuality of the pilgrims' passion and ineffability, and belies our ability to represent such cardinal human longings in words.

THE PROCESS FILM

This type of film deals with the chain of events that make up a significant process. Often it will show more than one strand of ongoing present, each serving as a cutaway from the others. Cutting between parallel stories allows each segment to be reduced to its essence and stimulates comparison—often ironic—between concurrencies.

Humphrey Jenning's poetic *Fires Were Started* (1943) focuses on the unsung heroes of the National Fire Service in their nightly battles to contain London's erupting inferno during the Blitz. Their cycles of struggle become metaphoric for those of a whole beleaguered island people.

Frederick Wiseman's *Titicut Follies* (1967) shows every stage, from induction to burial, at an institution designed to contain the criminally insane, including the attempts of one seemingly sane man to extricate himself from its nightmarish embrace. The film's episodes, which lead the viewer progressively deeper into the surreal logic of the institution's personnel and their "treatment," are organized as side trips from an ongoing show, the institution's annual review.

Les Blank's *Burden of Dreams* (1982) chronicles the shooting of *Fitzcarraldo* (1982), a Herzog feature about an opera impresario who contrived to bring a river steamer over the Andes (Figure 27-13). Through Herzog's own struggle in the jungle to get a steamer up a mountain side, Blank reveals Herzog's dictatorial obsessiveness and the risks to which he exposed his workers. By showing how realizing a vision can become more important than human life, Blank implies that totalitarianism can masquerade under the guise of art.

THE JOURNEY FILM

There is a saying in the film industry that no film set on a train journey has ever failed. The journey's allure, with its metaphoric overtones and inbuilt rhythms of movement, applies equally to the documentary film.

Pare Lorentz's *The River* (1937) has a clearly defined beginning, middle, and end, but with an inherent augmentation as, stage by stage, the film leads us from the beginning trickle all the way to the ocean. Henri Cartier-Bresson's *Le Retour* (1946) chronicles a river of a different sort, that of displaced humanity trudging the roads of Europe in search of home after World War II.

Ross McElwee's *Sherman's March* (1989) takes General Sherman's destructive journey during the American Civil War as its starting point and then, bored with his chosen subject, turns into a parallel journey by McElwee himself, encountering old girlfriends and new in a bid to end his status as a single man. McElwee discov-

FIGURE 27-13

Werner Herzog and the boat he hauls up a hillside in Les Blank's *Burden of Dreams.* (Maureen Gosling)

ers that the General is still with him, but more as an instructive metaphor who came to an ignoble end.

THE WALLED-CITY FILM

Groups and institutions tend to close in upon themselves and beget their own code of conduct. This, in turn, reflects the larger host society in miniature. The "walled-city" film, therefore, investigates a microcosm in order to imply criticism on a much wider scale.

Buñuel's *Land Without Bread* (1932), by concentrating on starving villagers in a remote Spanish village and by defining the various forces that prevent them helping themselves, angrily exposes the pattern of cynical neglect sanctioned by church, state, and landowners.

Any of Frederick Wiseman's films qualify, notably *Titicut Follies* (1967), *High School* (1968; Figure 27-14), and *Hospital* (1969). They, respectively, imply critical attitudes toward mental health and normality, toward preparing the young for democracy, and toward a society that condones violence, both self-directed and that visited on others.

FIGURE 27-14

High School by Fred Wiseman. A walled-city film that looks at our attitudes toward preparing the young for democracy. (Zipporah Films, Inc.)

FIGURE 27-15

The ladies in Nick Broomfield's *Chicken Ranch* pose with their Madame.

Two films by Nick Broomfield, *Soldier Girls* (1981) and *Chicken Ranch* (1982), also qualify as walled-city films but differ significantly in approach from both the narrated and the direct cinema observational approach. One is about women soldiers doing basic training and the other about women and their customers in a brothel (Figure 27-15). Each shows how institutional life attempts to condition and control its inmates, and each makes us more knowledgeable and critical. Neither film pretends to be neutral or unaffected by what it finds. By letting us see a discharged woman soldier embrace the camera operator or by including the brothel owner's harangue of the crew for filming what he wants kept confidential, both films let us see where the filmmakers' sympathies lie and let us guess at the arrangements, liaisons, and even manipulation that made each phase of shooting possible.

THE HISTORICAL FILM

To the degree that all films reanimate what is already past, all are historical. Consequently, film ought to be an inherently good historical medium. But though concerned with cause and effect through time, the historical film seldom keeps to chronology. It must often digress to consider other chains of cause and effect that affect whatever is currently being developed on-screen. Sometimes chronological events dominate and sometimes contributory aspects take precedence.

Film history functions very differently from written history. As Donald Watt and Jerry Kuehl say in their essays,[3] screen histories sometimes don't even satisfy their makers. Balance is fatally hampered when particular coverage is not available, and executives' terror of making intellectual demands on their audience makes programming play safe. Then again, the screen, by its realism and ineluctable movement through time, discourages contemplation and defeats any statement that cannot be illustrated. Because the meanings of history are abstractions, the screen seems a singularly poor vehicle.

Cultural and political history films founder for a variety of reasons: from trying to sidestep controversy, as school textbooks do; from failing to recognize that the screen is different from reading or an academic lecture; from the domination of suspect interpretation; and from grandiose desires to be comprehensive. Particularly when consortia are involved, the audience cannot tell what strings come with funding or to what degree television histories are dominated by the desire to build monuments.

Britain has produced some notable war series *(The Great War, The World at War)*, and America has produced its own blockbusters (e.g., *Vietnam: A Television History* and *The Civil War)*. Compressed and heavily mediated by narration, they function like encyclopedias and deluge the viewer in facts and concepts that require inhuman feats of memorization to keep straight. The viewer wilts under a sense of inferiority at being unable to comprehend the lesson. What one gains—a sense of virtue at having seen so much old footage, a sense of atmosphere and mood, patches of vivid and clearly remembered drama—is clearly not the balanced and comprehensive understanding the producers imagine.

The incisive historical documentary, on the other hand, is not primarily concerned with conveying a balanced overall grasp. Its focus is probably a main issue or character, and is likely to be more visibly fueled by a passion or smoldering sense of injustice. Good examples are extremely diverse both in purview and language. Pare Lorentz's early ecology films, *The Plow That Broke the Plain* (1936) and *The River* (1937), warn eloquently of the ecological and human disasters that follow in the wake of soil erosion and deforestation caused by opportunistic government action.

Alain Resnais' *Night and Fog* (1955) leads us to confront the implications of Auschwitz for the future. It resurrects the hellish life of the prisoners with concentrated imaginativeness and leaves us looking over our shoulders for those among us capable of administering another such system.

Since the 1960s, oral history for the screen has gained important ground. Its emphasis on the form and priorities of personal experience has set clear and useful limits, because here "history" means the particular experience of particular people, and this frees it from trying to contrive a settled overview. Stephen Peet's "Yesterday's Witness" BBC series in England (which I helped to start), made over a hundred films, but in the United States similar films have often been made by in-

---

[3]Watt, Donald and Jerry Kuehl. "History on the Public Screen I & II," in *New Challenges for Documentary,* Rosenthal, Ed. Berkeley: University of California Press, 1988, pp. 435–453.

dependents—probably because of the political self-censorship that afflicts even the noncommercial PBS. Notable independent films are Reichert and Klein's *Union Maids* (1976) and *Seeing Red* (1983), Connie Field's *The Life and Times of Rosie the Riveter* (1981), and Lorraine Gray's *With Babies and Banners* (1979). In France, Marcel Ophuls' *Sorrow and the Pity* (1972) and *Hotel Terminus: The Life and Times of Klaus Barbie* (1988, Figure 27-16) and Claude Lanzmann's *Shoah* (1985) have concentrated on the workings of Fascism. With the collapse of communism in eastern Europe, we can expect to see a wealth of extraordinary stories rising to the surface.

What distinguishes these films is that they don't approach history in the textbook way—as bygone events requiring closure by consensus pronouncement—but as the light of human experience showing the way ahead through contemporary predicaments.

There must be many other "families" of films to further diversify the possibilities for forms and structural types. Some others to mention only in passing are:

- *Biographical film* (Peter Watkins' *Munch* [1978]; Ken Russell's many short films made in the 1960s for the BBC, notably *Elgar, Debussy,* and *Rousseau;* and recently, the Kartemquin collective's *Golub* [1990] by Gordon Quinn and Jerry Blumenthal).

- *Thesis film,* which assembles evidence to argue a case (the socially conscious British documentaries of the 1930s; Julia Reichert and Jim Klein's *Union Maids* [1976] and *Seeing Red* [1983]).

- *Catalogue film* (many of the Les Blank films, such *Garlic Is as Good as Ten Mothers* [1977], *In Heaven There Is No Beer* [1984], and the delightful *Gap-Toothed Women* [1987]).

- *Screwball comedy,* which was Erroll Morris' initial partiality in *Vernon, Florida* (1982) and *Gates of Heaven* (1985). Both are about the wackiest imaginable locals.

- *Documentary noir* is from the ever-inventive Erroll Morris again; *The Thin Blue Line* (1988) stylistically links the world of its participants to the dark and fatalistic fictional world of the *film noir.*

- *Absurdist documentary* in *Complaints of a Dutiful Daughter* (1995), Deborah Hoffman uses surreal humor to explore what would otherwise be a crushingly sad situation as her mother descends into Alzheimer's disease.

This review of documentary language demonstrates, I think, that the genre is becoming less monological and more dialogical. Still, old habits of disseminating improving tracts to the unwashed masses die hard, and far too much that circulates as documentary has the aura of the classroom or the privileged traveler's slide lecture. A new generation of filmmakers is dragging the documentary away from corporate bureaucrats and embracing the audience's eager longing for films that provoke an active inner dialogue. Slowly and surely, documentary is acquiring the complexities of language, thought, and purpose that were once confined to more mature art forms such as literature and theater. The old order is giving way to documentaries made by men and women who see the audience as equals, and who are willing to share their inmost thoughts and feelings.

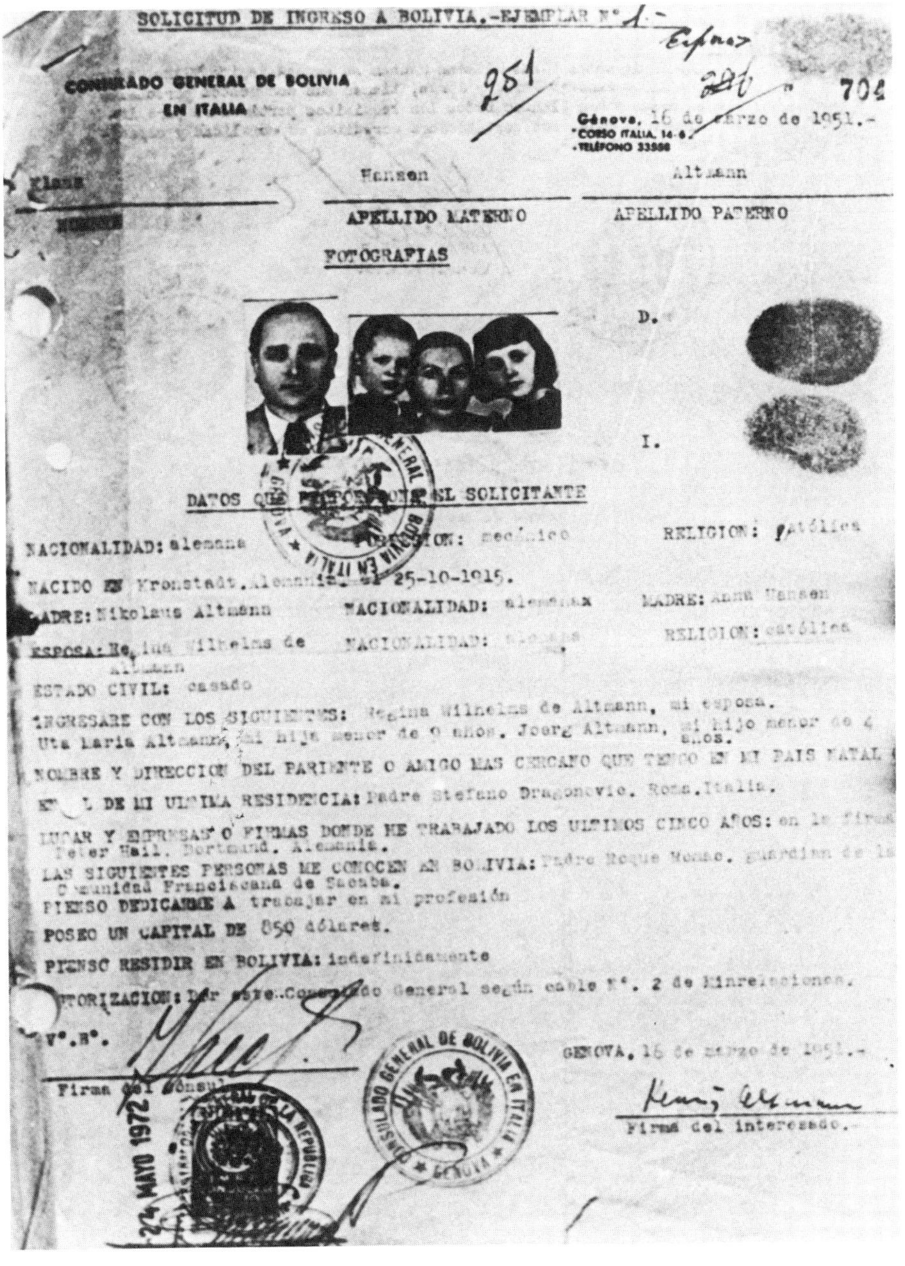
SOLICITUD DE INGRESO A BOLIVIA.-EJEMPLAR N° 1.-

CONSULADO GENERAL DE BOLIVIA
EN ITALIA

Génova, 16 de marzo de 1951.-
CORSO ITALIA, 14-6
TELEFONO 33588

Klaus — NOMBRE
Hansen — APELLIDO MATERNO
Altmann — APELLIDO PATERNO

FOTOGRAFIAS

D.

I.

DATOS QUE PROPORCIONA EL SOLICITANTE

NACIONALIDAD: alemana — PROFESION: mecánico — RELIGION: católica
NACIDO EN Kronstadt, Alemania, el 25-10-1915.
PADRE: Nikolaus Altmann — NACIONALIDAD: alemana — MADRE: Anna Hansen — RELIGION: católica
ESPOSA: Regina Wilhelms de Altmann — NACIONALIDAD: alemana
ESTADO CIVIL: casado
INGRESARE CON LOS SIGUIENTES: Regina Wilhelms de Altmann, mi esposa. Uta Maria Altmann, mi hija menor de 9 años. Joerg Altmann, mi hijo menor de 4 años.
NOMBRE Y DIRECCION DEL PARIENTE O AMIGO MAS CERCANO QUE TENGO EN MI PAIS NATAL
... DE MI ULTIMA RESIDENCIA: Padre Stefano Dragonovic. Roma, Italia.
LUGAR Y EMPRESAS O FIRMAS DONDE HE TRABAJADO LOS ULTIMOS CINCO AÑOS: en la firma Peter Hall. Dortmund. Alemania.
LAS SIGUIENTES PERSONAS ME CONOCEN EN BOLIVIA: Padre Roque Romac, guardián de la Comunidad Franciscana de Sacaba.
PIENSO DEDICARME A trabajar en mi profesión
POSEO UN CAPITAL DE 850 dólares.
PIENSO RESIDIR EN BOLIVIA: indefinidamente
AUTORIZACION: por este Consulado General según cable N°. 2 de Minrelaciones.

V°.B°.

Firma del Cónsul

GENOVA, 16 de marzo de 1951.-

Firma del interesado.

FIGURE 27-16

Incriminating document in *Hotel Terminus*—the false identity paper that allowed Klaus Barbie to enter Bolivia.

C H A P T E R   2 8

FORM, CONTROL, AND IDENTITY

This chapter, concerned with issues of form, control, and identity, will examine:

- The relationship between subject and form.
- The difficulties of authorial control over a world meant to be spontaneous.
- How topics may be easy or difficult to film and the effect of this on the documentary's reputation.
- How documentaries must be justified to participants and funding sources.
- How ethics are bound up with this.
- How broadcasting handles the independent viewpoint.
- How documentary language has influenced the fictional form.

In attempting point of view groupings in Chapter 27, I was unable to make reliably clear distinctions between types or families of films. Trying to categorize documentary confronts one with a confusingly circular interrelationship between its elements. Indeed, good documentaries seem successful mainly because someone has found a way to turn particular footage into a compelling narrative. Good films, being one of a kind, may have only limited usefulness as prototypes.

With this handicap in mind, it may still be useful to examine some of the issues and contradictions in the documentarian's environment, which inevitably influence which films get made and how. Some paradoxes lie in the medium, others in the ways that filmmakers have thus far used it. There are also anomalies in the framework of funding and audience interests, but these are somewhat outside our purview.

CONTENT INFLUENCES FORM

Some of the difficulties that face anyone trying to classify the documentary arise from the fact that each film owes its credibility to acts, words, and images plucked from life and *lacking central authorship*. In virtually every other expressive art form, the creative artist has more control over content and the form in which it is expressed. In documentary the filmmaker is in the position of a mosaic artist. Freedom is severely curtailed by the idiosyncratic nature of the materials, and unless the film is of the highly controlled essay type, the author is at the mercy of the materials he or she can acquire. To those who are not obsessed with control, there is actually a fascination in this relationship because it is analogous to our ambiguous relationship with destiny. We influence but cannot control it, and must harmonize and compromise with it.

FICTION AND DOCUMENTARY: AUTHORIAL CONTROL

While the fiction filmmaker can mold and compress material during the writing stage to make the intended inner qualities visible and compelling, the documentary director must imply an authorial point of view in more subtle and indirect ways. To avoid devaluing your own coin, documentary as a genre compels you to work from behind the appearance of verisimilitude. Stamp your work with too much of your own viewpoint, and you suggest there was not enough in the personalities and events you filmed to be interesting or persuasive. The observational documentary, in particular, must strike a balance between tracts of autonomous, unfolding realism, on the one hand, and signs and portents that make us want to peer beyond the veil of the material and the literal, on the other. A willingness to do so is probably initiated by three main factors, that the film's:

- Subject is gripping and original.
- Point of view is individual, flexible, and evident.
- Language and conventions are used effectively.

Most directors face challenges in one or all of these areas, and the measure of a film's originality is the energy and freshness with which they were tackled.

COMMON LIMITS ON THE RANGE OF SUBJECTS

The sheer difficulty of getting audiences to notice fragile and transient moments of significance, so easily accomplished by the writer, means that documentary often plays it safe by resorting to sensational subjects. War, family violence, urban problems, eccentrics, deviants, demonstrations, revolts, and confrontations all promise something heightened. In the long run this is self-defeating because by promising a showdown or a freak show, the genre has run out of steam and leaves us unfulfilled. Further, by so often dealing in fashionable causes, the documentary has become perceived as the "problem movie" and is saddled with some obligation to preach solutions, which are never profusely available.

Unfortunately documentaries seldom penetrate the heart of their subjects with the ease and precision we expect of literature. For the true feel of small-town life or for the authentic claustrophobia of a middle-class family reunion, we look instinctively to fiction and not the documentary film. This is not inevitable, but difficulties exist at every level. Not the least is raising money to budget a film about "minor" subjects. One must blame those who administer the bidding system by which films are proposed, weeded out, and funded. Just imagine how much major literature would exist if Jane Austen, Guy de Maupassant, Doris Lessing, and John Updike—writers specializing in the significance in unremarkable lives—were forced to first apply for huge sums of corporate funding. Libraries would contain only supermarket novels.

If filmmaking generally reflects its capitalistic foundations and thrives or fades according to audience figures, in the end it is futile and unproductive to complain, because other obstacles also discourage working on a small canvas.

PARTICIPANTS' COOPERATION

Some difficulties in making the "ordinary-life" documentary arise from participants themselves. How does one find any suitable explanation to offer participants for wanting to film what they themselves consider trivial? Fail to justify your purposes, and you fail to assure them of your underlying respect. On the other hand, when you do make your interests clear and justifiable, many people will spontaneously set aside considerations of privacy because your motives for making the film seem overridingly important. A rape victim may volunteer to appear in your documentary because she urgently wants others to know what she has experienced. She chooses to sacrifice her privacy in order to raise public awareness of rape and rapists, and of how society processes the raped woman's legal case. She does so wisely only *if you make her fully aware of the consequences*—not always easy.

RESISTANCE TO THE PERSONAL VIEWPOINT

A major obstacle to films finding the extraordinary in the ordinary is corporate television's unwillingness to countenance work expressing personal politics or beliefs, unless, of course, large viewing figures are assured. Television, for all its vaunted investigative journalism, generally avoids social criticism, no matter how well argued, unless it can be safely yoked to a famous name or a widely recognized movement. This serves a double purpose: it attracts viewers, and dissociates the channel from responsibility for the opinions expressed.

Pandering to audience figures can work in either direction. The Beatles were able to have quite silly work shown on national television because they were very popular, while at the other end of the scale, Louis Malle's thoughtful and critical series, *Phantom India* (1968), would not have been shown in Britain without his prior reputation as a director of controversial fiction films.

Other kinds of resistance to the personal viewpoint may be cultural and harder to pinpoint. Mark Wexler's widely shown and critically praised *Me and My Matchmaker* (1996) aroused a barely contained fury in one television buyer at a European festival, either because the film shifts focus from profiling its subject to reflecting on Mark's changing relationship with her, or because documentary itself is still expected to suppress its maker's persona (Figure 28-1.) The notion of

FIGURE 28-1

Mark Wexler and his subject, Irene Nathan, in *Me and My Matchmaker.* Autobiographical content, though popular with cinema audiences, is hard to get accepted by television (photo © Wexler's World).

television documentary as an objective public service lives on, and proponents remain hostile to individual cinematic authorship, particularly (I suspect) when the buyer is European and the author unremorsefully American.

DOCUMENTARY LANGUAGE

The documentary is a young genre in a young art form that is by no means limited to present forms. It need not even be a slave to realism. Its only limitation is that it relay aspects of actuality (past, present, or future) and imply a critical relationship to the fabric of social life.

To engage and hold an audience, the form seems compelled to draw on storytelling techniques and narrative compression, as Flaherty recognized at documentary's inception. This fact of life may be uncomfortable for the ethnographer or *cinéma vérité* purist, who sometimes protest that this is manipulative. Marxist filmmakers of the 1960s and 1970s were aware of this and attempted a more respectful presentation of participants by leaving what they said and did largely uncut. While this certainly made films look different (and seldom more coherent), it left the foundation of documentary unchanged. *Everything on the screen comes from choices and relationships, and these inescapably reflect the director's commitment to what is true and what needs to be said about those truths.*

Here we return to the notion of the contract with your audience. A film must promise something, deliver what it promises, and remain consistent in its relationship with the audience. This is the most difficult aspect to control and the one where the director grows only slowly, given the time it takes to complete (and therefore learn from) each project.

In previous editions of this book I lamented that documentary form had stagnated. Some of the great films that followed in the wake of the 1960s *cinéma vérité* explosion, such as Ophuls' *The Sorrow and the Pity* (1972), Kopple's *Harlan County, USA* (1976), and Wohl's *Best Boy* (1979), broke new ground in their depth and humane subject matter, but not in documentary language. After the novelty of spontaneously filmed actuality wore off, the documentary settled into a complacent middle age. Innovation came in the area of narrative editing rather than in directing or camera usage.

Now a renaissance in form and audience response is under way. Recent documentaries of significance show a strongly authorial point of view emerging. Neidik and Angelico's reflexive *Dark Lullabies* (1986) is told in the first person, and so is Moore's *Roger and Me* (1989)—a documentary picked by audience votes as "best film" at the Chicago International Film Festival over dozens of fiction films. Another popular success was Ross McElwee's long and playful autobiography of the heart, *Sherman's March* (1986). Following the success of Errol Morris' docudrama noir, *The Thin Blue Line* (1988), also shown in movie houses and on television, one can only rejoice that there's change afoot.

In television changes are also happening. Home Box Office (HBO) cable is showing and even commissioning documentaries, and video stores often have a documentary shelf. The BBC has its *Video Diaries* series and in America PBS has *POV*, so television is getting used to showing singly and independently produced, and even personal documentaries. Naturally, making films in the first person is more difficult and does not automatically make better films, but it helps to break the mold of forms held static far too long by conservatism, and to jolt filmmakers into greater self-awareness.

As always, technological change also impels artistic developments. We can expect nonlinear editing to contribute greater flexibility of form and film language to continue moving in more subjective and poetic directions, as so movingly evident in the PBS series *The Great War* (1996).

A large public following exists for the right films, but convention must give way to fresh approaches. Committees, commissioning editors, and panels who dispense public monies must revise their expectations and procedural habits if they are ever to seed films that rise above the institutional pabulum still thought appropriate for the masses.

Is standardization the inevitable cost of industrial timetables and management conservatism? Industrialization is sensible for making sitcoms and talk shows, but disabling to documentaries. Sadly, caution and self-censorship among filmmakers helps this standardization to evolve. Often insidious because unconscious, it comes from the freelancer's need to be acceptable to his paymaster and lifeline. While the breakup of the monolithic BBC and ITV in Britain would seem to enfranchise the many small, independent companies this has created, it has in fact concentrated power in the hands of a few commissioning editors, who call all the shots whether they like it or not.

DOCUMENTARY, FICTION FILMS, AND THE FUTURE

Fiction filmmaking, after the innovative and experimental silent days, became a profitable industry, and the creative process lost much of its immediacy and flexibility. This individuality never languished in the documentary, which has always been an improvisatory genre. From the 1950s, as lighter sync equipment made freer filming possible, improvisational methods were revived in British fiction by Free Cinema movement proponents such as Lindsay Anderson, Karel Reisch, and Tony Richardson. In France of the late 1950s and 60s, a willingness to improvise, to shoot in the streets and on the run, produced the great films of the New Wave. In America, Cassavetes and Altman were the pioneers, and the sustained subjective view of the handheld camera has since become standard in feature films with no intellectual pretensions whatsoever.

The independent-minded documentary has, I believe, influenced fiction directing relationships and styles of acting by provided a demanding benchmark for screen realism. The actor/director relationship has become more intimate and demanding, more revealing of the actor's self. The results are immensely hopeful and exciting because the most inventive directors are expecting, and getting, superlative creativity from their actors. They have abandoned the high-concept blueprint, with its stock characters, in favor of intensified character portraits whose roots are in the actual.

Experience in making documentaries is an excellent preparation for making features. Ken Loach has worked in theater, soap opera, and drama documentary on his way toward making his intensely compassionate films about English working-class life. Documentary experience evidently equipped Alain Tanner, the Swiss documentarian and feature film director, to make *In the White City* (1984) without a script and relying on an informal, extemporizing relationship with his actors. Mike Leigh, best known for *Naked* (1993) and *Secrets and Lies* (1996), is an English director who has arrived at similar working methods by way of theater directing, and whose mixture of dark comedy and strongly humanitarian themes has resulted in a major series of films about English working-class life that challenge documentary at its own game.

The growing amount of documentary, its separation from electronic journalism, and its developing cinematic voice may have far-reaching consequences. Because documentary can now be made fast and inexpensively using desktop technology, and because filmmakers are no longer dependent on studios and production centers, we can expect to see more films made speculatively, with a consequent rise in imaginative authorship, and some diversification away from power hubs toward regional centers. The Amber group in England is an illustration of this possibility. Their beautiful drama documentary, *Eden Valley* (1995), is an impressive outgrowth of their commitment to nonprofessional actors, documentary inventiveness, and their impoverished home area in England.

Documentary improvisation and experimental theater will inevitably come together as Fassbinder made them do with the Munich *action-teater,* and as Mike Leigh has done with spectacular success in England. If this avenue interests you, the possibilities are explored from a practical angle in this book's companion volume, *Directing: Film Techniques and Aesthetics.*[1]

---

[1]Rabiger, Michael. *Directing: Film Techniques and Aesthetics,* 2nd ed. Boston: Focal Press, 1996.

C H A P T E R   2 9

RE-ENACTMENT, RECONSTRUCTION, AND DOCUDRAMA

This chapter looks from a moral or ethical perspective at:

- reenacting and truth claims
- reconstructing or projecting situations
- reconstructing subjectivity
- fake documentaries as instruments of critique

A controversial aspect of the documentary is its ability to hypothesize actuality by reconstructing bygone situations or even by creating an entire biography for someone no longer living. To take the less radical situation first, it sometimes happens that some important biographical event has passed before you begin filming—a crucial career interview, say, for a job that one's main character has already begun.

If participants can credibly re-enact this scene, how important is it that you be totally truthful with your audience? There is no easy answer. Some films run a subtitle saying the scene is re-enacted, but this seems unnecessarily dramatic if the scene is only part of the exposition needed to get the film under way, and if it is already using a distancing past-tense narration or voice-over. It would, however, be highly misleading in a key evidence scene to let the audience think it was seeing actuality instead of a reconstruction. Recently I saw an explosive documentary made in the Netherlands national film school, which turned out, despite many clues to its being improvised, to have been wholly and masterfully fabricated—in fact, not a documentary at all. The audience (mainly, it must be admitted, of documentary teachers) was disturbed and even irate at being bamboozled, and this suggests how important it may be to keep the contractual relationship with the audience straight. We make different inferences from documented actuality than from material that is acted, and feel manipulated when someone transposes the labeling. Indeed, it was to illustrate this very point that the film was shown.

The dividing line seems to be one of good faith; there is nothing controversial about showing how a character got her job, if we know she got one. But if instead our character says that the personnel manager tricked her, whether we see the actual interview or only a re-enactment becomes crucially important because everyone's integrity is at stake.

To summarize, re-enacting important scenes that can be shown no other way is a useful and valid way to stimulate the audience's imagination and to fill what would otherwise be significant gaps in your story. If, however, the audience will be misled into making formative judgments from the re-enactment, it should be appropriately labeled either with a caption or by use of the voice track. Incidentally, you should encourage participants to approach a re-enactment not as acting but rather as an exercise in reliving the spirit of what truly happened.

In large-scale reconstruction you definitely need clear labeling. Here a scene, several scenes, or even a whole film is reconstructed from available sources. These might be eyewitness memories, documents, transcripts, or hearsay. British television once showed an acted reconstruction directed by Stuart Hood of the trial of Sacco and Vanzetti. It had been put together from court transcripts of the famous anarchists' trial. It was intelligent, restrained, and austerely memorable. Although all who appeared were actors, the piece was factually accurate and can only be described as documentary in spirit because there was no central authorship. Each of the participants—the actors portraying the two anarchists, the judge, and the legal representatives—used the actual ideas and language preserved in the court records.

Even Peter Watkins' famous *Culloden* (1964), an extremely hypothetical reconstruction of the 1746 Highlands battle in which Bonnie Prince Charlie and his Stuart cause were brutally put down by the English, is usually included with the documentary genre. Here historical accuracy is more than doubtful, and the words of the officers and foot soldiers who Watkins "interviewed" are a modernist guess at what soldiers—had documentary existed—might have said. Yet the attitude of the film toward its participants speaks of an overall respect and comprehension, not only to the distant historical actuality, but also to the tragic human process by which such events recur in human history. Although the film deals with power and politics, its true concern is subjugation and the process by which the humble get used as cannon fodder in the ideological struggles of their masters.

Where, then, is the dividing line between documentary and fiction? A short answer is that nobody knows and that any line is always being challenged.

THE DOCUDRAMA

There is a yet more imaginative—some would say fanciful—use of the real, known as *docudrama* or *dramadoc*. Two examples must suffice to describe this form, which, as its name signifies, is a hybrid straddling two worlds. One is an English dramatization of the plight of the homeless made in the 1960s, Jeremy Sandford's *Cathy Come Home* (1966). Working from case histories at a time when homelessness was new and shocking, Sandford and his wife, Nell Dunne, constructed a "typical" blue-collar couple who overspend and encounter bad luck. The family—evicted, then homeless—drifts rapidly down the social scale until dismembered by the welfare state "for the good of the children."

Coming hard on the heels of the successful Conservative re-election slogan, "You never had it so good," the British public was at first stunned, then appalled, to find that the drama was true to life in all its particulars. The force of public feeling even contributed to some amelioration in the law, rare for a film of any kind. The film's effectiveness was not only because of its documentary basis, it was also superbly acted and presented.

Anthony Thomas' *Death of a Princess* (1980) attempted to show how a member of the Saudi royalty could be publicly humiliated and executed for a sexual offense. From the highly critical reaction it raised on all sides, the film, which used actors to reconstruct the princess's life and death, seems to have taken altogether too many risks—first with the truth, which was insufficiently determinable, then with the authenticity of how it portrayed Islamic culture and assumptions, which were outside the producer's realm of experience. These uncertainties gave the film a contrived and speculative quality that made it successful neither as fiction drama nor as documentary.

The premise of a screen portrayal influences greatly the state of mind in which we assess and assimilate what is proffered as "true to life." If the premise seems unsupported or insupportable, the film's pretensions to documentary authenticity are likely to be indignantly rejected. It is interesting to compare *Death of a Princess* with Jack Gold's well-received re-enactment of Ruth First's imprisonment in South Africa, *Ninety Days* (1966). Because First played herself, the program apparently raised no questions over its premise as a subjective and authentic account. Her account must have illuminated South African police-state methods rather too well, because it prompted her murder in an act of brutal reprisal.

SUBJECTIVE RECONSTRUCTION

Some works of reconstruction deserve notice because their language successfully creates a heightened state of imaginative identification with the subjects. The National Film Board of Canada's *Volcano* (1977), by the brilliant and quirky Donald Brittain, reconstructs the life of Malcolm Lowry, author of the novel *Under the Volcano*. Lowry (like Brittain himself, an alcoholic) transmuted his own story into art and produced a novel of stunning depth after a life of tragicomic turmoil and self-destructiveness. In telling Lowry's life, Brittain uses some of the standard apparatus of screen biography, but the film uses no archive film and few photos of Lowry himself, concentrating instead on creating a sense of place and atmosphere akin to Lowry's own. This is counterpointed against the novelist's words and ideas. Afterward one seems to have lived through a destructive addiction oneself.

Erroll Morris' *The Thin Blue Line* (1988) investigates the indictment and trial of Randall Adams, who was on death row for killing a policeman in Texas many years earlier. Using minimalist music by Philip Glass and a camera that stares unblinkingly at a number of witnesses, each composed and lit as if for a feature film, Morris' tale gathers force as a formal work of intricate detection.

What really took place at the time of the murder? Morris re-enacts many versions according to each participant's testimony. The effect is like pondering a chess problem just as Morris, while groping for the truth, must have pondered the puzzle himself. The outcome is haunting: we see, from a prisoner's perspective, how he gets caught in a real-life *film noir* web and how idiosyncratically and unjustly the law can operate.

Marlon Riggs' *Tongues Untied* (1989) goes even further in creating an interior world. Using Brechtian vignettes by the filmmaker and gay associates, the film playfully and elliptically conveys what it is like to be black, gay, and invisible in a predominantly white heterosexual world. There is no through line of argument, only a series of forcefully stylish performances—everything from dance and body movement to inner monologue, street talk, and rap. The film defies description or analysis, except perhaps as a montage of moods, thoughts, ideas, and plaints when the tongue is untied by the imminence of death. Riggs himself later died of AIDS and the film is his last testament.

FAKE DOCUMENTARIES OR MOCKUMENTARIES

Mitchell Block's renowned short film about a female rape victim, *No Lies* (1973), shows how powerful a tool of inquiry *cinéma vérité* can be in the hands of an intrusively questioning filmmaker. Appalled at the pressure he applies and fascinated by the revelations he pries from the victim, the audience is disconcerted when the movie reveals that both are actors and that the exploitative relationship is a calculated performance. The film was made to "cinematically . . . demonstrate and commit rape—and it does so in such a way as to make the experience of being the unwary, unprepared victim of an aggressive assault on one's person, on one's pride, and on one's expectations of and security in familiar activity in familiar surroundings a very real experience accessible to anyone of *either* sex who views the film."[1]

Ken Featherstone's *Baba Kiueria* (1987) purports to be an Australian television documentary about how Aboriginal colonists discovered Australia back when the country was thinly peopled by primitive whites cooking meat in ritual places called barbecue areas (hence the film's title). Centering on a nervously compliant white family, it shows how they try to cooperate with the Aboriginal majority and, because of their fecklessness, are split up by Aboriginal social workers for their own betterment. By inverting predominant racial values in Australia, and by making the film a comedy, this fake documentary sets out to show what happens when liberal paternalism flows from blacks to whites instead of vice versa.

Woody Allen's *Zelig* (1983) is a fable in mock documentary style about a Depression-era Jewish celebrity with a penchant for assimilating himself, chameleon-like, into any situation. Through masterful photo processing, Allen appears at Babe Ruth games and Hitler rallies, always adapting himself to the mood and identity of those around him. Like so much comedy, it has an underlying critical

---

[1] Sobchack, Vivian C. *"No Lies:* Direct Cinema as Rape" in Rosenthal, Ed. *New Challenges for Documentary.* Berkeley: University of California Press, 1988, p. 332.

purpose, part of which is to lampoon the pompousness of stereotypical documentary.

These films are Trojan horses that appropriate the documentary form to test the audience's credulity, and to provoke questions about the worth and trustworthiness of documentary itself. They seem to warn us, "Buyer beware! No form and no author merits automatic trust."

In revising this chapter, I am indebted to enlightening discussions of docudrama and false documentaries led by Otto Schuurman and Elaine Charnov at the Sights of the Turn of the Century documentary conference at the Centro de Capacitación Cinematográfica in Mexico City in November 1996.

C H A P T E R   3 0

ETHICS, AUTHORSHIP, AND DOCUMENTARY MISSION

This chapter takes a practical approach to some of the issues that were raised more theoretically in preceding pages, particularly Chapter 26, Documentary Theory and the Issue of Representation. It addresses:

- Developing loyalties to the individuals one films and one's obligations to "truth."
- Responsibilities to participants' lives and what obligation exists to warn of the consequences of being filmed.
- Documentary as a catalyst of change in participants' lives, and your responsibility.
- Truth claims in both the transparent and the reflexive documentary.
- Explaining your purposes and laying a foundation of trust.
- Dealing with changes that alter or disable your working hypothesis.
- Participants' dependency.
- Responsibilities to truth in editing.
- Your judgments made public at a showing, and how to prepare participants for what they may consider "negative."
- Authorship as looking outward at the world.
- Authorship as looking inward.
- Making authorial judgments public and living with it.
- Being changed by one's work.
- Accepting one's incapacity for any ultimate truth or final word.

- Learning to live with your creative identity's limitations.
- Letting your last work prepare you for your next.

Anyone who directs even the briefest documentary soon discovers how loyalties and obligations develop between oneself and participants, and how authorship is inseparable from ethical dilemmas. A single example is as follows: You are making a film about the victims of a housing scam who you get to know and like. You also gain the confidence of the perpetrators and are offered hospitality by them. Because refusing might expose your judgment of them, you go out with them, eat an expensive dinner, and laugh at their jokes. Now you feel like a whore, especially when you next visit their victims.

How and why one works as a documentarian is doubtless anchored in one's sense of ethics and mission. At the beginning even the smallest decisions compel one to scared self-examination, but after a few years, particularly if you work in a news organization with older and cynical pros, you become more comfortable, and risk becoming professional in the worst sense. That is, you are in danger of turning into a skeptical bystander or of using people to illustrate foregone conclusions. Belonging to a powerful corporation makes it seductively easy to overvalue one's own importance and to devalue those who let you into their lives.

PARTICIPANTS HAVE TO LIVE WITH THE FILM'S CONSEQUENCES

By publicly showing footage—though not necessarily by taking it—one can conceivably harm someone's life irreparably. Unlike the fiction filmmaker paying actors, the documentarian generally offers no financial compensation, and even if a substantial sum changes hands, you can take little comfort from having settled moral obligations with cash. Checkbook documentary is still likely to be exploitation.

Where do the filmmaker's responsibilities lie? When does one owe loyalty to the individual, when to larger truths? Is there an accepted code of ethics? How much can one, and should one, say to participants before they become too alarmed to permit filming?

Directing a documentary sometimes feels like being a doctor advising patients about the procedure, complications, and consequences of an irreversible operation. Some documentary participants are not attentive or sophisticated enough to absorb all the implications, and although the release form discharges legal obligations, it doesn't meet those that are moral. In America during the 1970s, the Loud family consented to have their lives filmed (*An American Family*, 1973, PBS, 12 hour-long episodes). Exposure to the camera and criticism in the press (as though the family were performers) tore the family apart. They said afterward that the series' intentions were inadequately explained. In fact, the open-ended nature of the project made any kind of comprehensive explanation virtually impossible.

Regrettably none of these issues has a clear answer, so let's look at what usually comes up at different stages of production.

APPROACHING PARTICIPANTS

At the time you ask someone to participate in a project, you seldom have more than the sketchiest idea of who or what will be used in the film, what it will say, or how this individual will appear to the world. Given such a shadowy outcome, films can only be made on a basis of trust. Indeed, one probably "casts" particular people because they are cooperative and of good will. Unfortunately documentarians have been known to abuse this trust. When I worked at the BBC, a woman factory worker spoke candidly and trustingly in an interview about sexual morals among her female coworkers. Outraged when the film was transmitted, they beat her up the next day. The (male) director apparently knew this was a risk and gambled with her safety for the sake of a more sensational film.

For most participants, there is nothing comparable at risk. To read them a standardized list of possible consequences would scare the hell out of them, and for no good reason. In investigative filmmaking, where one's film is bound to be critical of someone, the case is probably different. If you suspect someone is going to run an undeserved risk, you should discuss all the possibilities with the participant, taking particular care when the person is unused to being in the public eye. Normally your problems will lie in the opposite direction, and you will find yourself trying to convince someone that their exaggerated fears are unfounded.

Occasionally the filmmaker, employing dubious practices that serve a larger purpose—as did Michael Moore while making *Roger and Me* (1989)—can discover his methods returning to haunt him. By simplifying and transposing cause and effect, Moore handed ammunition to his film's many enemies. Other times, subterfuge is thoroughly justified. Your loyalty to the truth effortlessly overrides any scruples when someone has just butchered 200 defenseless people. There is no moral dilemma about exposing this kind of person. Such clarity is rare; usually one is faced not with black and white but shades of pale gray. This takes more moral courage and more scruples, not less.

Documentary exists entirely through the voluntary cooperation of participants, so take every care to avoid unnecessary exploitation. Consider what it takes and what it will cost to do some good in the world, and decide *from your participant's vantage* whether it is worth it—a lonely calculation if ever there was one.

DIRECTING AND REFLEXIVITY

Because "the unexamined life isn't worth living," the documentary often justifies itself through the self-examination it brings one's participants. But especially when reflection and action are unfamiliar activities, this can serve to transform the very lives you wanted to record intact. So you face a conundrum, because filming can compromise, subvert, or even create the end result. In a genre that purports to show life spontaneously unfolding, this is analogous to Cousteau showing deep sea fish shoals when the presence of a frogman wielding lights and camera signified an alien invasion. He got around it by reflexively making a feature out of the sensation his men and equipment caused in the oceanic community.

Developments in 1980s and 1990s documentary show that reflexive acknowledgment like this is increasingly appropriate.

Reflexivity can be designed into a film, as in McElwee's *Sherman's March* (1986), or it can happen accidentally. A microphone lunging into shot, or a participant suddenly questioning the camera operator, punctures a film's "transparency." That is, it breaks our illusion of spying on spontaneous life and probably gives little of value in return. For ideological reasons, in the 1960s and 1970s some filmmakers would deliberately show crew members during a scene to "remind the audience they were watching a movie." But isolated gestures toward acknowledging "the process" generally break the audience's concentration and undermine the film's overall credibility with mixed messages.

Today's audience is quite aware that filming is a complex artistic process and is interested in the authorship process, and in what filming does to the situation under study. This makes the audience more of a friend to the responsible filmmaker than to those whose claims to truth rely on smoke and mirrors.

TRUTH CLAIMS

A film's validity as a truthful record is usually asserted in one of two ways. The traditional approach is to make a film that is honest to the spirit of one's best perceptions and to trust that the audience can infer how the filmmaking process has affected the outcome. Consciously or otherwise, spectators judge the film against their own instincts and knowledge of life.

In the second, reflexive approach, the director deliberately builds into the film whatever doubts and perceptions would not be adequately acknowledged through showing the material on its own. Such a film explores perception as well as what is perceived, and this usually means including some elements of self-portraiture by its makers. Robb Moss' touchingly autobiographical documentary, *The Tourist* (1991), examines the two dominant and concurrent aspects of his life—his job as a documentary cameraman, often filming in third world countries where people have too many children, and his marriage to a nurse specializing in neonatal care, with whom he wishes to have children. Without falsely reconciling any of the open questions in his life, Moss outlines the ironies that fate has dealt them, and finally, the joy of adopting a daughter.

How one sees, how one connects with others through making a film, represent a Pandora's box that cannot be half-opened. Autobiography always suppresses some truths and, by this subtraction, elevates others. As such, truth becomes provisional and, to some extent, fictionalized. We are seemingly incapable of telling all the truths about ourselves and settle for some, telling others by allusion or artfully by way of fiction.

SHOOTING PROCESS

The fear so many new directors express about "altering reality" is surely because they remain in awe of the objectivity affected by so much that appears on television. Leaving aside the invasiveness of cameras and equipment, it remains true that *every* set of relationships is changed according to who is present and observing. Even a family picnic is altered according to who arrives; a 10-year-old child will make a different impact and less change to the atmosphere than would, say, a man in sunglasses who silently takes photographs. If, however, the photographer first convinces the group that his interests are sympathetic and genuine, or if his arrival is mediated by a trusted member of the group, the newcomer will be trusted and welcomed.

Your presence, with or without crew and camera, cannot help altering an event. But the changes can be large or small according to who you film and how you handle the preparation. The documentary director must not only build bridges but must choose participants with care. Casting participants mistakenly can mean waking up to find you have committed yourself to someone who resists, distorts, or even manipulates the process. To guard against this, defer decisions about who is to participate until the latest possible moment. The longer you give yourself to see people in action, the less likely you are to miscalculate. Later, avoid all comment about what is likely to survive into the final film.

Other mishaps and twists of fortune will present both ethical and practical difficulties. Suppose the evidence you are getting does not support your hypothesis. Should you make a different film or stop shooting? Suppose somebody's basic situation changes—your lonely widow suddenly acquires a boyfriend, say. Do you collect materials to reconstruct the situation as it (interestingly) was, or do you alter your film to reflect the (less interesting) situation as it now is? The answers depend on what you have promised, what code of conduct you have set yourself, and what good story remains possible.

Interviewing poses an ethical responsibility. For instance, the thrill of the righteous chase can delude one into unfairly demolishing a person's defenses. Although there is a second chance in the cutting room to recognize and prevent this situation from becoming public, the damage to your relationship with your subject (and your coworkers) may remain. Especially if you don't have complete editorial control, you may be forced by your superiors to use something you regret shooting. Some documentarians even say, "If you shoot it, you'll use it."

Here is another interviewing dilemma. You take a participant up to an important, perhaps unperceived, threshold in his life. In a revealing moment, the interviewee crosses into territory never before penetrated. We see what Rouch calls a "privileged moment," where all notion of film as an artificial environment ceases for participant and audience alike. It is a wonderful moment, but it hinges on the revelation of some fact that should not become public.

Do you now lean on the person to permit its inclusion in the film? Perhaps the participant is so trusting that you alone can make the decision whether it will damage him. Here wise and responsible coworkers can help you carry the burden of decision. But if it is best to suppress the revelation, can you carry on with the film as though nothing new had taken place? Again, only you can finally decide, based on your own values and circumstances.

There is also an ethical responsibility that comes with causing change. The documentary often alters its subjects' lives merely by exposing them to scrutiny— their own and others. At first, participants will often maintain an "on the record" and an "off the record" relationship with you. Then the line becomes blurred as deepening trust or emotional dependency develop. One day the director of a film finds she has become responsible for the direction of a life. In a class of mine at the time of first writing this chapter, there were several projects where this was happening. One was about a man who, as a teenager, narrowly missed being the victim of a multiple sex murderer; another was about a middle-aged gang member who was dying of AIDS and wanted the film about him to become a posthumous message to his beloved daughter; another was about a young male prostitute whose activities existed through contempt for his own body; yet another concerned a *ménage à trois*.

All the directors expressed anxieties about their responsibilities, and this took considerable class discussion time. Invariably they needed support for their decisions more than any radical advice. Most films change the lives they record, and it is our responsibility to help make the chemistry a positive one. Conceivably, while doing this you may be told something that, were it to fall into the wrong hands, could lead to someone's injury or even death. This may be the time to stop the camera or to destroy footage. Filmmakers who broadcast revelations from people in danger in South Africa, Russia, and other benighted societies usually make absolutely certain that the individual knows the risks and is ready to take them.

A more usual level of responsibility is that of Loretta Smith, whose *Where Did You Get That Woman?* (1979) started from a chance encounter with an elderly lady in the cab that Loretta drove for a living. She remained a loyal friend to her film's subject for years after the film was finished—loyal, in fact, until Joan died.

EDITING PROCESS

There are more than a few dubious editing practices. One that can happen inadvertently is to allow acted or reconstructed material to stand unidentified in a film made of otherwise original and authentic materials. If there is any doubt about how the audience will take it, identify the material's origin either by narration or subtitle.

Most documentary editing involves compression, and a long statement can be unfairly reduced to serve the film but misrepresent the speaker's original pronouncement. Any participant who runs his own audio recording while you film (as happened to me when filming the leader of the British Union of Fascists, Sir Oswald Mosley) may be preparing to serve you up a legal challenge.

Apparent truths and bogus meanings can be manufactured by juxtaposing unrelated events or statements. What has happened may be invisible or insignificant to a lay audience, yet scandalize participants. Even the way you compress into three shots a long process, such as buying a house, may be attacked. You should be able to defend and justify every such device in your narrative flow.

Imagine that you must deal with a participant's fear-fantasy when, after weeks of anguish, she wants to retract some innocuous statement that is vital to your film. You have the legal right to use it, and you know it can bring no harm, but should you go ahead and override the participant's wish? Your good name and career may suffer, and at the very least your conscience will prick you for violating someone's trust. Then again, a real risk to a participant may emerge only at the editing stage, and one must face up to the conflict between releasing a good film that causes pain and danger to someone, and removing something important to the film's effectiveness, not to mention retarding one's career or even threatening one's survival as a filmmaker.

Most dilemmas do not lie in choosing between right and wrong, but between conflicting rights.

INTEGRITY OF THE EVIDENCE

Another ethical concern should be with the standard of argument you put forward. Strong and incontrovertible evidence is always more persuasive than opinion. A documentary is always more powerful when its themes and ideas arise out of an unfolding life situation than when you plunder actuality to illustrate a thesis. Interestingly, the same principle applies to fiction films and makes the difference between "signifying" a situation versus presenting it in the act of being. Once again, drama and the documentary share fundamentals.

Take care to show that a point your film makes is not contrived. In a film I made about an English country estate, *A Remnant of a Feudal Society,* a head groom spontaneously held out his deformed hand to demonstrate what happened (as he thought) to horsemen from holding reins at their master's pleasure in all kinds of weather. Because it was unclear what was wrong with the hand in the wide shot, the cameraman zoomed in close. I kept the zoom because cutting to the hand would have undermined the authenticity of his demonstration by making it look like something I had set up. Demonstrating the origin and authenticity of evidence, and acknowledging ambiguity where it exists, are also ethical considerations—ones in which you must maintain a good-faith relationship with your audience.

PUBLIC SHOWING

When should a participant have the right to see and veto a cut? If you agreed from the outset that editing would involve feedback from participants, they obviously have such a prerogative. Offering participation may be the only way to overcome the kind of distrust that can poison relations between races, say, or between feminists and well-meaning males. With only a little grief, I filmed women's liberation militants in the 1960s under such an agreement. Today, white filmmakers in Australia can no longer film Aboriginal people in the old unfettered way. That is, they are no longer free to imagine they can adequately represent that constituency. As groups and individuals become more sophisticated about film's process and purposes, and less trustful of those who elect to speak through film on their behalf, they become more discriminating about controlling the outcome. This represents not a loss of the filmmaker's rights, but a maturing relationship that takes more depth from the filmmaker and offers greater respect for the rights of others to control their own images.

If you have not worked out a consultative agreement with your subjects, you are ill advised to embark on one without strong cause. If you must show your cut to participants, do so only after clearly explaining any limitation to their rights. If you are willing to be advised but not instructed, make this absolutely clear, or there will be much bad feeling.

Before a public showing, get legal opinion about anything that might land either you or your participants in legal trouble. Be aware that lawyers look on the dark side, as their job is to look for snags and to err on the side of caution.

If you are showing your film when a participant sitting in the audience may feel betrayed by something critical in your film, you should prepare that person in advance, so he does not feel humiliated in the presence of family and friends. If you don't, that person may henceforward regard you as a traitor and all film people as frauds. Avoid renegade behavior at all costs, but keep in mind that participants see themselves on the screen with great subjectivity. To adjust oversympathetically to this would be to abandon documentary work for public relations. Usually, having a general audience and person's friends present can be an advantage, because their enjoyment and approval mitigate the subject's oversensitivity. All this is a matter of judgment.

PHILOSOPHY AND MISSION

The two approaches to making documentary outlined elsewhere—transparency and reflexivity—break down at their crudest into either directing the self to look outward at the world or employing the world as a mirror in which to examine some aspect of self interacting with the world. This difference is supposed to distinguish the classicist temperament from the romantic, but either can be valid and fascinating as long as you recognize at the outset your real purpose and priorities. Finally, of course, neither dimension is separable; there is no world without perception nor any perception without its object. Self and world are inextricably related, as I have argued all along. The decision about which route to take should arise from the subject and what you want to say about it. Often finding the right approach is a question of emphasis and of how, temperamentally, you function best as a storyteller.

Any philosophy of documentary must accommodate the inevitable: that your human subjects will make some adaptations for your camera and that your audience will make its own assessment of your relationship to truthfulness, no matter whether you assist them or not. The process of recording and interpreting needs to be justified, and you making your records need to be liked and trusted. When the complexities of the relationship affect important truths, they need to be acknowledged, either implicitly or explicitly, if credibility or even truth itself is not be impaired. These parameters put a lid on certain kinds of subjects: The recording process is too intrusive to document some intimate occasions, or at least it will seem so to the audience.

DOCUMENTARY AS EXPOSURE TO LIFE

Unlike some other arts, documentary is hard to make in retreat from life because—unless you make highly premeditated essay films—it is created by moving within life and by consciously and conscientiously living with the consequences. Because many issues and personalities remain unawakened and unresolved until the camera arrives, you must be ready when you begin exhibiting the film to argue passionately for your rights as judge and critic, and to do so when you are attacked for daring as one person to make an interpretive criticism.

Aesthetic and ethical decisions are seldom made from a position of cool intellectual neutrality; more often they are forged in discomfort and anxiety over conflicting moral obligations—to actual people who know and trust you, on the one hand, or to truths whose importance may transcend any individual's passing discomfort, on the other.

One thought I keep in mind when making a documentary, one that I find both comforting and liberating, is that my best efforts to make a film are still only what the French call *"une tentative"*—an attempt, bid, or endeavor that is no more than one little person's view at one moment in time. In the end, it is delusionary and productive of too much misery to saddle oneself with the responsibility for definitive truth. It is as irrational, as common, and as humanly foolish as demanding that one's children be perfect.

MISSION AND IDENTITY

Luckily, when you and I honestly take stock of ourselves, we find that we already carry certain knowledge and certain convictions. To give this imprint full recognition is really to say to oneself, "This is the heart of what I can pass on to others." If you feel the need to communicate it, you have the drive for authorship and to make art—a human need no less imperative than the need for shelter or sex.

To some, the "transparent" documentarian busily finding and illuminating a subject ends up negating his or her own importance as an author. This kind of filmmaker often aims to present life on the screen so that it exists with scarcely a trace of authorship. But he or she is still likely to be engaging in displaced autobiography, because rather than expressing, say, "I have been the victim of a violent society, and look like what has happened to *me*," the filmmaker searches out others whose diversity and experience give universality to what has already been discovered in the filmmaker's own limited but deeply felt experience.

This is a way of putting your convictions to a test—by finding other people and other situations that convey what you want to say. As such, it is your *vision* you share with the audience, rather than yourself as a subject. Your task is to identify the counterparts of your own experience floating unattached on life's stream, and to catch and tether them in a structured statement that will mirror the truths that life has taught you.

Obviously this is neither scientific nor objective, but the restraints on indulging a display of ego, and the fact that your own most enduring preoccupations must be found freestanding outside yourself, help to create a product with overtones of universality. Only with maturity can you identify the surrogates to your own values and temperament, and allow them to achieve a life of their own in a film. The discipline of such a process has its own rewards. Your work alters the way you see the fundamentals of your own life—the very source from which your documentary process sprang. In this way, each film lays the foundations for the next.

P A R T   8

CAREER TRACK

CHAPTER 31
Education   367

Planning a Career   367
Getting Started   367
To School or Not to School   368
What to Look for in a Good Film School   369
The Internet and Researching for the Right
   School   370
International Film Schools   372
Self-Help as a Realistic Alternative   380

CHAPTER 32
Getting Work   381

What You Can Do While You're Still in
   School   381
Internships   382
Craft Worker   382
The Search for Subjects and a Market   383
The Documentary Proposal   383
Funds   383
Journals and Associations   384
Presenting Yourself   385
Making a Job for Yourself   386
A Personal Message   387

C H A P T E R   3 1

EDUCATION

PLANNING A CAREER

How do you get started in any kind of film—or videomaking? And where should you expect to be after, say, three years of professional work? These questions deserve answers because they are often asked, but the latter is the most immediately important because it indicates a perilous misunderstanding.

Filmmaking does not have a career ladder with predictable promotion rates, like banking or retail management. It is a branch of show business: How far you get and how long you take getting there depend on your ability, energy, luck, and persistence. If your primary loyalties are to home, children, family, community, and affluence, then remaining committed to filmmaking may be difficult because the industry is informally structured, unpredictable, and expects an unusual degree of initiative and autonomy in the individual.

On the other hand, if you are interested in people, social movements, and politics, and if making your individual voice heard is worth investing a long, uphill, and impecunious struggle to gain recognition, you might really like the documentary filmmaker's way of life. You certainly will never have to wonder why you go to work every day.

GETTING STARTED

Old-timers used to scorn any form of schooling, but that has changed now that film school alumni are becoming pre-eminent. If schooling is out of the question, you can use this book to do a great deal of self-preparation outside the available educational structures, especially if you team up with other enthusiasts. The best education is self-education, because you'll never forget your lessons. Schools are seldom ideal because they have to cater to the common denominator—frustrating for those who learn either slowly or rapidly, or who are unusually motivated.

The other side of the coin, taking the "industry route" by getting into a ground-level apprenticeship program, can be fraught with restrictions, even though initially it looks very attractive.

In short, there are no sure routes, only intelligent traveling.

TO SCHOOL OR NOT TO SCHOOL

Though I received on-the-job training myself, I believe ardently in the value of a good filmmaking education. One example should tell you why: I regularly see students in 15-week classes absorbing techniques and insight that took me 10 years on the job to discover for myself. Maybe I was unlucky or unobservant, but most of what I hear confirms how isolated the apprentice usually is and how slowly he or she learns. The explanation is simple and stark: Know-how and experience are earning power in the freelance world, so workers systematically *avoid* enlightening juniors. Unfortunately, demarcation lines in people's working lives ensure that professionals develop mystiques about each other. In the long run, this discourages experiment and makes people overdeferential to real or claimed expertise.

Not knowing any of this, the ill-prepared youngster, weary of "more school" and gratefully taking the first job that comes along, finds himself still driving the company station wagon or answering the phones 5 years later. Most employers live pressurized lives and consider preparing the individual for more responsibility not to be part of their job. Either that individual comes *prepared through prior schooling* to assume more complex duties as opportunities arise or he/she must somehow extract an education while serving as the company peon.

Good schooling, on the other hand, gives:

- A cultural and intellectual perspective on your medium.
- Knowledge and history of your art and chosen role in it.
- Technical training in the use of the tools, techniques, and concepts.
- Help in exposing your true talents, abilities, and energies.
- Encouragement in collaboration and in expressing individual vision.
- An environment in which to safely experiment and make mistakes.
- Aspirations to use one's professional life to its fullest extent and for the widest good.
- Teammates with whom to face adversity (there's a lot of that), particularly after school in the working world.

Only by going through all the stages of making a film—no matter how badly—can the aspiring director see the faults or the strengths in his or her own (and other people's) work. Film is a dense and allusory language, so a director must develop rare abilities. One needs a slew of human and technical skills to put a well-exposed, well-composed series of shots on the screen and to make them add up to a coherent statement. Another competence is more profound, that of knowing and remaining true to yourself, even under attack.

A proper film school is an ideal place in which to have this experience. There is a structured program of learning, technical facilities, enthusiastic expertise, and contemporaries with whom to collaborate. Most importantly, in school one can experiment and afford failures, while unwise experiment in a commercial arena spells professional suicide.

School is where one can share enthusiasm, find peers, and fly high on exhilarating theories of life and of film. An established school also offers a formal and informal network of contacts, each of whom tends to aid the others after they become established.

WHAT TO LOOK FOR IN A GOOD FILM SCHOOL

Most countries, especially small ones, have few good film schools, and getting accepted is very difficult. In the United States, many schools, colleges, and universities now have film courses, but be careful and critical before committing yourself. Many are underequipped and underbudgeted, or situated where teachers are drawn from a hidebound local industry. Sometimes "film studies" is an offshoot of the English department, perhaps originally created to bolster sagging enrollments.

Avoid departments that seem lukewarm about student production or that insist on extensive theoretical studies before production. The literary and cerebral nature of much that passes as film study can seriously misdirect you and make production very difficult. The measure of a film school is what the students and faculty produce. Quite simply, you will learn best by studying with experienced filmmakers who are also dedicated teachers. Finding both qualities in a faculty is not easy.

A good film school offers a broad balance of technical education with a strong foundation in conceptual, aesthetic, and historical course work. It should have defined tracks for specialization, such as screenwriting, camera, sound, editing, directing, and producing. Documentary is rarely taught as a specialty, and this must be your prime concern. Animation is an advantage, but utterly separate from live-action filming and more akin to the graphic arts in its training. There should be a respectable contingent of professional-level equipment as well as enough basic cameras and editing equipment to support the beginning levels. Most importantly, a good school should be the center of an enthusiastic film-producing community, where students support and crew for each other as a matter of course (Figure 31-1).

In a longer standing teaching/production community, successful former students not only give visiting lectures but come back as teachers. In turn, they either employ or give vital references to the most promising students. The school filmmaking community tapers off into the young (and not so young) professional community to mutual advantage. In the reverse flow, mentors not only give advice and steer projects, but exemplify the way of life the student is trying to make his or her own. Be aware that even in the largest cities, the filmmaking community operates like a village, where personal recommendation is everything.

FIGURE 31-1 ───

A unit of women from Columbia College Chicago shooting in a Chicago shelter for the homeless. (Jane Stevens)

THE INTERNET AND RESEARCHING
FOR THE RIGHT SCHOOL

Much practical information can now be found on the Internet, some of it bracingly negative. For North America, try the Cyber Film School (http://www.cyberfilmschool.com) for information on schools, production and screenwriting tips, as well as bibliographical and miscellaneous information to be found in other website links. Cross-check every assertion you encounter because web publication seems to encourage more bravado than accuracy. A site of special interest to documentarians is the Motion Picture Archive http://lcweb2.loc.gov/papr/mpixhome.html), which contains Library of Congress 1897 to 1916 clips of early movies available as AVI files for downloading. New sites are coming on-line practically daily, and many of these are bulletin boards for special interest groups and mutual help.

For those outside the United States, study in America, though expensive, can be an invaluable investment. You get a film education that may be unavailable in your own country, an opportunity to make your English fluent, and an induction into an entrepreneurial culture that is a necessary mindset for working in the arts. This can wonderfully offset the fatalism that paralyzes young people growing up in hierarchically structured societies with social barriers that keep people down.

Much can be gleaned from the periodically published *American Film Institute Guide to College Courses in Film and Television* (Princeton, NJ: Peterson's Guides). Its standardized information allows one to make comparisons and to spot a department's emphasis. Even a promising statement of philosophy from a department of communications may be undercut when you add up equipment holdings and examine course structure. Here are some questions you should pursue to help you decide whether a film department fulfills your expectations:

- How big is the department and what does its structure reveal?
- How many courses are offered and how many sections are there per course?
- What is the total student population and the range of class size?
- What degree of specialization is made possible by the school's size?
- What do senior (and the most influential faculty) teach?
- How long is the program? (See model syllabus. Short is not necessarily bad and long isn't necessarily good, but short do-it-all summer courses are usually taster sessions to aid recruitment.)
- What do entry submission requirements reveal, and how well can you fulfill them?
- How much specialization is possible, and how far do upper-level courses go?
- How flexibly are you allowed to schedule your chosen courses?
- How much equipment is there, and what kind? (This is a real giveaway.)
- What are faculty members' qualifications, and what have they produced lately?
- What equipment and materials are supplied out of tuition and class fees, and how much is the student expected to supply along the way?
- What does the department say about its attitudes and philosophy?
- What does the place feel like? (Try to visit the facilities.)
- What do the students think of the place? (Speak with senior students.)
- How much of a specialty is documentary?
- In senior-level production classes, do all students direct? (In some otherwise prestigious schools, only a minority chosen by the faculty may direct, with the class losers becoming crew.)
- What films have the people teaching documentary produced themselves?

Locate good teaching by going to film festivals and noting where the good films are being made. A sure sign of energetic and productive teaching, even in a small facility, is when student or alumni work is getting awards. Keep abreast of festivals, conferences, and meetings by reading specialized journals, such as *Videomaker, The Independent, American Cinematographer,* and the *International Documentary Association Journal.* Subscribe to whatever you can afford—it's a painless way to become intimate with the world you want to enter.

INTERNATIONAL FILM SCHOOLS

Following are major film/video schools in country, then city, order. There is no guarantee that they run documentary filmmaking courses, nor that foreign students are accepted, so make appropriate inquiries. The + sign before a phone or fax number means you must first dial your country's overseas telephone code to make an international call. An asterisk denotes that the school is believed or known to teach documentary. (If you are already in a school with a good documentary track and it isn't asterisked or listed here, ask your teacher to e-mail me so it gets listed in the next edition.)

ARGENTINA

Centro de Experimentación y de Realización
  Cinematográfica (CERC)
Salita 327
1074 Buenos Aires
Tel: +54 1 38 11785
Fax: +54 1 8143 062

Universidad del Cine
Pasaje Giuffra 330
1063 Buenos Aires
Tel: +54 1 300 1413
Fax: +54 1 782 0473

AUSTRALIA

Victorian College of the Arts
School of Film & Television
234 St. Kilda Road
Melbourne, Victoria 3004
Tel: +61 3 685 9000
Fax: +61 3 685 9001

*Australian Film and Television School (AFTRS)
1st Floor, 144 Moray St.
PO Box 1008
South Melbourne, Victoria 3205
Tel: +61 3 9690 7111
Fax: +61 3 9690 1283

*Australian Film and Television School (AFTRS)
Corner Balaclava Road & Epping Highway
Box 126, North Ryde
N.S.W. 2113
Tel: +61 2 805 6611
Fax: +61 2 887 1030

AUSTRIA

Hochschule für Musik und Darstellende Kunst
  in Wien (HFMDK)
Abteilung "Film und Fernsehen"
Metternichgasse 12
1030 Wien
Tel: +43 1 713 52120
Fax: +43 1 713 52 1423

BELGIUM

Hogeschool voor Audiovisuele Communicatie
Naamsestraat 54
1000 Brussel
Tel: +32 2 511 93 82
Fax: +32 2 502 55 06

*Institut National Supérieur des Arts du
  Spectacle (INSAS)
Rue Thêrésienne 8
1000 Bruxelles
Tel: +32 2 511 9286
Fax: +32 2 511 0279

St. Lukas Hoger Instituut voor Beeldende Kunsten
Paleizenstraat 70
1210 Brussel
Tel: +32 2 217 05 89

Institut des Arts de Diffusion (IAD)
Rue des Wallons, 77
1348 Louvain-la-Neuve
Tel: +32 10 47 80 18
Fax: +32 10 45 11 74

BRAZIL

*Universidade Federal Fluminense (UFF)
Departamente de Cinema e Video R. Lara Vilela
126-Niterói
24220 590 Rio de Janeiro
Fax: +55 21 211 2752

*Escola de Comunicaçoes e Artes
Universidad de Sao Paulo
Av. Prof. Lucio Martins Rodrigues, 443
Cidade Universitaria CEP 05508-900
Sao Paulo
Tel: +55 11 818 4020
Fax: +55 11 211 2752

BULGARIA

Nacionalna Academia za Teatraino i Folmovo
   Izkoustvo (NATFIZ)
"Krustyo Sarafov" - Sofia
Rakovski Street 108a
Sofia 1000
Tel: +359 2 87 98 62
Fax: +359 2 89 73 89

New Bulgarian University
Dept. of Mass Communications
47 Gurko Street
Sofia 1000
Tel: +359 2 891 203
Fax: +359 2 880 902

CANADA

Université du Québec à Montréal (UQAM)
Module de Communications
Case Postale 8888, Succursale A
Montréal (Québec) H3C 3P8
Tel: +1 514 987 3759
Fax: +1 514 987 4650

Canadian Film Centre
Windfields
2849 Bayview Avenue
North York, Ontario, Canada M4W 3E2
Tel: +1 416 445 1446
Fax: +1 416 445 9481

*York University
Faculty of Fine Arts
Dept. of Film & Video
4700 Keele Street
North York, Ontario M3J 1P3
Tel: +1 416 736 5149
Fax: +1 416 736 5710

*Ryerson Polytechnic University
Film & Photography Dept.
Faculty of Applied Arts
350 Victoria Street
Toronto, Ontario M5B 2K3

Tel: +1 416 979 5167
Fax: +1 416 979 5341

CHINA

Beijing Film Academy (BFA)
Xi Tu Cheng Lu 4
Haidian District
Beijing
Tel: +861 201 2132
Fax: +861 201 2132

CROATIA

*Akedemija Dramske Umjetnosti (ADU)
Trg Marsala Tita 5
41000 Zagreb
Tel: +385 1 446 633
Fax: +385 1 446 032

CUBA

*Escuela Internacional de Cine y TV (EICTV)
Ap. Aéreo 40/41
San Antonio de los Baños
Tel: +53 7 335196
Fax: +53 7 335341

CZECH REPUBLIC

*Akedemie Múzickych Umeni (FAMU)
   (Planning a summer English-language course)
Filmová a televisni fakulta
Smetanovo Nábr. 2
116 65 Prague 1
Tel: +42 2 24 22 94 68
Fax: +42 2 24 22 23 02 85

DENMARK

*Den Danske Filmskole
St. Sondervoldstræde 4
1419 Copenhagen K
Tel: +45 31 57 65 00
Fax: +45 31 57 65 10

EGYPT

Academy of Arts
High Cinema Institute
Pyramids Road
Gamal El Din El Afghany Str.
Giza
Tel: +20 2 537 703
Fax: +20 2 560 1034

FINLAND

*Taideteollinen Korkeakoulu
Elokuvataiteen Laitos
Pursimiehenkatu 29-31B
00150 Helskinki
Tel: +358 0 636982
Fax: +358 0 634303

FRANCE

*Ecole Nationale Supérieure Louis Lumière
"Ecole de Vaugirard"
Allée du Promontoire
B.P. 22
Marne-la-Vallée
93161 Noisy-le-Grand Cédex
Tel: +33 1 48 15 40 10
Fax: +33 1 43 05 63 44

*Institut de Formation et d'Enseignement pour
  les Metiers de l'Image et du Son (FEMIS)
6 rue Francoeur
75018 Paris
Tel: +33 1 42 62 20 00
Fax: +33 1 42 62 21 00

*Atelier de Réalisation Cinématographique
  (VARAN)
6 Impasse Mont-Louis
75011 Paris
Tel: +33 1 43 56 64 04
Fax: +33 1 43 56 2902

*Ecole Supérieure d'Audiovisuel (ESAV)
Université Toulouse Le Mirail
5 Allées Antonio Machado
31058 Toulouse Cédex
Tel: +33 61 50 44 46
Fax: +33 61 50 49 34

GEORGIA

The Russian State Institute of Theatre and Film
Rustaveli Avenue 19
380004 Tbilisi
Tel: +7 8832 990438
Fax: +7 8832 931824

GERMANY

Deutsche Film-und Fernsehakademie Berlin
  (DFFB)
Pommernallee 1

14052 Berlin
Tel: +49 30 30 30 71
Fax: +49 30 301 9875

Hamburger Filmwerkstatt e.V.
Friedensallee 7-9
22765 Hamburg
Tel: +49 40 3982 6136
Fax: +49 40 3982 6149

*Kunsthochschule für Medien
Television and Film Dept.
Peter-Weller Platz 2
D-50676 Köln
Tel: +49 221 201 890
Fax: +49 221 201 89124

Filmakademie Baden-Württemberg
Mathildenstr. 20
71638 Ludwigsberg
Tel: +49 7141 969 102
Fax: +49 7141 969 298

*Hochschule für Fernsehen und Film
Frankenthalerstr. 23
D-81539 München
Tel: +49 89 68 000 40
Fax: +49 89 68 000 436

*Hochschule für Fernsehen und Film "Konrad
  Wolf"
Karl-Marx-Str. 33/34
14482 Potsdam
Tel: +49 331 789 81
Fax: +49 331 75073

GHANA

National Film & Television Institute (NAFTI)
Private Mail Bag - GPO
Accra
Tel: +233 21 71 76 10
Fax: +233 21 77 45 22

GREECE

Hellenic Cinema and Television School Stavrakos
26 Ioulianou Str.
104 34 Athens
Tel: +30 1 8230 124
Fax: +30 1 8237 648

*School of Cinema & Television (ETCEH)
Eugégie Hadjikou
Asimaki Fotila Str. 7
114 73 Athens
Tel: +30 1 82 34 236
Fax: +30 1 88 30 871

HONG KONG

Hong Kong Baptist College
School of Communication
Dept. of Cinema & Television
224 Waterloo Road
Kowloon
Tel: +852 339 7395
Fax: +852 336 1371

The Hong Kong School for Performing Arts
1 Gloucester Road
GPO Box 12288
Wanchai
Tel: +852 584 1593
Fax: +852 802 4372

HUNGARY

*Szinház - es Filmmüvészeti Föiskola
Szentkirályi U. 32/a
1088 Budapest
Tel: +36 1 118 5533
Fax: +36 1 138 4560

INDIA

Development and Educational Communication
  Unit (DECU)
Indian Space Research Organization
ISRO
SAC P.O.
Jodhpur Tekera
Ahmedabad 380 053
Gujarat
Tel: +91 079 42 39 54
Fax: +91 079 42 85 56

Film and Television Institute of India (FTII)
Law College Road
Pune 411 004
Tel: +91 212 33 10 10
Fax: +91 212 33 0416

INDONESIA

Institut Kesenian Jakarta (IKJ)
Fakultas Film dan Televisi
Jl. Cikini Raya No. 73

Jakarta 10330
PO Box 4014
Jakarta 10001
Tel: +62 21 324 807
Fax: +62 21 323 603

Yayasan Citra
Film Centre "Usmar Ismail"
Jl HR Rasua Said
Jakarta 12950
Tel: +62 21 52 07390
Fax: +62 21 51 5027

IRELAND

National Association for Audio-Visual Training
  in Ireland
c/o Irish Film Institute
6 Eustace Street
Dublin 2
Tel: +353 1 679 5744
Fax: +353 1 679 9657

ISRAEL

*The Sam Spiegel Film & Television School
4 Yad Harutzim St.
P.O.B. 10636
Jerusalem 91103
Tel: +972 2 731950
Fax: +972 2 731949

Tel Aviv University
Department of Film and Television
Ramat-Aviv
P.O.B. 39040
Tel: +972 3 640 9483
Fax: +972 3 640 9935

Camera Obscura
School of Art
4 Rival Street
Tel Aviv 67778
Tel: +972 3 537 1871
Fax: +972 3 381 025

ITALY

Ippotesi Cinema
Instituto Paolo Valmarana
Via S. Giorgio, 24
36061 Bassano del Grappa (VI)
Tel: +39 424 500 007
Fax: +39 424 502 139

*Zelig Scuola di Televisione e Cinema
Via Carducci, 15a
Bolzano
Tel: +39 471 977930
Fax: +39 471 977931

Centro Formazione Professionale per le Techiche
    Cinetelevisive
Viale Legioni Romane, 43
20147 Milano
Tel: +39 2 4048455
Fax: +39 2 48700392

Centro Sperimentale di Cinematografia (CSC)
Via Tuscolana 1524
00173 Rome
Tel: +39 6 72 29 41
Fax: +39 6 72 11 619

JAMAICA

University of the West Indies (CARIMAC)
The Caribbean Institute of Mass Communication
Mona
Kingston 7
Tel: +1 809 927 1481
Fax: +1 809 927 5353

JAPAN

Japan Institute of Visual Arts
1-16-30 Manpukuji
Kawasaki-shi
Kanagawa 245
Tel: +81 44 951 2511
Fax: +81 44 951 2681

Nihon University
College of Art
Department of Cinema
2-42-1 Asahigaoka
Nerima-Ku
Tokyo 176
Tel: +81 3 5995 8220
Fax: +81 3 5995 8229

KENYA

Kenya Institute of Mass Communication (KIMC)
Film Production Training Department
PO Box 42422
Nairobi
Tel: +254 2540 820
Fax: +254 2556 798

LEBANON

Institut d'Etudes Scéniques et Audiovisuelles
    (IESAV)
Université St. Joseph
Faculté des Lettres et Sciences Humaine
Rue Huvelin
Beyrouth
Tel: +961 1 200629
Fax:+961 1 423369

MEXICO

*Centro de Capacitación Cinematográfica (CCC)
Czda. de Tlalpan 1670 Esq Rio Churubusco
México 21, D.F. 04220
Tel: +52 5 544 8007
Fax: +52 5 688 7812

*Centro Universitario de Estudios
    Cinematográficos (CUEC)
Universidad Nacional Autónoma de México
Adolfo Prieto 721 (Colonia del Valle)
México D. F. 03100
Tel: +52 5 536 02 30
Fax: +52 5 536 17 99

NETHERLANDS

*Nederlandse Film en Televisie Academie
Ite Boeremastraat 1
1054 PP Amsterdam
Tel: +31 20 683 02 06
Fax: +31 20 612 62 66

NORWAY

*Statens Studiesenter for Film
Filmens Hus, Droningens Gate 16
Boks 904, Sentrum
N-0104 Oslo
Tel: +47 22 82 24 00
Fax: +47 22 82 24 22

PHILIPPINES

Mowelfund Film Institute
No. 66 Rosario Drive
Cubao, 111 Quezon City
Metro Manila
Tel: +63 2 721 7702
Fax: +63 2 722 8628

University of the Philippines
Film Center
UP Film Center
Magsaysay Avenue
PO Box 214
Diliman
Quezon City 1101
Tel: +63 2 96 27 22
Fax: +63 2 99 26 25

POLAND

*Panstwowa Wyzsza Szkola Filmova i Teatralna
   (PWSFTV i T)
Targowa 61/63
90-323 Lódz
Tel: +48 42 74 35 38
Fax: +48 42 74 81 39

PORTUGAL

*Escola Superior de Teatro e Cinema
Rua dos Caetanos, 29
1200 Lisboa
Tel: +351 1 342 36 85
Fax: +351 1 347 02 73

ROMANIA

*Academia de Teatru si Film
Facultatea de Film si TV
Str. Matei Voievod 75-77
Sector 2
73224 Bucuresti
Tel: +40 1 642 47 26
Fax: +40 1 250 98 80

RUSSIA

*Russian State Institute of Cinematography
   (VGIK)
Wilhelm Pieck Str. 3
Moscow 129226
Tel: +7 095 181 3868
Fax: +7 095 187 7174

*St. Petersburg Institute of Cinema and
   Television (SPIC&T)
Pravda Str. 13
191126 St. Petersburg
Tel: +7 812 315 72 85
Fax: +7 812 315 01 72

SERBIA (and MONTENEGRO)

Fakultet Dramskih Umetnosti (FDU)
Ho Si Mina 20

11070 Beograd
Tel: +38 11 140 419
Fax: +38 11 130 862

SINGAPORE

Ngee Ann Polytechnic
Film, Sound, & Video Dept.
535 Clementi Road
Singapore 2159
Tel: +65 460 6992
Fax: +65 468 6218

SLOVAKIA

Vysoka Skola Muzickych Umeni (VSMU)
Filmová a Televisna Fakulta
Ventúrska 3
813 01 Bratislava
Tel: +42 7 332 306
Fax: +42 7 330 125

SLOVENIA

Akademija za Glendalisce Radio Rilm in
   Televizijo (AGRFT)
Nazorjeva 3
Ljublijana
Tel: +38 61 210 412
Fax: +38 61 210 450

SOUTH AFRICA

Newtown Film & Television School
1 President Street
Newtown, 2113
Johannesburg
Tel: +27 11 838 7462
Fax: +27 11 838 1043

SPAIN

Escuala de Cine y Video (ESKIVI)
Vada. Ama Kandida s/n.
20140 Andoain (Guipúzcoa)
Tel: +34 43 59 41 90
Fax: +34 43 59 40 52

Escola Superior de Cinema i Audiovisuals de
   Catalunya (ESCAC)
Immaculada 25-35
08017 Barcelona
Tel: +34 3 212 40 76
Fax: +34 3 417 86 99

Escuela des Artes Visuales
Fuencarral 45
28004 Madrid
Tel: +34 1 523 17 01
Fax: +34 1 523 17 63

Centro Imagen y Nuevas Tecnologias (CINT)
Adriano VI-9
01008 Vitoria - Gasteiz
Tel: +34 45 13 44 64
Fax: +34 45 14 61 48

SRI LANKA

Sri Lanka Television Training Institute (SLTTI)
100 A Independence Square
Colombo 7
Tel: +94 1 699 720
Fax: +94 1 699 791

SWEDEN

*Dramatiska Intitutet (DI)
University College of Film, Radio, Television,
    and Theatre
Borgvägen 5
Box 27090,
102-51 Stockholm
Tel: +46 8 665 13 00
Fax: +46 8 662 14 84

SWITZERLAND

*Ecole Cantonale d'Art de Lausanne (DAVI)
46 rue de l'Industrie
1030 Bussigny
Tel: +41 21 702 92 22
Fax: +41 21 702 92 09

Ecole Supérieure d'Art Visuel
2 Rue Général Dufour
Genève 1204
Tel: +41 22 311 05 10
Fax: +41 22 310 46 36

Focal
Fondation de Formation Continue pour le
    Cinéma e l'Audiovisuel
Stiftung Weiterbildung Film und Audiovision
33 rue St. Lauent
1003 Lausanne
Tel: +41 21 312 68 17
Fax: +41 21 323 59 45

TAIWAN

National Taiwan Academy of Arts
No. 59 Section 1 Da-Kuan Rd.
Pan-Chao Park
Taipei
Tel: +886 2 966 3154
Fax: +886 2 968 7563

UKRAINE

Fakultet Kinomystetstva
Kyïvskoho Instytutu Teatrainoho Mystetstva
    Imeni I.K. Karpenha-Karoho
Yaroslaviv Val St. 40
252034 Kiev
Tel: +7 044212 10 32
Fax: +7 044 210 10 03

UNITED KINGDOM

*National Film and Television School (NFTS)
Beaconsfield Film Studios
Station Road,
Beaconsfield, Bucks HP9 1LG
Tel: +044 4946 71234
Fax: +044 4946 74042

*London International Film School (LIFS)
24 Shelton Street
London WC2H 9HP
Tel: +44 171 240 0168
Fax: +44 171 497 3718

*London College of Printing
School of Film & Video
6 Back Hill
Clerkenwell Road
London EC1R 5EN
Tel: +44 171 278 7445
Fax: +44 171 833 8842

National Association for Higher Education in
    Film & Video ((NAHEFV)
City of London Polytechnic
Dept. of Communication Studies
31 Jewry Street
London EC3N 2EY
Tel: +44 181 840 2815
Fax: +44 171 320 3040

Royal College of Art
Dept. of Film & Television
Kensington Gore
London SW7 2EU
Tel: +44 171 584 5020
Fax: +44 171 589 0178

University of Westminster
School of Communication
18-22 Riding House Street
London W1 P7PD
Tel: +44 171 911 5000
Fax: +44 171 911 5127

UNITED STATES OF AMERICA

*Grand Valley State University
1 Campus Drive
Allendale, MI 49401-6611

*University of Texas at Austin
Department of Radio, Television and Film
School of Communications CMA6.118
Austin, TX 78712-1091
Tel: +1 512 471 4071
Fax: +1 512 471 4077

Emerson College
Division of Communication
100 Beacon Street
Boston, MA 02116
Tel: +1 617 578 8800
Fax: +1 617 578 8804

*Columbia College Chicago
Film/Video Department, Columbia College
600 S. Michigan Avenue,
Chicago, Illinois 60605-1996
Tel: +1 312 663 1600 Ext. 306
Fax: +1 312 986 8208

American Film Institute (AFI)
PO Box 27999
2021 North Western Avenue
Los Angeles, CA 90027
Tel: +1 213 856 7664
Fax: +1 213 464 5217

Loyola Marymount University
Communications Arts Dept.
Los Angeles, CA 90045
Tel: +1 310 338 3033
Fax: +1 310 338 3030

University of California, Los Angeles
School of Theater, Film and Television
East Melnitz
405 Hilgard Avenue
Los Angeles, CA 90024
Tel: +1 310 825 7741
Fax: +1 310 206 1686

*University of Southern California (USC)
School of Cinema and Television
University Park
Los Angeles, CA 90089-2211
Tel: +1 213 743 2235
Fax: +1 213 740 7682

Columbia University
Film Division
513 Dodge Hall, School of the Arts
116th Street and Broadway
New York, NY 10027
Tel: +1 212 854 1681
Fax: +1 212 854 1309

*New York University (NYU)
Institute of Film and Television
721 Broadway, Room 1042
New York, NY 10003
Tel: +1 212 998 1700
Fax: +1 212 995 4040

Film School
A3100 University Center
Florida State University
Tallahassee, FL 32306-2084
Tel: +1 904 644 7728

California Institute of the Arts (CALARTS)
24700 McBean Parkway
Valencia, CA 91355
Tel: +1 805 253 7825
Fax: +1 805 253 7824

VIET NAM

Truong Dai Hoc San Khau Va Dien Anh
Mai Dich
Tu Liem
Ha Noi
Tel: 43397 (operator service)

Most non-American film schools, and many American, have extremely competitive entry requirements. Self-support through part-time work in foreign countries is usually illegal. Check local conditions with the school's admissions officer and with the country's consulate before committing yourself. Occasionally, when teaching is for an international group, it will be in English, but normally teaching is in the language of the country, as one would expect.

SELF-HELP AS A REALISTIC ALTERNATIVE

Many can afford neither time nor money to go to school, and so must find other means to acquire the necessary knowledge and experience. Werner Herzog has said that anyone who wants to make films should waste no more than a week learning film techniques. Given his flair for overstatement, this period would appear a little short, but fundamentally I share this attitude. Film and video is a practical subject and can be tackled by the intelligent do-it-yourselfer. This book should encourage you to learn filmmaking by making films, by learning through doing, and, if absolutely necessary, through doing it alone.

Self-education in the arts, however, is different from self-education in a technology because the arts are not finite and calculable. Instead, they are based on shared tastes and perceptions that even at an early stage call for the criticism and participation of others. The painter, novelist, poet, photographer, or animator—each an artist who usually creates alone—is not complete until the work is submitted for public interaction. What seems like a career of pleasantly removed creation is really a long, isolated preparation to finally engage with the public. This usually includes rejection as an important preparation for the next attempt.

Somewhere along the way you will want a mentor—someone to give reliable, knowledgeable, and reasonably objective criticism of your work, and who can help you solve the problems that arise. Don't worry if none is in the offing right now, because you can go far under your own steam. It is a law of nature that we only find who we need when we really need them.

C H A P T E R   3 2

GETTING WORK

WHAT YOU CAN DO WHILE YOU'RE STILL IN SCHOOL

Let's imagine that you now have knowledge and some experience in film- and videomaking, graduation is on the horizon, and the scary world of work is hurtling toward you. How will you make the transition from student to paid worker in the medium?

First, in addition to your directing aspirations, you must emerge from school with one or more highly developed *craft skills* such as camera or sound operator, editor, or production manager. If your school has a producing track, try to set up a partnership with a keen producer. Your development work and future production will need solid producer skills, and it is debilitating (though often necessary) to do it yourself.

You need a respectable *portfolio* of work that makes your production skills manifest. From these you should be able to earn short-term money at crewing while you deploy a longer term plan to get established as a director. Would-be documentary directors seldom find positions awaiting them; they have to make jobs for themselves. Your degree will count for nothing in the world of production but your production work, if good, will help you get *job interviews* and, especially if you have won awards, maybe some modest commissioned work or better.

The film and television industries are downsizing their permanent staffs and employing freelancers, so in principle, there are now more opportunities for small, self-starter companies. But work goes to those with a track record of accomplishment, which is catch-22 for the beginner. If you are lucky and get commissioned directing straight from school, it will probably still be too sporadic and ill paid to initially cover your bills. So while you pursue your own projects you will need paid crewing work, and this requires building up your résumé with film-related jobs.

INTERNSHIPS

Well-established schools have an internship system with local media employers, and temporary (usually unpaid) positions often turn into one's first paying job. A steady flow of graduates get work as a grip, assistant editor, production assistant, or camera assistant via an internship where an employer can, at low risk, try you out in places where you can't do much harm. This will happen only if you have developed the appropriate social skills. To gain acceptance anywhere you need *professional level skills, professional discipline, and good references*. Initially the latter will come from your teachers.

CRAFT WORKER

Unless you are lucky enough to be studying in a national film school with assured jobs at graduation, you will have to enter the marketplace as a freelancer. There are regional and national differences to the film and television industries, but developing a track record as a freelancer is similar everywhere. To find openings, you will need to *network* through friends, associates, and any professional contacts acquired during your schooling and internships.

To begin with, and perhaps for a long time after, you will work at fulfilling mundane commercial needs; expending lots of imagination and effort crewing for industrial, training, or medical films; or shooting conferences and weddings. Learning to do this reliably, well, and inventively will teach you a great deal. Such a training served Robert Altman and many another director well.

If you do good work, on time, within the projected cost, and with a good spirit, your reputation as an OK person slowly spreads through the grapevine. Such "work ethic" requisites don't impede creative work, but they do exclude the undisciplined and immature personality who imagines that going to film school means a place should await him. It doesn't. You may have become somebody big in film school, but you become nothing and nobody in the working world until your work and a lengthening track record prove otherwise. So at the start you should be ready to do any level of work cheerfully so you are well placed when "something opens up."

Your aim is to make a living as a freelance crew person and invest any spare time and cash in making films with contemporaries who, like you, are struggling to gain experience and recognition. Each level of accomplishment as a group equips you to seek more interesting and demanding work. By developing your talent together to a point where you have concrete, proven results, you then have something to offer an employer, fund, or sponsor.

If the emphasis on becoming known and fitting in seems like the slipway to compromise, it need not be. The films on which we were all raised were produced under identical conditions (for profit), and some were good art by any standards. The entire cinema has its roots in commerce, and each new venture is predicated on day-to-day ticket sales.

THE SEARCH FOR SUBJECTS AND A MARKET

At the time of writing the market is changing rapidly as cable television and VCR rentals present a rapidly evolving set of new circumstances. Television networks, especially in Europe, are relying more on coproductions to spread the high cost of making documentaries over larger audiences. At the same time, desktop broadcast-quality digital production is rapidly developing, and the proliferation of production will produce still more change and democratization of production.

For your own projects you will need to define subjects that interest a sizable audience. This need not be a cynically conceived or fixed commodity, however. On the one hand, there is a subject, and on the other, there is *a way of seeing*. How a film sees may be more important than *what* it sees. Creativity in form is as important, or more so, than finding unique content.

The best way to find subjects is to uncover what deeply interests you, and then to propose it, argue it out, and discover all its possibilities, depths, and difficulties through conversations with filmmaking colleagues. Pitch your ideas to nonfilmmakers too; they need only be the kind of people for whom discussion of the world's affairs is an enjoyable part of living.

Go through distributors' catalogues, looking for your own areas of interest, and make your own market study to decide where your interests could fit into the existing commercial structure.

Attend festivals and conferences so you find out what others are producing, how they present themselves publicly, and what TV networks and distributors seem to buy. Pitching sessions, where proposers are publicly grilled by a panel, are particularly revealing. Bear in mind that there is a separation, by and large, between producers and distributors akin to that between authors and publishers. You can only expect funds from a distributor if you already have a commercially marketable product. For a film in the planning stages you are unlikely to get distributors' or television money without a proven track record.

THE DOCUMENTARY PROPOSAL

With films of your own to show, particularly if you have won some awards, you have a visible identity and are in a good position to approach the various funds. Naturally competition is keen, but you would be surprised how poorly most prospective filmmakers represent themselves on paper, and how often they don't read the fund's guidelines carefully. Would you give money to someone who can't follow a few rules?

Carefully read the sections of this book on proposal writing, draft and redraft your proposal until it is perfect, and try your luck.

FUNDS

When funding organizations make awards they usually grant up to 50 percent of a budget. The proposal has to be well written, unusually interesting, and businesslike. With your application, send a specially edited sample reel of around 5 minutes. This is a trailer showing your best and most applicable work, especially sections from material already shot for the proposed film.

In the United States, there is a complex and shifting system of *federal, state, and private funding agencies*. Each has guidelines and a track record in funding some special area. Usually only local organizations will fund first films. Fund money is good money because you usually are not required to pay it back, so making use of local or national funds is an important means of financing documentary filmmaking. As a general rule, private grant funds prefer to give completion money to films that are shot and may be viewed, while government agencies are a little more likely to fund research and preproduction.

If your track record is slender (perhaps a short film that has won a festival award), and you are seeking either preproduction, production, or completion money, you should investigate your *state or city arts council*. Each state in the United States has a *state humanities committee*, which works in association with the *National Endowment for the Humanities* (NEH.) This agency works to fund groups of accredited individuals (usually academics) producing work in the humanities. National guidelines can be obtained from The National Endowment for the Humanities, 1100 Pennsylvania Avenue, Rm. 406, Washington, D.C. 20506.

Many states and big cities have a *film commission or bureau* that exists to encourage and facilitate filmmaking (because it's good business). These bureaus develop formal and informal relationships with the whole local filmmaking community and can be an excellent source of information on all aspects of local production. A full list of those in the United States, as well as a wealth of other documentary-related information, is in the International Documentary Association's Membership Directory and Survival Guide, obtainable from the International Documentary Association (IDA; see later).

The Independent Television Service has been authorized by Congress to oversee the distribution of $6 million to independent producers and to encourage innovative programming for underserved audiences, in particular, minorities and children. For information and guidelines, contact: Independent Television Service, PO Box 65797, Saint Paul, MN 55165.

Survey organizations exist to help you find the appropriate private fund or charity to approach. Chicago has the Donors Forum, a clearinghouse that periodically publishes local information (53 West Jackson Blvd., Chicago, IL 60604, tel.: +1-312-431-0260). New York has the Foundation Center (79 Fifth Avenue, New York, NY 10003-3076), which serves as a center for nationwide reference collections for study by those wishing to approach donors and donor organizations.

JOURNALS AND ASSOCIATIONS

The International Documentary Association is based in Los Angeles and has a strong program of events in that area. It publishes *International Documentary*, an important quarterly journal with featured articles on new films, filmmakers, trends, festivals, and technology. At the back is a directory of upcoming festivals and competitions, funding, jobs and opportunities, classes/seminars/workshops, distributors looking for new films, new publications, and classifieds. The IDA also publishes a superb *Membership Directory and Survival Guide.* Contact: International Documentary Association, 1551 S. Robertson Blvd., Los Angeles, CA 90035 (Tel: +1-310-284-8422, fax: +1-310-785-9334, e-mail: idf@netcom.com). Students get a special price.

Another good move is to take out a subscription to *American Cinematographer,* a monthly publication, mainly for feature fiction workers, but which keeps one abreast of the latest methods and technical innovations. It also includes news, interviews, and a great deal of useful "who's doing what" information. Contact: *American Cinematographer,* American Society of Cinematographers, Inc., P.O. Box 2230, Hollywood, CA 90078.

Videomaker is an excellent monthly magazine that reviews new equipment in the prosumer range (i.e., high-end consumer, low-end professional) and is particularly good for its accessible explanations of techniques and technical principles. Subscription info: P.O. Box 469026, Escondido, CA 92046-9938, Tel: +1 619 745 2809, e-mail: Icraft@videomaker.com, Web site: http://www.videomaker.com

The production section of this book's bibliography lists books that contain a vast amount of interlocking information on the structure of the film/video industry, job descriptions, pay scales, funding agencies, proposals, grants, budgeting, contracts, and distribution. Most pertain to the independent feature film industry, but those of particular use to documentary-makers are as follows:

Jan Bone, *Opportunities in Film Careers* (Lincolnwood, IL: VGM Career Horizons, 1990)

Michael Wiese, *The Independent Film and Videomaker's Guide, 2nd ed.* (Boston: Focal Press, 1990)

Michael Wiese and Deke Simon, *Film and Video Budgets, 2nd ed.* (Studio City, CA: Michael Wiese Productions, 1995)

With case histories and examples, these works represent a mine of information. Wiese's *The Independent Film and Videomaker's Guide,* dealing as it does specifically with documentaries, is particularly valuable. He corrects the myth that any worthy film can be sold to the Public Broadcasting System (PBS) and tells how Byzantine this sprawling, bureaucratic organization is. "If you have the idea that PBS is a benevolent network serving public and education interests," warns Wiese in an earlier version of the book, "a renewed study is suggested." You can get a *Program Producer's Handbook* from: PBS Programming, 1320 Braddock Place, Alexandria, VA 22314-1698. *The Producer's Guide to Public Television Funding* is available from the Corporation for Public Broadcasting, 901 E Street, NW, Washington, D.C. 20004-2006.

PRESENTING YOURSELF

A professionally laid out résumé is a must when you seek work, and the best reference, apart from letters of recommendation from established filmmakers, is awards won at festivals. The IDA and American Film Institute (AFI) list upcoming festivals, and you should enter your work in as many as you can afford. Most film and video competition entries are abysmal, so if you do good work, it is realistic to hope to win. Prizes are inordinately important in swinging votes during a funding application process or in securing an interview.

Whomever you plan to approach, learn all you can about the business, organization, and individual that you are approaching. People who deal with job seekers distinguish rapidly between those who are realistic and the dreamers adrift in alien seas. This judgment is made not on who you are but on how you present yourself, both on paper and in person. You will only do this well if your homework includes resourceful reading and lots of networking on the phone.

When you send your résumé to an individual or company, send a brief, carefully composed, *individual* cover letter that describes your goals and how you might best contribute to the organization. Call up after a few days and ask if you might have a brief chat with someone in case a position opens up in the future. If you are called for an interview, dress conservatively, be punctual, know what you want, and show you are willing to do any kind of work to get there. Let the interviewer ask the questions, and when you reply, be brief and to the point. Say concisely what skills and qualities you think you have to offer. This is where you can demonstrate your knowledge of (and therefore commitment to) the interviewer's business. Interviewers often ask if you have any questions; have two or three good ones ready so you can demonstrate your knowledge of the company or group.

If shyness holds you back, do something about it now. Get assertiveness training, or join a theater group and force yourself to act, preferably in improvisational material. Only you can do what it takes to start believing in yourself. Almost all human problems boil down to a matter of courage.

MAKING A JOB FOR YOURSELF

I don't remember ever seeing an advertisement for a documentary filmmaker, but this does not mean there are no jobs. It simply means that one must find or create a job rather than expect one ready made. Selling one's services is initially a grisly business, and rejections hurt. But they help make you better at what's unavoidable: talking people into letting you use their money to make your films.

Some interesting facts emerged in a colloquium at my institution (Columbia College Chicago) given by former students now working in various capacities in the film industry. Everyone:

- took about the same (long) time to get established and to begin to earn a reasonable amount of money
- had moved up the ladder of responsibility at roughly the same (slow) pace
- found that greater responsibility came suddenly and without warning
- was scared stiff when it came, feeling they were conning their way into an area beyond their competence
- felt they grew into their new levels of responsibility
- loved their work and said they felt privileged to be working in such an important area of public life

A PERSONAL MESSAGE

Documentary is a growing field in which the levels of inventiveness, humor, courage, and humanism are all going up. Documentary people *en masse* are remarkable for their conviviality and helpfulness (try a conference or festival). They have chosen documentary film as the work that matters to them most in all the world, be it political, humanitarian, or celebratory. I hope that you, dear reader, join this community and use the wonderful art of the screen to help create a better world.

Thank you most sincerely for using this book, and please send me any comments that could help me make the next edition better. Write either to Columbia College Chicago (address in film schools list, Chapter 30) or by e-mail (MRabiger@aol.com). I will try to reply, but if I don't it is probably because I am on the road giving workshops or seminars. Please don't send me proposals or films. I simply don't have time to review them (or to do lots of other good things too!).

May you have good luck, good filming, and good friends.

PART 9

OTHER INFORMATION

Filmography of Director Michael
Rabiger   391

Glossary   393

Bibliography and Film Sources   407

Index   413

FILMOGRAPHY OF DIRECTOR MICHAEL RABIGER

BBC "Breakaway" Series

Au Pair to Paris	(30 min, GB [Great Britain] and France)
Kibbutzniks	(30 min, GB and Israel)

BBC "Faces of Paris" Series

Gerard et Regine	(30 min, France and Austria)
César	(30 min, France)

BBC "Yesterday's Witness" Series

Prisoners of Conscience	(30 min, × 2, GB)
The Cramlington Train Wreckers	(30 min, GB)
Breaking the Silence	(30 min, GB)
Tolstoy Remembered by his Daughter	(30 min, USA)
The Battle of Cable Street	(45 min, GB)
A Remnant of a Feudal Society	(30 min, GB)
A Cause Worth Fighting For	(45 min, GB)
Charlie Smith at 131	(30 min, USA)

BBC "One Pair of Eyes" Series

Dr. Spock: We're Heading for Destruction	(45 min, USA)
Idries Shah: The Dreamwalkers	(45 min, GB)
Leonardo Ricci: Cities of the Future	(45 min, Italy/Sicily)

BBC "Voices of the Seventies" Series
    Our Time Is Coming Now   (30 min, GB)

BBC "Cameron Country" Series
    Prejudice: on the Face of It   (45 min, GB)
    Patriotism   (45 min, GB)

BBC "In the Limelight" Series
    Ronald Fraser: Having a Lovely Time   (30 min, GB)
    Barry Took: Working Men's Clubs   (30 min, GB)

Independently Produced
    Can You Live Like That?   (45 min, GB, Krishnamurti Foundation)
    Gravity Is the Therapist   (53 min, USA, Rolf Foundation)
    The Memorial Day Massacre   (20 min, USA)
    Bishop Hill Celebrates   (30 min, USA, DePaul University)
    The Temptation of Charles C. Charley   (26 min, USA, fiction pilot)
    Portrait of a Director   (30 min, USA, Columbia College)
    Ro Raises His Roof   (30 min, USA)
    A Child's Journey through Auschwitz   (58 min, USA)
    Lotte on Lotte   (13 min, Norway)
    Australian Cousins   (Australia, work in progress)

GLOSSARY

More information can often be found by using the index.

A & B rolls Two or more rolls of film camera-original from which release prints are struck.

Acetate sheet Clear plastic sheet used in making titles or animation cels.

Action match cut Cut made between two different angles of the same action using the subject's movement as the transition.

AD Assistant director.

Adaptation The unique way each person adapts to the changing obstacles that prevent him or her from gaining his ends and a prime component in externalizing his or her conflicts.

Address track A spare track in a videotape recording system that can be addressed by the user, and is usually accessed to record time code data.

ADR Automatic dialogue replacement. *See* Postsynchronization.

Aerial shot Shot taken from the air.

AFI American Film Institute.

Ambient sound Sound naturally occurring in any location. Even an empty, quiet room has its own special atmosphere because no space is truly silent.

Analogue recording Any sound or picture recording that records its waveforms as an analogue representation, rather than digitally, when the waveform is registered by digital numbers, as in the coordinates for a graph.

Angle of acceptance The height and width of the subject filmed by a particular lens at a given distance, expressed in a lens table either in degrees or as measurements. Photographed image also depends on aspect ratio of the format in use. Wide-screen format will have longer horizontal measurement.

Anticipating When an actor (and a documentary participant who is temporarily in the role of actor) speaks or acts in advance of the appropriate moment.

Anticipatory sound Sound brought in ahead of its accompanying picture.

Aspect ratio The size of a screen format expressed as the ratio of the width in relation to the height. Films made for television are photographed at a ratio of 1.33:1. *See also* Angle of acceptance.

Atmosphere track   Sound track providing a particular atmosphere (cafe, railroad, beach, rain, for example).

Attack (sound)   The beginning portion of any sound.

Audio sweetening   The level and equalization adjustment process that accompanies sound mixing.

Auteur theory   The concept that one mind controls the creative identity of a film.

Axis   *See* Scene axis.

Baby legs   A miniature tripod for low angle shots.

Back lighting   Lighting from behind the subject.

Back story   The events stated or implied to have happened prior to the period covered in the screenplay.

Bars   Standard color bars generated in video systems, usually by the camera.

BCU   Big close-up.

Beat   Point in a situation where a buildup of pressure produces a major and irreversible change in one or more characters' consciousness(es) (theater term).

BFI   British Film Institute.

BG   Background.

Blocking   Choreographic arrangement of movements by participants and camera in relation to the location.

Body copy   Nondialogue descriptive portion of screenplay, usually consisting of stage directions and physical description.

Boom   Support pole suspending the microphone close to the speakers but just out of shot.

Boxcar cutting   Crude method of assembling sound and action segments as level-cut segments for speed and convenience.

Broad lighting   Lighting that produces a broad band of highlight on a face or other three-dimensional object.

Butt splice   Taped film splice made without the overlap necessary to cement splicing.

Buzz track   *See* presence.

Camera left/right   Method of specifying movement or the placement of objects in relation to the camera: "Davy turns away from camera and walks off camera left." Also expressed as *screen right* or *left*.

Camera motivation   A shot or a camera movement must be motivated within the terms of the scene or story if it is not to look alien and imposed. Camera motivation is often answered by asking, "What is the point of view here?"

Camera-to-subject axis   The invisible line drawn between the camera and the subject in the composition. *See also* Scene axis.

Capturing   *See* Digitizing.

Cement splice   A film splice made by cementing two overlapping portions of film together.

Character generator   An electronic device for producing video titles.

Checkerboarding   The practice, during conforming, of alternating film scenes with black leader in each A & B roll of camera original. Sound tracks prior to mixing are likewise alternated between two or more channels, with silence separating sound segments. Both black frame and silence allow the operator a grace period in which to adjust printer or sound channel settings before the arrival of the next segment.

Cinéma vérité   Documentary shooting method in which the camera is subservient to an actuality that is sometimes instigated by the director.

Clapperboard   Marker board used at the beginning of takes whose bar closing permits separate sound to be synchronized. Also called the *slate*.

Climax   The dramatic apex or turning point of a scene.

Color bars   Standard electronic video color test, usually generated by the camera.

Color chart   Chart attached to film slate board as color reference for laboratory processing technicians.

Color temperature   Light color quality is measured in degrees Kelvin. Common light sources in moviemaking contain a different mix of colors. The eye compensates effortlessly, but film and video cameras (or lighting itself) must be adjusted to prevailing color temperature if white objects are to be rendered as white on-screen. Mixing daylight (around 5400°K) and studio lights (3200°K) in the same scene leads to an unnatural lighting effect. One source must be filtered to make its output match the other, and the camera must likewise be filtered or electronically color balanced for all scene colors to be rendered faithfully.

Comm   Commentary.

Complementary shot   A shot compositionally designed to intercut with another.

Composite print   A film print combining sound and picture.

Compression   Sound with a wide dynamic range can be proportionately compressed so that the loudest and softest sounds are closer in volume. All TV transmissions and most radio transmissions, with the exception of high-fidelity music stations, are compressed. Cinemas usually give you the authentic range between whispers and the roar of battle.

Concept   The dramatic *raison d'être* underlying the whole screenplay.

Conforming   The process in which the film camera original is edited in conformity with the fine-cut workprint prior to making release prints.

Confrontation   Bringing into final collision those people or forces representing the dramatic situation's main conflict.

Contingency percentage   A percentage, usually between 10 percent and 15 percent, superadded to a budget to provide for the unforeseeable.

Contingency planning   Scheduling alternative shooting for any scenes threatened by weather or other imponderables.

Continuity   Consistency of physical detail between shots intended to match.

Continuity script   Script made after postproduction as record of film contents. Useful in proving piracy or censorship.

Continuity supervisor   *See* script supervisor.

Contrast   Difference in brightness between highlight and deep shadow areas in an image.

Contrast ratio   Ratio of lightest to darkest areas in an image.

Controlling point of view   The psychological perspective (a character's or the storyteller's) from which a particular scene is shown.

Counterpoint   The juxtaposing of antithetical elements, perhaps between sound and picture, to create a conflict of impressions for the audience to resolve.

Coverage   The different angles from which a given scene is covered in order to allow variations of viewpoint in editing.

Crab dolly   Wheeled camera support platform that can roll in any direction.

Craning   A boom supporting the camera that can be raised or lowered during the shot.

Crash zoom   Very fast zoom in or zoom out.

Crib notes   Director's notes listing intentions and "don't forgets" for a scene.

Crossing the line   Moving the camera across the scene axis. Can be problematical.

CS   Close shot.

CU   Close-up.

Cutaway   A shot, often a character's physical point of view, that allows us to cut away momentarily from the main action.

Dailies   The film unit's daily output, processed and ready to be viewed. Also called *rushes* because of the rush involved in readying them.

DAT recorder   Digital audio tape recorder.

Day for night   Special photography that allows a sunlit day shot to pass as moonlit night.

Decay   The tapering away of a concluding sound.

Deep focus   Photography that holds objects both near and far in sharp focus.

Degradation   A picture, either video or photo, becomes degraded when it passes through several generations of analogue copying.

Depth of field   Depth of the picture that is in acceptably sharp focus. Varies widely according to lens and f-stop in use.

Diegetic sound   Sound that belongs in the natural world we see in the picture.

Diffused light   Light composed of disorganized rays that casts an indistinct shadow.

Digitizing   (also known as *capturing*) Process of turning an analogue signal, whether audio or video, into a digital record. This usually involves using an algorithmic formulation to compress the information to avoid wasteful recording of similarities in one frame to the next. *See also* JPEG and MPEG.

Direct cinema   A low-profile documentary style of shooting that disallows any directorial intrusion to shape or instigate incidents.

Dissolve   Transitional device in which one image cross-fades into another. Also called a *lap dissolve*. One sound can dissolve into another.

DOF   Depth of field.

Dolby   A proprietary electronic recording system that produces low-noise sound recording, that is, having a lowered systemic hiss.

Dolly shot   Any shot on a wheeled camera support.

Double-system recording   Camera and sound recorder are separate instruments.

DP   Director of photography.

Dramatic dynamics   The ebb and flow of dramatic pressure through the length of a scene or of a whole film.

Dramatic tension   The unresolved knowledge, hopes, fears, and expectations that keep us wanting to know "And what happens next?" Vital component in any storytelling. Wilkie Collins said, "Make them laugh, make them cry, but make them wait."

Dub   To copy from one electronic medium to another. Can be sound or video picture.

Dutch angle   Shot made with camera deliberately tilted out of horizontal.

DV   Digital video, or video and sound recorded digitally. Tape may be as small as 6mm wide.

Dynamic character definition   Defining a participant like a dramatic character—by what he or she wants and is trying to accomplish.

Dynamic composition   Pictorial composition as it changes within a moving shot.

Echo   Sound reflections that return after a constant delay time.

Edge numbers   Code numbers imprinted on the edge of camera original film and printing through to the workprint.

Edit decision list   Sound and picture edit decisions in a movie, defined as a list of time code or Keycode© numbers. Taking camera originals and a standard EDL to a postproduction facility allows the making of a clean facsimile of the workprint.

EDL   *See* Edit decision list.

Effects   Sounds specially laid to augment the sound track of a film.

Ellipsis   In filmmaking, the editing out of superfluous steps in a lengthy process in order to produce a shorthand version whose missing parts can be inferred by the audience (e.g., car stops at garage, gas pump nozzle into gas tank, money given to clerk, car rejoins road)

EQ   *See* Equalizing.

Equalizing   Using sound filters to reduce the discrepancy between sound tracks that are supposed to match and sound seamless.

Establishing shot   A shot that establishes a scene's geographical and human contents.

Exposition   The part of a scene or a story in which basic information is relayed to the audience. Good exposition is buried within the action and goes unnoticed.

Expressionism   A mode in art in which verisimilitude is laid aside in favor of techniques that evoke the subjective vision, either of a character or of the storyteller.

Ext   Exterior.

External composition   The compositional relationship between two images (shots) at the point of transition between them, usually a cut.

Eyeline   The visual trajectory of a character in a scene.

Fade down   Lower sound level.

Fade to white   Fade an image to white instead of to black.

Fade up   Raise sound level.

Falling action   *See* Resolution.

FG   Foreground.

FI   Fade in.

Fill light   Diffused light used to raise light level in shadows cast by key light.

Flash forward   Moving temporarily forward in time; the cinematic equivalent of the future tense. This quickly becomes a new form of the present.

Flashback   Moving temporarily backwards in time; a cinematic past tense that soon becomes an ongoing present.

Floor plan   *See* Ground plan.

FO   Fade out.

Focal distance   Distance between camera and subject.

Focus (acting)   In acting it means seeing, hearing, thinking in character. When a documentary participant loses focus, he or she becomes self-conscious and aware of participating in a make-believe world.

Foley   Generic name for a stage where sound is recreated to picture.

Foreshadowing   A somewhat fatalistic narrative technique by which an outcome is hinted at in advance. Helps to raise expectant tension in the audience.

Form   The means and arrangement chosen to present a story's content.

Freeze frame   A single frame arrested and held as a still picture.

Frontal lighting   Key light coming from the direction of the camera and showing the subject virtually without shadows.

FTs   Footsteps. Sometimes recreated for stylized documentaries.

FX   Sound effects

Generation   Camera original (in film or video) is the first generation, and copies become subsequent numbered generations. Each in analogue recording will have increased degradation of the original's fidelity. Many digital generations are possible before degradation sets in.

Genre   A kind or type of film (essay, reflexive, direct cinema in documentaries, for example, and horror, sitcom, cowboy, domestic drama, etc. in fiction).

Grading   *See* Timing.

Graduated tonality   An image composed of midtones and having neither very bright nor very dark areas.

Gray scale   Test chart useful to camera and lab technicians that shows the range of gray tones and includes absolute black and white.

Grip   Location technician expert in handling lighting and set construction equipment.

Ground plan   Diagram showing placement of objects and movements of actors on a floor plan. Also called *floor plan.*

Gun/rifle mike   Ultradirectional microphone useful for minimizing the intrusiveness of ambient noise.

Hard light   *See* Specular light.

Headroom   Compositional space left above heads.

High angle   Camera mounted high, looking down.

High contrast   Image with large range of brightnesses.

High down   Camera mounted high, looking down.

High-key picture   Image that is overall bright with few areas of shadow.

Highlight   Brightest areas in picture.

Hi-hat   Ultralow camera support resembling a metal top hat.

Improv   Improvisation. A dramatic interaction that deliberately permits an outcome to emerge spontaneously. Improvs can involve different degrees of structure, or may set a goal to be reached by an undetermined path. Improv drama and documentary directing methods are often interchangeable.

Insert   A close shot of detail to be inserted in a shot containing more comprehensive action.

Int   Interior.

Interior monologue   The interior thoughts voice an actor will sustain to help himself or herself stay in character and in focus.

Internal composition   Composition internal to the frame as opposed to the compositional relationship existing between adjacent shots, called *external composition*.

Irony   The revelation of a reality different from that initially apparent.

Jam sync   Refers to videotape copying method that transfers not only all video and audio data but time code data as well, with frame-to-frame accuracy.

JPEG   An electronic algorithm standard used to compress video up to a 20:1 ratio for recording. Each frame is discrete, unlike MPEG compression, which achieves up to 100:1 compression while maintaining quality. JPEG allows editing to any particular frame, MPEG may not.

Jump cut   Transitional device in which two similar images taken at different times are cut together so that the elision of intervening time is apparent. From this the audience infers that time has passed.

Juxtaposition   The placing together of different pictorial or sound elements to invite comparison, inference, and heightened thematic awareness on the part of the audience.

Keycode©   Kodak's proprietary system for bar coding each camera's original film frame. This facilitates digitizing by assigning each frame its own time code. Later, after digital editing, the coding permits negative cutting (conforming) from a digitally produced EDL.

Key light   A scene's apparent source of illumination, and the one creating the intended shadow pattern.

Key numbers   *See* Edge numbers.

Keystone distortion   The distortion of parallel lines that results from photographing an object from an off-axis position.

LA   Low angle

Lap dissolve   *See* Dissolve.

Lavalier mike   Any neck or chest microphone.

Lead space   The additional compositional space allowed in front of a figure or moving object photographed in profile.

Legal release   A legally binding release form signed by a participant in a film that gives permission to use footage taken.

Leitmotiv   Intentionally repeated element (sound, shot, dialogue, music, etc.) that helps unify a film by reminding the viewer of its earlier appearance.

Lens speed   How fast a lens is depends on its maximum aperture and is a measure of light-transmitting capacity.

Level   Sound volume.

Lighting ratio   The ratio of highlight brightness to shadow illumination.

Limiter   Electronically applied upper sound limit, useful for preventing momentary transient sounds, such as a door slamming, from distortion through over-recording.

Line of tension   Invisible dramatic axis, or line of awareness, that can be drawn between protagonists and important elements in a scene.

Lip sync   Recreated speech that is in complete sync with the speaker. Singers often lip sync to their recordings and fake a singing performance on television.

Looping   *See* ADR.

Lose focus   *See* Focus.

Low angle   Camera looking up at subject.

Low-contrast image   Image with small differences of brightness between highlight areas and shadow.

Low-key picture   A scene that may have high contrast but that is predominantly dark overall.

LS   Long shot.

Magazine   Removable lightproof film container for a film camera.

Mannerisms   An actor or participant's idiosyncratic and repeated details of behavior. Very hard to change or suppress.

Master mix   Final mixed sound, first generation.

Master shot   Shot that shows most or all of the scene and most or all of the characters.

Match cut   *See* Action match cut.

MCS   Medium close shot.

Metaphor   A verbal or visually implied analogy that ascribes to one thing the qualities associated with another (e.g., the shop assistant, catlike behind her potted plants).

Midtones   The intermediate shades of gray lying between the extremes of black and white.

Mise-en-scène   The totality of lighting, blocking, camera use, and composition that produces the dramatic image on film.

Mix   The mixing together of sound tracks.

Mix chart   Cue chart that functions like a musician's score to assist in the sound mix.

MLS   Medium long shot.

Modulations   Any electrical or electronic waveforms by which sound or picture are relayed and recorded.

Montage   Originally meant editing in general, but now refers to the kind of sequence that shows a process or the passage of time.

Montage sequence   *See* Montage.

MOS   Short for "Mit Out Sound," which is what the German directors in Hollywood called for when they intended to shoot silent. In Britain this shot is called *mute*.

Motif   Any formal element repeated from film history, or from the film itself, whose repetition draws attention to an unfolding thematic statement. *See also* Leitmotiv.

Motivation   Whatever logic (in drama, of the plot) that impels a character to act or react in a particular way, usually a combination of psychological makeup and external events.

MPEG An electronic algorithm standard used to compress, by up to a 100:1 ratio, large amounts of video into a smaller amount of information. Each frame is not discrete, like JPEG compression, but achieves greater compression while maintaining quality. MPEG may not allow editing to any particular frame.

MS Medium shot.

Murphy's Law "Whatever can go wrong will go wrong." Applies also to people.

Mus Music.

Music sync points Places in a film's action where music must exactly fit. Also called *picture-pointing* and can be overdone.

Mute shot *See* MOS.

Narr Narration.

Narrow lighting Lighting that in portraiture produces a narrow band of highlight on a face.

Negative cutting *See* Conforming.

Noise Noise inherent in a sound recording system itself.

Noise reduction Recording and playback technique that minimizes system noise. *See also* Dolby.

Normal lens A lens of a focal length that, in the format being used, renders distances between foreground and background as recognizably normal.

Obligatory moment In documentary, as in drama, the moment of maximum dramatic intensity in a scene, for which the whole scene exists.

Off-line edit Manual, noncomputerized video editing. *See also* On-line edit.

Omniscient point of view A storytelling mode in which the audience is exposed to the author's capacity to see or know anything going on in the story, to move at will in time and space, and to freely comment upon meanings or themes.

On-line edit Video editing assisted by a computer that can locate and line up specific time-coded frames in the process of assembling a final cut.

Optical Any visual device, such as a fade, dissolve, wipe, iris wipe, ripple dissolve, matte, superimposition, etc.

Optical house A company specializing in visual special effects.

Optical track A sound track photographically recorded.

OS Offscreen.

Overlap cut Any cut in which picture and sound transitions are staggered instead of level cut.

Pan Short for *panorama*. Horizontal camera movement.

Parallel storytelling The intercutting of two separate stories proceeding in parallel through time. Useful for abridging each and for making ironic contrasts.

Participant Someone who takes part in a documentary who would, in a fiction film, be an actor playing a character.

Perspective The size differential between foreground and background objects that causes us to infer receding space. Perspective that is obviously distorted makes us attribute subjectivity to the point of view being expressed.

Picture pointing Making music fit picture events. Walt Disney films used the device so much that its overuse is called *Mickey Mousing*.

Picture texture   This can be hard or soft. A hard image has large areas in sharp focus and tends toward contrastiness, while a soft image has areas out of focus and lacks contrast.

Pitching   The oral presentation of a film proposal in a brief, comprehensive, and attractive form to a committee or interested party. Comes from the idea of the sales pitch.

Playwriting   In drama, one actor's tendency to take control of a scene, particularly in improv work, and to manipulate other actors into a passive relationship. Happens in documentaries too.

Plot   In drama, the arrangement of incidents and the logic of causality in a story. Plot should create a sense of momentum and credibility, and act as a vehicle for the thematic intention of the piece. Same architecture of logic is necessary in documentaries.

PM   Production manager.

Point of view   Sometimes literally what a character sees (e.g., a clock approaching midnight) but more usually signifies the outlook and sensations of a character within a particular environment. This can be the momentary consciousness of an unimportant character, or that of a main character (*see* Controlling point of view). It can also be the storyteller's point of view (*see* Omniscient point of view).

Postsynchronization   Dialogue or effects shot in sync with existing action. Abbreviated as *postsync*.

POV   Point of view. When thus abbreviated, it often means a shot reproducing a character's eyeline view.

Practical   Any light source visible in the frame as part of the set.

Premise   *See* Concept.

Premix   A preliminary pass in which subsidiary sound elements are mixed together in preparation for the final mix.

Preroll   The amount of time a camcorder or video editing rig needs to reach running speed prior to recording or making a cut.

Presence   Specially recorded location atmosphere to authentically augment "silent" portions of track. Every space has its own unique presence.

Prop   Property.

Property   Physical object handled by participants or present for authenticity in a set. A term also used to describe a script or proposal to which someone has secured the rights.

Rack focus   Altering focus between foreground and background during a shot. Prompts or accommodates an attention shift (e.g., a figure enters a door at the back of the room).

Radio microphone   A microphone system that transmits its signal by radio to the recorder and is therefore wireless. Famous for picking up taxis and CB enthusiasts at inopportune moments.

Reconnaissance   Careful examination of locations prior to shooting.

Release print   Final print destined for audience consumption.

Research   Library work and observation of real life in search of authentic detail to fill out one's knowledge of participants, situations, historical events, or anything else one must know to direct knowledgeably.

Resistance   Human evasion mechanisms that show up in actors under different kinds of stress. Similar situations happen in shooting documentary.

Resolution   The wind-down events following the film's climax that form the final phase of its development. Also called *falling action.*

Reverberation   Sound reflections returning in a disorganized pattern of delay.

Rising action   The documentary story developments, including complication and conflict, that lead to a scene or a film's climax.

Room tone   *See* Presence.

Rushes   Unedited raw footage as it appears after shooting. Also called *dailies.*

Rushes book   Log of important first reactions to rushes footage.

Scene axis   The invisible line in a scene representing the scene's dramatic polarization. In a labor dispute scene, this might be drawn between the main protagonists, the plant manager and the union negotiator. Coverage is shot from one side of this line to preserve consistent screen directions for all participants. Complex scenes involving multiple characters and physical regrouping may have more than one axis. *See also* Crossing the line.

Scene breakdown or crossplot   In fiction, a chart displaying the locations, characters, and script pages necessary to each scene. Used in complex re-enacted documentaries, or any film using actors.

Scene dialectics   The forces in opposition in a scene, which in documentary are likely to be externalized through body language, action, and behavior. A sense of the pressures in each scene, even one lacking human presence, is invaluable to documentary makers.

Scene geography   The physical layout of the location and the placing of the participants. *See also* Master shot.

Screen direction   The orientation or movement of characters and objects relative to the screen (screen left, screen right, upscreen, downscreen).

Screen left/right   Movement or direction specifications. *See also* Screen direction.

Screenplay   Standard script format showing dialogue and stage direction but no camera or editing instructions.

Script supervisor   Also called *continuity supervisor,* this is the person who notes the physical details of each scene and the actual dialogue used so that complementary shots, designed to cut together, will match. Seldom used in documentary unless recreation and actors are being used.

Segue   (pronounced "seg-way") Sound transition, often a dissolve.

Set light   A light whose function is to illuminate the set.

Setup   The combination of particular lens, camera placement, and composition to produce a particular shot.

SFX   Sound effects.

Shooting ratio   The ratio of material shot for a scene in relation to its eventual edited length. 8:1 is a not unusual ratio for dramatic film, 20:1 or above is common for documentary.

Shooting script   Screenplay with scenes numbered and amended to show intended camera coverage and editing. Used only in docudrama.

Side coaching   In drama the director, during breaks in a scene's dialogue, quietly feeds directions to the actors, who incorporate these instructions without breaking character. Rarely used in documentary, but everything is possible.

Sightlines   Lines that can be drawn along each character's main lines of vision that influence the pattern of coverage so that it reproduces the feeling of each main character's consciousness.

Silhouette lighting   Lighting in which the subject is a dark outline against a light background.

Single shot   A shot containing only one character.

Single-system recording   Sound recording made on film or video that also carries the picture. *See also* Double-system recording.

Slate   *See* Clapperboard.

Slate number   Setup and take number shown on the slate, or clapper, which identifies a particular take.

Soft light   Light that does not produce hard-edged shadows.

Sound dissolve   One sound track dissolving into another.

Sound effects   Nondialogue recordings of sounds intended either to intensify a scene's realism or to give it a subjective heightening.

Sound mix   The mixing together of sound elements into a sound composition that becomes the film's sound track.

Sound perspective   Apparent distance of sound source from the microphone. Lavalier mikes, for instance, give no change of perspective when characters move or turn because they remain in a fixed relationship to the wearer.

Specular light   Light composed of parallel rays that casts a comparatively hard-edged shadow.

Split-page format   A script format that places action on the left-hand side of the page and its accompanying sound on the right. This format allows an extremely precise transcription of relationship between words or sounds and images.

Stage directions   In drama and docudrama, nondialogue screenplay instructions, also known as *body copy*.

Stand in   In drama and docudrama, someone who takes the place of an actor during setup time or for shots that involve special skills, such as horseback riding, fights, etc.

Static character definition   Giving a character static attributes instead of defining him in terms of dynamic volition.

Static composition   The composition elements in a static image.

Steadicam   Proprietary body brace camera support that uses counterbalance and gimbal technology so the camera can float while the operator walks.

Step outline   Synopsis of a screenplay expressed as a series of numbered steps, and preferably including a definition of each step's function in the whole.

Sting   Musical accent to heighten a dramatic moment.

Storyboard   Series of key images sketched to suggest what a series of shots will look like.

Strobing   The unnatural result on-screen caused by the interaction of camera shutter speed with a patterned subject, such as the rotating spokes of a wheel or panning across a picket fence.

Structure   The formal organization of the elements of a film, story, or any kind of discourse, principally the handling of time, and the arrangement of these elements into a dramatically satisfying development that includes a climax and resolution.

Style   An individual stamp on a film, the elements in a film that issue from its makers' own artistic identity.

Subjective camera angle   An angle that implies the physical point of view of one of the characters.

Subtext   The hidden, underlying meaning to what is said or done. It is supremely important and the director must usually search for it.

Superobjective   In drama, the overarching thematic purpose of the director's dramatic interpretation. Documentarians make the same identifications from life.

Surrealism   Concerned with the free movement of the imagination, particularly as expressed in dreams, where the dreamer has no conscious control over events. Often associated with helplessness. Also a movement in art and literature.

Sync coding   Code marks to help a film editor keep sound and action in sync.

Tag   An irreducibly brief description useful for its focus upon essentials.

Take   One filmed attempt from one setup. Each setup may have several takes.

Telephoto lens   Long or telescopic lens that foreshortens the apparent distance between foreground and background objects.

Tense, change of   Temporary change from present to either past, future, or conditional tenses in a film's narrative flow. Whatever tense a film invokes speedily becomes a new, ongoing present. For this reason, screenwriting is always in the present tense.

Tension   *See* dramatic tension.

Thematic purpose   The overall interpretation of a complete work that is ultimately identified and decided by the director. *See also* Superobjective.

Theme   A dominant idea made concrete through its representation by the characters, action, and imagery of the film.

Three-shot/3S   Shot containing three people.

Thumbnail character sketch   Brief character description useful either in screen writing or in writing documentary proposals.

Tilt   Camera swiveling in a vertical arc, for example, tilting up and down to show the height of a flagpole.

Time code   Electronic code number unique to each video frame.

Timebase correction   Electronic stabilization of the video image, particularly necessary to make it compatible with the sensitive circuitry used in transmission over the air.

Timing   The process of examining and grading a negative for color quality and exposure prior to printing. Also called *grading*.

Tracking shot   Moving camera shot in which the camera dolly often runs on tracks, like a miniature railroad.

Transition   Any visual, sound, or dramatic screen device that signals a jump to another time or place.

Treatment   Usually a synopsis in present-tense, short story form of an intended documentary. It summarizes expected dialogue and describes only what an audience would see and hear. Can also be a puff piece designed to sell the script rather than to give comprehensive information about content.

Trucking shot   Moving camera shot that was originally shot from a truck. The term is used interchangeably with *tracking*.

Two-shot/2S   Shot containing two people.

Unit   The whole group of people shooting a film.

VCR   Videocassette recorder.

Verbal action   In drama as in life, words conceived and delivered so as to act upon the listener and instigate a result.

Video assist   A video feed taken from the film camera's viewfinder and displayed on a monitor, usually for the director to watch during shooting.

Visual rhythm   Each image, depending on its action and compositional complexity, requires a different duration on-screen to look right and to occupy the same audience concentration as its predecessor. A succession of images, when sensitively edited, exhibits a rhythmic constancy that can be slowed or accelerated like any other kind of rhythm.

VO   Voice-over.

Volition   The will of a character to accomplish something. This leads to constant struggle of one form or another, a concept vital in making dramatic characters come to life. Important concept to a documentary director as he or she struggles to see more deeply into the characters and situations being filmed.

VT   Videotape.

WA   Wide angle.

Whip pan   Very fast panning movement.

White balance   Video camera setup procedure in which circuitry is adjusted to the color temperature of the lighting source so that a white object is rendered as white on-screen.

Wide-angle lens   A lens with a wide angle of acceptance. Its effect is to increase the apparent distance between foreground and background objects.

Wild   Nonsync.

Wild track   A sound track shot alone and with no synchronous picture.

Window dub   A transfer made from a time-coded video camera original that displays each frame's time-code number in an electronic window, usually near the bottom of frame.

Wipe   Optical transition between two scenes that appears on-screen as a line moving across the screen. An *iris wipe* makes the new scene appear as a dot that enlarges to fill the screen. Optical effects are overused on the TV screen.

Wireless mike   *See* radio microphone.

WS   Wide shot.

WT   Wild track.

XLS   Extra long shot.

Zoom lens   A lens whose focal length is infinitely variable between two extremes.

Zoom ratio   The ratio of the longest to the widest focal lengths. A 10 to 100mm zoom would be a 10:1 zoom.

BIBLIOGRAPHY AND FILM SOURCES

FINDING DOCUMENTARIES ON VIDEOTAPE

Documentaries are hard to find. Be aware that in the United States, all tapes are NTSC and cannot be played on PAL or SECAM equipment. Well-stocked videotheques are:

- Facets Multimedia, Inc., 1517 West Fullerton Avenue, Chicago, IL 60614 (Toll-free telephone: 1-800-331-6197, or 1-312-281-9075. e-mail: sales@facets.org). 26,000 films with reasonable prices. 300-page catalogue, knowledgeable and friendly staff, and tapes can even be rented by mail.
- Movies Unlimited, 3015 Darnell Road, Philadelphia, PA 19154. 24-hour mail order line: 1-800-466-8437. fax: 1-215-637-2350. Customer service: 9 am to 5 pm Eastern Standard Time at 1-800-668-4344. e-mail: movies@moviesunltd.com. Movies Unlimited has 50,000 films for sale and a 750-page catalog.

FINDING BOOKS

Bookstores are putting their list of wares on the Internet. An outstandingly useful site, with a million books listed, is that of Amazon of Seattle (http//:www.amazon.com), whose film section is very strong and even includes reviews by readers and comments by authors.

Writing and Directing

Rabiger, Michael. *Directing: Film Techniques and Aesthetics, 2nd ed.* Boston: Focal Press, 1997.

Rosenthal, Alan. *Writing, Directing, and Producing Documentary Films.* Carbondale, IL: Southern Illinois University Press, 1990.

Lighting

Box, Harry. *Set Lighting Technician's Handbook: Film Lighting Equipment, Practice, and Electrical Distribution, 2nd ed.* Boston: Focal Press, 1997.

Brown, Blain. *Motion Picture and Video Lighting, Revised ed.* Boston: Focal Press, 1996.

Carlson, Verne and Sylvia. *Professional Lighting Handbook, 2nd ed.* Boston: Focal Press, 1991.

Ferncase, Richard K. *Basic Lighting Worktext for Film and Video.* Boston: Focal Press, 1992.

Fitt, Brian and Joe Thornley. *Lighting by Design: A Technical Guide.* Boston: Focal Press, 1993.

Fitt, Brian and Joe Thornley. *The Control of Light.* Boston: Focal Press, 1993.

Lyver, Des and Graham Swainson. *Basics of Video Lighting.* Boston: Focal Press, 1995.

Malkiewicz, Kris. *Film Lighting.* New York: Prentice Hall, 1986.

Millerson, Gerald. *The Technique of Lighting for Television and Film, 3rd ed.* Boston: Focal Press, 1991.

Ritsko, Alan J. *Lighting for Location Motion Pictures.* New York: Van Nostrand Reinhold, 1979.

Samuelson, David W. *Motion Picture Camera and Lighting Equipment: Choice and Technique.* Boston: Focal Press, 1986.

Viera, David and Maria Viera. *Lighting for Film and Electronic Cinematography.* Belmont, CA: Wadsworth, 1993.

Video Cameras and Recording

Hodges, Peter. *The Video Camera Operator's Handbook.* Boston: Focal Press, 1995.

Lyver, Des and Graham Swainson. *Basics of Video Production.* Boston: Focal Press, 1995.

Millerson, Gerald. *Video Camera Techniques.* Boston: Focal Press, 1994.

Millerson, Gerald. *Video Production Handbook, 2nd ed.* Boston: Focal Press, 1992.

Ward, Peter. *Basic Betacam Camerawork.* Boston: Focal Press, 1994.

Watkinson, John. *Digital Compression in Video and Audio.* Boston: Focal Press, 1995.

Watkinson, John. *The Art of Digital Video, 2nd ed.* Boston: Focal Press, 1994.

Watkinson, John. *The Digital Videotape Recorder.* Boston: Focal Press, 1994.

Motion Picture Techniques

Arijon, Daniel. *Grammar of the Film Language.* Los Angeles: Silman-Janus, 1991.

Beacham, Frank, ed. *American Cinematographer's Video Manual*. Hollywood, CA: American Society of Cinematographers (issued regularly).

Bernstein, Steven. *Film Production, 2nd ed.* Boston: Focal Press, 1994.

Carlson, Verne and Sylvia. *Professional Cameraman's Handbook, 4th ed.* Boston: Focal Press, 1993.

Detmers, Fred, ed. *American Cinematographer's Handbook*. Hollywood, CA: American Society of Cinematographers (issued regularly.)

Happe, L. Bernard. *Basic Motion Picture Technology*. Boston: Focal Press, 1978.

Maier, Robert G. *Location Scouting and Management Handbook*. Boston: Focal Press, 1994.

Malkiewicz, J. Kris. *Cinematography: A Guide for Film Makers and Film Teachers, 2nd ed.* New York: Prentice Hall, 1989.

Pincus, Edward and Steven Ascher. *The Filmmakers Handbook*. New York: Plume, 1984.

Samuelson, David W. *"Hands-On" Manual for Cinematographers*. Boston: Focal Press, 1994.

Samuelson, David W. *Motion Picture Camera Techniques*. Boston: Focal Press, 1979.

Ward, Peter. *Picture Composition for Film and Television*. Boston: Focal Press, 1995.

Sound

Baert, Luc, Luc Theunissen, and Guido Vergult. *Digital Audio and Compact Disk Technology, 3rd ed.* Boston: Focal Press, 1995.

Bartlett, Bruce. *Stereo Microphone Techniques*. Boston: Focal Press, 1991.

Borwick, John. *Loudspeaker and Headphone Handbook, 2nd ed.* Boston: Focal Press, 1995.

Borwick, John. *Microphones: Technology and Technique*. Boston: Focal Press, 1990.

Borwick, John. *Sound Recording Practice, 4th ed.* Oxford: Oxford University Press, 1994.

Clifford, Martin. *Microphones: How They Work and How to Use Them.* Blue Ridge Summit, PA: Tab Books, 1977.

Ford, Ty. *Advanced Audio Production Techniques*. Boston: Focal Press, 1993.

Forlenza, Jeff and Terri Stone, eds. *Sound for Picture: An Inside Look at Audio Production for Film and Television*. Milwaukee, WI: Hal Leonard Publishers, 1993.

Hubatka, Milton C., Frederick Hull, and Richard W. Sanders. *Audio Sweetening for Film and TV*. Blue Ridge Summit, PA: Tab Books, 1985.

Huber, David Miles. *Microphone Manual: Design and Application*. Boston: Focal Press, 1988.

Lyver, Des. *Basics of Video Sound*. Boston: Focal Press, 1995.

Nisbett, Alec. *The Sound Studio, 6th ed.* Boston: Focal Press, 1995.

Nisbett, Alec. *The Technique of the Sound Studio, 3rd ed.* Boston: Focal Press, 1989.

Nisbett, Alec. *The Use of Microphones, 4th ed.* Boston: Focal Press, 1994.

Pendergast, Roy M. *Film Music, A Neglected Art, 2nd ed.* New York: W.W. Norton, 1992.

Pohlmann, Ken C. *Principles of Digital Audio.* Carmel, IN: Sams, 1991.

Rumsey, Francis. *An Introduction to Digital Audio.* Boston: Focal Press, 1994.

Rumsey, Francis. *Digital Audio Operations.* Boston: Focal Press, 1991.

Rumsey, Francis. *Sound and Sound Recording: An Introduction, 2nd ed.* Boston: Focal Press, 1994.

Watkinson, John. *The Art of Digital Recording, 2nd ed.* Boston: Focal Press, 1994.

White, Glenn D. *The Audio Dictionary.* Seattle: University of Washington Press, 1987.

Editing

Anderson, Gary H. *Video Editing and Post Production: A Professional Guide.* Boston: Focal Press, 1993.

Browne, Steven E. *Video Editing: A Postproduction Primer, 3rd ed.* Boston: Focal Press, 1997.

Burder, John. *The Technique of Editing 16mm Films.* Boston: Focal Press, 1988.

Dancyger, Ken. *The Technique of Film and Video Editing, 2nd ed.* Boston: Focal Press, 1997.

Hollyn, Norman. *The Film Editing Handbook.* Beverly Hills, CA: Lone Eagle, 1990.

Kerner, Marvin. *Art of the Sound Effects Editor.* Boston: Focal Press, 1989.

Ohanian, Thomas A. *Digital Nonlinear Editing.* Boston: Focal Press, 1993.

Reisz, Karel and Gavin Millar. *The Technique of Film Editing.* Boston: Focal Press, 1995.

Rosenblum, Ralph. *When the Shooting Stops . . . the Cutting Begins.* New York: Penguin, 1980.

Walter, Ernest. *The Technique of the Film Cutting Room.* Boston: Focal Press, 1982.

Documentary Theory, History, and Criticism

Andrew, Dudley. *Concepts in Film Theory.* New York: Oxford University Press, 1984.

Barsam, Richard Meran. *Nonfiction Film: A Critical History, 2nd ed.* Bloomington, IN: Indiana University Press, 1992.

Barsam, Richard Meran, ed. *Nonfiction Film Theory and Criticism.* New York: Dutton, 1976.

Barsam, Richard Meran. *The Vision of Robert Flaherty: The Artist as Myth and Filmmaker.* Bloomington, IN: Indiana University Press, 1988.

Barnouw, Erik. *Documentary: A History of Non-Fiction Film, 3rd ed.* New York: Oxford University Press, 1993.

Barnouw, Erik. *Nonfiction Film Theory and Criticism.* New York: Dutton, 1976.

Bordwell, David and Kristin Thompson. *Film Art: An Introduction, 3rd ed.* New York: McGraw Hill, 1990.

Burton, Julianne, ed. *The Social Documentary in Latin America.* Pittsburgh, PA: University of Pittsburgh Press, 1990.

Hardy, Forsyth. *John Grierson: A Documentary Biography.* London: Faber & Faber, 1979.

Jacobs, Lewis. *The Documentary Tradition: From Nanook to Woodstock.* New York: W. W. Norton, 1971.

Levin, G. Roy. *Documentary Explorations: Fifteen Interviews with Filmmakers.* Garden City, NY: Doubleday, 1971.

Lorentz, Pare. *Lorentz on Film: Movies 1927–1941.* Norman, OK: University of Oklahoma Press, 1986.

Moscovitch, Arlene. *Constructing Reality: Exploring Media Issues in Documentary.* Resource book and package of six videotapes. Education Office, Marketing D-5, National Film Board of Canada, PO Box 6100, Station A, Montreal, Quebec, H3C 3H5, Canada.

Nichols, Bill. *Representing Reality.* Bloomington, IN: Indiana University Press, 1991.

Papers presented at a conference at McGill University, Montreal, 1981. *John Grierson and the NFB.* Toronto: ECW Press, 1984.

Peyton, Patricia, ed. *Reel Change: A Guide to Social Issue Films.* San Francisco: Film Fund, 1979.

Renov, Michael, ed. *Theorizing Documentary.* New York: Routledge, 1993.

Rosenthal, Alan. *New Challenges for Documentary.* Berkeley, CA: University of California Press, 1988.

Rosenthal, Alan. *The Documentary Conscience: A Casebook in Filmmaking.* Berkeley; CA: University of California Press, 1980.

Rosenthal, Alan. *The New Documentary in Action.* Berkeley, CA: University of California Press, 1971.

Rotha, Paul. *Documentary Film.* London: Faber & Faber, 1939.

Finance and Distribution

Gates, Richard. *Production Management for Film and Video, 2nd ed.* Boston: Focal Press, 1995.

Goodell, Gregory. *Independent Feature Film Production.* New York: St. Martin's Press, 1982.

Levison, Louise. *Filmmakers and Financing: Business Plans for Independents.* Boston: Focal Press, 1994.

Matza, Aleks. *The Video Production Organizer.* Boston: Focal Press, 1995.

Singleton, Ralph. *Film Scheduling.* Los Angeles: Lone Eagle, 1991.

Wiese, Michael. *Film and Video Financing.* Boston: Focal Press, 1991.

Wiese, Michael. *Film and Video Marketing.* Boston: Focal Press, 1989.

Wiese, Michael. *The Independent Film and Videomaker's Guide, Revised and Enlarged Edition.* Boston: Focal Press, 1990.

Wiese, Michael and Deke Simon. *Film and Video Budgets.* Boston: Focal Press, 1995.

Education, Career Possibilities, and Career-Helpful Periodicals

Angell, Robert. *Film and Television: The Way In.* London: British Film Institute, 1988.

Bayer, William. *Breaking Through, Selling, Dropping Dead.* New York: Limelight Editions, 1989.

Bone, Jan. *Opportunities in Film.* Lincolnwood, IL: VGM Career Horizons, 1990.

Horwin, Michael. *Careers in Film and Video Production.* Boston: Focal Press, 1990.

International Documentary. Journal of the International Documentary Association, 1551 S. Robertson Boulevard, Suite 201, Los Angeles, CA 90035. Phone: +1-284-8422. Fax: +1-310-785-9334. e-mail idf@netcom.com

The Independent. AIVF Publications, 625 Broadway, 9th Floor, New York, NY 10012.

Lazarus, Paul. *Working in Film.* New York: Prentice Hall, 1992.

Petersons Guides to Graduate Programs in the Humanities, Arts, and Social Sciences. Princeton, NJ: Petersons (regularly published).

Videomaker. P.O. Box 469026, Escondido, CA 92046-9938.

INDEX

Abstraction, 65
Acknowledgments, 300–302, 312
Action
  deciding the, 130
  different angles on same, 63–65
  mobile coverage of complex, 218–19
Actor and the acted upon, 60–61
Actuality, creative treatment of, 201
Adams, Randall, 353
Address track, 259
Alekan, Henri, 92
"All in a Day," 250
Allen, Woody, 354
Alter egos, 41
Altman, Robert, 80, 211, 272, 349, 382
Amber group, 349
America, 319
American Cinematographer, 371, 385
American Dream, 29, 217
American Family, An, 357
*American Film Institute Guide to College
  Courses in Film and Television*, 371
American Society of Cinematographers, 385
Amps (rate of flow), 162
Analysis format, 77
Analysis projects, 70–96
Anderson, Lindsay, 349
Anderson Platoon, The, 27, 250, 331
Andrew, Dudley, 318
Angelico, Irene Lillienheim, 348
Angle of throw, 88
Anthem, national, 231–32
Anticipatory sound, 275
Antonia, 49
Apted, Michael, 135, 220, 229, 251, 327–28

Arthur, Paul, 319
Assembly, first, 245–48, 309
Associations, 384–85
Attitudes, negative, 204–5
Auden, W.H., 19–20
Audiences
  as active participants, 272
  contract with, 8–9
  contracts with, 250
  in direct relationship to interviewees, 183
  participation by, 184
  response of, 311
  witnessing interviewee and implied
    interviewer, 183–84
Auditions, voice, 283
Austen, Jane, 346
Authorial control, 345
Authority
  believing in one's, 182
  problem of having, 206
Authorship, 207–11, 356–64
  central, 345
  concessions and risk, 211
  covering important aspects, 210–11
  defining and fulfilling one's intentions, 208–9
  digging below surface, 209
  finding real meaning, 209
  measuring progress, 209
  scripting, 207–8
Authorship and factual footage, 14–16
Automatic controls, 156–57
Axis
  camera, 59–60
  camera-to-subject, 59–60
  the, 59–60

Baba Kiueria, 354
Backgrounds, overbright, 168
Backlighting, 91, 167
Ballard, Carroll, 77
Bar code, 260
Barbie, Klaus, 343
Barnouw, Eric, 25, 316
Barsam, Richard Meran, 316
Batteries, rechargeable, 157
Battle of Cable Street, The, 191
Battleship Potemkin, The, 21
BBC, 144, 349
   "All in a Day," 250
   Debussy, 342
   Elgar, 342
   Golub, 342
   One Pair of Eyes, 174
   Rousseau, 342
   Video Diaries, 32–33
   Video Diaries series, 348
   Warrendale, 29–30
   Yesterday's Witness, 175, 341
BCU (big close-up), 215
Beatles, 346
Beauty and the Beast, 92
Behalfers defined, 319
Being, habits of, 192
Bell, Martin, 214
Bennett, Alan, 45
Bergman, Ingmar, 92
Berlinger, Joe, 216
Best Boy, 9, 179, 216, 222, 348
Birth of a Nation, 15
Black Stallion, The, 77
Blank, Les, 251, 337–38, 342
Block, Mitchell, 354
Blocking, 82–83
Blumenthal, Jerry, 342
Bone, Jan, 385
Bookends time structuring, 250
Boot, Das, 13
Bounce cards, 165
Brecht, Bertolt, 19
Breitrose, Henry, 319
Bresson, Robert, 50
Brico, Antonia, 49
Brief History of Time, A, 84
British Union of Fascists, 361
Brittain, Donald, 353
Britten, Benjamin, 19
Broad lighting, 91
Broomfield, Nicholas, 5–6, 137, 190, 222, 340

Brother's Keeper, 33, 216
Brown, Jim, 18, 326
Budget control, and logs, 169
Budget planning forms, 119–24
   budget summary, 124
   budget worksheet, 120
   postproduction costs, 123
   preproduction costs, 120
   production costs, 121–22
Bulbs, quartz, 167
Buñuel, Luis, 21–22, 334, 339
Bunyan, John, 252
Burden of Dreams, 337–38
Burns, Ken, 208, 230, 331
Bus, The, 28
Buzz tracks, 187, 204, 285
Bystanders, 142
Böll, Heinrich, 250

Cable television, 30
Camcorders and sound, 158–59
Camera-to-subject axis, 59–60, 88
Camera
   axis, 59–60
   bodies, 155
   compromises for, 192–93
   handheld, 199
   handling projects, 105
   handling theory, 104–5
   how people alter in front of, 131–32
   movements, 196
   operators, 146–47, 186–87
   panning, 60
   perceptions by, 59
   placement, 182–84
   positioning, 196
   support systems, 157–58
   tripod-mounted, 199
   use of, 80
Cardioid mikes, 158
Cards, bounce, 165
Career, planning a, 367
Cartier-Bresson, Henri, 337
Cassavetes, John, 26, 349
Casting the players, 130
Catalyst cinema, 219–27
Cathy Come Home, 352–2
Cavalcanti, Alberto, 21
CDs (compact disks), 31–32
Central authorship, 345
CG (character generator), 259, 301

Character in film, 324–26
Characters within films, multiple, 326–28
Charlie, Bonnie Prince, 352
Charnov, Elaine, 355
Charts
    mix, 296–97, 311
    flow, 288–90
Checkerboard fashion defined, 258
Checking, double, 132
Checklist, preproduction, 149–52
Chest mikes, 158
Chicken Ranch, 340
Childhood stories, 46
Chronicle of a Summer, 224, 229, 334–35
Churchill, Joan, 5–6, 137, 222
Cinéma vérité, 25–29, 219–27, 348, 354
    elements, 325
    movement, 334
Cinemas
    catalyst, 219–27
    compilations, 213
    direct, 25–29, 212–19
    eclectic, 213, 233–38
    essays, 213, 230–33
    observational, 212–19
    reflexive, 227–30
Citizen Kane, 91
Civil War, The, 208, 230, 331, 341
Clarification, 6–7
Cleo from Five Till Seven, 250
Coal Face, 19
Cocteau, Jean, 92
Code, bar, 260
Collins, Judy, 49
Collins, Wilkie, 139
Color balance, 156–57
Color temperatures, 156
    problems, 165
    working with different, 165–66
Compilation cinema, 213
Complaints of a Dutiful Daughter, 227, 342
Composition
    dynamic, 73–74
    external, 74–75
    form, and function, 75–76
    internal, 74–75
    static, 71–72
Concentration, 66
Concepts in Film Theory, 318
Concerned Observer, 59
Conflicts, 135–36, 221–23
Confrontation, 135–36

Consciousness, how editing mimics, 268–69
Constructs, 56
Contact number, prearranged, 140
Content influences form, 244–45
Contracts with audiences, 250
Contrast problems, 165
Control, 344–50
Controls
    authorial, 345
    automatic, 156–57
    exposure, 156
Conversation, two-person, 221–23
Cooperation, participants, 346
Corporation for Public Broadcasting, 385
Costs
    postproduction, 123
    preproduction, 120
    production, 121–22
Counterpoint, 270–71
Cousteau, Jacques Yves, 358
Craft skills, 381
Craft workers, 382
Cramlington Train-Wreckers, The, 196
Creative identity
    finding one's, 37–43
    finding one's life issues, 39
    finding one's work path, 42–43
    projects, 39–42
        alter egos, 41
        goals summary, 43
        self-inventory, 39–41
        using dreams to find one's preoccupations, 42
Creative treatment of actuality, 201
Crew
    defining areas of responsibility, 145
    developing a, 143–52
    directing, 202–6
    drawing up a want list, 149–52
    equipment selection, 149–52
    human breakdowns, 171
    preproduction checklist, 149–52
    roles and responsibilities, 145–49
        camera operators, 146–47
        directors, 145–46
        gaffers, 147
        grips, 148
        production managers (PMs), 148–49
        sound recordists, 147–48
    temperaments of, 144
    thanking, 200
    using people with experience, 143

Crib notes, 197–99
Critics
    making use of what they say, 291–92
    surviving one's, 291–92
Cross-checking people's impressions, 132
Crumb, 33, 223, 328
Crumb, Robert, 328
CS (close shot), 102
Culloden, 352
Cut-ins defined, 204
Cutaway shots, 204
Cuts
    final, 293
    fine, 293, 310–11
    L, 275
    lap, 275
    overlap, 272–75
    rough, 309
Cyber Film School, 370

Dailies, 11–12, 56
Dark Lullabies, 348
Davis, Peter, 28, 132, 331
Day for Night, 113
Death of a Princess, 353
Death of a Salesman, 26
Debussy, 342
Desktop production, digital, 12
Development
    need for, 135–36
    psychological, 136
    time and structure, 336–43
Devices, transitional, 67
Diagnostic form, editing, 289
Dialectics, finding, 133–34
Dialogue sequences, 272–74
Digital desktop production, 12
Digital production, from tape to, 261
Digital video, 30–31
Digitizing for nonlinear editing, 261–62
Direct Cinema, 20, 25–29, 212–19
Directing: Film Techniques and Aesthetics, 350
Directing and
    crews, 202–6
        communication, 202–3
        instructing, 203–4
        maintaining communication, 203
        monitoring, 203–4
        negative attitudes in profession, 204–5
        problem of having authority, 206
        scheduling, 202–3
        working atmosphere, 205

participants, 188–201
    and camera movement, 196
    and camera positioning, 196
    chance...?, 196–97
    compromises for camera, 192–93
    crib notes, 197–99
    habits of being, 192
    handheld cameras, 199
    limits to the form, 201
    maintaining screen direction, 193–95
    mindbody connection, 189–90
    obstacles, 192
    scene breakdown, 197–99
    in search of naturalness, 188–89
    self-consciousness, 190–91
    self-image, 190–91
    special photography, 200
    thanking crew and participants, 200
    tripod-mounted cameras, 199
    using social times and breaks, 200
    why motives for filming matter,
        191–92
    wrapping, 200
    reflexivity, 358–59
Direction
    maintaining screen, 193–95
    screen, 62–63
Directional mikes, 158
Directors, 145–46
    craft of, 7–8
    evolution of good, 38
Discovery Channel, 30
Dissonance, 270
Distributors, 17
Docudrama, 351–55, 352–53
Documentaries
    fairness and, 6–7
    fake, 354–55
    and television, 29–30
    and time, 3
    video, 10–12
    what are, 201
*Documentary: A History of the Non-Fiction
    Film,* 25, 316
Documentary
    as an organized story, 4
    bearing witness to present time, 12
    coinage of term, 16
    contract with audience, 8–9
    as creative treatment of actuality, 3
    defined, 3–6
    director's craft, 7–8
    elements of, 321–43

European, 21
as exposure to life, 363–64
and fiction, 345
fidelity to actual versus realism, 4
film, 10–12
filmmakers and media, 10
form, control, and identity, 349–50
history of, 13–34
    advances in form, 23–24
    authorship and factual footage, 14–16
    cinéma vérité, 25–29
    developments in technology, 30–33
    direct cinema, 25–29
    documentaries and television, 29–30
    on film language, 13–14
    future of documentaries, 33–34
    invention of, 16–23
individualities and points of view, 4
is often wrongly labeled, 7
is subjective construct, 7
issues, 316–18
language, 347–49
makers as dramatists, 265–66
mission, 356–364
objectivity, 6–7
point of view (POV), 322–36
    character in film, 324–26
    intercession, 323–24
    multiple characters within films, 326–28
    observation, 323–24
    omniscient, 328–31
    personal, 331–33
    reflexive, 333–36
    single point of view, 324–26
as presence and consciousness, 5–6
project proposal helper, 117–19
proposals, 113–26, 383
range of forms, 4
sizing up ingredients, 321–22
    picture, 321–22
    sound, 322
as social art, 6
as socially critical, 3–4
theory, 315–20
    and film, 318
    history, 316
    issue of representation, 315–20
    it comes down to point of view, 319–20
time, development, and structure, 336–43
Documentary Conscience, The, 316
Dollies, 157
Dollying, 62
Donors Forum, 384

Don't Look Now, 76
Double-checking one's findings, 132
DP (director of photography), 145
Dr. Spock: We're Sliding Towards Destruction,
    174, 285
Dramadoc, 352–53
Dramatic curve, 136–39
Dramatic tension, 138–39
Dramatist, documentary maker as, 265–66
Dramatizing a location, 213–15
Dreams, using to find one's preoccupations,
    42
Drew, Robert, 24
du Maurier, Daphne, 76
Duration, 66
DV (digital video), 256–59
Dynamic composition, 73–74

Eclectic cinema, 213, 233–38
Eden Valley, 349–50
Edit
    assembling paper, 253–54
    paper, 249–54
        story structures, 251–53
        time and structural alternatives, 250
        why a structure matters, 249–50
Editing, 307
    analysis, 76–83
        point of view (POV), 82
        use of camera, 80
    changing technology, 256–59
    complex projects, 306–12
    counterpoint, 271
    diagnostic form, 289
    digitizing for nonlinear, 261–62
    ellipses, 216, 305
    end game, 288–302
        mix charts, 296–97
        acknowledgments, 300–302
        diagnosis, 288–90
        fine cut, 293
        first showing, 290–91
        getting titles made commercially, 302
        making flow charts, 288–90
        making use of what critics say, 291–92
        preparation, 294–95
        sound mix, 291–94
        sound track hierarchy, 295–96
        surviving one's critics, 291–92
        titles, 300–302
        try, try again, 292–93
        uses of procrastination, 292

Editing (*Cont.*):
first assembly, 255–67
  after the dust settles, what next?, 266–67
  after the first viewing, 263
  changing editing technology, 256–59
  deciding on an ideal length, 263
  diagnostic questioning, 264
  digitizing for nonlinear editing, 261–62
  documentary maker as dramatist, 265–66
  finding equipment, 255
  making visible significant, 266
  material that doesn't work, 264–65
  putting first assembly together, 262
  return to innocence, 262–63
  time code: off-line to on-line editing,
    259–61
  video: from tape to digital production, 261
linear video, 11
machine-to-machine tape, 256
nonlinear, 11–12
off-line to on-line, 259–61
process, 243, 361–62
process of refinement, 268–75
  an analogy in music, 269–70
  audience as active participants, 272
  counterpoint in practice, 270–71
  dialogue sequences, 272–74
  editing rhythms, 269–70
  how editing mimics consciousness, 268–69
  looking at and looking through, 269
  overlap cut, 272–75
  problem of achieving a flow, 268
  sequence transitions, 274–75
  understanding editing, 275
  unifying material into a flow, 270–71
theory, 241–42
understanding, 275
Editors
control of sound levels, 291
role and responsibilities, 242–43
EDL (edit decision list), 160, 262
Education, 367–80
getting started, 367–68
good film schools, 369–70
international film schools, 372–80
and Internet and researching for right school,
  370–71
planning a career, 367
researching for right school, 370–71
self, 367
self-help as a realistic alternative, 380
to school or not to school, 368–69

Egos, alter, 41
Eisenstein, Sergei, 21
Eisler, Hans, 286
Electret mikes, 158
Elgar, 342
Ellipsis
editing, 216, 305
shooting for, 184–85
Equipment
breakdowns, 170–71
finding, 255
selection, 149–52, 155–63
  automatic controls, 156–57
  camcorders and sound, 158–59
  camera bodies, 155
  camera support systems, 157–58
  color balance, 156–57
  exposure controls, 156
  lenses, 155–56
  lighting instruments, 160–62
  monitors, 159
  picture gain, 156–57
  power calculations, 162
  power supplies, 157
  sound equipment, 158
sound, 158
Essay cinema, 213, 230–33
Ethics, 356–64
European documentaries, 21
Events
centered films, 336–37
one-shot, catalyzed, 224
perception of, 65
Evidence, integrity of, 362
Experience, using people with, 143
Exposure controls, 156
Exteriors, voice recording experiments for,
  101–3
External composition, 74–75
Eyes on the Prize, 331

f-stop, 156
"Faces of Paris," 251
Facts and narration, 139
Factual footage, and authorship, 14–16
Fairness, 6–7
Fake documentaries, 354–55
Family stories, 46
Fassbinder, Rainer Werner, 350
Featherstone, Ken, 354
Fellini, Federico, 133

Fiction, 47
  and documentary, 345
  films, 349–50
Field, Connie, 179, 220, 342
Fill lights, 165
Film
  at location facilities, 141–42
  bureaus, 384
  character in, 324–26
  commissions, 384
  and documentary theory, 318
  event-centered, 336–37
  historical, 340–43
  journey, 337–39
  language, 13–14, 55
  participants living with consequences of,
    357
  process, 337
  schools, 369–70, 372–80
  technique, learning, 55–56
  walled-city, 339–40
Film noir, 354
Film and Video Budgets, 2nd ed., 385
Filming, why motives matter, 191–92
Filmmakers
  responsibilities of, 357
  and media, 10
Filmography of Michael Rabiger, 391–92
Films
  always in present tense, 57
  developing thematic structure of, 132
  fiction, 349–50
  multiple characters within, 326–28
  New Wave, 349
  popularity of, 34
  subject-driven, 50–51
  subject-driven versus character-driven,
    50–51
  trying out, 292–93
  and videotapes compared, 169–70
Final cut, 293
Fine cut, 293, 310–11
Fires Were Started, 20, 24, 337
First assembly, 309
  editing, 255–67
  selecting sections for, 245–48
First impressions, 78–79
First, Ruth, 353
First showing, 290–91
First viewing, 77
Fishpole defined, 158
Fitzcarraldo, 337

Fixture, lighting, 160
Flaherty, Robert, 16–17, 23, 324–27
Floor plan, making and using a, 77–78
Flow charts, 288–90
Focusing lamps, 160
Form, 75–76
  advances in, 23–24
  budget planning, 119–24
  content influences, 344–45
  control, and identity, 344–50
    authorial control, 345
    content influences form, 244–45
    documentary, 349–50
    documentary language, 347–49
    fiction and documentary, 345
    fiction films, 349–50
    future, 349–50
    limits on range of subjects, 345–46
    participants cooperation, 346
    resistance to personal viewpoint, 346–47
  editing diagnostic, 289
  personal release, 140–41
  and self-expression, 38
Format, analysis, 77
Forms
  budget planning, 119–124
  personal release, 187
Free cinema movement, 349
Fresnel lights, 160–62
From the Journals of Jean Seberg, 45
Frontal lighting, 88–90
Function, 75–76
Funds, 383–84

Gaffers, 147
Gap-Toothed Women, 251, 342
Garlic Is as Good as Ten Mothers, 251, 342
Gates of Heaven, 342
Germany, Nazi, 13
Gilbert, Peter, 4
Gimme Shelter, 26–27
Glass, Philip, 286, 353
Godard, Jean-Luc, 133, 193
Godmillow, Jill, 49
Gold, Jack, 353
Golub, 342
Grab shooting, 143
Graininess, 157
Gray, Lorraine, 342
Great War, The, 14, 331, 341, 348
Grierson, John, 3, 16, 18–19, 201

Griffith, D. W., 15
Grips, 148

Habits of being, 192
Handheld cameras, 199
Hard lights, 160, 166–67
Hard-edged shadows, 166
Harlan County, USA, 28–29, 215, 217, 327–28, 348
Harmony, 270
HBO (Home Box Office), 30, 348
Headphones, 158
Heaney, Seamus, 173–74
Hearts and Minds, 28, 132, 331
Height of shadow, 88
Helfand, Judy, 336
Help, self, 380
Herzog, Werner, 13, 113, 224, 325–26, 336, 380
High School, 252, 339
High school students, 33
Historical films, 340–43
History, 45
   making, 230–31
   social, 46–47
Hitler, Adolf, 6, 22, 336
Hoffman, Deborah, 227, 342
Holdover sounds, 275
Hood, Stuart, 352
Hoop Dreams, 4–5, 10–11, 33
Hospital, 130, 252, 339
Hotel Terminus: The Life and Times of Klaus Barbie, 342–43
How the Myth Was Made, 18, 326
Human breakdowns, 171
Hypothesis, working, 133–35

IDA (International Documentary Association), 384
IDA Membership Directory and Survival Guide, 385
Ideas, developing story, 44–51
Identity, 344–50
   creative, 37–43
   and mission, 364
Implied interviewer, 183–84
Impressions, first, 78–79
In Heaven There is No Beer, 251, 342
In the White City, 349
Independent Film and Videomaker's Guide, 2nd ed., 385

Independent Television Service, 384
Independent, The, 371
Innocence, return to, 262–63
Inserts, 204
Instruments, lighting, 160–62
Intentions, defining and fulfilling one's, 208–9
Interactive video, 30–31
Intercession, 323–24
Interference, radio frequency (RF), 158–59
Interiors, voice recording experiments for, 100–101
Internal composition, 74–75
International Documentary, 384
International Documentary Association Journal, 371
International film schools, 372–80
Internet, 370–71
Internships, 382
Interviewers
   and camera placement, 182–84
   editing out voices of, 179
   implied, 183–84
Interviewing, 173–87
   audience participation, 184
   believing in one's authority, 182
   brevity, 180–81
   briefing camera operators, 186–87
   concluding interview, 187
   editing out interviewer's voice, 179
   framing questions, 177–78
   guidelines for effective, 178–79
   in-depth interviews, 180
   interviewer and camera placement, 182–84
   preparation and basic skills, 176
   pushing boundaries, 181
   right order for questions, 181–82
   setting people at ease, 176–77
   shooting alternatives, 185–86
   shooting for ellipsis, 184–85
   types of situations, 175–76
   who interviews, 174
   why it matters, 173–74
Interviews
   in depth, 219–20
   job, 381
   one subject, 105–6
   simple, 284–85
Interviews with My Lai Veterans, 28
Introduction to the Enemy, 28
Inventory structuring, 251
ITV, 349
Ivens, Joris, 21, 330

Jam sync defined, 262
James, Henry, 68
James, Steve, 4
Janacek, Leos, 66
Jennings, Humphrey, 20, 23–24, 337
Job interviews, 381
Journals, 44–45, 384–85
    American Cinematographer, 371
    Independent, The, 371
    *International Documentary Association
        Journal,* 371
    Videomaker, 371, 385
Journey films, 337–39

Key light direction, 167
Keycode, 160
Kimbrell, Marketa, 37
King Lear, 47
Kissinger, Henry, 131
Klein, Jim, 342
Kopple, Barbara, 29, 215, 217, 327–28
Koyaanisqatsi, 286
Kuehl, Jerry, 341

L cuts, 275
La Soufrière, 336
Lamps; *See also* Lighting; Lights
    focusing, 160
    open-face quartz, 160
Land of Silence and Darkness, 224, 325–26
Land Without Bread, 21–22, 334, 339
Language
    documentary, 347–49
    film, 13–14
Lanzmann, Claude, 223, 342
Lap cuts, 275
Lavalier microphones, 100, 158
Leacock, Ricky, 24
Leader, The Driver, and the Driver's Wife, The,
    190
Legends, and myths, 45–46
Leigh, Mike, 349–50
Lenses, 155–56
Lessing, Doris, 346
Letter, video, 232–33
Life, documentary as exposure to, 363–64
Life experiences, dramatic, 38
Life issues, finding one's, 39
Life and Times of Rosie the Riveter, The, 179,
    342

Lighting, 164–68
    adding to a base, 166
    analysis, 84–96
    avoiding overbright backgrounds, 168
    back, 91
    broad, 91, 167
    color-temperature problems, 165
    contrast problems, 165
    defining shadows, 166–67
    fixtures, 160
    frontal, 88–90
    how much is enough light?, 167–68
    instruments, 160–62
    key light direction, 167
    narrow, 91
    reactions to, 168
    setups, 88–91
    silhouette, 91
    terminology, 84–88
    using a key light, 166
    when one needs it, 164
    working with different color temperatures,
        165–66
    working with light sources, 165–66
Lights; *See also* Lamps; Lighting
    fill, 165
    fresnel, 160–62
    hard, 160, 166–67
    key, 166
    quartz bulbs, 167
    shadowless working, 167
    soft, 160, 166–67
Linear video editing, 11
List, drawing up a want, 149–52
Listen to Britain, 20
Listening, 131
Literature and Film, 133, 265–66
Loach, Ken, 349
Locations
    dramatizing, 213–15
    filming at, 141–42
Logging, 308
Logs and budget control, 169
London Labour and the London Poor,
    15–16
Long Journey to Guadalupe, A, 337
López, Ana M., 319
Lorentz, Pare, 18, 138, 230–31, 330–31, 337,
    341
Lost Honor of Katharina Blum, The, 250
Loud family, 357
Louisiana Story, 23–24, 324

Lowry, Malcolm, 353
Lumieres brothers, 69
Luminaire defined, 160
Luther, Martin, 45

*M*A*S*H*, 272
McElwee, Ross, 32, 190, 223, 251, 335–36, 337–39, 348, 359
Machine-to-machine tape editing, 256
Madness of King George, The, 45
Magazines, 45
Malle, Louis, 92, 250–51, 332, 346
Man of Aran, 17, 326
Man with the Movie Camera, The, 20–21, 334
Marker, Chris, 32–33
Markets, search for, 383
Marx, Fred, 4
Materials
    collecting raw, 44–47
    that do not work, 264–65
    that misfire, 264–65
    unifying into a flow, 270–71
Maupassant, Guy de, 346
Mayhew, Henry, 15–16
Maysles, Albert, 25–27, 137, 215, 217, 252, 324–25
Maysles, David, 25–27, 137, 215, 217, 252, 324–25
Me and My Matchmaker, 228, 346–47
Meaning, finding real, 209
Media, and filmmakers, 10
Medium Cool, 28–29
Medium, using the, 49–50
Metaphoric journey structuring, 251
Metaphorical roles, 130–31
Microphones
    cardioid, 158
    chest, 158
    directional, 158
    electret, 158
    lavalier, 158
    omnidirectional, 158
    operators of, 158
    radio, 158
    reception patterns, 100
        cardioid, 100
        directional, 100
        omnidirectional, 100
Mikes; *See* Microphones
Mindbody connection, 189–90

Minh-ha, Trinh H., 319
Mission, 356–64
    and identity, 364
    and philosophy, 363
Mix
    charts, 296–97, 311
    sound, 293–94, 312
Moana, 16
Mockumentaries, 354–55
Moments, privileged, 182
Monitors, 159
Moore, Michael, 226–27, 231, 348, 358
Morin, Edgar, 229
Morris, Erroll, 5, 84, 179, 185, 226, 286, 342, 348, 353–54
Mosley, Sir Oswald, 191, 361
Moss, Robb, 359
Motion Picture Archive, 370
Motivation
    for camera movement, 196
    for camera positioning, 196
Motives for filming, 191–92
Movement
    horizontal, 62
    motivation for camera, 196
    physical, 135–36
    in time, 135–36
    vertical, 62
Munch, 333, 342
Munich action-teater, 350
Murphy's Law, 146, 245
Music
    part of postproduction checklist, 310
    using, 286–87
Myths and legends, 45–46

Naked, 349
Nanook of the North, 16–18, 49–50, 324–25
Narration, 276–87, 309–10
    as an option, 276
    creating improvised, 284–85
        improvising from an identity, 284
        improvising from rough scripts, 284
        simple interviews, 284–85
    drawbacks and associations of 276–77
    and facts, 139
    fitting, 285
    positive aspects of, 277
    recording presence track, 285

scripted, 278–84
    accommodating sound features, 280
    adjusting syntax, 279
    auditioning, 283
    complement, don't duplicate, 282
    operative words, 281–82
    power in each first word, 280–81
    recording and directing narrators, 283–84
    scratch recording, 282
    scripts for narrators, 282
    trying it out, 282
    tryouts, 279
    voice auditions, 283
    writing, 278–79
  two approaches to, 278
  using music, 286–87
Narrators
  recording and directing, 283–84
  scripts for, 282
Narrow lighting, 91
Nashville, 211
Nathan, Irene, 346
National anthem, 231–32
National Film Board of Canada, Volcano, 353
Naturalness, in search of, 188–89
Nazis, 13, 22–23
Negative attitudes, 204–5
NEH (National Endowment for the
    Humanities), 384
Neidik, Abbey, 348
New Challenges for Documentary, 316–17, 333,
    354
New Documentary in Action, The, 316
New Wave films, 349
Newspapers, 45
Nichols, Bill, 319
Night and Fog, 23, 230, 286, 341
Night Mail, 19, 327
Ninety Days, 353
Nixon, Richard, 132
No Lies, 354
Noise, picture, 157
Nonchronological structures, 250
Nonfiction Film: A Critical History, 316
Nonlinear editing, 11–12
Nonlinear editing, digitizing for, 261–62
Notes, crib, 197–99
Nykvist, Sven, 92

Objectivity, 6–7, 66
Observation, 323–24

Observational cinema, 212–19
Observer
  concerned, 59
  observing, 228
Off-line rig, 260
Olympia, 22, 336
Olympiad, 330
Omnidirectional mikes, 158
Omniscient, 328–31
"One Pair of Eyes," 174, 285
Open-face quartz lamps, 160
Operators
  camera, 146–47
  mike, 158
Ophuls, Marcel, 28, 211, 342, 348
Opportunities in Film Careers, 385
Opticals defined, 307
Orchestra Rehearsal, The, 133
OS (over-the-shoulder), 217
Osborne, John, 45
Overlap cut, 272–75
Owen, Wilfrid, 174

Panning, camera, 60
Paper cuts
  preparing for a, 308
  structural considerations, 308
Paper edit, 249–54, 308–9
Parallel storytelling, 184–85
Participants
  approaching, 358
  audience as active, 272
  cooperation of, 346
  directing, 188–201
  thanking, 200
Partnership, research, 139
PBS (Public Broadcasting System), 33,
    385
  A Program Producer's Handbook, 385
  An American Family, 357
  Eyes on the Prize, 331
  POV, 33, 348
  The Great War, 14, 331, 348
Peet, Stephen, 49, 341
People
  cross-checking impressions of, 132
  how they alter in front of camera,
    131–32
  setting at ease, 176–77
  using experienced, 143
  voice of, 224–27

Perceptions
  by cameras, 59
  of events, 65
Personal release forms, 140–41, 187
Petersen, Wolfgang, 13
Phantom India, 151, 332, 346
Philosophy and mission, 363
Photography, special, 200
Physical movement, 135–36
Picture gain, 156–57
Picture noise, 157
Pilgrim's Progress, 252
Players, casting the, 130
Plow That Broke the Plains, The, 18–19,
  230–31, 330–31, 341
PMs (production managers), 148–49
Portfolio, 381
Postproduction, 241–48
  case for making transcripts, 244
  checklist, 307–12
    mix charts, 311
    acknowledgments, 312
    assembling paper edit, 308–9
    diagnostic method, 311
    editing, 307
    evoking a trial audience response, 311
    fine cut, 310–11
    first assembly, 309
    logging, 308
    music, 310
    narration, 309–10
    paper cut structural considerations,
      308
    preparing for paper cuts, 308
    rough cut, 309
    selecting sections, 308
    sound mix, 312
    titles, 312
    track laying, 311
    transcripts, 308
  costs, 123
  editing process begins, 243
  editing theory, 241–42
  editor's role and responsibilities, 242–43
  logging rushes, 244–45
  overview, 241–48
  projects, 303–12
    complex editing projects, 306–12
    conversation, two or more persons, 304
    editing for ellipses, 305
    interview, 303–4
    varying image sizes, 303–4

  selecting sections for first assembly, 245–48
  viewing rushes, 243
POV, 348
POVs (points of view), 82–83, 217, 269, 319–20
  shots, 306
  subjective structuring, 250–51
Power consumption in amps, 162
Power supplies, 157
Practicals defined, 89, 166
Preinterview, 131–32
Premix defined, 258
Preproduction, 113
  checklists, 149–52
  costs, 120
Presence, 187
Presence tracks
  defined, 204
  recording, 285
Presenting oneself, 385–86
Pretty Baby, 92
Prisoners of Conscience, 210
Privileged moments defined, 182
Problems
  avoiding, 169–72
    equipment breakdowns, 170–71
    having alternatives, 72
    human breakdowns, 171
    logs and budget control, 169
    shooting ratios, 170
    videotapes and film compared, 169–70
  finding, 98–99
Process films, 337
Procrastination, uses of, 292
*Producer's Guide to Public Television Funding,
  The,* 385
Production
  checklist, 235–38
    authorship, 238
    before interviewing, 235
    crew and scheduling, 237–38
    ensuring variety, 236
    preparation to get proper coverage, 236
    shooting in general, 237
    social skills, 237
    when interviewing, 235–36
  costs, 121–22
  digital desktop, 12
  from tape to digital, 261
  projects, 212–38
    catalyst cinema, 219–27
    cinéma vérité, 219–27
    compilation cinema, 213

compilation and essay cinema, 230–33
covering a conversation (exterior), 216–18
direct cinema, 212–13
direct or observational cinema (handheld), 216–19
direct or observational cinema (tripod), 213–15
dramatizing a location, 213–15
eclectic cinema, 213, 233–38
ellipsis editing, 216
essay cinema, 213
final project, 233–38
interview in depth, 219–20
making history, 230–31
metaphoric counterpoint, 224–27
mobile coverage of complex action, 218–19
national anthem, 231–32
observational cinema, 212–13
observing observer, 228
one-shot, catalyzed event, 224
reflexive cinema, 227–30
self-portrait, 227–28
story, question, and suggestion, 228–30
three-person conversation (interior), 215
two-person conversation with conflict, 221–23
unbroken five-minute story, 223–24
video letter, 232–33
vox populi interviews, 224–27
Profession, negative attitudes in, 204–5
Program Producer's Handbook, A, 385
Progress, measuring, 209
Projects
analysis, 70–96
basic shooting, 97–110
production, 212–38
VISIONS, 224
Propos de Nice, A, 330
Proposals
documentary, 116–19, 383
helper, 117–19
and treatments, 119
Prospectus, 124–26
Proust, Marcel, 68
Psychological development, 136
Public interest, 33
Public showing, 362–63

Quartz bulbs, 167
Quartz lamps, open-face, 160
Questioning, diagnostic, 264

Quinn, Aiden, 190
Quinn, Gordon, 342

Rabiger, Michael, 134, 174, 181–82, 285, 350, 391–92
Radio mikes, 158
Rain, 330
Rappoport, Mark, 45
Raw, materials collecting, 44–47
Re-enactment, 351–55
Reagan, Ronald, 132
Realism, fidelity to actual versus, 4–5
Rechargeable batteries, 157
Recognition, shock of, 44
Reconstruction, 351–55
Recording
and directing narrators, 283–84
presence track, 285
scratch, 282
Recordists, sound, 147–48
Red Shoes, The, 334
Reflexive cinema, 227–30
Reflexivity
and directing, 358–59
and filmmaker, 334–36
Reggio, Godfrey, 286
Reichert, Julia, 342
Reisch, Karel, 349
Release forms, personal, 140–41, 187
Remnant of a Feudal Society, A, 134, 175, 362
Renov, Michael, 318
Representing Reality, 319
Research
and documentary proposals, 113–26
leading up to shoot, 127–42
overview, 114–15
partnership, 139
relationships, 128
strategies, 128–29
Resistance to personal viewpoint, 346–47
Resnais, Alain, 23, 230, 341
Responsibility, defining areas of, 145
Retour, Le, 337
RF (radio frequency) interference, 158–59
Rhythm, 66, 73
Richardson, Robert, 133, 265–66
Richardson, Tony, 349
Riefenstahl, Leni, 22, 330, 336
Rig, off-line, 260
Riggs, Marlon, 354
River, The, 18, 20, 138, 230, 330–31, 337, 341

Roeg, Nicholas, 76
Roger and Me, 33, 225–27, 231, 348, 358
Roles, assigning metaphorical, 130–31
Room tone, 187, 204, 285
Rosenblum, Ralph, 242–43
Rosenthal, Alan, 316, 354
Rosie the Riveter, 220
Rostock, Suzanne, 336
Rouch, Jean, 25, 182, 224, 229, 334–35
Rough cut, 309
Rousseau, 342
Rubbernecks defined, 142
Rubbo, Michael, 228, 250–51, 335
Ruby, Jay, 226, 333
Rushes, 11–12, 56
   logging, 244–45
   viewing, 243
Russell, Ken, 342
Rustling of Leaves, 6
Ruttmann, Walter, 21

Sacco and Vanzetti, trial of, 352
Sad Song of Yellow Skin, 228, 250, 335
Salesman, 26, 137, 215, 252, 324
Sandford, Jeremy, 352–53
Scene breakdown, 197–99
Schindler, Oskar, 45
Schindler's List, 13, 45
Schlesinger, John, 214
Schlöndorff, Volker, 250
Schoendoerffer, Pierre, 27, 250, 331–32
Schools
   good film, 369–70
   international film, 372–80
   Internet for researching, 370–71
   to school or not to, 368–69
Schuurman, Otto, 355
Science, social, 46–47
Scratch recording, 282
Screen direction, 62–63
   changing, 63
   maintaining, 193–95
Screen grammar, 55–69
   abstraction, 65
   actor and acted upon, 60–61
   the axis, 59–60
   concentration, 66
   different angles on same action, 63–65
   duration, 66
   horizontal movement through space,
      62
   rhythm, 66

screen direction, 62–63
screen language in summary, 67–69
sequence, 67
shots
   denotation and connotation, 57
   in juxtaposition, 57–58
subjectivity versus objectivity, 66
subtext, 62
transitional devices, 67
transitions, 67
vertical movement through space, 62
Screen language in summary, 67–69
Screencraft
   analysis projects, 70–96
   editing analysis, 76–83
      analysis format, 77
      defining blocking, 82–83
      defining point of view, 82–83
      definition and statistics, 79–80
      first impressions, 78–79
      first viewing, 77
      making and using a floor plan, 77–79
      strategy for study, 78
      use of sound, 80–81
   lighting analysis, 84–96
      setups, 88–91
      strategy for study, 91–92
      terminology, 84–88
   picture composition analysis, 70–76
      composition, form, and function,
         75–76
      dynamic composition, 73–74
      external composition, 74–75
      internal composition, 74–75
      static composition, 71–72
      strategy for study, 71
      visual rhythm, 73
Scripting, 207–8
Seberg, Jean, 45
Secrets and Lies, 349
Seeing Red, 342
Selection, equipment, 149–52
Self-expression and form, 38
Self-help as a realistic alternative, 380
Self-portrait, 227–28
Sequence, 67
Sequence transitions, 274–75
Shadowless working light, 167
Shadows, 26
Shadows
   defining, 166–67
   hard-edged, 166
   height of, 88

Sherman's March, 32–33, 190, 223, 251, 335,
    337–39, 348, 359
Shoah, 223, 342
Shock of recognition, 44
Shoot
    research leading up to, 127–42
        assigning metaphorical roles, 130–31
        casting the players, 130
        deciding the action, 130
        developing film's thematic structure, 132
        developing working hypothesis, 133–34
        double-checking one's findings, 132
        dramatic curve, 136–39
        facts and narration, 139
        finding dialectics, 133–34
        how people alter in front of camera,
            131–32
        logistics and the schedule, 139–40
        need for development, conflicts,
            confrontation, 135–36
        permission to film at location facilities,
            141–42
        personal release form, 140–41
        preinterview, 131–32
        research partnership, 139
        research relationships, 128
        sample subject for discussion, 127
        setting up shoot, 139–40
        two research strategies, 128–29
        working hypothesis as a necessity, 135
    setting up, 139–40
Shooting
    for ellipsis, 184–85
    grab, 143
    process, 359–61
    projects, 97–110
        camera handling projects, 105
        camera handling theory, 104–5
        finding problems, 98–99
        finding solutions, 99–100
        handheld: tracking backward with moving
            subject, 108–10
        handheld: tracking on static subject,
            107–8
        handheld tracking forward on moving
            subject, 108
        sound theory, 97–98
        tripod: interview, one subject, 105–6
        voice recording experiments for exteriors,
            101–3
        voice recording experiments for interiors,
            100–101
    ratios, 170

Shots
    cutaway, 204
    denotation and connotation, 57
    in juxtaposition defined, 57–58
    the, 56–57
Showing
    first, 290–91
    public, 362–63
Side-coaching defined, 209
Signs of Life, 13
Silhouette lighting, 91
Simon, Deke, 385
Sinofsky, Bruce, 216
Six O'Clock News, The, 335
Skills, craft, 381
Smiley, Jane, 47
Smith, Loretta, 361
Sobchack, Vivian C., 354
Social history, 46–47
Social science, 46–47
Soft light, 160, 166–67
Soldier Girls, 5, 137–38, 222, 340
Solutions, finding, 99–100
Sorrow and the Pity, The, 28, 342, 348
Sound
    anticipatory, 275
    mix, 293–94, 312
    and camcorders, 158–59
    equipment, 158
    features, accommodating, 280
    holdover, 275
    levels, editor control of, 291
    recordists, 147–48
    theory, 97–98
    use of, 80–81
Sound tracks
    cutting and laying, 294–95
    hierarchy, 295–96
Sound-mix strategy, 298–300
Space
    horizontal movement through, 62
    vertical movement through, 62
Spielberg, Steven, 13, 45
Spock, Benjamin, 174, 176, 200, 285
Spotlights, 160
Stanislavski, Konstantin, 189
Static composition, 71–72
Static subjects 107–8
Steadicam systems, 158
Stoney, George, 18, 326, 336
Stories
    childhood, 46
    family, 46

Story
  development and editing, 44
  discovery, 44
  question, and suggestion, 228–30
  structures, 251–53
  unbroken five-minute, 223–24
Story boards, 73
Story ideas, developing, 44–51
  collecting raw materials, 44–47
    childhood stories, 46
    family stories, 46
    fiction, 47
    history, 45
    journals, 44–45
    magazines, 45
    myths and legends, 45–46
    newspapers, 45
    social history, 46–47
    social science, 46–47
  displace and transform, 51
  local can be large, 50
  subject-driven versus character-driven films,
      50–51
  subjects to avoid, 51
  testing subjects, 47–49
  using the medium, 49–50
Storytelling, parallel, 184–85
Straubinger, Fini, 325
Streetwise, 214
Strick, Joseph, 28
Strike, 21
Structure, development and, 336–43
Structures
  and contracts with audiences, 250
  designing, 249–54
  no time, 251
  nonchronological, 250
  story, 251–53
  why they matter, 249–50
Structuring
  bookends time, 250
  inventory, 251
  metaphoric journey, 251
  subjective POV, 250–51
Students, high school, 33
Study, strategy for, 78
Subject-driven films, 50–51
Subjective reconstruction, 353–54
Subjectivity versus objectivity, 66
Subjects
  limits on range of, 345–46
  search for, 383

  testing, 47–49
  to avoid, 51
  tracking on static, 107–8
Subtext, 62
Sundance Festival, 33
Supplies, power, 157
Sync, jam, 262
Synecdoche defined, 65
Syntax, adjusting, 279
Systems, Steadicam, 158

Tanner, Alain, 349
Tape editing, machine-to-machine, 256
Tape to digital production from, 161
TBC (time-base corrector), 261
Teaching Documentary in Europe, 213
Technology
  changing editing, 256–59
  developments in, 30–33
  new, 23–24
Television
  cable, 30
  and documentaries, 29–30
Temperaments, crew members', 144
Temperatures, color, 156
Tension, dramatic, 138–39
Terminology, lighting, 84–88
Terminus, 214
Terreblanche, Eugene, 190
Test, working, 171
Testing subjects, 47–49
Thames Television, 331
Thatcher, Margaret, 132
Theorizing Documentary, 318
Thin Blue Line, The, 5, 33, 179, 185, 226, 286,
      342, 348, 353
35 Up, 135, 229, 328
Thomas, Anthony, 353
Thompson, Virgil, 231
Thousand Acres, A, 47
Time, 336–43
  development, and structure
    event-centered films, 336–37
    historical films, 340–43
    journey films, 337–39
    process films, 337
    walled-city films, 339–40
  and documentaries, 3
  movement in, 135–36
Time coding defined, 259
Titicut Follies, The, 27–28, 218, 337, 339